The 27 Celestial Portals

The 27 Celestial Portals

The Real Secret Behind the 12 Star Signs Revealed

Prash Trivedi

Illustrations by Veno

Copyright © 2004 by *Prash Trivedi*

Edited and Illustrated by *Veno*

Distributed By:
Lotus Brands Inc.
P.O. Box 325
Twin Lakes, WI 53181 USA
www.lotuspress.com

ISBN : 0-940985-84-5

Published for Prash Trivedi by
Sagar Publications
72, Janpath Ved Mansion
New Delhi - 110 001

and Printed at
The Artwaves
A-487, Double Storey
Kalkaji, New Delhi-110019

Contents

S. No.	Description	Page No.
	Introduction	vii
1.	Ashvini	3
2.	Bharani	21
3.	Krittika	37
4.	Rohini	53
5.	Mrigashira	69
6.	Ardra	85
7.	Punarvasu	103
8.	Pushya	119
9.	Ashlesha	137
10.	Magha	153
11.	Purvaphalguni	169
12.	Uttaraphalguni	185
13.	Hasta	201
14.	Chitra	217
15.	Swati	233
16.	Vishakha	249
17.	Anuradha	265
18.	Jyeshta	281
19.	Mula	299
20.	Purvashadha	317
21.	Uttarashadha	333
22.	Shravan	349
23.	Dhanishta	367
24.	Shatabhisha	385
25.	Purvabhadrapada	403
26.	Uttarabhadrapada	421
27.	Revati	437

Abhijit   453

Afterword   455

Bibliography   456

Sexual Compatibility Table   457

Marriage Compatibility Table   458

OSFA   460

Illustrations

1.   Ashvini   1
2.   Bharani   19
3.   Krittika   35
4.   Rohini   51
5.   Mrigashira   67
6.   Ardra   83
7.   Punarvasu   101
8.   Pushya   117
9.   Ashlesha   135
10. Magha   151
11. Purvaphalguni   167
12. Uttaraphalguni   183
13. Hasta   199
14. Chitra   215
15. Swati   231
16. Vishakha   247
17. Anuradha   263
18. Jyeshta   279
19. Mula   297
20. Purvashadha   315
21. Uttarashadha   331
22. Shravan   347
23. Dhanishta   365
24. Shatabhisha   383
25. Purvabhadrapada   401
26. Uttarabhadrapada   419
27. Revati   435

* * *

Om Shree Ganeshaye Namah

Om Shree Durgaye Namah

Om Shree Laxmiaye Namah

Om Shree Svarasvatve Namah

Om Shree Taraye Namah

Om Shree Nakshatrayee Namah

Lunar Month & Day

It can be seen as the co-ruler of the month *Shravan*, which is generally said to be ruled by Shravan. One can expect the energies of this asterism to be stronger during the last 9 days of the lunar month of *Shravan*, a period which corresponds to the month of August in the solar calendar.

Shatabhisha is also related to the *Chaturdashi* (14th or 14th) of the waxing and waning phases of the Moon's monthly cycle.

Auspicious Activities

Good for signing business deals & resolving matters; Education or learning activities; Travel (especially over water); Bike riding; Acquiring new vehicles; Recreational ventures; Meditation & Yog; Sexual activity; Studying asterisms & astronomy; Therapies; rejuvenation & life enhancing activities; Media events; Technological activities; Visiting the seaside.

Inauspicious Activities

Not good for beginnings in general; Marriage; Childbirth; Family disagreements, conflicts, arguments; Negative or wrathful action; Not beneficial for religious activities unless it is well initiated; Not good for financial matters; Not good for buying new clothes; Not good for domestic activities.

Planetary Ruler

Shatabhisha is ruled by the planet of Saturn, Rahu and Varuna. Being the fourth asterism of the asterism, Shatabhisha is the abode of Rahu's energy.

In its mundane aspect this Nakshatra deals the more worldly insights and administrative side. Rahu, being one of the two pole of spiritual self, this Nakshatra tends to the spiritual aspiration and completion trends. The humanitarian qualities and idealistic aspiration of this asterism

Om Shree Ekakshara Namah!

Om Shree Durgaye Namah!

Om Shree Laxmaye Namah!

Om Shree Syanasvaye Namah!

Om Shree Nakshatrayee Namah!

Introduction

In Vedic system of Astrology, known in sanskrit as *Jyotish*, the 27 constellations and not the 12 star-signs form the core of understanding celestial influences on our planet. These 27 constellations are known as the 27 *Nakshatras*.

The term *"Nakshatra"*, when broken down into its constituent parts :— *"naks"* meaning "sky" and *"shetra"* meaning "region", translates into "Sky Map". Another translation is arrived at by a different dissection :— *"nakhsa"* is "map" and *"tara"* is "star" and so Nakshatra is "Star Map".

Both meanings clearly shows that in the eyes of the ancient vedic seers it is the 27 *nakshatras* (constellations) and not the 12 *rashis* (zodiacal star-signs), which map the sky.

Jyotish (Vedic Astrology) without nakshatras is as incomplete as the human body is without eyes. If *Jyotish* is the *"eye of the Vedas"*, then *Nakshatras* are the *"eyes of Jyotish"*.

The 27 *nakshatras*, in a way, represent our journey from the moment of birth to the moment of death. The ideal path of one's passage in life can be viewed through the 27 *nakshatras* in a short, general way : -

"Ashvini relates to the first year or so of our lives, where we are totally dependant on outside support for our survival and operate from a purely instinctual awareness.

Bharani represents the time, when as infants, we start growing teeth and undergo other transformative processes like change of diet. Here we have to take on more responsibility, such as starting to learn to eat by ourselves. One notices that a sense of primeval will, which usually relates to wanting and not wanting, is seen here.

Next comes the stage of the learning process where we learn to walk, talk etc. All this initial learning process happens under the influence of *Krittika*. This stage can extend up to four or five years of age. The process of learning to write is also part of this stage. A sense of discipline is required at this stage and one has to outgrow the purely primordial awareness of Ashvini and Bharani.

After this follows *Rohini,* where one starts understanding and enjoying the material world with their newfound knowledge gathered in the previous stage.

Mrigashira is the point where we follow wherever our curiosity takes us and in *Ardra* it is time to analyze and understand our experiences.

Purnavasu is where emotions come into being for the first time. One begins to understand one's role in family and society. Playfulness is combined with a sense of caring.

Pushya represents the stage when more responsibility is taken. This is the age around 16, where one falls in love with life and everything seems so full of promise and wonder.

Ashlesha comes into picture at around 18 -20 years, where the harsh realities of the world dawn upon us and we have to wriggle our way through. There is no place for naievete, as one tries to find one's own way through the jungle of life. This coincides with Rahu's maturity age.

Once we find our way, our identity and individuality are established under the auspices of *Magha*. This usually takes place around 21. Here, one also becomes aware of one's roots and how they are relevant in the scheme of things.

After one's individuality is established, one tends to relax and be creative under the impulses of *Purvaphalguni*. The search for a partner begins. Some might marry and think of having children at this time.

Uttaraphalguni follows, making one concentrate on having a fixed role in society and on family issues. It is about finding one's social individuality, rather than personal individuality, which occurs in Magha.

In *Hasta,* one immerses themselves in worldly responsibilities and affairs and tries to be clever and crafty in it. This is the time for making plans and starting projects.

Chitra is where we create our works, the plans having being formed in Hasta are now manifested in reality.

Swati is where we sell our creations to the world. In other words, we relate to the world through business.

After the business is done and riches are acquired, a longing arises for something more meaningful. This catharsis happens within the domain of *Vishakha.*

This longing is only fulfilled in *Anuradha,* through the wisdom gained in understanding the secrets of nature.

Once this is achieved, one begins to be seen as a respected and responsible elder-figure, under the energies of *Jyeshta* and a feeling of pride and superiority sets in.

Mula crushes whatever we have built so far, and shows us that there is a lot more left to unravel and understand. In a way this is the beginning of the impersonal.

In the *Purvashadha* stage which follows, one feels invincible as the results of overcoming the trials and transformations experienced in Mula. One begins to share its wisdom and experience with the world, but still in a somewhat individualistic way.

In *Uttarashadha,* one is forced to look at the bigger picture and sublimate one's individuality for collective purposes.

After one's individuality is sublimated, one becomes receptive to the fainter but deeper universal voices under the auspices of *Shravan.*

Whatever we have learnt from our receptivity in *Shravan,* is used for working in tune with the rhythm of the universal mind, as symbolised by *Dhanishta.* This often bestows wealth, abundance and fulfillment on all levels.

After one has enjoyed the abundance, there is a longing for something even more fulfilling. This catharasis takes place in *Shatabisha*, a place where one ponders over the question of existence itself.

This questioning ultimately leads one to severe penance and austerities under the influence of *Purvabhadrapada*. One is ready to sacrifice everything on a material, mental and emotional plane, in order to gain the ultimate knowledge.

The real path to gaining this knowledge is shown in *Uttarabhadrapada*, which shows that the ultimate wisdom and knowledge can be gained through easier, milder and more peaceful means. This is where the understanding of the middle-way or the middle-path comes into being.

The following of the middle way finally leads to attainment of complete enlightenment under the care of *Revati*, the final nakshatra. All dualities, complexities, philosophies, actions and reactions merge in the celestial ocean represented by *Revati*, and like *Vishnu*, one rises above this ocean free from all of them. "

It goes without saying, that for most people, the stages represented by the *nakshatras*, hold more meaning, depending on those *nakshatras* which are occupied by the planets or ascendant in an individual's horoscope. Especially in today's out-of-balance society, the ideal path outlined by the *nakshatras*, as described above, only applies partially to the majority of us.

Nakshatras, however, still form the core of understanding a nativity. For example, if a learned astrologer sees a chart with Aquarius rising on the ascendant and goes about making a character sketch of the native on the basis of the general traits of Aquarius as a sign, they would find that their derivations are too general, non-specific and even completely wrong in some aspects. This is because Aquarius carries energies of three nakshatras - *Dhanishta*, *Shatabhisha* and *Purvabhadrapada* - all of which have totally different nature, characteristics and functionings. The same applies to all the planetary placements.

One cannot expect a person to have an amiable and harmonizing nature just because their Moon is posited in the sign Libra. This would be the case if the Moon was placed in the *Swati* part of

Libra, but the scenario would be entirely different if Moon was placed in the relatively more complicated nakshatra, *Vishakha*.

In this work, the study of each *Nakshatra* has been divided into 23 sections, which simplifies the process of dealing with the multifarious aspects of their functionings.

It is the author's hope, that this work will fuel further research on these cosmic transmitters and in time we would be able to attain the clear and complete understanding, which our forefathers possessed.

* * *

Throughout this work :

* The term 'Ketu' refers to South Node of the Moon

* The term 'Rahu' refers to the North Node of the Moon

1. Ashvini   0°0' - 13°20' Aries

1.

Ashvini

(00°00' Aries - 13°20' Aries)

In the Sky :

Ashvini, the beginning of everything, especially Ketu's energies, is represented in the celestial firmament by two bright stars in the constellation of Aries. The ancient vedic seers saw the constellation of Aries as forming a horse's head, and thus these two stars were seen as making a similar pattern. These stars are known in modern astronomy as *Alpha-Arietes* (*Hamal*) & *Beta-Arietes* (*Sheratan*). Alpha-Arietes is slightly brighter with a visual magnitude of 2.02, while Beta-Arietes has a visual magnitude of 2.66. These relatively bright stars lie very close to the planetary ecliptic, right below the bright constellation of *Andromeda*, and are easy to locate in the night sky.

Name :

"Ashvini" can be translated into either "Born of a Female Horse" or the "Horse-Woman". The first meaning is clear but the second one leaves one confused as to whether the woman is riding a horse, or is she a mythical creature with a horse's head and woman's body. As we shall discover later, it is probably the latter.

Its alternative name is *Asvayuj*, which translates into "she who yokes horses". Once again a strong emphasis on the horse and a female is seen, the root of which we would discover when we get to its ruling deities.

Symbol :

Ashvini's main symbol is a "horse's head". This symbol, as we can see, is in keeping with its name. A horse's head conveys the idea of "a beginning". One can notice how riders pat their horse's neck before beginning any journey. From time immemorial a horse has been seen as a symbol of power, courage, movement and vitality. A horse's head signifies an eagerness to act and a swiftness of approach. A horse as we know is always ready to make journeys, not for its own ends, but for the ends of its rider or others in general.

If one has had the chance of being close to a horse, one will realize that a horse's head conveys a certain amount of sensitivity and alertness. Since Ashvini lies in the beginning of the sign Aries, which is seen as representing the head of the *kala purush* (the eternal being), it makes sense that Ashvini be related to a head of some kind. The head of course relates to the brain, the controlling organ of all body functions. Thus Ashvini automatically relates to mental impulses and leadership. Horses are nervous, fidgety and highly strung animals. Therefore this nakshatra carries all of these qualities in good measure.

Its alternative symbol is a 'horse carriage consisting of two horses carrying two people'. This symbolism relates to the presiding deities of this nakshatra. This symbol once again emphasizes a need for movement and relates to transportation of all kinds. This movement can relate to material transportation on the earth or travelling between different worlds, realms or planes.

Deity :

The *Ashvini Kumars,* the two celestial horsemen, are regarded as the main presiding deities of this nakshatra. Their names are *Dashra* and *Nasatya,* which translate into "bringing help" and "truthfulness" respectively. There's no ancient culture where one cannot find stories and legends carrying their symbolism. The tales often show two heroic brothers travelling around solving the problems of whosoever they encounter in their travels.

In the Vedic legend they are twin brothers, who were born out of the union of Sun and his wife *Sanjana*, when they were in the form of a stallion and a mare. One can refer to the previous author's book "*Sun - The Cosmic Powerhouse*" (*Sagar* Publications, India) for the full story. These two brothers are seen as the celestial physicians in ancient Vedic texts. This is where the healing and rejuvenating aspect of this nakshatra stems from.

The Ashvini Kumars are supposed to have knowledge of all herbs on the physical and astral plane; and are supposed to possess supernatural powers to cure any disease or fix any problem. They are particularly concerned with friction or obstacles which might come up between married couples. Thus Ashvini is a nakshatra which promotes marital harmony. Ashvini Kumars are also invoked to aid childbirth. They are also very well known in the ancient legends for curing impotence and other types of sexual disorders.

This nakshatra reflects the divine qualities of these two beings as best as it can be done on the material plane. The Ashvini Kumars are considered so powerful that they can make the old become young and even bring the dead back to life. They themselves have a youthful appearance and never age. This explains the ageless quality of this nakshatra. The generosity and compassion of the Ashvini Kumars extends to the animals as well. There are a lot of stories of them saving gentle animals like lambs from preying creatures like wolves.

In our view, *Brahma*, the creator among the Trinity, can be regarded as the overseer of this nakshatra. Not many scholars have shed light on this aspect, but the fact remains that this nakshatra represents the beginning of all things, including creation. Brahma is the architect of the universe and is responsible for all types of beginnings.

Ganesh, the elephant headed son of *Parvati* and *Shiv*, is also strongly attached with this asterism. Ganesh also represents the beginnings of all things and is regarded as the remover of obstacles. It is interesting to note that this nakshatra can be summed up by the phrase "Remover of obstacles". Ganesh is also the main presiding deity of Ketu, the planet ruling this nakshatra. His four main qualities - purity, auspiciousness, innocence and supreme devotion to the Universal Mother principle, can be seen manifested through the functionings of Ashvini.

Nature & Functioning :

'Spontaneous' is the word which sums up this nakshatra's nature and functioning. It is a nakshatra which is way ahead of all the other nakshatras as far as initiating anything is concerned. It is also the quickest amongst the nakshatras. All associated qualities with quickness like agility and speediness form the core of Ashvini's functioning. One can see that in order to be quick one has to be direct and to the point. This nakshatra has a straightforward, no nonsense approach to dealing with things and life in general.

The natives with prominent Ashvini never lose a minute in converting their impulses into thoughts and their thoughts into action. This often results in an impulsive behaviour pattern, which in its negative aspect often leads to rashness. All the phrases like "Hurry causes delay, and haste makes waste", seem to be aimed directly at Ashvini natives.

Ashvini natives are usually brimming with life, have lively intelligence, a quick comprehension ability and a happy go lucky disposition. Their appearance is usually youthful and eager. They seem to age less quickly than other nakshatra types. When Ashvini is rising on the Ascendant, it makes the person short, athletic, robust and charming in an innocent sort of way. In fact natives with prominent Ashvini can be singled out by their innocent looks and childish demeanour. Since the Ashvini Kumars are known for their charm, elegance, style and extravagance - these qualities are reflected in the mental and physical makeup of Ashvini natives.

Ashvini natives usually have a strong spirit of adventure and revel in encountering the unknown. A spirit of adventure always requires courage and this nakshatra has loads of it. It is a fearless nakshatra which derives satisfaction from heroic pursuits. For example, a person bungy jumping at the age of ninety could only be an Ashvini type. In its negative aspect, this quality often comes out as foolhardiness, and Ashvini natives have a tendency to suffer a lot as a result. The lesser evolved among such natives show a marked tendency not to learn from their mistakes, and can be seen to be repeating the same mistake over and over again. There is definitely a lack of reflection associated with this nakshatra and the bad news is that things don't usually improve with age.

There's a distinct sense of humour associated with this nakshatra. Natives have a light hearted and jovial humour and possess an ability to laugh at themselves and others.

The constant need for movement makes the Ashvini natives completely useless at all activities requiring stillness and patience. This is the reason why they are very rarely seen to bring to completion what they have begun. They have enough motivation when it comes to initiating new activities, but they find it hard to stick it out.

Ashvini natives are known for having an eye for the needs of others and a helpful nature, but in our experience they are more likely to be helpful in short term things or those requiring quick bursts of energy. If something requires long term attention, Ashvini natives are likely to transfer their responsibilities to some other nakshatra type and move onto the next thing.

Their innate urge to quickly move onto the next thing makes them lose out as far as attaining enduring knowledge and wisdom is concerned. This is especially the case with younger and less evolved souls. In today's hyper-materialistic day and age, such natives can easily scatter their lives away moving from one triviality or distraction to the next. 'Naivete' is the keyword which sums up such Ashvini types. Ashvini natives usually have an independent and confident spirit and don't like to be told what to do. This quality is similar to that of a wild or untamed horse. This is alright in evolved souls who know exactly which path to follow, but for those who have not reached that level it makes them want to do things their own way, without even knowing what to do. Such Ashvini types can be very stubborn and unyielding, and are likely to ignore all good counsel. Just like the wildest horse can be tamed, all Ashvini natives can be made to tow the line if handled with a certain degree of sensitivity and caution, mixed with aggression and firmness.

Ashvini natives usually like to dress well and can be seen spending a considerable amount of time on their wardrobe. They are direct, straightforward people and appreciate the same quality in others. They are always fascinated by all affairs related to healing, rejuvenation and self-improvement practices of all kinds. They can be easily found in the local health club and most of the bodily improvement advertisements seem to be directed at them.

Ashvini natives like to be unique in whatever they do and how they are seen. All Ashvini natives have a marked tendency to feel unique in comparison to others. They like to think that they have some special gifts which others do not possess. It is true that they have a pioneering approach to things, which makes them a step ahead of the rest. In the present day and age they are the ones that are likely to catch on to the new trends and happenings first.

One peculiarity of Ashvini natives is that they are moderate eaters and are modest in any circumstance. Despite their unique qualities, they are not the show off types and are not likely to gloat over their accomplishments. They have a thing about being self sufficient and don't like to be dependant on others. Ashvini is a very resourceful nakshatra. Natives under its influence always seem to come up with the required resources under the most adverse circumstances, as if by magic. They are competent and sincere about whatever they do, although they may lack the discipline and endurance required to achieve perfection. Ashvini natives who have endurance are often very successful at whatever they choose to do. This endurance factor usually comes from other factors in a chart rather than Ashvini itself.

Mode of Functioning :

In keeping with its basic nature and disposition, ancient Vedic seers saw this as an Active asterism. This comes as no surprise as this nakshatra relates to the very beginning of all activities. It is the basic primordial force which introduces activity into passivity of time and space. The original creative spark cannot be anything but active.

Caste :

It belongs to the *Vaishya* or merchant caste of nakshatras. It might surprise some to know that the original creative spark is a business man, but the ancient Vedic seers did not have the above indication in mind when they designated the Vaishya caste to this asterism. Doing any kind of business requires a lot of initiative and there is no nakshatra with more initiative than Ashvini, so it automatically gets connected to all kinds of business activities on the material as well as other planes of existence. Business out here cannot just be seen as buying and selling goods, as is mostly the case nowadays. It relates to interaction and exchange on many different levels, and the primordial, unconscious motivations underlying all activity. In the present context however, Ashvini natives can be seen to be good at doing business and making money.

Gender :

It is a male nakshatra, since it is the first nakshatra and the number '1' relates to the male aspect in nature. This nakshatra projects the archetypical masculine qualities like drive, ambition, logic and initiative. It is also mainly connected to male planets like Sun and Mars. All its presiding deities are also male.

Bodyparts & Humor (Ayurvedic Constitution) :

Knees and the top portion of the feet are the main body parts ruled by this nakshatra. Its association with knees is evident from its association with movement. Knees are the body parts which provides us our capacity for walking, running and jumping. Horses can run fast because they have strong knees. The feet again are related to our ability to move.

It is a primarily "Vata" (airy) nakshatra. Vata as we know carries a very moveable energy in tune with this nakshatra's basic nature. All very moveable creatures in nature, like birds, have a Vata disposition.

Direction :

Its main directions are centre, east, south and northwest.

Padas (Quarters) :

The first pada or quarter of this asterism 00° 00' - 3° 20' Aries, falls in Aries Navamsa and is ruled by Mars. This is the pada which relates to the most pioneering, courageous and physically active part of this nakshatra. This pada is full of initiative and bestows abundant energy and drive.

The second pada or quarter of this asterism 3° 20' - 6° 40' Aries, falls in Taurus Navamsa ruled by Venus. This pada relates to the more practical and resourceful aspect of this nakshatra. It is connected to the splendorous, graceful and indulgent aspect of the Ashvini Kumars. This pada likes to see the material manifestation of its thoughts and ideas.

The third pada or quarter of this asterism 6° 40' - 10° 00' Aries, falls in Gemini Navamsa ruled by Mercury. This pada relates to the light, humorous, communicative aspect of this nakshatra. This pada gives a very quick comprehension and makes one adept at all kinds of mental activity. It can be said to be the speedy jack of the zodiac.

The fourth pada or quarter of this asterism 10° 00' - 13° 20' Aries, falls in Cancer Navamsa ruled by Moon. This pada relates to the healing part of Ashvini. This pada has an eye for people's needs, and is usually very in tune with the pulse of the collective consciousness at any given point in time. It is the birth place of the emotional faculty which manifests itself as empathy.

Professions :

Equestrian professions, Horse Trainers & Keepers and all those involved in Equine jobs or sports; Horse Racing Enthusiasts/Gamblers; All types of Healing Professions (in the present day and age - Physicians, Therapists, Chemists, Counsellors, Physiotherapists, Druggists & Surgeons); Marriage Counsellors and Childbirth Specialists; Those involved in Promotional & Motivational jobs & campaigns; Physical Arts like Dancing; Those involved in the Transportation Industry; Athletes and all Sport related jobs; Herbologists; Gardeners; Teachers & Educators for Beginners; All those involved in Racing Professions like Motor Sports; Adventure Sports; Explorers; Stunt men; Researchers & Pioneers; Concreters & all those involved in laying foundations in the building industry; People in Law Enforcement

Agencies; Soldiers; Generals; Mechanical Engineers & those involved in Engineering Professions in general; Jewellers especially Goldsmiths; Small business owners and Shopkeepers in general.

Places :

All places related to Equine professions - Grazing Lands, Stables, Horse Tracks etc.; Hospitals and Places associated with the Medical Profession; Places where Herbs grow; Botanical Gardens; Sporting Grounds; Race Tracks of all kinds; Roads, Railway Tracks and all other types of Paths meant for Transportation; Military Bases; Research Centres; Technological & Industrial Centres; Health Clubs & Gymnasiums; All places where Initiations and Beginnings are done; Kindergartens & Primary Schools.

Guna (Essence) and Tattwa (Element) :

This is a *Sattwic* nakshatra. It's Sattwic quality relates to the purity and innocence attached with all types of beginnings, including the creation of our universe. What ancient Vedic seers are saying through this is that - "In the beginning only *Sattwa* exists, and *Rajas* and *Tamas* manifest themselves afterwards."

It belongs to the Earth element. All beginnings including the beginning of our universe have one and only one objective - material manifestation.

Gana (Type) :

It is considered a godly or *Deva* nakshatra. This comes as no surprise as all of its presiding deities are predominantly godly in nature.

Orientation & Disposition :

It is a Level nakshatra. Level nakshatras are useful for levelling things. This applies almost literally to this asterism, as it is associated with all kinds of levelling activities such as laying foundations for houses, buildings etc. We can see that the levelling aspect is very important in Ashvini when it comes to places like racetracks, roads etc.

It is a Moveable or Ephemeral nakshatra. This means that it relates to travelling and change in all its forms. One doesn't have to think twice before assigning a moveable disposition to this nakshatra. This is the most restless among all the nakshatras and is happy only in movement. This movement normally expresses itself through the mental and physical planes.

Lunar Month & Day :

It relates to the first half of the lunar month of *Ashvin*. This usually relates to the month of September or October in the solar calendar.

Ashvini is also related to the *Prathma* (1st tithi or day) of the waxing phase of the Moon's monthly cycle.

Auspicious Activities :

Good for all types of beginnings and initiations, especially those involving learning new things; Laying foundation stones; Taking medicines; Good for all healing, rejuvenation and exercise; Good for improving physical appearance, self improvement on other levels, and age prevention techniques; Good for all activities requiring quickness of thought and action; Equine related activities; Favourable for buying or selling; Travelling; Repairing vehicles or machinery of any kind; Putting on clothes & jewellery; Planting seeds; Learning astrology and other spiritual, occult sciences; Especially good for installing sacred items such as altars, statues, temples etc.; Legal activities; Favourable for taking up a new name.

**The first pada of this nakshatra can be avoided for performing activities in general.

Inauspicious Activities :

Unfavourable for marriage; All kinds of endings; All kinds of activities requiring patience and perseverance; Sexual activity; Not good for activities which are heavy on the emotional plane; Intoxication; Not good for completions of any kind.

Planetary Ruler :

The planetary ruler of this nakshatra is Ketu. Ketu as we know relates to all types of beginnings and thus is directly related to the initiatory impulse inherent in this nakshatra. Among the planets, Ketu is the only one which represents the power of the past, which can be utilised to heal the person in the present. Ketu's power of rejuvenation and regeneration is akin to the phoenix rising from the ashes, and as mentioned earlier, this nakshatra's ruling deities can even bring the dead back to life.

The creativity of this nakshatra corresponds to Ketu's primordial creative potential arising from the will aspect of nature. However this creative force can sometimes be so strong and overwhelming that it becomes difficult to control or channel. This is where things go wrong with this nakshatra. Its downfall usually comes through attempting close to impossible feats without proper consideration. However when it succeeds, it gets the pioneer label. This nakshatra has a strong faith in magic and the dictum - "anything is possible". For a more detailed understanding of its connection with Ketu, the readers can refer to the author's previous work, "*The Rahu-Ketu Experience /The Astrology of the Lunar Nodes*" (*Sagar Publications*, India) or "*The Key Of Life*" (*Lotus Press*, USA).

Mars connects to this nakshatra, being the planetary ruler of the sign Aries. Mars as we know is the planet of energy, and energy is a must for any kind of initiatory impulse. Without energy there can be no movement. In a way it can be said that Mars is the engine which drives Ashvini's car.

This nakshatra also has a close relationship with Sun, since Sun reaches maximum exaltation here. In numerology Sun is related to the number '1', and since this is the first nakshatra, it is also directly connected with the number '1'. This nakshatra has an independent spirit in much the same way as Sun. It is interesting to note that Sun is also a continuously moving entity, which is supposed to ride on a chariot of seven horses. The readers can also recall that the two Ashvini Kumars are the sons of our Sun.

Sun, Ketu and Mars express themselves strongly when placed in Ashvini. Mercury, Venus, Jupiter and Rahu are good here as long as Ketu is well placed. Conjunctions of Sun/Ketu; Sun/Mars and Mars/ Ketu carry energies similar to Ashvini.

Vowels and Alphabets :

The first pada or quarter of this asterism 00° 00' - 3° 20' Aries corresponds to "Chu" as in Chuck or Church.

The second pada or quarter of this asterism 3° 20' - 6° 40' Aries corresponds to "Che" as in Cherry.

The third pada or quarter of this asterism 6° 40' - 10° 00' Aries corresponds to "Cho" as in Chocolate.

The fourth pada or quarter of this asterism 10° 00' - 13° 20' Aries corresponds to "La" as in Larry or Las Vegas.

In the Sanskrit alphabet Ashvini corresponds to "Am", "Aam" & "Im", consequently its mantras are "Om Am", "Om Aam" & "Om Im".

Sexual Type and Compatibility :

Its sexual animal is a Horse. Horses are sensitive and passionate creatures and these qualities find expression in Ashvini's sexuality. The natural grace of horses gives Ashvini natives appeal and sexiness. Ashvini is most compatible with other horse nakshatras like Shatabishak.

For sexual & marriage compatibility with other nakshatras please refer to the tables on pages 468 & 469 .

Esoteric :

Ashvini represents the primordial, initiatory urge which created both the manifest and unmanifest universes. Being the beginning of all things, it has the power to set anything right. This is why in later times, the physicians of the gods, the Ashvini Kumars, were intertwined with the energies of this nakshatra. In almost all ancient cultures, the roots of which of course are the same, one can find the 'divine physician' archetype. Astoundingly, all these divine physician archetypes are very similar to the Ashvini Kumars in the sense that - they are always riding horses, they are mostly twins, they are born out of a water goddess or a water source of some sorts. The Ashvini Kumars are very learned in Ayurveda, the original healing system. They revived the sage Dadhichi. Indra warned Dadhichi not to teach the Kumars Brahma-Vidya (knowledge of creation) since their occupation placed them outside that realm. He promised to cut off Dadhichi's head should he not heed the warning. Dadhici relayed this to the Kumar's. With their great medical abilities however they removed Dadhici's head and replaced it with a horse head. Dadhichi then spoke to them through the horse's mouth. They were then able to replace the original human head of Dadhichi after Indra cut off the horse head.

The Ashvini Kumars restoring the youth of Cyavana Muni. Through this service to a powerful Muni, the twins were granted the right to drink Som Ras, an immortalizing drink, with the other demigods. In Mahabharat, Nakul & Sahadev the youngest amongst the 5 Pandava brothers were sons of Ashvini Kumars.

An ancient Welsh legend, which still holds relevance today in the minds of the Welsh people, illustrates this fact. According to this legend, three sons were born from a lady who had emerged from a lake called *Lannefann*. These semi -divine beings, known as the "Physicians of *Myddfal*", were known to be able to cure every disease and were even able to slow down the ageing process. The lake can still be visited today. This story definitely supports the assumption, which is gaining ground now, that the ancient Celtic religion was the same as the ancient Vedic religion. It corroborates well with the puranic story of the birth of Ashvini Kumars. Vivasvan's (the Solar Deity) wife Samjna once ran away from her husband and in order to hide from him took the body of a mare while she performed austerities on Earth. Vivasvan, who was searching for her, finally found her by the side of a lake and turned himself into a horse and out of their union these twin sons, the Ashvini Kumars, were born.

Whilst discussing the asterism Shatabishak, we came across the fact that oceans are known to carry enough herbs to cure every known disease, besides carrying other types of magical herbs. In the ancient Vedic legend concerning the "Churning of the Ocean ", (please refer to the author's previous work - "*The Rahu-Ketu Experience*" *Sagar* Publications, India or "*The Key of Life*" *Lotus Press*, USA), the Ashvini Kumars were born out of this churning of the ocean. We can see that the Ashvini Kumars and Shatabhishak have a strong connection due to the correlation between their ruling deities. It is said that diseases which are caused under the influence of Shatabhishak can only be cured under the influence of Ashvini. Since every beginning is a kind of rejuvenation, Ashvini has the power to overcome any affliction on the physical, mental, emotional and higher planes.

In the universal scheme of things, Ashvini relates to "*shidravyapani shakti*" or the power to quickly attain one's objective. It is clear from the above that Ashvini is representative of the universal energy which assists everyone in need without hesitation or delay.

Gotra (Celestial Lineage) :

This nakshatra is related to the Sage *Marichi*, one of the seven celestial sages looking after the affairs of our galaxy. The name of this sage translates into "light". This comes as no surprise as Ashvini is the lightest and swiftest amongst the 27 nakshatras.

Remedial :

For those suffering from bad effects resulting from afflictions to this nakshatra, the best remedial measure is worship of "*Lord Ganesh*".

Repetition of the root mantra of this nakshatra - "Om Am" and "Om Im" 108 times when Moon transits this nakshatra and in its corresponding lunar month, is sure to reduce suffering and bring enlightenment into a person's life.

Persons who are benefiting from the positive energy of this nakshatra can also increase the good effects through the above mentioned ways. It is helpful for them to wear various shades of red and bright variegated colours. They should use Ashvini's directions, lunar month and the days when Moon transits Ashvini to undertake all important actions.

Example :

Ashvini's sound and light can be experienced at -

http://osfa.org.uk/ashvini.htm

Miscellaneous :

According to *Varahamihira*, "Moon in Ashvini gives good appearance, manners and intelligence. The native is fond of dressing up and ornaments. The native is skilled in their chosen field. "

2. Bharani 13°20' - 26°40' Aries

2.

Bharani

(13°20' Aries - 26°40' Aries)

In the Sky :

Bharani, the heralder of Venusian energy, is represented in the celestial firmament by a group of three faint stars forming a triangle in the constellation of Aries. The ancient vedic seers saw these stars as forming the female sexual organ. These stars are known in modern astronomy as *35-Arietes*, *39-Arietes* & *41-Arietes*. 41-Arietes is the brightest among the three, with a visual magnitude of 3.62, which explains the faintness of the stars of this asterism. It is only through being privy to some direct universal (galactic, in this case) knowledge, that the ancient seers were able to attach such importance to these relatively faint group of stars. In order to locate these stars in the night sky, one has to focus in the region between the bright star Alpha-Arietes (belonging to the previous asterism, *Ashvini*) and the bright group of stars of *Pleiades* star cluster (belonging to the next asterism, *Krittika*). It is easier to locate 41-Arietes, while the other two can be seen lying in a straight line on its right hand side.

Name :

"Bharani" can be roughly translated into either "Bearing" or "She who Bears". It must be noted, however, that it doesn't necessarily mean bearing a child as in the case of pregnancy, even though we would discover later how this asterism is directly related to the womb. The name, which conveys a major part of this asterism's energy, relates primarily to the feminine side of nature and its capacity to receive, hold, nurture and destroy.

Symbol :

The main symbol of this asterism is a "vagina", the female sexual organ. In effect all the female reproductive organs can be seen as the symbols of this nakshatra. In all ancient cultures these organs as symbols were seen to represent the fertility aspect of nature. In the Egyptian civilization, the vagina is symbolically represented as the *Buckle of Isis* and is seen as the doorway between different worlds. The Vedic point of view also ascribes birth, death, transformation and regeneration to the feminine reproductive symbols. They are also seen to represent restraint, caution, jealousy, secrecy, forbearance, struggle, sacrifice, catharsis, sexuality, nurturing and maternal love. Bharani therefore carries all the above mentioned attributes.

Since a soul finds its entry from the astral plane to the physical world of the living through the female sex organ, it is not very hard to see the 'doorway' connotation associated with this symbolism. As we shall discover later, *Yama*, the lord of death and one of the eight door keepers between the physical and the other worlds, is the ruling deity of this nakshatra. The womb as we know carries the new life in the form of a foetus for several months, before it finally finds itself manifested in the world. In the same way, Bharani allows things to brew on subtle planes, before they suddenly take outer material forms. In the case of childbirths, it is usually very hard to predict which day the water is going to break. The same is the case with revolutions, which usually brew within the hearts and minds of people for a while before suddenly erupting. The same is applicable to death as well. This makes Bharani an unpredictable nakshatra, which operates in hidden ways and revels in secrecy.

A "boat" is the alternative symbol of this nakshatra. It again symbolizes transportation between different planes and realms of existence. Bharani is thus a nakshatra directly related to the process of birth, death and regeneration, at least on the earthly plane of existence.

Deity :

Yama, the lord of death, is considered the main presiding deity of this asterism. He is supposed to be one of the eight celestial gatekeepers, who guard the eight directional doorways or exits through which the souls travel from the earthly plane to other planes of existence. In the Vedic texts, he is mostly seen as the Lord of *Dharma*. This apparent mixing of the deities of Death and Dharma may not be instantly clear to the western reader. However when seen in the light of the fact it is Yama's duty to assign the life paths for the souls who have left their earthly bodies, it becomes clear that he has to be well versed in the laws of *karma* and dharma.

Yama, despite being the lord of death, is a very jovial deity. His lightheartedness finds expression through Bharani's playfulness and joyousness. It is up to Yama to weigh our actions in the present life so that we can be assigned an appropriate new life. He is thus a benevolent deity and should not be feared. Yama is only feared by those who fear death and those whose karmas are not good. Yama is privy to many of the secret functionings of *Maya*. Bharani also holds within itself the complete understanding of the process of life, birth and death.

Kali, the dark and destructive form of *Parvati*, is one of the three main feminine deities upholding our universe. Just like Yama, Kali is also considered a deity to be feared. Kali's function however is just to kill the demons within and without. Her form has to be terrifying because the entities she deals with are themselves cruel and fierce. Her involvement with this nakshatra implies that Bharani is a sort of battle field between the opposing qualities of nature. It is here where the distinction between right and wrong, good and bad, godly and demonic is made. The process of uprooting the negative side begins. Bharani deals with extremes and in the process becomes the most extreme amongst nakshatras.

Nature & Functioning :

'Extreme' is the one word which sums up Bharani's essential nature and functioning. It swings between polar opposites like puritanism and bohemia, naivete and wisdom, maturity and immaturity and life and death. Bharani is representative of the desire aspect of nature. It is thus in a way a lust for life and a fear of death. Bharani is a 16 year old girl on the verge of deflowering, a baby in the womb or a person facing the *Yamadutas* (celestial angels whose task it is to guide souls through the afterlife process) after one's death. Because of its childlike quality Bharani is one of the most eager nakshatras. Just like a child wants to experience all of its surroundings, Bharani natives have a desire to experience their surroundings to the fullest. There is a primeval innocence in how they experience things, people and places. They might go through instinct rather than reason. Most of their feelings and desires are so overwhelming that very little can be done to restrain or placate them. Once again the evolutionary status of the soul in question comes into picture.

Evolved Bharani types would channel their immense primeval energy into positive and wholesome universal pursuits, while the less evolved types will be akin to a moth madly hopping about from one light source to another. In the present day and age where confusion and chaos reign supreme, Bharani can be a very difficult energy to handle. This can be easily understood through the mental dilemmas and naiveties which young girls and boys go through after puberty. Without proper guidance and understanding, Bharani natives are ready to jump into anyth' g and everything without caution or consideration.

Bharani natives are often strong characters who can withstand the many turbulences which life has to offer. They do get down and moan and cry like infants sometimes, but nothing holds them down for too long. They are often seen to undergo huge transformations and radical changes throughout their lives. This comes about due to their longing for extremes. When they get set on a path, they want to experience every aspect of it until they have exhausted all possibilities and have no option left but to tip over to something completely new. There's no set boundary in 'Bharani universe'.

All Bharani natives have a creative urge inside them. The feminine sex usually expresses this creativity through bearing children, while the male sex tries to be creative on other levels. Bharani is a nakshatra where the interplay between the male and female takes place. This makes it one of the most sexual nakshatras of the zodiac. Bharani is representative of nature's force which creates attraction between the opposites. Bharani natives experience, indulge in, fall prey to and try to understand this force. *Sigmund Freud*, the famous psychoanalyst, had prominent Bharani placements and it was no wonder then that he deduced every activity on the earthly plane to sexuality. However the more evolved Bharani types realize that this force of attraction has more to do with love, harmony and conscious unity. Sexuality is just one of its many expressions.

Bharani natives usually have large, expressive eyes, a prominent head, medium sized lips and a spooky deathly smile. Their smile is their most distinguishable feature. It encapsulates all their sexuality, mystery and the processes of life and death itself. Just like the sunset emanates a stillness over nature, Bharani natives have the ability to put up a calm countenance, even if their insides are a raging torment. Their childlikeness is quite helpful when it comes to exploration and learning, but it makes for a distinct type of cruelty and morbidity. Everyone knows how children can be more cruel than grownups on many different levels. Bharani's cruelty comes from a lack of responsibility for one's own actions. It is very easy for Bharani natives to move from one action to the next without caring about the longterm implications.

Bharani types are usually enthusiastic and energetic in their approach to life. They have a strong sense of adventure in the fields they pursue. It is seen that they can only achieve their goals if they are under constant guidance from a more mature and wiser source.

Mode of Functioning :

Bharani is considered to be a Balanced nakshatra. Bharani is in actuality an extreme nakshatra, but it is classified as 'Balanced' because of its tendency to balance opposing extremes like birth and death. Bharani natives often lead double lives, touching two different extremes. Thus on a whole, their lives can be seen as balanced. Sunrise (conveying a sense of birth) or Sunset (conveying a sense of death), which forms a part of this nakshatra's symbolism (as seen in its image), is the time when nature's energies are very delicately balanced. This is the reason why these times are seen as the best time for occult/spiritual practices. Bharani, as we shall discover, carries a lot of occult potential due to its relationship with the planet Venus.

Caste :

It belongs to the *mleccha* (outcaste) nakshatras. It is Bharani's tendency to go towards extremes, which probably made the ancient Vedic seers classify it as an outcaste. Bharani almost always tries to break the social norms or taboos one way or the other. It is a highly explosive energy, which cannot usually be controlled within any societal structure.

Gender :

It is a Female nakshatra. This comes as absolutely no surprise as Bharani stands for all that is feminine. It is the second nakshatra and the first feminine nakshatra. Just like the number '2' in numerology, it is the initiator of the feminine principle on all levels of existence. It is the beginning of duality and maya, and within it lies the essence of the complex functionings of the feminine principle.

Bodyparts & Humor (Ayurvedic Constitution) :

The Head and Bottom Parts of the Feet are the body parts related to this nakshatra. It is interesting to note that in childbirth (a Bharani activity), it is either the head or feet which come out of the womb first.

It is a primarily "*pitta*" (fiery) nakshatra. Since all of Bharani lies within the pitta sign of Aries, this classification comes as no surprise. Bharani represents the original creative fire, which produces the world of matter. It is its pitta quality which makes it very active on the material plane, despite its earthy bulkiness.

Direction :

It is related primarily to the arc covering the directions east, south-east and south.

Padas (Quarters) :

The first pada or quarter of this asterism 13° 20' - 16° 40' Aries falls in Leo Navamsa ruled by Sun. The focus here is on creativity and self-immersion. Planets here can be extremely self-centric and can often offend others without meaning to. The drive and will-power inherent in this pada can be used for positive ends if the nativity as a whole allows for it. Sun, Mars & Jupiter are especially strong in this pada.

The second pada or quarter of this asterism 16° 40' - 20° 00' Aries falls in Virgo Navamsa ruled by Mercury. The emphasis here is on service and hardwork. Planets here function in an altruistic way. A certain degree of organization is seen even in typically extreme and chaotic Bharani mode. Mercury, Mars and Rahu are better suited for giving good results here.

The third pada or quarter of this asterism 20° 00' - 23° 20' Aries falls in Libra Navamsa ruled by Venus. The ability to relate and harmonize opposites characterizes this pada. There is however no sense of any limits here when it comes to sex and relationships, which can be either a good thing or a bad thing depending upon the evolutionary level of the nativity in question. Being a pushkara navamsa pada it allows for fulfilment of one's desires. Mercury, Venus & Rahu are best suited for utilizing the energies of this pada.

The fourth pada or quarter of this asterism 23° 20' - 26° 40' Aries falls in Aries Navamsa ruled by Mars. The energy here is extreme in every sense of the word. Planets here work in an uninhibited primeval fashion. It can be a highly inventive and original pada if its explosive energy can be channelled properly. Sun, Mars & Ketu are strong here but may not always give beneficial results. Only the natural benefics Jupiter and Venus are suited for utilizing the energies of this pada in a wise, non self-destructive way.

Professions :

Babysitters, Nannies, Nursery School Teachers; All professions involving children; Professions connected with Amusement, Theme Parks; Children's Toys Industry; Gynaecologists; Midwives; All professions connected with birth & death; Professions related to Fertility Clinics; Morticians; All those connected with Morgues and Funerals; Coffin Makers; Obituary Writers; Officials handling Birth/Death Records; Homicide Detectives; Dancers from all schools and styles; Tobacco, Coffee and Tea Industry; Cooks, Caterers, Hoteliers; Professions connected to Slaughterhouses; Veterinarians; Fire Fighters;

Automobile Industry; Motor Sports; Stuntmen; Coal & Petroleum Industry; Heavy Industries; Surgeons; Film & Entertainment Industry; Photographers; Models; All professions involving the use of sex and glamour; Exotic professions; Strip tease artists; Pornography Industry; Prostitution; Occultists & Tantriks using sexual energies; Judges; Those in Elite positions requiring extreme secrecy; Volcanic & Earthquake Experts; Geophysicists; Biologists & Microbiologists; Seed & Fertilizer Industry.

Places :

Extreme Exotic Landscapes; Volcanoes; Areas with Volcanic Soil; Volcanic Tropical Islands like Hawaii and Polynesian Islands; Farmlands; Kindergartens, Nurseries, Nursery Schools; Children Parks; Amusement Parks; Morgues; Cemeteries; Funeral Homes; Maternity & Child Wards in Hospitals; Intensive Care Units; Gynaecology Hospitals; Film & Photography Studios; Exotic Nightclubs; High Courts; Fertility Clinics; Streets and roads with busy traffic; All places connected with the abovementioned professions.

Guna (Essence) and Tattwa (Element) :

It is supposed to be a *Rajasic* nakshatra. This can be easily assessed from Venus's rulership of Bharani. Venus is seen as the most rajasic among planets. Its relation to the terrestrial life processes is very strong. In a way it can be said that it is only Venus which makes life worth living. Since Bharani heralds the Venusian energy, its expression here is primal, highly charged and explosive (all rajasic expressions).

It belongs to the Earth element. Bharani can be said to represent the point in creation where the fire element (spewed forth by Ashvini) transmutes into the Earth element. Bharani has everything to do with the process of materialization. It is the force which puts a material sheath around the astral body, so that it can experience the terrestrial plane. The earthy quality of Bharani can be easily understood by the fact that its representative animal, the elephant, is the largest and heaviest land animal.

Gana (Type) :

It is considered a *Manusha or* Human nakshatra. Bharani relates to the second and seventh houses in a chart. These are the houses which sum up what human life is about for most people. One's partner, family and resources are all what the common man cares about. These are the houses of both life and death (2nd and 7th are the maraka (killer) houses). Venus is the karaka for both these houses and together they convey Bharani's intense involvement in human affairs, whether it be life or death.

Orientation & Disposition :

It is Downward Looking nakshatra. This classification relates to the hidden aspect of Bharani. As we have discussed earlier, events brewing up under Bharani's influence don't come to the surface until the very last moment. Just like the act of sex or a foetus developing in a womb, Bharani likes to keep its activities hidden from view of others.

It is a Fierce or Severe nakshatra. The intent behind this classification is clear from Bharani's ruling deities. Yama and Kali are both fierce deities interested in jobs requiring fierce actions like cutting the lifeforce of lifeforms against their will. Even the process of childbirth (ruled by Bharani) is a painful process. In fact it is considered to be the most painful experience amongst all natural processes on the earthly plane.

Lunar Month & Day :

It relates to the second half of the lunar month of *Ashwin*. This period usually falls in the month of October in the solar calendar.

Bharani is also related to the *Chaturtithi* (4th tithi or day) of the waxing and waning phases of the Moon's monthly cycle.

Auspicious Activities :

All Creative Activities are favoured; Good for Severe, Cruel, Destructive, Competitive or Warlike activities; Sexual, Amorous & Procreative Activity; Fertility Rites & Agricultural Activities; Beginnings & Endings; Gardening; All type of activities which require use of fire; Good for taking care of postponed or neglected activities; All activities requiring spontaneity; Ascetic activities requiring self-discipline; Fasting & other purificatory rites; Dealing with children.

Inauspicious Activities :

Most unfavourable for travel (Bharani relates to traffic jams and accidents); Not good for slow & gentle activities requiring calmness or serenity; Not good for Initiations; In the present day & age it is better for endings than beginnings.

Planetary Ruler :

The main planets connected with this nakshatra are Mars and Venus. Mars is ruler of the sign Aries, and Venus is the main planetary ruler of this nakshatra. Venus can be said to be born in Bharani. As discussed in the Esoteric Section, Venus is a planet strongly connected with birth and renewal. Venus in Bharani acts as a 'bringer of life'. In combination with Mars, which, being the ruler of the sign Scorpio signifies death, Venus signifies the universal cyclic process of life and death on all levels of existence, especially biological.

According to one school of thought, both Mars & Venus are connected to the outer planet Pluto. Pluto has always been seen as the hidden, creative source and is equated with *Shiv*. In Greek legends, it is supposed to hide in the underbelly of the earth and is responsible for the fertility of earth. Mars & Venus are the two planets most concerned with fertility and interplay with the sexes. Nowadays, it has become fashionable to associate men with Mars and women with Venus, but the truth is that it is the male who creates the sperm (Venus), while it is women who create and house (Mars) the newborn.

Conjunctions of Mars and Venus in a nativity carries an energy similar to that of Bharani. Saturn reaches its maximum debilitation in this nakshatra. Bharani is the warm place of creativity and fertility, while Saturn is a cold planet of obstruction and delay. It is easy to see how they don't go together. Other planets usually do well in Bharani, as long as Venus has a refined placement in the chart.

Vowel s and Alphabets :

The first pada or quarter of this asterism 13° 20' -16° 40' Aries corresponds to "Lee" as in Lisa.

The second pada or quarter of this asterism 16° 40' - 20° 00' Aries corresponds to "Lu" as in Lulu.

The third pada or quarter of this asterism 20° 00' - 23° 20' Aries corresponds to "Lay" as in Layla.

The fourth pada or quarter of this asterism 23° 20' - 26° 40' Aries corresponds to "Lo" as in Logan.

In the Sanskrit alphabet Bharani corresponds to "Eem" and consequently its mantra is "Om Eem".

Sexual Type and Compatibility :

Its sexual animal is an Elephant. Elephants are slow moving and somewhat sensual creatures. The elephant as a sexual animal represents elephantine appetites in sex. It is very hard for other nakshatras, with the exception of *Revati* (the other elephant), to satisfy Bharani. Bharani is the most sexual amongst nakshatras and promotes sex in all its different forms. However in its extreme aspect it can shun sex completely or immerse itself in it to the point of perversion.

For sexual & marital compatibility with other nakshatras please refer to the tables on pages 468 & 469.

Esoteric :

Most of Bharani's esoteric understanding can be arrived at from the study of the planet Venus. Besides the Sun (which is a star and thus cannot be seen as a planet), Venus is the only planet which periodically undergoes a process of birth and death.

The Mayan calendar was based on Venus's 584 day cycle, which it makes from being the morning star to being the evening star. Venus illumines the skies as the morning star for a 236 day period. After that Venus disappears for 90 days. It reappears as the evening star for 250 days, and then there is the second relatively brief disappearance of 8 days before it reappears in the east. This makes a total of 584 days.

We can see that just like the Sun , Venus too rises in the in the east, to disappear in the west, to one day reappear in the east. Because it dies and is born again, all ancient cultures saw Venus as representing the rejuvenative principle. Its connection with the well spring of life is the reason why Venus is considered an occult planet.

In Vedic texts *Shukracharya*, the preceptor of the *Daityas* (celestial demonic beings) and the presiding deity of Venus, is supposed to be an adept at *Sanjivini Vidya*, the knowledge to raise the dead to life. Even *Brihaspati,* the preceptor of the *Devas* (celestial godly beings) doesn't have this knowledge, a fact which renders the Devas weaker in comparision to Daityas.

All goddesses, especially the fertility goddesses, are connected with Venus. The May Day celebration on 1st of May forms an integral part of the Celtic traditions. The interesting thing to note is that Sun is transiting through Bharani on 1st of May every year. This is why the Celts saw this as an opportune time to practice fertility rites, just like the Mayans chose to do it in the 8 day disappearance of Venus. One must realize that all cultures, which placed strong importance on Venus above all else, had roots in the celestial Daitya lineages. The harsh and cruel behaviour of the Daitya race in Puranic legends can also be understood from the cruel and severe nature of Bharani.

Birth and death are complementary processes, in the sense that every death is a beginning and every birth is an ending. When a balance is achieved between birth and death the soul finds easy evolutionary progress. However if the soul finds it hard to confront one or the other, severe situations and turmoil are the result. Bharani is the nakshatra of karma and reincarnation, one of the least understood concepts in modern times, especially in the western world. Bharani is the name for the stage where the masculine and the feminine, which have come out of a single genderless source, copulate, and in doing so, carry forward the process of creation.

Gotra (Celestial Lineage) :

This nakshatra is related to the Sage *Vashishta*, one of the seven celestial sages looking after the affairs of our galaxy. The name of this sage translates into "possessor of wealth ", which is in keeping with this asterism. Bharani has a tendency to be financially well off, as implied by the sage's name. On the other hand, we can infer that this particular sage has a lot to do with life and death processes within our galaxy.

Remedial :

One good way of getting in touch with the energies of this nakshatra is to meditate on death. Worship of Yama, the god of death and dharma is also helpful. However the best way to master the energies of Bharani is through the worship of Kali, the dark goddess. Worship of any feminine deity, especially fertility goddesses is also auspicious (especially for material gains).

Repetition of the root mantra of this nakshatra - "Om Eem" 108 times when Moon transits this nakshatra and in its corresponding lunar month is sure to reduce suffering and bring enlightenment into a person's life.

Persons who are benefitting from the positive energy of this nakshatra can also increase the good effects through the above mentioned ways. It is helpful for them to wear mixtures of white, red and black and generally dark shades. They should use its directions, lunar month and the days when Moon transits Bharani to undertake all important actions.

Example :

Bharani's sound and light can be experienced at -

http://osfa.org.uk/bharani.htm

Miscellaneous :

According to *Varahamihira*, Moon in Bharani natives are "resolute, resourceful, honest, healthy and happy".

* * *

3. Krittika   26°40' Aries - 10°00' Taurus

3.

Krittika

(26°40' Aries - 10°00' Taurus)

In the Sky :

Krittika, the seed of solar energy, is represented in the celestial firmament by a well known group of seven bright stars huddled together in the star cluster of *Pleiades*. The ancient Vedic seers saw these seven stars as forming a necklace and attached immense importance to their role in galactic affairs. These stars are known in modern astronomy as *27-Tauri* (*Atlas*), *Eta-Tauri* (*Alcyone*), *23-Tauri* (*Merope*), *17-Tauri* (*Electra*), *28-Tauri* (*Pleione*), *19-Tauri* (*Taygeta*) & *20-Tauri* (*Maia*). Alcyone is the brightest among this group, with a visual magnitude of 2.88. These stars are very easily visible in the night sky because of their close proximity to each other. In fact they stand out in the night sky more than any other object because of this uniqueness. In order to locate these stars in the night sky, one has to focus in the region to the right of the the bright star *Alpha-Tauri* (*Aldebaran*, belonging to the next asterism, *Rohini*).

Name :

"Krittika" translates simply into "The One Who Cuts" or in a plural sense "The Cutters". This simple, direct and straightforward name is very much in keeping with the essential quality of this asterism. "The Cutters" here relates to a feminine aspect rather than a male aspect and as we shall discover later, this asterism is related to the 'seven Krittikas' (or the seven wives) of the seven main sages looking after the affairs of our galaxy.

Symbol :

Its main symbol is an axe, razor or any sharp edged instrument like a blade or knife. This symbolism obviously relates to its name, which implies cutting and penetration. All sharp instruments can be used for both constructive or destructive purposes. A knife, for example, can be used for cutting vegetables or hurting someone. In the same way, Krittika's penetration can be used for cutting through superficial layers of mental and emotional functionings. On the other hand, it can be used for causing harm out of anger or enmity. In some cases, its destructive aspect is constructive from a universal point of view, especially when those at the end of the blade are crooked or evil.

A flame of any type is another widely used symbol for Krittika. This as we shall see in the next section, relates to its association with *Agni*, the lord of the fire element.

Peacock is another alternative symbol of this nakshatra. The elaborately ornate feathers of the male peacock relate to the exuberant martial nature of the masculine part of this nakshatra. A peacock is the chosen vehicle of the male ruling deity of this nakshatra (please refer to the image). *Krishn* always wore a peacock feather on top of his head and his early life, under the care of his foster parents, reveals the essence of this nakshatra (refer to the Deity Section).

Deity :

Karttikeya, the commander of the celestial godly forces, is the primary ruling deity of this asterism. He is one of the most prominent among *Shiv's* sons and was raised by the aforementioned Krittikas (the seven wives of the seven celestial sages). As we can see the name "Krittika" and "Karttikeya" have common roots, and it is automatically implied that Krittikas are the foster mothers of a boy called Karttikeya. Thus this nakshatra is related to foster care and nurturing of all types.

The circumstances preceding Karttikeya's birth, as mentioned in Puranic texts, are as follows:-

"At one point in time, the gods had lost all of their territory to the demons, and in their desperation asked Lord Shiv to help them. Shiv expressed his disability to intervene directly, but promised that he would produce a son who would deal with their problems. There are many different versions on how Karttikeya was actually born (please refer to the Esoteric section for a common version). However all texts agree with the fact that he was sent away to the Krittikas (Pleiades star cluster) in order to hide him from the demons. The demons had come to know that this child was born for destroying them and were searching all over to find him, so that they could destroy him first, while he was still a baby. Hidden from everyone's eyes, the seven wives of the seven rishis took care of Karttikeya, and as soon as he reached boyhood, he fulfilled his purpose by destroying the demonic forces and restoring the heavens to the gods. "

If properly understood, all of Krittika's nature and functioning can be understood from the above legend. Krittika relates to a sense of imminent danger, which leads to secrecy, seclusion and hiding as a result. It relates to the care and nurturing of anything in its young, delicate state and this is the reason why Moon reaches its maximum exaltation in the second pada of this nakshatra. Karttikeya's heroic valorous deeds are mirrored in its functioning as well.

Agni, the god presiding over the "fire" element in nature, is the secondary ruler of Krittika. Fieriness is definitely required for the combative and militaristic nature of this nakshatra, as suggested by the war general post of Karttikeya. The fire symbolism here can be interpreted at a variety of levels. On a physical level it represents the digestive fire, which converts the food we eat into usable energy. This makes Krittika an energetic and physically active asterism. On a mental plane, fire relates to the ability of the mind to assimilate new knowledge. The mental fire constantly seeks knowledge and experience in order to keep itself burning. This nakshatra therefore relates to curiosity and an inclination to venture out into unknown areas.

On the astral and more subtle planes, fire relates to the purifying principle in nature. It burns away the karma from previous lives, so that a sense of unity with the original creative source may be achieved.

Krittika, on an esoteric level, serves the function of purifying the soul through the fires of knowledge and experience.

We must not forget the seven wives of the seven sages, as they represent the actual stars of this constellation. Krittika is a semi-maternal nakshatra and all its maternal qualities come from these seven women. These seven women can in a way be seen as the five senses, the mind and the consciousness. Their child Karttikeya, then represents the limitless perceptivity of the innocent mind.

There are many legends associated with the reasons behind the separation of these wives from their husbands (the seven celestial sages). We will touch upon one of these legends in the Esoteric Section. In the meantime, we just need to acknowledge the fact that these seven wives trained and educated baby Karttikeya in the various systems of knowledge. This fact reveals the "educational" and "institutional" aspect of Krittika. Krittika is a sort of celestial training ground or university, where one receives training necessary to pursue one's life purpose.

Nature & Functioning :

It is clear that the English word 'critical', has its roots in the sanskrit word 'Krittika' and this one word sets the tone for Krittika's basic nature and functioning. Krittika's piercing quality lends itself to the criticizing and faultfinding part of human nature. Krittika aims to get to the root of any action or situation and consequently it comes across all the imperfections, which often lie between the apparent and the real. Krittika doesn't tolerate imperfections because it sees them as obstacles in achieving its decidedly fixed goals.

Planets placed in Krittika give one pointed action and fiery bursts of energy. They act in a sudden and explosive manner. Krittika natives have a direct and straightforward approach and don't like to beat about the bush. They usually have cutting and blunt manners which often offends or intimidates those around them. One must however remember that Krittika natives are good at putting up social graces and do not act in a cutting or sharp manner all the time. They do so only when roused. They have an extreme temper, but it does not last for more than a few seconds.

Krittika exemplifies Sun's anger rather than Mar's anger. Sun's anger doesn't last for very long, while Mar's anger lingers on with an avenging attitude. The King (Sun), does not need to stay angry for long to declare war, while the Soldiers (Mars), who actually fight the battle, need sustained anger to keep them interested in battles.

Krittika natives usually hide their caring, nurturing and maternal side beneath hard, stern exteriors. Fire, despite its dangerous and destructive potential, cooks our food, warms us up on a cold day and helps make most of the things we require for a comfortable living. In other words fire is what makes civilization possible. Going one step further, we find that Sun's fire makes life possible on earth. This is the reason why Krittika natives are usually the life-sustaining element within their social sphere. They like to support others around them through their warmth, independence and will-power. In some cases this may be excessive and the result is similar to overcooked food. Krittika natives can alienate those around them by their sharp tongue and nature even though they don't have any real malefic intent.

In the universal scheme of things, *Krittika* relates to "*dahana shakti*" - the power of the astral body to cut its ties with the physical body. Its symbolism has heat above and light below. This relates Krittika to all the functions of fire - purification, cooking, melting, moulding etc. Fire also suggests the creative potency of the nakshatra and it is said to have a strong association with the Moon. In this way the Moon represents a receptive field or channel through which the creative potential of the Sun can unfold. Krittika only acts when it has some kind of direction to go in and so individuals with the nakshatra prominent in their charts, have a peculiarly startling and sudden way of erupting when their Krittika energy is activated.

On a spiritual level this nakshatra can provide intense awareness and allows one the ability to undergo extreme forms of purification. On a spiritual level Krittika is forever devoted to cutting its way along a clear path towards the development of one's true inner nature and therefore will slay any obstruction, inner or outer which blocks its path. When it is strong in a nativity it indicates sudden transformations/ups and downs in life.

Mode of Functioning :

Krittika is considered to be an Active nakshatra. It is sacrosanct that the commander of the celestial armies be anything but active. No matter which way one looks at Krittika, all one finds is restless activity, whether it be in the field of leadership, nurturing, education or battle.

Caste :

It belongs to the priestly or *brahminical* caste. One may have expected Krittika to be classified as a *kshatriya*, considering Karttikeya's heroic, warrior-like nature. The reason why the seers saw this nakshatra as brahminical, is because of its intense involvement with learning, knowledge and education. It is naturally philosophical, altruistic and concerned with purity.

Gender :

It is a Female nakshatra. This classification obviously relates to the maternal nature of this nakshatra, as exemplified by the seven wives of the seven sages.

Bodyparts & Humor (Ayurvedic Constitution) :

Hips, Loins and the Crown of the Head are the body parts related to this nakshatra.

It is a primarily "*Kapha*" (watery) nakshatra. Its kapha quality must arise from its relationship with Venus, a primarily kapha planet. The fact that Moon, another kapha planet, finds maximum exaltation in this nakshatra, re-emphasizes this. Its ruling deity, Karttikeya, is supposed to have a lustrous body, which is normally associated with the kapha humor.

Direction :

It is related primarily to the arc covering the directions from east, south-east to south.

Padas (Quarters) :

The first pada or quarter of this asterism 26° 40' - 30° 00' Aries falls in Sagittarius Navamsa ruled by Jupiter. This is a highly moralistic, generous and altruistic pada. There's a daredevil element to this pada, which connects it to one type of military pursuit or the other. It is the explorer of the zodiac. Planets here give a lot of will power, strength and stamina. Sun, Mars, Jupiter and Ketu are especially strong here.

The second pada or quarter of this asterism 00° 00' - 3° 20' Taurus falls in Capricorn Navamsa ruled by Saturn. This pada also has a strong sense of ethics but its vision is more material rather than mental or spiritual. Even its spirituality is expressed through matter. The emphasis here is on arranging matter to create a nurturing and motherly environment. The maternal aspect of Krittika's functioning is at its peak here. Natives under a strong influence of this pada get and provide sustenance when it matters the most. Moon reaches its maximum exaltation in this pada. Mars and Saturn also function strongly here. However Mar's placement here has more to do with receiving nourishment rather than providing it.

The third pada or quarter of this asterism 3° 20' - 6° 40' Taurus falls in Aquarius Navamsa ruled by Saturn. This is also a humanitarian and altruistic pada. It combines futuristic visions and ancient knowledge on a weave of fixed principles. The emphasis here is on 10th house significations like one's collective duty. This pada promotes all types of learning and can thus be called the university of the zodiac. Since no planet gets debilitated in Aquarius, all planets can function well here relating to their own specific domains.

The fourth pada or quarter of this asterism 6° 40' - 10° 00' Taurus falls in Pisces Navamsa ruled by Jupiter. This pada has the ability to manifest its deep sensitivity on a material plane. It promotes groupwork of all types in a joyful, benevolent way. Planets here are more creative under group situations. This is a Pushkara navamsa pada and so all planets are capable of conferring good results here. Jupiter, Venus and Ketu can make the fullest use of the energies of this pada, while Mercury is a little out of sorts here.

Professions :

Critics; Managers; Generals & People in authority positions; Technical professions in general; Teachers; Educators; University related professions; Lawyers; Judges; Surgeons; Swordsmen; Fencers; People who make swords, knives and other sharp instruments; Blacksmiths; Creative Arts involving the use of fire based processes; Jewellers and Glassmakers; All Military Professions; Police; Fire Fighters; Explosive Experts; Those who work in Foster Homes & Orphanages; Professions connected to Rehabilitation of Addicts of all kinds whether it be related to drug addiction, smoking, alcoholism, weight problems; Professions involved in promoting methods & techniques for Self-Improvement or Self Assertiveness; Spiritual Teachers who promote strong purificatory measures or worship involving the Sun or Fire; Professions involving fire like Fire dancers or Fire Sacrifices; Professional Dart players or Archers; Barbers & Hairdressers; Tailors; Work involving use of needles like Embroiderers or Vaccinators; Gold diggers & Miners; Cooks of all varieties; Those who make clay objects like bricks for building houses or ceramic objects; Furnace makers; Those who make Cooking Utensils or Trade tools; All professions involving use of fire and sharp objects.

Places :

Places with hot climates; Deserts & Arid lands; Agricultural lands; Cattle ranches; Meadows; Tropical forests; Volcanic areas; Military Bases & testing grounds; Government Buildings; Universities; Rehabilitation Centres; Orphanages; Mines in general; Factories & Industrial areas using fire in one form or the other; Fireplace, Furnaces, Heating devices within homes; all places connected with the abovementioned professions.

Guna (Essence) and Tattwa (Element) :

Krittika is a *Rajasic* nakshatra due to its association with dynamic qualities like individuality, projection, motivation, leadership and initiative.

It belongs to the Earth element. This doesn't come as a surprise because three fourths of this nakshatra lie in the earth sign, Taurus. The fieriness of this nakshatra manifests itself through the earth element. One way to understand this is to see Krittika as "cooked food". Krittika represents all matter which is made useful in some way by the action of the fire element, just as food is made palatable by the process of heating.

Gana (Type) :

It is considered a *rakshasa* or demonic nakshatra. Its demonic quality relates to its cold-blooded, merciless approach to acts of violence like killing etc. It works by the "tit for tat" dictum and is usually unforgiving.

Orientation & Disposition :

It is a Downward nakshatra. In keeping with its penetrative nature, Krittika is always more interested in what is below the surface. For example, in relation to our planet, Krittika would relate to the fiery core, which keeps the surface in place. On a more personal level, one will find that the latent fieriness of a Krittika native remains hidden, unless provoked by some external agency.

It is a Mixed nakshatra i.e. it alternates between sharp and soft. Its sharper side is exemplified by Karttikeya, who as the general of the celestial armies, indulges in sharp actions like attacks, wars and battles. Krittika usually uses its sharper side for commanding purposes. Its softer side relates to the nurturing and maternal qualities of the seven wives. (Please refer to the Deity section).

Lunar Month & Day :

It relates to the first half of the lunar month of *Karttika*, which usually falls in late October, early November.

Krittika is also related to the *Shashti* (6th tithi or day) of the waxing and waning phases of the Moon's monthly cycle.

Auspicious Activities :

Fire worship; Purification rites; Giving up old habits; Making swift changes and sudden endings; Acts requiring initiative, courage, leadership and executive ability; Making important decisions; Military Activities and Interests; Debating; Standing up for oneself; Cooking; Sewing & Embroidery; Cutting; Shaving; All activities involving the use of fire or heat; All mothering & nurturing activities; Good for starting educational ventures; Good for commencing new ventures in general; Good for activities requiring a sense of discrimination, honesty and frankness; Drumming & Percussion; Most activities are favourable in this nakshatra.

Inauspicious Activities :

Socializing; Diplomatic activities; Rest or relaxation; Water based activities.

Planetary Ruler :

The Sun is the main ruler of this nakshatra, giving it a lot of energy, independence and power. Sun's rulership indicates the penetrating insight, pride, ambition and self motivation which characterise Krittika. Just like the Sun, Krittika goes on about its objectives in a straight and relentless fashion. The first pada is co-ruled by Mars. The combined energies of the two military planets make it harsh in its approach and functioning. It can ruthlessly conquer any obstacles or enemies that come in its path.

The rest of the padas are co-ruled by Venus. Sun and Venus are natural enemies and thus the Taurus part of Krittika has more to do with harmonizing the Apollonian and Dionysian extremes rather than having a cutting no nonsense militant approach. It helps to understand that in Krittika the solar energy is stronger in comparision to venusian energy and this is the reason why Moon (Sun's Queen in the planetary hierarchy) gets exalted here. The dynamics between Sun and Venus are not easy to understand. Venus is usually described as the hidden minister or the Queen's (Moon's) minister in the planetary hierarchy and thus the King's (Sun's) relationship with it is obscure. Venus however brings in love, caring and harmony into Krittika's hot, strict domain making it a more balanced nakshatra. Sun and Venus are both creative planets which strive for knowledge and forms the core of Krittika's functioning.

Sun/Venus, Sun/Mars conjunction or exchange in a horoscope carries energies similar to Krittika. Sun, Mars and Venus usually give strong results here but as always a lot depends on the pada they occupy.

Vowel s and Alphabets :

The first pada or quarter of this asterism 26° 40' -30° 00' Aries corresponds to "A" as in Arden.

The second pada or quarter of this asterism 00° 00' - 03° 20' Taurus corresponds to "Ee" as in Eagle.

The third pada or quarter of this asterism 3° 20' - 6° 40' Taurus corresponds to "Oo" as in Uzbekistan.

The fourth pada or quarter of this asterism 6° 40' - 10° 00' Taurus corresponds to "Ay" as in Elliott.

In the Sanskrit alphabet Krittika corresponds to "I", "Oo"and "U" consequently its mantras are "Om Im ", "Om Oo" and "Om U".

Sexual Type and Compatibility :

Its sexual animal is a Sheep or Goat, an animal which is seen as a rather passive creature, however the Ram, the animal symbol of the sign Aries, is capable of much aggression and fighting qualities when roused.

For sexual & marriage compatibility with other nakshatras please refer to the tables on pages 468 & 469 .

Esoteric :

There are many stories relating to the birth of Karttikeya. One of them says that Karttikeya was born as a result of Shiv's sperm falling on earth. Shiv here can be equated with Sun and the original masculine principle in the form of the sign Aries, while the earth is represented by the sign Taurus. This tale therefore suggests a mingling of these energies, and Krittika, as we know, is the nakshatra which bridges the signs Aries and Taurus, and is the initiator of solar energy. Krittika is the point in creation where the Fire element converts itself into the Earth element.

The star cluster Pleiades, which as we know represents Krittika in the skies, has been an object of veneration since ancient times. It is the place where the seven wives (represented by the seven brightest stars among the seventeen stars that are part of the Pleiades star cluster) of the seven sages (represented by the seven stars of the constellation *Great Bear*) are supposed to reside. These wives are supposed to be nannies to Shiv's younger son Karttikeya. Karttikeya, as we know, is the deity presiding over the planet Mars. This symbolism makes Krittika a harbinger and nourished of the Martian energy. In fact it can be seen as a cosmic university of sorts where the souls with predominantly Martian qualities are trained. This association with Martian energy is reinforced by the fact that Krittika begins in Aries, a sign ruled by Mars. The fact that the remainder of this asterism lies in the sign Taurus, representing earth itself, connects this asterism strongly with earthly activities.

A lot of ancient texts point towards a direct connection between Pleiades and evolution of life on earth. This relates to the benefic part of this asterism as the nourisher and well wisher of life on earth. This is why Moon is exalted in the first three degrees of Taurus, which are governed by this asterism. We can see the last three quarters of this asterism as carrying the feminine principle illustrated by the symbolism of the seven wives. Krittika is more or less the representation of the feminine matrix of life. The first quarter of this asterism relates more to its martian aspect, as illustrated by its symbolism of Karttikeya.

Gotra (Celestial Lineage) :

This nakshatra is related to the *Sage Angiras*, one of the seven celestial sages looking after the affairs of our galaxy. The name of this sage translates into "the fiery one". The relationship between Krittika and this sage is immediately clear from the name of the sage.

Remedial :

For those suffering from bad effects resulting from afflictions to this nakshatra, the best remedial measure is worship of Karttikeya. Worship of Sun along with the recitation of *Gayatri* mantra is also helpful in bringing the best out of this nakshatra. Having a reverential attitude towards the seven wives every time one gets to see the constellation of Pleiades also helps.

Repetition of the root mantras of this nakshatra - " Om Im ", "Om Oo" and "Om U" 108 times when Moon transits this nakshatra and in its corresponding lunar month is sure to reduce suffering and bring enlightenment into a person's life.

Persons who are benefiting from the positive energy of this nakshatra can also increase the good effects through the above mentioned ways. It is helpful for them to wear all bright fiery colours like gold, orange, red, yellow and variegated colours like those seen on peacock feathers. They should use its directions, lunar month and the days when Moon transits Krittika to undertake all important actions.

Example :

Krittika's sound and light can be experienced at –

http://osfa.org.uk/krittika.htm

Miscellaneous :

According to *Varahamihira*, Moon in Krittika gives one "a bright appearance, fondness for other's spouses, extreme appetite and widespread fame".

* * *

4. Rohini 10°00' Taurus - 23°20' Taurus

4.

Rohini

(10°00' Taurus - 23°20' Taurus)

In the Sky :

Rohini, the seed of lunar energy, is represented in the celestial firmament by a very bright pale rose star in the constellation of Taurus. This star is known in modern astronomy as *Alpha-Tauri* (*Aldebaran*). Aldebaran is one of the brightest stars in the night sky, with a visual magnitude of 0.99. In fact this unique pale rose star can even be spotted in the evening sky. The ancient vedic seers revered this star because this was supposed to be the abode of *Brahma* and the *Prajapatis.*

Name :

"Rohini" translates into - the "Reddish One" or the " Growing One". The "one" here carries a feminine tone and can be read as "celestial woman". The colour 'Red' evokes notions of warmth, passion and liveliness. The fact that in ancient cultures it was seen as the colour of abundance and prosperity, reveals some of the essential characteristics of Rohini. Its alternative names - *Vidhi* and *Viranchi,* a name which relates to *Brahma* (the Creator among the Trinity) - reveal more sides of this fascinating nakshatra.

Symbol :

Rohini's main symbol is an Ox-Cart pulled by Two Oxen. Oxen have been used as fertility symbols by all ancient cultures. Even Taurus, the sign representing 'bounties of the earth', has a bull, ox or cow as its symbol. In countries like India, where Vedic civilization flourished, an ox cart was one of the only ways to transport various earth produces like crops over large distances. They serve the same function which trucks serve in the present day and age.

Just as the ox-cart carries the harvested and ready to use produce, Rohini is supposed to be the carrier of all the fruits of creation. Its relationship with the ox cart immediately suggests that it has a lot to do with all aspects of agriculture, cattle rearing and all other activities involving material produce. The "carrier" aspect of the ox-cart relates Rohini to all kinds of conveyances. An ox-cart is a very earthy symbol and as a matter of fact, Rohini is the most materialistic amongst the nakshatras. In ancient times ox-carts were the "wheels of commerce". Thus in the present day and age, Rohini relates to all kinds of commerce and financial dealings.

All the qualities normally associated with oxen like steadiness, fixidity and ability to romp over anything which comes in its way, find expression through Rohini. As a result of the ox cart symbolism, Rohini relates to the 'development of agriculture' and therefore 'civilization' itself. All the qualities normally ascribed to the sign Taurus such as - earthiness, fixidity, stability, creativity, productivity, material security, acquisitiveness, refinement, accumulating, luxury loving, indulgence, idealism in love, beauty and relationships - are mostly derived from Rohini's essential qualities.

Deity :

Brahma, the creator among the governing Trinity of the universe, is the main presiding deity of Rohini. There are only three nakshatras which have one of the Trinity as its main presiding deity. This says a lot regarding the importance of this nakshatra, especially in regards to the affairs of *Bhuloka* (the earthly realm).

There are a lot of legends connecting Brahma to this nakshatra. The main legend relates to an earlier point of time in the history of the universe, when Brahma, after creating a daughter named Rohini, fell in love with her. From the Vedic point of view, every constellation is seen as a feminine goddess entity. Rohini's extraordinary charm and magnetism is made clear by the fact that Moon, whose duty it is to spend only a certain amount of time with each of these feminine figures in his monthly travel through the zodiac, at one point, refused to leave Rohini's abode. So it is not hard to see why Brahma fell for her and pursued her, despite the stigma attached with engaging in "cosmic incest"! However, he was stopped short in his chase by *Shiv* and had to be satisfied with just having the rulership of this nakshatra (please refer to the Esoteric Section of "*Ardra*").

From this story it is clear that Rohini is the most alluring amongst all nakshatras. Just as money in the present day world spins people around, Rohini makes people and even Gods chase after it in every which way possible. Rohini relates to the wish-fulfilling creative aspect of nature, embodied by goddesses of prosperity like *Laxmi*, the spouse of *Vishnu*. Due to its association with Brahma, it has the ability to create anything which constitutes 'prosperity' and 'abundance' on any plane of existence. All Brahma does is "create, create and create" and the same is the case with Rohini. It is thus not hard to see that its services are much in demand in all the *lokas* (planes of existence). Rohini is that important productive aspect of *Maya*, which keeps the game of life worth playing for those involved.

Nature & Functioning :

Rohini is the harbinger of agriculture and consequently "civilization", as we understand it. It is a very productive nakshatra which supports all types of growth. The growing of plants when we put seeds into the earth is a Rohini process. Rohini relates to the production of all types of amenities required for civilized living. When working through its higher plane, Rohini is only interested in use of products derived directly from nature. In its low aspect it indulges in all types of chemical, synthetic and man made products. The evolved Rohini types are usually true environmentalists and conservationists, while the lesser evolved ones promote unwholesome products like those of the present day cosmetic industry.

Rohini natives usually have large, clear and expressive eyes, refined feminine features, thick lower lip and a smiling countenance. They have a stable, earthy and well balanced way about them. They are as unresponsive to external stimuli as a cow. They only open up in extremely intimate situations. Their unflinching quality often comes out as stubbornness. Despite their calm exteriors, they can be very expressive with their voice and gestures. They can act well, whenever necessary. They are smooth talkers and have gentle, seductive mannerisms.

They seek attention and more often than not are able to get it. They are extremely popular within their social circle because of their charisma. They often use their charm and social ease for manipulating situations to suit their own ends. This is obviously a good thing if their personal ends are in line with universal ends, but when this is not the case, they can be the most self-serving of all people. It is very easy for them to gain the trust of others, and in the present day and age, this is often used to derive some sort of material benefit.

They are both sexually alluring and indulgent at the same time. On the whole they have simplistic personalities. This makes them appear dull and boring to those natives who are ruled by more complex nakshatras. In *Kali-Yug* they often turn out to be plain materialists and sensualists. Rohini natives are always very concerned about being constructively productive in one way or the other. They want to be of use to their home, community or the world in general depending upon their level of soul functioning. The essential fertile nature of Rohini helps them achieve their goals without much fuss.

Rohini always facilitates the materialization of one's thoughts and desires. This ability to give expression to feelings and thoughts makes it artistic. Rohini is a true patron of the arts; and therefore the level of artistic sensibilities at any given point of time among the collective, defines the level where Rohini is working from. These days when the standards in arts have declined to really putrid or abominable levels, one can easily see that Rohini is working through its lower, baser expression in the majority of the populace.

Rohini natives have a tremendous fixidity of purpose and persevere until their will is done. They usually have strong family values and tend to support those within their close circle. It is not possible for those outside their inner circle to hold their attention for long as they are very quick to spot weaknesses in others. Despite their naturally fixed nature, they like to quickly flit through people when it comes to social and communal interactions. When working through their lower natures, Rohini natives are cool and suave opportunists who have a knack for extracting favours and financial support from others.

Rohini natives are usually conservative to a degree, but at the same time are open to new influences. The word 'conservative' is used here in all its implications. The conservation part of their nature comes out strongly when it comes to preserving the body. Rohini is very strongly related to the life force within us. Most natives with a prominent Rohini are usually very careful about their health and live up to a ripe old age. In younger souls Rohini can cause a fear of death and dislike for the ageing process. The mantra of Rohini is to - create, create and create. Natives with Rohini connected to the 5th house in some form like to have lots of progeny.

Common english words like "robust", "romantic", "romeo", "rosy", "rose" seem to have the same root as the word "Rohini". All these terms give us clues to Rohini's functioning at different levels, especially in regards to the matter of enjoyment. Rohini is one of the most enjoyment-oriented nakshatras. It believes in making the most of the good things in life.

In the universal scheme of things, Rohini relates to "*rohana shakti*" or the power to make things grow. Its symbolism has plants above and water below. This is obviously a representation of the fertility aspect of nature. Rohini is the force which makes possible the materialization of the astral impulses.

Mode of Functioning :

Rohini is considered to be a Balanced nakshatra. Those who are involved in any productive activity will understand the importance of balance in achieving desired results. Just as nature is creative and productive through the balance of heat and cold, light and dark, rain and shine, winter and summer etc., Rohini is methodical and balanced in its actions. In its negative aspect however, Rohini, like other balanced nakshatras, makes one go through life with the least amount of adventure possible. It can be ultra-conservative and reluctant to try new things which add to its wisdom and experience. On the positive side, it knows how to stay within the assigned life path, without unnecessary strain.

Caste :

It belongs to the *shudra* caste. It may surprise some that Rohini is assigned this lowly caste. One has to understand that Rohini relates to the 'salt of the earth' people who are involved in activities directly dealing with the earth. Farmers (those who actually work in the fields) and construction workers, were all seen as belonging to the shudra caste in ancient times.

Gender :

It is a Female nakshatra. Its association with the two feminine planets Moon and Venus make Rohini a primarily feminine energy.

It is also the fourth nakshatra and the number 4 represents the mothering principle in nature. Rohini is the asterism most related to the Earth, which is seen as a feminine entity in all ancient cultures.

Bodyparts & Humor (Ayurvedic Constitution) :

The Forehead, Ankles, Shins and Calves of the Legs are the body parts related to this nakshatra.

It is a primarily "*Kapha*" (watery) nakshatra. This stems from its association with two primarily kapha planets, Moon and Venus. Among the three humors, kapha is most closely related to the earth element. This automatically makes Rohini a kapha nakshatra.

Direction :

It is related primarily to south, south east and northwest.

Padas (Quarters) :

The first pada or quarter of this asterism 10° 00' - 13° 20' Taurus falls in Aries Navamsa and is ruled by Mars. Passions and carnal nature are heightened here. The focus is on indulgence and extravagance. Planets here want quick-fire material results. Only a well placed Sun and Mars do well here. In its higher aspect this pada can make one a spiritual warrior fighting against exploitation on a material plane. On that level it is a purifying energy which combines spirtuality with matter without differentiation.

The second pada or quarter of this asterism 13° 20' - 16° 40' Taurus falls in Taurus Navamsa ruled by Venus. This pada best exemplifies all what Rohini stands for. Planets here usually give abundance and ability to conjure up required resources in the worst of conditions. The native however may tend to suffer from extreme materialism. This pada allows one to give expression to their thoughts and feelings through material means. Being a Vargottama pada it gives very strong results. This is the strongest pada in the zodiac when it comes to actualization and fulfilment of desires. Moon, Mercury, Venus and Saturn are especially strong here.

The third pada or quarter of this asterism 16° 40' - 20° 00' Taurus falls in Gemini Navamsa ruled by Mercury. The focus of this pada is on arts, sciences and business. It is the most flexible and shrewd amongst Rohini's padas and has the power to accumulate wealth equivalent to the second pada. This is a lighthearted and jovial pada and has less chances of getting stuck on purely material issues in comparison to the previous pada. Mercury, Venus and Saturn give strong results in this pada.

The fourth pada or quarter of this asterism 20° 00' - 23° 20' Taurus falls in Cancer Navamsa ruled by Moon. The focus here is on home and material security. Money comes in through short travels. Planets placed here have a maternal quality to them but can get excessively possessive and narrow-minded. A lot of the worst qualities of Rohini like unnecessary hoarding are relayed through this pada. Only a well placed Moon or Jupiter function well here.

Professions :

Farming; Agriculturists of all types; All professions relating with growing, processing and handling food; Botanists; Herbalists; Artists; Musicians; Entertainment and Leisure Industries; Fashion & Cosmetic Industry; Beauticians; Sex Therapists; Jewellers; Gemstone Dealers; Interior Decorators; Bankers and Financiers; Transportation Business; Tourism Industry; Automobile Industry; Oil & Petroleum Industry; Textile Industry; Shipping Industry; Food Production, Packaging & Distribution industry; All professions connected with Aquatic products and Liquids of all types.

Places :

Farms, Orchards, Gardens, Agricultural Estates, Places where herbs grow; Bus Stations, Train Stations & Shipping Yards; Ponds & Swimming Pools; Banks & Financial Institutions; Marketplaces; Bars, Restaurants, Hotels; Tourist Resorts; Studios for creative arts of all kinds; Places where gemstones are founds; All places connected with the above professions.

Guna (Essence) and Tattwa (Element) :

It is supposed to be a *Rajasic* nakshatra. This classification is obvious considering the materially productive quality of this nakshatra. The fact that it is related to Moon and Venus, two primarily rajasic planets, settles the issue.

It belongs to the Earth element. This is an obvious classification considering Rohini falls completely within the earth sign of Taurus. We have already touched upon its earthy quality many times throughout this chapter.

Gana (Type) :

It is considered a *Manusha* or human nakshatra. Rohini's earthy quality and its association with agriculture and civilization makes it strongly involved in human affairs. It represents earth's bounties without which human beings cannot survive. It is the nakshatra which most strongly supports human life.

Orientation & Disposition :

It is an Upward nakshatra. If we recall, one of the translations of Rohini's name is "the growing one". Thus it relates to all things which grow upwards like crops and buildings. We have already stated that any activity started in this nakshatra experiences growth, increase and expansion.

It is a *dhruva* (fixed or permanent) nakshatra. Its fixed nature is best exemplified by the behaviour pattern of oxen, its main animal symbol. Its permanence relates to the defined quality of nature, which ensures that the trees bear fruit every growing season and that the rivers flow from their source to the sea. In modern times, nature has become unreliable to an extent, only due to the destructive functionings of mankind. Still, she can be more or less relied upon to sustain the six billion of us.

Lunar Month & Day :

Rohini relates to the second half of the lunar month of *Karttika*, which usually corresponds to the month of November in the solar calendar.

Rohini is also related to the *Dvitiya* (2nd tithi or day) of the waxing and waning phases of the Moon's monthly cycle.

Auspicious Activities :

Extremely favourable for initiating activities of all types; Favourable for farming activities like planting, sowing; Trading & financial dealings of all types; Good for marriage; All healing & self-improvement measures; Nature exploration and travelling in general; Beginning construction; Romance and sexual activity; Putting the material world in order; Purchase of clothes, jewellery, automobiles etc.

Inauspicious Activities :

Not unfavourable for any action except those related to death, demolishing and destruction.

Planetary Ruler :

Moon and Venus are the two planets connected with Rohini. Moon is Rohini's main planetary ruler. The lunar energy imbues Rohini with primordial feminine energy. Venus is also related to shakti, the universal feminine force. The confluence of two feminine planets make Rohini a portal for material expression of *shakti*.

Moon's natural grace, nurturing ability and maternity combines with Venusian charm, creativity and productivity to make Rohini one of the most fruitful nakshatras. It is the most feminine amongst all the nakshatras and therefore the most receptive and productive. Just like Mother Earth, it provides for all without bias. In the present times however, Rohini is exploited, just as women and Mother Earth in general are exploited at the hands of dark forces which rule our planet. Rohini's bountifulness has been exploited to extreme levels through unbounded greed. This is the reason why most of the earth is polluted and most of the women troubled and unhappy. The ruling forces of the planet deliberately corrupt the feminine principle through the use of media.

Moon-Venus conjunction carries energy similar to Rohini. Moon, Mercury, Venus and Saturn express themselves strongly when placed in Rohini.

Vowels and Alphabets :

The first pada or quarter of this asterism 10° 00' -13° 20' Taurus corresponds to "O" as in Omega.

The second pada or quarter of this asterism 13° 20' - 16° 40' Taurus corresponds to "Va" as in Value.

The third pada or quarter of this asterism 16° 40' - 20° 00' Taurus corresponds to "Vi" as in Victor.

The fourth pada or quarter of this asterism 20° 00' - 23° 20' Taurus corresponds to "Vu" as in Wood.

In the Sanskrit alphabet Rohini corresponds to "Rm" and "Lrm" consequently its mantras are "Om Rm" " and "Om Lrm".

Sexual Type and Compatibility :

Its sexual animal is a Cobra. This makes Rohini exhibit serpent qualities in sexual union. The *sarpas* (celestial serpent beings) are regarded as being adepts at sexual activity. In fact Rohini is supposed to be the most sexually adept among all nakshatras. This is probably the reason why the Moon god was not ready to leave Rohini's abode. The representative goddess figurine of this nakshatra is supposed to be the master of all thirty-two principles of sexual union. Rohini is most compatible with *Mrigashira*, the other serpent nakshatra.

For sexual & marital compatibility with other nakshatras, please refer to the tables on pages 468 & 469.

Esoteric :

Since Rohini is the fourth nakshatra, all the qualities normally associated with the number '4' in Numerology form the basis of this nakshatra's universal role. '4' is the number of structure and concreteness. The material universe takes form under the energies of this nakshatra. The fire of *Krittika* is transformed into the earth element. In the language of physics we can say that pure energy condenses to form physical atoms, molecules etc. Rohini is representative of *Brahma's* power to turn energy into mass (tangible matter).

In the modern day *Tarot* pack, the fourth card called *"The Empress"* represents Rohini's role in the game of life, as the "Great Fruitful Mother Goddess" representing fertility, warmth, passion and abundance. She is supposed to represent *Maia* as she creates an earthly or material paradise. Rohini therefore can be seen as a channel through which the divine expresses itself through matter.

It is interesting to note that "The Empress" card carries the symbol of Venus, a planet very strongly connected with Rohini. The truth of the matter is that the word "Tarot" is derived from the word "*Taro*", which in turn comes from the Sanskrit term "*Tara*" meaning "Star". All the 21 cards of the Major Arcana in this pack have been derived from the 21 main attributes of the great mother goddess "Tara" or "*Jagdamba*" in charge of universal affairs.

We all have to admit that pleasure and enjoyment on varying levels is the basis of the game of life. If it wasn't for Rohini, the universal mind would have a hard time sustaining the drama of life, as very few souls would be willing to play it.

Gotra (Celestial Lineage) :

This nakshatra is related to the *Sage Atri*, one of the seven celestial sages looking after the affairs of our galaxy. The name of this sage translates into "one who consumes ". Atri seems to be a sage with a dual nature. He has rulership over two creative nakshatras and two destructive nakshatras. Rohini obviously relates to his productive side. From another point of view, Rohini can be seen as a devouring nakshatra, in the sense that it consumes souls through its excessive materialism.

Remedial :

Reverence towards cows, earth and nature in its various forms is the best way to get on the right side of Rohini's energy. Worshipping *Brahma*, its presiding deity, is not sanctioned by Vedic texts. Brahma is under the curse of *Shiv*, which doesn't allow for his worship on the earthly plane.

Repetition of the root mantras of this nakshatra - "Om Rm and "Om Lrm" 108 times when Moon transits this nakshatra and in its corresponding lunar month is sure to reduce suffering and bring enlightenment into a person's life.

Persons who are benefiting from the positive energy of this nakshatra can also increase the good effects through the above mentioned ways. It is helpful for them to wear all reds, whites, crèmes and bright pastel shades. White fabrics with flower designs are suitable. They should use its directions, lunar month and the days when Moon transits Rohini to undertake all important actions.

Example :

Krishn, Vishnu's 8th incarnation, was born with both his Ascendant and Moon in Rohini. Most Indians are aware of Krishn's personality and life and can therefore easily relate his life with Rohini's functionings. Krishn was known for his beautiful eyes, strong personal magnetism and the ability to find material manifestation of all his thoughts and desires.

Queen Victoria, the lady who was seen as the crowning monarch of 75% of the earth, was also born with both her Ascendant and Moon in Rohini. In her case the expansive and acquisitive material aspect of Rohini is brought to light.

Rohini's sound and light can be experienced at -

http://osfa.org.uk/rohini.htm

Miscellaneous :

According to *Varahamihira,* those born with Moon in Rohini are "honest, pure, beautiful, have steady minds and pleasant speech." This applies to Krishn totally.

5. Mrigshira 23°20' Taurus - 6°40' Gemini

5.

Mrigashira

(23º20' Taurus - 6º40' Gemini)

In the Sky :

Mrigashira, the initiator of Martian energy, is represented in the celestial firmament by a bright star and three not so bright stars in the constellation of *Orion.* These stars are known in modern astronomy as *Pi2-Orionis, Pi3-Orionis, Pi4-Orionis* & *Gamma-Orionis* (*Bellatrix*). Bellatrix is the bright star among them, with a visual magnitude of 1.66. It is easy to locate, as Orion is one of the most prominent and easily noticeable constellations in the night sky. Bellatrix is the bright star at the top right hand corner of Orion, while the three faint stars can be seen aligned in a bowlike formation a little away on the right hand side of Bellatrix. The ancient vedic seers however saw these stars to be forming a deer's head and we would soon know "why".

Name :

"Mrigashira" translates into - the "Deer's Head". One can immediately see the correlation between the shape formed by its stars and its name. The legend behind this name is dealt with later in the Esoteric Section. One can also make an obvious inference that this asterism's nature and quality should be akin to that of a deer. Its other names - *Saumya* meaning "benevolent" or relating to *Som* (Divine Nectar), *Arghayani* meaning "start of the year", *Chandra* meaning Moon and *Udupa,* which also is another name for Moon; each reveal a part of Mrigashira's functioning, as will shall discover in the course of our exploration.

Symbol :

Its main symbol is a Deer. Some scholars choose to have a deer's head as its symbol, as is literally apparent from its name. The association with a deer makes this nakshatra possess all deer like qualities such as timidity, lightness, fragility, fickleness, wandering etc. The deer is seen as a primarily lunar animal. In all ancient Vedic texts, deers are associated with gentle aspects of nature and often play major roles in romantic lores. Deers are portrayed as elusive, magical, divine and enchanting creatures.

In the Vedic epic of *Ramayan*, it was a magical deer (actually a demon posing as a deer), that caught *Sita's* attention; and her craving to possess it resulted in the disruption of her and Ram's marital felicity. This is the reason why Mrigashira is associated with problems in married life through illusion, undue suspicion or plain misunderstanding. The readers can refer to the Ramayan for the complete story. There are other legends associated with the deer aspect of this nakshatra. We will cover the most important among them in the Esoteric Section.

Deers have a constant searching and seeking quality about them, which forms the essence of this nakshatra. As most hunters know, deers often roam around predictable trails. Thus this nakshatra is related to all types of defined travel by road, air etc. Deers more often than not like to be in scenic habitats. Similarly this nakshatra feels comfortable only in scenic surroundings.

Its alternative symbol is a 'pot full of *Som'*. Som is the preferred drink of the gods. It is a kind of celestial nectar associated with the Moon. In fact Som is one of the sanskrit names of the Moon. As we shall discover later, Moon has a strong connection with this nakshatra.

Deity :

The main deity of this nakshatra is the Moon. All the primary qualities of the Moon - inconstancy, fickleness, changeability, tenderness, persuasiveness, gentleness, sensuality, perceptivity - apply in total to this nakshatra.

This nakshatra relates the most to the "Som" aspect of Moon. Moon is known by many names, each reflecting a different aspect of its functioning. As we discussed earlier, Som represents the nectar aspect of Moon. Moon is the ruler of all kinds of fluids on the material as well as astral plane. Fluids in turn are the essence of life, which we can observe through the functioning of our own bodies. As we know our physical bodies are comprised of more than 60% water and are biologically alive only because of the circulation of vital juices. The physical counterpart of mind, the brain, is also dependent upon the transmission and interaction of fluids for its functioning. Moon, in its Som aspect, is related to this essential lifeforce on the physical, mental, etheric and astral plane. This nakshatra thus relates to our life force and vitality through the presence and circulation of these vital fluids.

Moon relates to the feminine aspect of nature, a fact which connects this nakshatra directly to the feminine goddess energy. Ancient vedic seers saw this nakshatra as a seat of *Shakti* (the primordial goddess energy). In fact, *Parvati*, the wife of *Shiv* and one of the three main representatives of universal Goddess energy, is the main presiding deity of this nakshatra. It is her own personal nakshatra, as can be gauged from the fact that ancient texts say that her Moon is in Mrigasira. All her qualities like benevolence, charm, changeability, compassion, playfulness and joyousness are relayed through this nakshatra. Her timidity and gentleness is not to be confused with cowardice, as she can be very strong, unyielding and wrathful if necessary. Her fierce forms like *Durga* and *Kali* illustrate this fact. Most scholars usually neglect the fixed, strong willed and wrathful aspect of this nakshatra. The name "Parvati" translates into "she who has many parts". This translation exemplifies the multifarious, multifaceted persona of Mrigashira.

Moon in its Som aspect, is an indulgent character with hundreds of romantic liaisons. He is often seen getting into trouble due to his affairs with other's wives. According to one very famous legend, Mercury was produced out of the union of Moon with Jupiter's wife, *Tara*. In a way this story can be seen as the birth of intellect (Mercury), as a result of the union of mind and wisdom. Intellect is a more conscious force, which governs over the largely unconscious mind. In the universal scheme of things, mind couldn't have just been by itself without a governing faculty for long.

Nature & Functioning :

The essence of the nature and functioning of Mrigashira can be summed up by one word - "searching". This searching can have any level or aspect to it - it can relate to Mrigashira's ruling deity Parvati searching for her perfect spouse; a spiritual aspirant searching for true knowledge; or a soul searching for new mental, emotional or physical experiences.

Mrigashira is the most curious amongst all nakshatras and thus makes one seek new areas of experience. This aspect of Mrigashira is very similar to that of the planet Rahu (please refer to the author's previous work "*The Rahu-Ketu Experience*" *Sagar Publication,* New Delhi; "*The Key Of Life*" *Lotus Press,* USA for a comprehensive understanding of the nature and functioning of Rahu). This seeking brings contentment, fulfilment and enlightenment only when it is in keeping with one's life purpose. In other cases, it only brings about temporary satisfaction, which usually gives way to sorrow and disillusionment.

This seeking quality, however, makes Mrigashira natives good at artistic pursuits of all types. On a higher level, Mrigashira may allow one to find one's life path or destiny and on a lower level, it can just make one prance about like a deer from one transitory experience to the next. This is akin to a person in a desert chasing one mirage after the other. This negative quality gives rise to many other negative traits like fickleness, inconstancy and superficiality. Mrigashira natives often have to learn to stick at a thing until some sort of completion is achieved.

The whole emphasis of Mrigashira is on the mental rather than the physical. Mrigashira natives usually have great dexterity of mind, which gives them the ability to grasp various subjects with effortless ease. They have a great capacity for all types of mental work, but they often stretch themselves, and as a result suffer from mental and nervous exhaustion. They usually need a lot of clean air and physical exercise like walking to balance their mental energy. A lot of Mrigashira types are prone to physical lethargy, which besides making them functionally useless, makes them susceptible to physical ailments.

Mrigashira natives are usually thinly built with youthful delicate features; a smiley, jovial and lighthearted disposition; and warm, gentle manners. They are the restless type and may appear as flaky or fidgety to others. They usually convey a sense of fragility through their appearance and mannerisms. Their mind is always roaming about, which in many cases takes the form of daydreaming. They are charming, spontaneous, enthusiastic types who enjoy meeting and relating with people. They are good conversationalists, advisors and enjoy all vocal activities like talking and singing. They have a poetic soul and enjoy beauty in both spoken and written forms of communication. They are natural satirists and have a strong sense of humour which comes about due to their varied experiences. Despite their conversational skill and sociability, they are naturally shy. Their shyness has to do with their inherent timidity. They don't like confrontations and therefore are very cautious regarding whom they mingle with.

They love life and know how to suck delight out of it, just like gods take delight out of drinking *som* (celestial nectar). A honey bee buzzing about sucking juice from different flowers, sums up Mrigashira's functioning in this regard. Mrigashira natives are often quite whimsical in their approach, just like a honey bee would choose not to suck juice from a particular flower for no apparent rhyme or reason. Mrigashira craves excitement in all its mild and benevolent forms and is not prone to go to self-destructive extremes like cruel nakshatras.

Mrigashira natives often display a highly suspicious nature. This comes about due to their high alertness levels and their ability to sense danger, just like deer or stags do in their forest environment. This suspicious nature is especially troublesome in regards to marital felicity. Like all the nakshatras ruled by Mars, Mrigashira promotes domestic bickering due to suspicion and an inability to be attentive to their partner's needs. Their partners usually get more attached to them than they do. Mrigashira is a part bohemian nakshatra and doesn't like restricting its affections to one person. Those having a strong influence of this nakshatra in their charts, usually experience marital disharmony in one form or the other. However if both partners give each other enough space, Mrigashira through its lovingness and delightfulness, promotes profound marital stability like that of Parvati and Shiv.

Since Mrigashira signals the arrival of Mercurial energy through beginning the sign Gemini, it is the place where discrimination is born. It is also the first nakshatra where conclusions are drawn and fixed opinions are formed as a result of experiences. Mrigashira, despite its lightness, is a very fixed nakshatra when it comes to attitudes and opinions. It will never back down in any civilized argument.

In its highest functioning, Mrigashira makes one very conscious of their life path and purpose. The whole point of this nakshatra is to make one go through a variety of experiences, for finding one's true path in life. For example, if one was born to be a singer, one may dabble around with a lot of other things like painting, writing, or just plain nine to five jobs before their true niche is discovered. In the case of highly evolved souls, the varied experiences generated through the energy of this nakshatra, all fit a definite and singular purpose, while in the case of younger less evolved souls, these experiences are an endless maze without a final destination.

In the universal scheme of things, *Mrigashira* relates to "*prinana shakti*" or the power to give fulfilment. Its symbolism has extension above and weaving below. This is obviously a representation of fabric undergoing the weaving process. If we take this fabric to be the fabric of life, then Mrigashira is the structure and principles which create beauty in the chaotic process which is life.

Mode of Functioning :

It is a Passive nakshatra. Its passivity relates to a strong awareness of others. Mrigashira usually doesn't have the spotlight on itself and has its attention concentrated on the outside. In a way it is a passive nakshatra in relation to the dynamics of the self.

Caste :

It belongs to the Farmer caste. In ancient times Mrigashira was often related to artisans, agricultural workers and community in general.

Gender :

It is a Neutral nakshatra. Mrigashira is basically a hermaphrodite energy and has the ability to function both as a male or female. This dual functioning is clear from its ruling deities Moon and Parvati. Moon is seen as a male deity by the Vedic seers while Parvati is the female companion of *Shiv*.

Bodyparts & Humor (Ayurvedic Constitution) :

Eyes and Eyebrows are the body parts related to this nakshatra.

It is a primarily "*Pitta*" (fiery) nakshatra. This stems from the fact that it is the birthplace of Martian energy. Mars as we know is a primarily Pitta planet. One must however keep in mind that Mrigashira's fiery quality is not fierce or hurtful. It can be related to the fire which cooks our food, or the digestive fire which digests the food in our stomach, but not the cremation pyre fire which burns our bodies.

Direction :

Its range is the arc between south west and northwest.

Padas (Quarters) :

The first pada or quarter of this asterism 23° 20' - 26° 40' Taurus, falls in Leo navamsa and is ruled by Sun. This pada relates to the fixed and unyielding side of Mrigashira, which however has the ability to express its experiences through creative and artistic activities.

The second pada or quarter of this asterism 26° 40' - 30° 00' Taurus, falls in Virgo Navamsa ruled by Mercury. This pada represents the discriminatory, calculative, satirical and humorous side of Mrigashira. The conversational acumen and the strong mental ability of Mrigashira is more evident here. The fusing of the planetary energies of Mercury and Venus takes place here in such a way that the more grounded practical side of Mrigashira is expressed.

The third pada or quarter of this asterism 00° 00' - 3° 20' Gemini, falls in Libra Navamsa ruled by Venus. This is the first pada of Mrigashira which falls in the sign Gemini. The emphasis here is on sociability and a penchant for exploring the mental side of all types of relationships. Just like the previous pada, a fusing of Mercurial and Venusian energies takes place here, but on a whole, this pada is more airy in comparison to the previous pada; and thus cannot give strong material results.

The fourth pada or quarter of this asterism 3° 20' - 6° 40' Gemini, falls in Scorpio Navamsa ruled by Mars. This pada relates to the intellectual, argumentative, suspicious, flaky and whimsical part of this nakshatra. This pada is not as superficial as the previous Libra pada, but tends to over-intellectualize matters, rather than getting to the root of anything. Most of the negative qualities of Mrigashira find expression through this pada. It can function wisely only in evolved souls and thereto through proper guidance.

Professions :

Artists of all types; Singers & Musicians; Painters; Poets; Linguists; Romantic Novelists; Writers; Thinkers and Seekers; Gemstone dealers; Dealers in Earth related products; Those involved in the Textile & Garment Industry; Fashion Designers & Trendsetters; Veterinarians; All professions dealing with animals as pets; Salespersons of all kinds; Advertising agencies; Administrators; Landscapers; Farmers & Gardeners; Forestry workers; Real Estate developers; Map makers & Navigators; Travellers & Explorers; Psychics and Astrologers; Teachers especially those dealing with beginners; Artisans & Clerks; Commentators.

Places :

Forests, Fields & Meadows; Deer Parks; Villages and Small Towns; Bedrooms; Playgrounds; Nurseries; Nursery Schools; Recreation rooms; Entertainment places of all kinds; Streets, Footpaths & Roads; Lawns & Gardens; Forest trails; Art & Music studios; Small shops; Markets and other sales places; Astrological & Psychic institutions; All places connected with the above professions.

Guna (Essence) and Tattwa (Element) :

It is supposed to be a *Tamasic* (inert) nakshatra. This however shouldn't be taken in any negative sense, as it is basically a divine nakshatra (see Gana). It is associated with tamas because of its association with the tamasic planet Mars. The basic significations of Mars were seen as tamasic by the ancient Vedic seers. The "I can't get no satisfaction" aspect of Mrigashira is what makes it tamasic. However this nakshatra will behave in a predominantly tamasic way only if predominantly tamasic planets like Rahu, Mars and Saturn inhabit it.

It is the last among the nakshatras whose dominant element is Earth. This basically relates to this nakshatra's capacity for producing quick results on the material plane.

Gana (Type) :

It is seen by the ancient seers as a Divine/*Deva* nakshatra. It relates more to the beings on the astral plane than us humans. This classification reflects upon the refinement oriented focus of Mrigashira.

Orientation & Disposition :

It is a Level nakshatra. This reiterates the fact that Mrigashira is not an extreme energy and stays within limits. It is always trying to achieve a balance between expansion and contraction.

It is a *Mridu* (soft, mild and tender) nakshatra. This is pretty evident from the fact that Mrigashira is most suitable for seeking and enjoying pleasure on all planes of existence. Its pursuit of knowledge also takes place in an easygoing, enjoyable fashion.

Lunar Month & Day :

It relates to the first half of the lunar month of *Margashirsha*. This month usually corresponds to the month of December in the solar calendar. This month is also known as *Arghayana* because of

Mrigashira's alternative name *Arghayani*. It refers to an era when this month denoted the start of the year. In the present age the lunar month of *Chaitra* represents the start of the year.

Mrigashira is also related to the *Panchami* (5th tithi or day) of the waxing and waning phases of the Moon's monthly cycle.

Auspicious Activities :

Generally favourable for all lighthearted activities; Especially good for travel, exploring nature, sightseeing; Sexual activity; All types of artistic work; Healing and rejuvenation practices; Commencing educational ventures; Excellent for socializing; Changing residence; Good for all activities requiring communication; Good for setting up altars, religious items and performing spiritual initiations; Good for advertising and sales activity; Taking a new name.

Inauspicious Activities :

Unfavourable for marriage ceremonies (Vedic texts reveal that Shiv married Parvati when Moon was transiting through this nakshatra, and consequently their marriage went through many upheavals); Bad for hard and harsh actions of any kind; Not favourable for confrontations or making longterm important decisions of a serious nature.

Planetary Ruler :

The main planetary influences affecting this nakshatra are Mars, Venus and Mercury. Mars is the main ruling planet of Mrigashira. In fact as we mentioned earlier, martian energy comes into being through Mrigashira. Mars is the source, which provides energy for Mrigashira's "search". Mars here acts as an impulse planet, which encapsulates all the meanings associated with the word "desire".

We have already seen in the discussions on previous nakshatras, how the original creative fires (represented by the sign Aries), solidify into the earth element (represented by the sign Taurus). In

Mrigashira, these creative fires, which are now encased in an earthy, material sheath, try and mobilize matter. One way to understand this is to take a look at how modern day automobiles function. The average car is a heavy, metallic object, which is incapable of moving on its own, and its movement is only possible due to the fire/spark based internal combustion engines. In the same way, the martian energy here, becomes the force that drives matter, thus instilling a sort of life into it.

Mrigashira forms a bridge between Taurus and Gemini, and consequently relates to the fusing of Mercurial and Venusian energies. It is interesting to note that besides *Chitra* (14th nakshatra) and *Dhanishta* (23rd nakshatra), Mrigashira is the only nakshatra, which lies equally divided among two signs. Mrigashira has thus a strong sense of duality about it as it tries to resolve the conflict between earth and air, two naturally incompatible elements. Venus relates to the more earthy, Taurus part of this nakshatra, while Mercury relates to the airy Gemini part of this nakshatra. All the desirable qualities of Mrigashira like its artistic abilities and zest for life, ability to find the true life path or purpose, all come about only when the energies of Mercury and Venus are properly merged.

Planetary conjunctions like Mars/Mercury, Mercury/Venus, Mars/Venus and Mars/Mercury/Venus carry energies similar to Mrigashira. The presence of Mars or Saturn in this nakshatra is usually not auspicious for marital felicity. Both of them however can give good material results in the Taurus part of Mrigashira. In fact barring Jupiter, all other planets can usually give good material results in the Taurus part.

Vowel s and Alphabets :

The first pada or quarter of this asterism 23° 20' - 26° 40' Taurus corresponds to "Ve" as in Vega.

The second pada or quarter of this asterism 26° 40' - 30° 00' Taurus corresponds to "Vo" as in Vocal.

The third pada or quarter of this asterism 00° 00' - 3° 20' Gemini corresponds to "Ka" as in Katherine.

The fourth pada or quarter of this asterism 3° 20' - 6° 40' Gemini corresponds to "Kee" as in Key.

In the Sanskrit alphabet Mrigashira corresponds to "Em" and consequently its mantra is "Om Em".

Sexual Type and Compatibility :

Its sexual animal is a Serpent. Mrigashira is one of the experts in lovemaking. In all ancient cultures snakes or snakelike beings have been regarded as symbols of sexual potency and are seen as adepts at the art of sexual union. It is most compatible with the other serpent nakshatra *Rohini*.

For sexual & marriage compatibility with other nakshatras please refer to the tables on pages 468 & 469 .

Esoteric :

The most ancient tale relating to the formation of this nakshatra goes thus:-

"*Brahma*, the creator among the trinity, became obsessed with his own daughter *Rohini* (Brahma as we know is in a very funny position as every woman is his daughter). He was chasing Rohini in the form of a deer. *Shiv*, the destroyer among the trinity, cut the deer's head off with an arrow and thus the deer head's stars of Mrigashira came into being."

If one looks at the relative placements of Rohini, Mrigashira and *Ardra* (the nakshatra which is supposed to be the residence of Shiv), the story immediately makes sense. The deer head of Mrigashira faces Rohini in the night sky.

The constellation of *Orion* as a whole has always been regarded as an Archer. There are hundreds of tales of Parvati watching on as Shiv used his archery skills to kill demons or demonic cities, or the head of Brahma as we saw in the above mentioned story.

The fact that Mrigashira is supposed to be Parvati's abode, makes sense as it gives Parvati the right vantage point to observe Shiv's adventures in his *Rudra* form. Also the fact that Mrigashira can be seen either as a deer's head or an arched bow, reveals the dual functioning of this nakshatra as both the hunter and the hunted.

In all ancient cultures, Orion was supposed to be the abode of *Prajipati*. Prajipatis are the progenitors of all kinds of species inhabiting the universe. In this sense Brahma is the original Prajipati. This fact in the above mentioned story establishes a strong connection between Brahma and that portion of the celestial sky. Brahma however seems to have shifted his abode to the neighbouring Rohini. Please refer to the Ruling Deity section of Rohini.

Mrigashira relates to the point where curiosity is born in the process of creation. From a material point of view, we can see that all motion in the physical universe, even on an atomic level is dependent upon a physical quantity known as heat. Since Mrigashira is the initiator of Martian energy, it relates to the point in time where the temperature of the universe reaches the appropriate value for life to flourish. Heat and motion are the primary aspects of the planet Mars and they have their roots in this nakshatra.

Gotra (Celestial Lineage) :

This nakshatra is related to the *Sage Pulasthya*, one of the seven celestial sages looking after the affairs of our galaxy. The name of this sage translates into "having smooth hair". One can immediately see that Pulasthya has strong connection with the soft, refined aspect of Mrigashira.

Remedial :

For those suffering from bad effects resulting from afflictions to this nakshatra, the best remedial measure is worship of Parvati. Worship of the Moon is also favourable in increasing the favourable effects of this nakshatra.

Repetition of the root mantra of this nakshatra - "Om Em" 108 times when Moon transits this nakshatra and in the lunar month of Margashirsha is sure to reduce suffering and bring enlightenment into a person's life.

Persons who are benefiting from the positive energy of this nakshatra can also increase the good effects through the above mentioned ways. It is helpful for them to wear colours like red and white, green and light bright sparkly shades. They should use its directions, lunar month and the days when Moon transits Mrigashira to undertake all important actions.

Example :

Mrigashira's sound and light can be experienced at –

http://osfa.org.uk/mrigashira/htm

Miscellaneous :

According to *Varahamihira,* Moon in Mrigashira is "fickle, clever, timid, shrewd, energetic, wealthy and delighting in enjoyment."

Parvati, the presiding deity of this nakshatra and consort of Shiv, is supposed to have her Moon placed in the Taurus part of this nakshatra. A lot of her qualities, as revealed by the various puranic stories involving her, fit Varahamihira's description. Since she is an archetypal goddess, she can assume new forms like Durga and Kali, which embody completely different characteristics.

* * *

6. Ardra   6°40' Gemini - 20°00' Gemini

6.

Ardra

(6º40' Gemini - 20º00' Gemini)

In the Sky :

Ardra, the seed of Rahu's energy, consists of the bright star in the constellation of *Orion*, known in modern astronomy as *Betelguese* (*Alpha-Orionis*). With a visual magnitude of 0.57, this red giant is one of the brightest stars in the night sky. Betelguese is the bright star at the top left hand corner of Orion. It is revered in most ancient cultures as a very important star as it is supposed to have a strong influence on our planet. The ancient vedic seers saw this bright red star as being the abode of *Rudra*, the fierce red form of *Shiv*.

Name :

Ardra can have many varied English translations like - "green", "fresh", "the moist one". It's not hard to notice that all these translations are connected and carry a feeling of renewal. For example, the word "moist" may refer to the moisture in the air which forms the clouds, which in turn cause rain. The rain in turn brings life to the earthly vegetation and makes them "fresh" and "green".

Tears are one image which comes across instantly to one's mind when moisture is related with human feelings. A "teardrop" in fact is one of the most well-known symbols of this asterism. Sweat is another physical phenomenon which can be linked with moisture and the ancient texts associate this asterism with the oppressive heat of the Sun, which as we know is responsible for the sweating process.

Symbol :

Its main symbol is a Diamond, even though many scholars see a Teardrop as its primary symbol.

As we have already seen, the name of this nakshatra relates to moisture and wetness. The symbolism of the tear drop associates it with all kinds of sorrow. The tear drop symbolism also relates to water in all its droplet forms, like the early morning dew drops on the leaves or the thousands of drops left around after the rain has come and gone. These dew drops, as we can see, symbolise freshness and renewal. Even tear drops are part of a cleansing process and relate more to the dispersal of sorrow rather than the actual production of it. This cathartic process is similar to that of a baby, which can cry one minute and be smiling the next as if nothing happened.

This is a futuristic nakshatra, which tends to release one from the decaying past through a series of stormy events. It must be remembered though that all these storms are usually of a very short duration and don't last very long. If one does not try to cling to the past one can sail through this phase with ease and be rewarded with a renewal akin to the freshness of the leaves after the rain. For example, one feels disappointed when one loses a job, but this might provide a new opportunity for one to pursue one's favoured vocation and find success there in. This is the reason why 'a diamond' is the main symbol of this nakshatra.

A diamond, as we know, is formed after been acted upon by extreme heat and pressure for millions of years. In the same way, this asterism can produce a glowing personality after one has successfully gone through the storms that wash away the old. The diamond symbolism also relates to the hard work required to extract the shining and brilliant jewel of knowledge from the stormy vicissitudes of this nakshatra.

A diamond is mainly a mental and intellectual symbol, with its reflective multi-dimensional layers, signifying the multifarious aspects of *Manomayakosha* (mental/intellectual plane). Just as the brilliance of a diamond depends on the amount of light falling on it, the brilliance of the mind and intellect depends upon the amount of light the soul has. Ardra's alternative symbol, "a man's head", also conveys a similar idea of mind and mentality.

The diamond is also the hardest known substance on the material plane and this hardness in turn relates to the unyielding and determined aspect of this nakshatra. This nakshatra has a sharp, piercing quality to it and can cut through anything with ease in much the same way as a diamond can. Getting to the root of the matter is very important to this nakshatra. Ardra is therefore directly connected to one's depth of perception.

Deity :

Its presiding deity is *Rudra*, which translates into 'the terrible', 'the ruddy red', 'the transformer' or the 'the howler'. The reference to red colour gains significance from the fact that astronomers actually refer to Betelgeuse (the primary star of this nakshatra) as "the Red Giant". Rudra represents the destructive and transformative aspect of *Shiv* (the destroyer among the Vedic trinity).

Rudra is also seen as the Storm God by some Vedic texts, which again points towards a sense of commotion and upheaval. Rudra relates to chaos, disorder, confusion, anarchy and havoc. However most wise men will agree, that in fact, it is these terrible things which more often than not turn people around. Very few embrace change unless put against the wall!

The primary essence of Ardra is 'change' and Rudra knows exactly what is required to bring it about. The period before the storm, where the dark clouds gather accompanied by lightning and thunder, is the atmosphere Rudra revels in and relates to (refer to the image). Ardra can be seen as an expert at producing these kinds of situations, bringing in such experiences into a person's life.

Storm is an important phenomenon through which nature finds its release. Ardra can be seen as marking the period just before, during and after a rainstorm. Rudra is intimately connected with the constellation of Orion, "The Hunter". Orion is supposed to be the most important constellation in terms of its effect on earth and humanity. It is revered in all the Vedic texts as the gateway from where the souls descend to begin their earthly life and is thus called the "Giver of Life". It aids in the evolutionary process of humanity through triggering important changes. Some of these changes may appear destructive on an individual or collective level like a violent storm, but they are always auspicious in the sense that they always trigger new growth.

Rudra has many legends attached to him in the ancient Vedic texts. We will deal with the most famous amongst these and other aspects of Orion's importance in the Esoteric Section.

Nature & Functioning :

The nature of Ardra is like the nature of a child. Natives under its influence have an ability to flit from intense joy to intense sorrow, to somewhere in between within a matter of minutes. Ardra is always involved in a churning process. This makes the natives under its strong influence to be undergoing constant transformation. In some cases, this process produces good things like gems of knowledge and in some cases it produces negative things like poisonous thoughts and confusion.

Ardra is the first nakshatra where an attempt is made on a mental/ intellectual plane to understand the functionings of *maya*. This is the place where intellect is born. In the previous nakshatra, *Mrigashira*, mind develops its capacity to roam and wander. In Ardra an intellect is developed to synthesize the experience gained through these wanderings. Ardra is still pretty much as curious as Mrigashira, the only difference being that Ardra likes to know the cause behind the effect, while Mrigashira is mostly content with observing and enjoying the effect.

It can be said that Mrigashira "enjoys" and Ardra "dissects". This is probably the reason why all natives born under its influence have research orientated and probing intellects. When an Ardra native enters a room one can immediately recognise their probing quality. Even seven year old children like to observe and understand people around them. This observing is usually without any regards for courtesy and they can be quite upfront about voicing their findings.

In the universal scheme of things, *Ardra* relates to "*yatna shakti*" - the power to make efforts. Its main theme is searching and reaching the desired goal. Ardra thus finishes off the searching that began in Mrigashira. Achievement is the result of Ardra's energy.

It is easy to see that that the english words like - "arduous" and "ardent" have been derived from "Ardra" and thus relate to its functionings. In fact, English as a language has a lot to do with the energies of Ardra.

Ardra is the nakshatra where mental sensitivity and impressionability develops as the stormy vicissitudes of this nakshatra make the mind active and reactive. This sensitivity makes Ardra natives susceptible to all kinds of hurts and in some cases gives a strong desire to help those who are suffering or hurt. The underlying emotional thirst of Ardra is based upon empathy. Even Rudra, its ruling deity, came into being to protect *Rohini* from *Brahma* (please refer to the story in the Deity section of Rohini).

Even a thunderstorm is nothing but nature's way of relieving Earth's vegetation of its misery. Ardra is the first nakshatra where emotions are encountered by the mind. There is a constant need for balancing the mental and emotional impulses in this nakshatra.

Natives born with Ardra rising on the Ascendant usually have large faces, curly hair and sullen expression. The eyes have a particular piercing quality about them and the expression, "going red with anger", literally applies to Ardra natives. The mad, absentminded professor archetype is an Ardra character. They have good memory and are quick to respond to facts and figures. It must be noted that Ardra natives don't usually verify the facts before they speak. Although they may appear calm outside there is usually some raging storm going on in their heads. Their lives are full of extreme changes and complete turn-arounds.

Ardra natives are intense and unrelenting observers of both themselves and others. This quality, coupled with the fact that they usually put their thoughts into speech, makes them appear impolite and critical. In some cases their sarcasm can cause much pain or agony to others. In lesser evolved souls, Ardra displays its childlike tendency to serve selfish ends through lying, unscrupulousness etc. They are, however, courageous like Rudra and don't mind any type of confrontation.

Ardra people are like storms running around and the reactions they get from other people is as varied. They are good at scaring people, especially the softer types. Their physical constitution is usually quite strong, which makes them good at physically oriented jobs. On the material prosperity scale, they tend to fluctuate between extremes. They are, however, usually not good with finances, as they are likely to spend all of their earnings. Just like a seven year old child, Ardra is not very concerned about money.

Because of the illusionary energies of Rahu, Ardra can create a whole lot of confusion and make Ardra natives scatter away their intellectual and mental energies in meaningless pursuits. It can also make them stubborn, arrogant and reckless. In the present day and age, where science and technology have a strong hold over the mass consciousness, Ardra natives usually waste their potential on these material sciences, which in most cases don't bring about any evolution on the soul level. It is seen that a lot of physicists make the shift from physics to metaphysics late in their lives, after exhausting all its possibilities. This shows how people can waste their whole lives before coming to any meaningful conclusion. All Ardra natives get a chance to transform their lives for the better, but in today's hyper materialistic age, where all types of illusions abound, it is no easy task.

In the case of highly evolved souls, Ardra functions in a different way. In such cases, the universal mind tests them through stormy conditions and situations, in order to test their resolve and understanding. History is the proof that all great personalities have undergone many storms in their lives. Besides testing our faith, these storms clear away the dust of negative karmas from previous lives. Ardra is the storm which wakes us from our stagnating slumber and makes us howl and cry out the most important question "Why!"

Mode of Functioning :

Ardra is considered to be a Balanced nakshatra. Its balanced nature stems from its mental and intellectual acumen. Those who think, analyze and contemplate, don't usually go to extremes. All of Ardra's diffusion, chaos and storminess is nothing but nature's way of restoring balance. If we are facing some tormenting situation in the present life, its only purpose is to dissolve and balance out our karmas from previous lives. The thunderstorm is also a typical manifestation of nature's way of restoring balance.

Caste :

It belongs to the Butcher caste. It is Ardra's job to remove or put an end to whatever has outlived its usefulness. Ardra's presiding deity Rudra, is well known for getting the universe rid of unwanted demonic forces. As we will see in the Esoteric section, Rudra didn't think twice about a very serious issue like cutting off one of Brahma's heads.

Gender :

Ardra is a Female nakshatra. Even though its presiding deity, Rudra is male, all of this nakshatra's background and Rudra's functioning, relate to the chaotic, wrathful state of nature. The terms associated with Ardra like 'tenderness', 'moistness' and 'freshness' can only be regarded as being feminine. The renewal which the earth's vegetation experiences after rainfall is also one of nature's feminine phenomenas.

Bodyparts & Humor (Ayurvedic Constitution) :

The body organs it relates to, the Eyes and the Back and Front of the Head, highlight its perceptive and analyzing quality. As neurologists are now discovering, most of the brain's controlling mechanisms are located in the front and back of the head.

It belongs to the *Vata* (airy) humor. This is clear from the fact that all of this nakshatra lies within the vata sign of Gemini. Its planetary ruler Rahu is also a primarily vata planet. There can be no storm without air!

Direction :

It is related primarily to southwest, west and north.

Padas (Quarters) :

The first pada or quarter of this asterism 6° 40' - 10° 00' Gemini, falls in Sagittarius Navamsa and is ruled by Jupiter. This pada relates to the exploratory and curious side of Ardra. Planets placed here have a happy go lucky disposition, but are prone to material excesses. This is the beginning of the storm and thus conditions here are not very unfavourable.

The second pada or quarter of this asterism 10° 00' - 13° 20' Gemini, falls in Capricorn Navamsa ruled by Saturn. This pada gives a strong interest in all types of materialistic pursuits and frustration therein. Most of the negative qualities of this nakshatra are manifested through this pada. The storm has gained momentum here and thus the planets placed here give constant troubles and misfortunes.

The third pada or quarter of this asterism 13° 20' - 16° 40' Gemini, falls in Aquarius Navamsa ruled by Saturn. This pada relates to the electrical, scientific and research oriented part of Ardra's functioning. The storm here is at its peak lightning stage and thus the planets posited here can give short sudden bursts of inspiration. Mental activity is at its peak in this pada.

The fourth pada or quarter of this asterism 16° 40' - 20° 00' Gemini, falls in Pisces Navamsa ruled by Jupiter. This is the Pushkara Navamsa pada of Ardra. It relates to the sensitive and compassionate aspect of Ardra. It has a strong desire to help those less fortunate than itself in the process of evolution. The storm is ending here and so the conditions are mild and peaceful in comparison to the two previous padas. Planets posited usually give benefic expansive results.

Professions :

Electrical Engineers and Electricians; Electronic & Computer Industry; Computer Software Developers; Sound Engineers & Technicians; Musicians, especially those involved in Electronic Music; English Language Experts; Weapon Experts; Photographers; Special Effects people in the Film Industry; Computer Game Designers & Sci Fi Buffs; 3D & Virtual Reality Experts; Manual Labourers of all types; Physicists, Mathematicians & Researchers; Scientists; Profound Thinkers & Philosophers; Writers &

Novelists, especially of the science fiction genre; Surgeons; Physicians who administer poisons in small amounts as remedies like Homeopaths; Allopathic doctors; Those involved in mental sports like Chess, Scrabble, Bridge etc.; Morticians; Chemical & Fertilizer industry; Pharmaceutical Industry; Professions involving handling poisons of any type; Those working in Nuclear Power Plants; Eye & brain Specialists & Surgeons; Psychoanalysts & Psychotherapists; Those specializing in healing or curing Brain & Head disorders; Investigators, Detectives & Mystery Solvers; Analysts of all types; Lighting experts; Xray Specialists & Radar Personnel; Food Processing Places which produce canned, frozen & junkfood; Thieves; Legal & Illegal Drug Dealers; Sales people adept at lying and double talk; Biotechnologists; Chemotherapists; Politicians & Manipulators; Snipers & Hitmen.

Places :

Geographical places where natural phenomena like thunderstorms, hurricanes and tornadoes are common; Research laboratories of all types; High tech studios and shops; Hospitals; Communication centres like radar facilities, radio stations, television studios, telegraph offices; Nuclear power plants; All factories dealing with poisonous chemical processes; Escalators; Military bases where weapons are stored & maintained; All places connected with the above mentioned professions.

In today's day and age every home has its share of Ardra because of electrical wirings and appliances.

Guna (Essence) and Tattwa (Element) :

It is a *Tamasic* nakshatra. Its tamasic quality arises due to its association with the tamasic graha, Rahu. Its tamasic quality manifests itself as chaos, diffusion, disturbance and fuzziness.

It belongs to the Water element. Its wateriness is evident from its symbolism and imagery. This shows that there are strong underlying emotions involved within the intellectualism of Ardra.

Gana (Type) :

It is a *Manusha* or human nakshatra. Its association with Mercury, the planet which forms a bridge between the lower and higher worlds, relates it to the plane of humanity which lies right in the middle of the fourteen planes (realms) of existence. This asterism carries the illusory aspect of its ruler Rahu, which is very involved with humanity and its struggle on the material plane on the planet earth.

Orientation & Disposition :

Ardra is an Upward nakshatra. Just like Rudra aims his arrow towards the sky (refer to image), Ardra sets its goals high. It seeks intellectual challenges and higher knowledge in all its forms. Whenever we encounter troublesome situations in our life, we are often forced to question the why behind it all. This is usually the time when many among us turn our gaze upwards towards the sky, where all the answers lie.

It is a *Tikshna* or sharp and forceful nakshatra. This is evident from its ruling deity, the Storm God. It functions in a sudden sharp manner akin to a snake bite. Rahu as we know is a harsh planet. Biting sarcasm and distressful events are associated with this asterism. Even when giving good results it gives them in a sudden sharp manner.

Lunar Month & Day :

It relates to the second half (the middle 9 days) of the lunar month of *Margashirsha*. This period usually corresponds to the month of December in the solar calendar.

Ardra is also related to the *Ekadashi* (11th tithi or day) of the waxing and waning phases of the Moon's monthly cycle.

Auspicious Activities :

Only auspicious for activities related to its profession and places; Favourable for destructive activities like demolishing old buildings; Discarding old and wornout habits and objects; Good for confronting underlying issues and difficult problems which have been lurking around; Good for research and creative activities within its domain; Good for propitiating fierce deities like Rudra and Kali.

Inauspicious Activities :

Unfavourable for any type of beginning; Generally inauspicious for all auspicious activities like marriage, travel, giving and receiving honours, religious ceremonies and the like.

Planetary Ruler :

Even though Rahu is the main planetary ruler of Ardra, it can be seen as a combination of the energies of Mercury and Rahu. Mercury and Rahu are both intellectual planets dealing with the duality of life and nature. Rahu's Mercurial side is relayed through this nakshatra. This heightens the intellectual and thinking capacity of Ardra natives, and involvement in activities which emphasize communication, thinking or use of the hands. It ensures abundant mental and nervous energy and mercurial qualities like wit, versatility, quickness of thought and communication ability. Just like a diamond, Ardra's intellectualism is usually piercing and multifaceted.

In its negative aspect the Rahu-Mercury influence of this nakshatra will make one misuse their skills for selfish ends or harming others. In some cases the intellect is distorted to an extent that the native doesn't think twice about indulging in criminal actions. However one must be careful regarding what one does under the influence of Ardra, because the consequences usually have to be faced within this lifetime. This is also a good thing in the sense that we don't have to carry our baggage into future lives and possibility of redemption within the present life itself cannot be ruled out. Rahu and Mercury's energy can also get one caught up in the present day information boom, which has very little to do with real knowledge. In its higher aspect, it can give true knowledge and the ability to look through illusions. It can also connect one's intellect to the unseen realms and as a result give intuitive or psychic perception.

Ardra is the birthplace of Rahu's mysterious energy. Here nature deliberately introduces chaos and diffusion, in order to facilitate the process of creation and manifestation. We can see that the creative process has been quite ordered in the previous nakshatras. Ardra is thus related to that random x-factor in the universe which can never be grasped. In the language of physics, this is best exemplified by the "uncertainty principle" and "quantum theory", both of which broadly state that nothing is certain and everything is just a probability. In other words, *Maya* is unfathomable. It however reveals itself through true enlightenment - a process which involves all the 27 nakshatras.

Vowel s and Alphabets :

The first pada or quarter of this asterism 6° 40' -10° 00' Gemini corresponds to "Ku" as in Kubrick.

The second pada or quarter of this asterism 10° 00' - 13° 20' Gemini corresponds to "Kha" as in Khalsa.

The third pada or quarter of this asterism 13° 20' - 16° 40' Gemini corresponds to "Nga" as in Nancy.

The fourth pada or quarter of this asterism 16° 40' - 20° 00' Gemini corresponds to "Chha" as in *Chhatri* (hindi for umbrella).

In the Sanskrit alphabet Ardra corresponds to "Aee" and consequently its mantra is "Om Aeem".

Sexual Type and Compatibility :

Its sexual animal is a Dog. As is clear from the image, the dog is an aggressive howling hound and not a friendly Scottish terrier! Dogs are supposed to be sexually active animals and thus Ardra can be excessively indulgent in regards to sexual matters. It is most compatible with Mula, the other dog asterism.

For sexual and marital compatibility with other nakshatras please refer to the tables on pages 468 & 469 .

Esoteric :

Recent findings have shown that the constellation presently known as *Orion*, or the hunter, was of special interest to the ancient Egyptians. It has been assigned special status in Vedic mythology as well. This constellation houses two asterisms, Mrigashira and Ardra. Mrigashira is represented by the front three stars which form the bow of the hunter. Ardra, as we have discussed earlier, is represented by the bright star of Betelguese, which is situated at the top left part of Orion. We also know that Ardra is ruled by Rahu, which connects Rahu with Orion.

According to some Vedic scholars, Betelgeuse is supposed to be the abode of Shiv. Orion was supposed to come into being when Shiv assumed the form of a hunter and took out one of Brahma's heads with his arrow. This makes sense when one sees that Brahma is the ruling deity of the neighbouring constellation Rohini. We have already seen that Vedic seers think of Mrigashira, the neighbouring nakshatra, as *Parvati's* (consort of Shiv) abode. Though not well recognized by scholars, the fact is that Mrigashira and Ardra form a sort of a pair like *Purva Phalguni* (11th nakshatra) and *Uttara Phalguni* (12th nakshatra).

As we have already discussed, Rudra, the fierce form of Shiv, is the presiding deity of Ardra. This establishes a relation between Rahu and Shiv, the destroyer among the Trinity. Some Vedic texts have gone to the extent of saying that Rahu resides in the heart of *Neelkanth*, another name for Shiv. We can see that Rahu and Shiv are relatives, as Shiv is the husband of the sister of the mother of Rahu. His closeness with Shiv is one of the reasons why Rahu co-rules Aquarius, the sign most related to Shiv. They even share the same electric blue complexion, a colour associated with Aquarius.

The significance of Orion lies in the fact that it stands right in the middle of the galactic gateway between Taurus and Gemini. It is said that all the souls incarnating on planet Earth come through this galactic gateway. We can understand this astronomically in the sense that the gateway points away from the centre of our galaxy and can thus be seen as a doorway into our galaxy.

This is why Vedic texts relate Orion with the *Prajapati*, the progenitor of human race. Even ancient Egyptians saw Orion as *Osiris*, the father of all humanity. Orion is also situated very close in the night sky to *Sirius*, the star around which our Sun is supposed to revolve, but a detailed discussion on the importance of Sirius lies beyond the scope of this book.

In the universal scheme of things, Ardra relates to "yatna shakti" - the power to make effort. The effort is exemplified by the shooting of the arrow. Its symbolism has hunting above, and the goal below.

Gotra (Celestial Lineage) :

This nakshatra is related to the *Sage Pulahu*, one of the seven celestial sages looking after the affairs of our galaxy. The name of this sage translates into "connector of space". Ardra as we have discussed before, gives a fascination for space and all spacey things like sci-fi adventures. It makes sense therefore that this spacey nakshatra would relate to this sage, who is known to connect space.

Remedial :

For those suffering from bad effects resulting from afflictions to this nakshatra, the best remedial measure is worship of Shiv, in his terrible Rudra form.

Repetition of the root mantra of this nakshatra - "Om Aeem" 108 times when Moon transits this nakshatra and in its corresponding lunar month is sure to reduce suffering and bring enlightenment into a person's life.

Persons who are benefiting from the positive energy of this nakshatra can also increase the good effects through the above mentioned ways. It is helpful for them to wear colours like red, green, shiny metallic colours emulating lightning, all storm colours like silvers, dark greys and black. They should use its directions, lunar month and the days when Moon transits Ardra to undertake all important actions.

Example :

Ardra's sound and light can be experienced at -

http://osfa.org.uk/ardra.htm

Miscellaneous :

According to *Varahamihira*, Moon's placement in Ardra makes one "ungrateful, wicked, violent and proud".

* * *

7. Punarvasu   20°00' Gemini – 3°20' Cancer

7.

Punarvasu

(20°00' Gemini - 3°20' Cancer)

In the Sky :

Punarvasu, the root of Jupiterian energy, consists of the two bright stars in the constellation of Gemini, known in modern astronomy as *Castor* (*Alpha-Geminorium*) & *Pollux* (*Beta-Geminorium*). With visual magnitudes of 1.58 and 1.22 respectively, *Castor* & *Pollux* are easily visible in the night sky. They can be located at the top left hand corner above *Orion* within the constellation of Gemini. In most ancient cultures these stars were seen as twins (brothers or lovers). The ancient vedic seers however saw this asterism as a "quiver of arrows".

Name :

Punarvasu translates into "Good Again", "Wealthy Again" or the "Visible Infinity". The *Vasus* are demigods carrying all the desirable qualities like goodness, strength, prosperity etc. (refer to the Deity section of *Dhanishta*, the 23rd asterism). The fact that the term "Punarvasu" literally translates into "Becoming Vasu Again", reveals its first two meanings. We also get an impression of some positive transformation from darkness into light. This duality and interplay between the opposites is the essence of Punarvasu. Its "visible infinity" meaning is more profound and relates to its ruling deity.

Symbol :

The most accepted symbol of Punarvasu is a 'quiver full of arrows'. Sometimes one single arrow is taken is its symbol, but in both cases the arrow symbolism dominates the discussion of this nakshatra.

An arrow has been traditionally associated with every aspect of human nature and functioning - arrow of desire, arrow of ambition, *Eros'* arrow and not to forget the arrow of time. In all these cases the arrow is always associated with some sort of movement, striving or objective. The arrows in the Punarvasu quiver are not normal arrows. They are supposed to be like the divine *astras* (weapons), used in ancient times, which magically return after fulfilling their function or mission. This conveys the idea of renewal, regeneration and endless beginnings.

Punarvasu's quiver basically represents energy and resources at one's command. It is up to us to choose the purpose and timing of their use. Punarvasu thus has a distinction of returning safely from any mission it undertakes. This mission may be as simple as going to the neighbourhood shop or as arduous as climbing Mt Everest. The mission can take place on any plane - mental, physical, emotional, astral or causal. It is Punarvasu's function to ensure safe return to the starting point. No wonder that Punarvasu became synonymous with 'safety' in the eyes of the wise men. Its alternative symbol, "a house", once again reiterates the idea of safety.

One can also easily infer from the above that Punarvasu has a lot to do with any kind of motion, movement and searching. All the qualities normally associated with the sign Sagittarius, which also has an arrow as its symbol, can be applied to Punarvasu as well. The fact that the journey always ends where one started leads us to the idea of a circle. Time and reality are cyclical and not linear, as most in the modern world believe it to be. The modern Darwinian theory of evolution suggests that the human race is in a state of unhindered evolution by the process of natural selection. This implies that we, as a race, are becoming more intelligent than our ancestors with each passing generation. The theory further suggests that we are in a state of perpetual progress, through linear time, which only moves forward. This is in opposition to the view held by all ancient civilisations, who knew that time is cyclical, and that nature renews itself through perpetual repetition. This repetition has a helical (as is the case with DNA strands which make up the genetic code), rather than a purely circular nature, but for symbolic purposes the circle has always been used as the imagery which conveys this eternal reality. *Shatabhisha* (24th nakshatra) and Punarvasu are the two main nakshatras which reveal and deal with this aspect of the universal functioning.

Deity :

Aditi, the mother of the 12 Adityas (solar deities), is the main ruling deity of Punarvasu. Aditi translates into "unbounded". She is often seen as the goddess of abundance. She is a sky goddess who is said to be the mother of all the godly beings in the universe. In a way she relates to all space. The manifest universe, as we know, is basically a function of space and time. Space like time has an infinite quality to it and for all purposes can be taken as unbounded. The "visible infinity" translation of Punarvasu starts to make some sense when seen in the above light.

The reality however is that both space and time are finite quantities bounded by the circular aspect of nature discussed earlier. Aditi or space is the sinequanon for any motion or movement. If there is no space there is no motion. In fact there can be no concept of existence either. Space has always been the receptive, feminine principle as opposed to time, which is seen in a more masculine light. Going by this line of thinking, Aditi should be the mother of all that exists, if it were not for her sister *Diti.* Diti, the bounded space, is the mother of all ungodly or demonic beings in the universe.

Diti, like the night, can be seen as dark space, which harbours the dark, mysterious and evil side of nature. Aditi relates to the space, which like the day, is full of light, and is thus the harbinger of the benevolent side of nature. Aditi's rulership of Punarvasu imparts it with a maternal, caring, sensitive, reasonable and accommodating approach. Just like the space which accommodates all, Punarvasu is very accommodating of people, situations, circumstances and energies.

Nature & Functioning :

In the universal scheme of things, *Punarvasu* relates to "*vastuva prapana shakti*" - the power to gain or retrieve objects or objectives. Its main theme is triumphant return and renewal. The arrow which hits its target in Ardra now returns back. Its symbolism has wind, which carries the clouds above and rain, which revitalizes the plants below. Just like the rain, Punarvasu brings renewal. Another way of seeing this is that the wind carries the clouds to where they need to be after the rain is over.

The essence of Punarvasu's nature and functioning lies in two words, "Nurturing" and "Harmony". Since it represents the first light after the storm, Punarvasu represents harmonious conditions in nature. Nature seems to be at its happiest in the period after a storm, when the chirping of birds and the fresh smell from the rejuvenated earth creates a buzz in the air. Consequently, Punarvasu represents favourable conditions for life to thrive on all levels. The inherent calm of this nakshatra makes natives strongly under its influence, contented people, who get satisfied easily. They believe in living a simple, spiritual life and strive hard to get rid of any negative energies, feelings or thoughts, which may obstruct their evolutionary process.

Punarvasu is a nakshatra where the interplay of the mental with the emotional is at its most fascinating, as both have the same amount of strength. In the previous nakshatra, Ardra, the mental is much stronger, while the emotional part is in the process of developing. The quality which arises out of this fine balance of mental and emotional is "reasonability". Punarvasu represents the stage in life when a child outgrows its tempestuous and naughtiness and settles into a mindset which is more aware of the needs of others. This usually takes place between the ages of '9' and '14'. Children at this age have the unique ability to live in the moment and are friendly and good natured at the same time. This ability is retained by those under strong influence of this nakshatra throughout their lives. '9' to '14' are the right age to get a child interested in spiritual writings and philosophies, as they are more likely to take them seriously. Punarvasu is related to all kinds of spiritual practices meant to foster self understanding and enlightenment. The interplay of mental and emotional gives rise to a very active, profound and inspired imagination. Punarvasu natives thus excel in arts like poetry and writing.

Those with Punarvasu rising on the Ascendant are usually of short to middle stature, have a serene countenance and benevolent expression. One can refer to the many images of Ram, incarnation of Vishnu, to understand the appearance of this nakshatra (especially the part which lies in Cancer). The words - quiet, patient, devout, temperance, contrary views, amiability, adaptability, self-understanding and nobility sum up Punarvasu natives essential nature and functioning. It must be mentioned that Punarvasu's generosity is conditional and works on the principle of "give and take". This part of their nature actually accounts for their safety in today's tumultuous times.

Punarvasu natives usually lack the strong mental capacity of Ardra and have a much simpler approach to life. They lack foresight, a negative quality which gets them into complications, but they are always lucky to get out of them unscathed. In fact 'safety' is one of the keywords of this nakshatra. One can easily rule out any serious misfortune in relation to the significations Punarvasu influences in a nativity. For example, having Ascendant lord placed in Punarvasu would rule out any serious disease, accidents, bodily malfunctions and so forth. On a whole, Punarvasu natives usually lead comfortable lives filled with intermittent periods of adventure and upheaval.

Punarvasu natives are usually very attached to their homes, but at the same time are ever ready to travel if required. In some negative cases, Punarvasu natives may shun travel completely. Such natives usually end up confused and disillusioned as they have avoided following their natural life path. Punarvasu natives always need to guard against a tendency to stagnate. Their inward orientation usually gives them a lack of drive and focus required to attain their goals. Many such Punarvasu natives can be heard saying statements like, "What's the use?", "Why bother?" etc. In other words, they tend to philosophize their inactivity. In its higher aspect, Punarvasu gives a capacity to achieve its goal no matter how difficult or challenging it is. Just like an arrow fired by a good bowman, the evolved Punarvasu types never miss their mark.

One strange quality of Punarvasu is that everything happens in two goes for the natives under its strong influence. They almost always tend to fail or not get far in their first attempt at any pursuit, but the funny part is that they almost always succeed if they try a second time. This relates to the opposing natures of the two stars, Castor and Pollux, which make up the constellation of Punarvasu.

These stars are regarded as twin brothers, one of whom (Castor) is naughty and cruel, and the other (Pollux) is generous and wise. Punarvasu natives tend to encounter the first one in their first try, and the latter one in their second try.

It is Castor, which creates all types of losses for Punarvasu natives, while Pollux brings back all that is lost. Thus Punarvasu, in keeping with its name translation "Good Again", relates to all kinds of repetition and recycling. In its negative aspect, Punarvasu natives find it hard to discard anything just because they think that it might serve some purpose in some future time. The more evolved souls however, know when to let go of things which have outlived their usefulness.

Common English words like "punctual", "punitive", "pun", "puny" seem to have their root in the word "Punarvasu". We can easily see that their meanings relate to Punarvasu's functioning at some level or the other.

Mode of Functioning :

Punarvasu is considered to be a Passive nakshatra. Space by itself is a very passive entity. Unless stirred by some external agency, Punarvasu's philosophy is very much to "just be". It requires courage to stick to one's life path and finish off the task assigned to one. Punarvasu has been blessed with a moveable quality for that very purpose. However in its negative aspect, it can fail to commence the journey of fulfilling one's life purpose through procrastination, excessive idealism or pure laziness. The arrow usually has no problem travelling after it has been shot from an outstretched bow, but sometimes the archer may lack the strength or resolution to even string his bow. This is what happened to *Arjun* (character from the Vedic epic "*The Mahabharat*") at the very beginning of the epic world war known as Mahabharat. He refused to string his bow because of his idealistic compassion towards his kith and kin.

Caste :

It belongs to the *Vaishya* or Merchant caste. This classification obviously comes about because of its close association with the mercantile planet, Mercury. All of Punarvasu's generosity and kindness lie within the framework of reasonability. Punarvasu works on the principle of reciprocation. In today's world one has to be reasonable with one's generosity as people are bound to take undue advantage of you. It is probably this adherence to a reciprocal trader's mentality, which accounts for the fact that Punarvasu natives rarely get their hands burnt. Punarvasu is supposed to be the safest among nakshatras.

Gender :

It is a Male nakshatra. This classification must relate to its strong connection with the male planet Jupiter. Punarvasu has a feminine overseer in Aditi, but its impulses and functioning are masculine as illustrated in the nakshatra's image of the boy shooting the arrow.

Bodyparts & Humor (Ayurvedic Constitution) :

Fingers and Nose are the body parts related to this nakshatra.

It is a primarily "*Vata*" (airy) nakshatra. This definitely relates to its association with the Vata planet Mercury. Punarvasu represents space and Vata is the humor which gets closest to space or nothingness.

Direction :

It is related primarily to the arc made by west, north and north east.

Padas (Quarters) :

The first pada or quarter of this asterism 20° 00' - 23° 20' Gemini, falls in Aries Navamsa and is ruled by Mars. This pada relates to the moveable, adventurous and pioneering side of Punarvasu. Focus here is on friendships, goals and group work.

The second pada or quarter of this asterism 23° 20' - 26° 40' Gemini, falls in Taurus Navamsa ruled by Venus. This pada relates to the materialistic, earthy and fixed aspect of Punarvasu. It is connected with hotels, restaurants, tourism, import and export industry.

The third pada or quarter of this asterism 26° 40' - 30° 00' Gemini, falls in Gemini Navamsa ruled by Mercury. The focus here is on mental activities, imagination and science. Since this is a Vargottama pada, planets placed here give strong results, especially in the mental/intellectual realm.

The fourth pada or quarter of this asterism 00° 00' - 3° 20' Cancer, falls in Cancer Navamsa ruled by Moon. This pada is considered to be one of the strongest and most beneficent parts of the whole zodiac. Planets placed here are Vargottama and Pushkara Navamsa both. This is a maternal, nurturing and expansive pada, which brings out the mothering quality of Punarvasu to the fullest. Jupiter finds its maximum exaltation here.

Professions :

Trades & Sales people of all types; Artisans; Fairy Tale Writers; Writers dealing with Astrology & other Esoteric Subjects; Visionaries; All professions involving Travel & Tourism; Recycling Experts; Hotel & Restaurant Industry; Transport Industry; House Construction Companies; Architects; All Science related professions; Civil Engineers; Teachers in Schools, Colleges & Universities; Psychologists; Philosophers; Priests, Monks & Gurus; Preachers involved with self-enhancement techniques; Importers & Exporters; Historians; Antique Dealers; Farmers; Cattle & Sheep Farmers; All professions requiring an innovative approach; Communications Jobs; Radio & Telephone Industry; Courier Companies; Postal Service; Newspaper Industry; Mail Order & Home Delivery Businesses; Landlords; Keepers of Temples, Churches and other Religious Buildings; Home Maintenance Services; Archery & Target

Shooting; All sports involving use of hands; Patriots; Aviators; Astronauts & All Space/Satellite Professions.

Places :

Areas near Ponds, Lakes & Rivers; Farmlands; Pilgrimage Spots; Villages & Small Towns; Post Offices; Transportation Places like Bus Stations & Train Stations, Airports; Space Stations; Renovated Buildings; Public Parks; Homes; Home Land; Hostels; Hotels, Bed & Breakfast Places, Inns, Motels etc.; Restaurants; Temples & Treasuries; Markets; Rehabilitation Centres; Missions; Educational Institutions; Public & Political Assembly Places; Roads; Science Museums; Antique Shops; Community Halls.

Guna (Essence) and Tattwa (Element) :

It is supposed to be a *Sattwic* nakshatra. The reason behind this classification can be easily assessed from Punarvasu's association with Jupiter, a primarily sattwic planet. The qualities which make it godly, are the qualities which make it sattwic as well. However its most sattwic quality is that it never deliberately means harm to anyone.

It belongs to the Water element. Its association with the watery planet Jupiter, accounts for its watery quality. Punarvasu is a nakshatra akin to nourishing, nurturing and other such qualities associated with the water element.

Gana (Type) :

It is considered a *Deva* or godly nakshatra. It is clear from its nature and functioning that it is a very benign, generous, kindly and compassionate nakshatra. All these qualities are seen as being godly by ancient Vedic texts. The first ray of sunlight after a storm must obviously relate to the divinity aspect of nature and creation.

Outlook and Disposition :

It is Level nakshatra. The level nakshatras are neither too expansive nor too contracting. In other words, they have a sense of balance and reasonability. It is clear from Punarvasu's nature and functioning that it is a very balanced and reasonable nakshatra and thus fits this classification perfectly. Another way to see this, is that the archer needs to keep a level posture and level state of mind in order to hit its target.

It is a *Chara* or moveable nakshatra. As we have discussed in its Nature & Functioning, Punarvasu is related with all types of movement, especially the kind which ends where it begins. It is the first among the moveable nakshatras, even though Mrigashira can be said to be moveable in some respects.

Lunar Month & Day :

It relates to the first half of the lunar month of *Pausha,* which usually falls in the solar month of December, i.e. late December.

Punarvasu is also related to the *Ashtami* (8th tithi or day) of the waxing and waning phases of the Moon's monthly cycle.

Auspicious Activities :

Travelling & Exploring; Making Pilgrimages; Taking Medicines & all Healing Activities; Good for "Starting Over Again" in Projects, Relationships etc.; All Agricultural & Gardening Activities; All activities requiring Imagination & Innovation; Buying Cars & Homes; Starting work on a building; Starting Educational Activities; Auspicious for Marriage; Good for dealing with Children; Philanthropic Activities like Donations, Teaching etc; Good for Spiritual Activities like Fasting, Installing Altars, Meditation & Self Reflection; A time for enjoying life's simple pleasures; Very good for worship of the divine Mother Goddess.

Inauspicious Activities :

Unfavourable for Borrowing or Lending Money; Legal Activities or other activities requiring pushiness or conflict.

Planetary Ruler :

Jupiter is the main planetary ruler of this nakshatra. In fact, Jupiterian energy is heralded by this nakshatra. It is the first nakshatra where a sense of ethics is developed and the focus shifts from the self to communal well-being. Jupiterian energy manifests itself through a sense of accommodation, a quality which makes this the most reasonable amongst the nakshatras. As mentioned earlier, Punarvasu represents the stage in life when a child outgrows its tempestuous and naughtiness and settles into a mindset which is more aware of the needs of others.

Since this nakshatra falls in the signs of Mercury and Moon, both these planets are also associated with this nakshatra. Mercury relates to the communicating and moveable aspect of this nakshatra, while Moon relates to its nurturing, mothering quality and its connection with the universal mother principle.

Conjunctions like Jupiter/Moon, Jupiter/Mercury and Jupiter/Moon/Mercury carry an energy similar to that of Punarvasu.

All planets do well in this nakshatra, especially if Jupiter is well placed in the horoscope.

Vowels and Alphabets :

The first pada or quarter of this asterism 20° 00' -23° 20' Gemini corresponds to "Kay" as in Katie.

The second pada or quarter of this asterism 23° 20' - 26° 40' Gemini corresponds to "Ko" as in Kodak.

The third pada or quarter of this asterism 26°40 ' - 30° 00' Gemini corresponds to "Ha" as in Hart.

The fourth pada or quarter of this asterism 00° 00' - 3° 20' Gemini corresponds to "Hee " as in He-man.

In the Sanskrit alphabet Punarvasu corresponds to "Om" and "Aum", consequently its mantras are "Om" and "Aum". It is interesting to note that the beginning sound of the universe, which is most respected by all Vedic texts, is the root sound of this nakshatra. This once again reiterates its strong relation with the beginning of material manifestation.

Sexual Type and Compatibility :

Its sexual animal is a Cat. Cats are independent creatures and this attitude permeates the sexual nature of Punarvasu. Punarvasu can be aggressive sexually, but not to the extent of *Ashlesha* (the other cat nakshatra), which is the asterism it is most compatible with.

For sexual & marital compatibility with other nakshatras please refer to the tables on pages 468 & 469 .

Esoteric :

Being the 7th nakshatra, Punarvasu relates to the balancing aspect of nature. Space is the empty cloth on which the patterns of the universe are embroidered. Punarvasu allows for manifestation by providing a medium. Those familiar with chemistry will realize that the medium is always a balancing element in any reaction. At another level Punarvasu gives souls a chance to redeem themselves from whatever negative actions they might have done in the past. It is the most efficient karma recycler amongst the nakshatras. Due to its relationship with Aditi, mother of the gods, Punarvasu is a very nurturing nakshatra, which always gives a second chance. It harmonizes the opposing tendencies inherent in the universal scheme.

The twins Castor and Pollux represent two extreme sides of human nature and Punarvasu establishes a happy medium. It can be said that *Vishnu Tattwa* begins in Punarvasu. This is the first nakshatra where a sense of harmony and equilibrium is established between the existing elemental forces on all planes of existence. None of the nakshatras prior to Punarvasu engage in the above mentioned task. *Ram*, the 8th incarnation of Vishnu, was born with Punarvasu rising and his whole life was nothing but an effort to create an equilibrium on planet Earth in his day and age.

The two sons of Ram, *Luv* and *Kush* are the archetypal twin brothers who have been used to symbolize the twin stars Castor and Pollux through different names in various cultures. Their reign on Earth, after they took over from their father, is regarded as one of the most peaceful times in the tumultuous history of *Prithvi* (Mother).

Gotra (Celestial Lineage) :

This nakshatra is related to the Sage *Kratu*, one of the seven celestial sages looking after the affairs of our galaxy. The name of this sage translates into "the inspirer". Punarvasu, because of its association with Jupiter, has a preachy and inspiring quality about it. Punarvasu inspires by setting an example through its inner gentleness.

Remedial :

For those suffering from bad effects resulting from afflictions to this nakshatra, the best remedial measure is worship of any goddess figure like *Durga*, *Laxmi*, *Saraswati*, Aditi etc.

Repetition of the root mantras of this nakshatra - "Om" or " Aum" 108 times when Moon transits this nakshatra and in its corresponding lunar month is sure to reduce suffering and bring enlightenment into a person's life.

Persons who are benefiting from the positive energy of this nakshatra can also increase the good effects through the above mentioned ways. It is helpful for them to wear green, yellow and white.

They should use its directions, lunar month and the days when Moon transits Punarvasu to undertake all important actions.

Example :

Ram, incarnation of Vishnu in the Silver Age and widely celebrated and hailed in the Vedic thought as the perfect man, was born with Punarvasu rising. His life, which is documented in the legendary epic "*Ramayan*", sheds light on the nature and functionings of Punarvasu. He always got everything right only in two goes (he lost his kingdom and wife and regained them), as suggested by the expression "good again".

Punarvasu's sound and light can be experienced at –

http://osfa.org.uk/punarvasu/htm

Miscellaneous :

According to *Varahamihira*, Moon's placement in Punarvasu makes one "easily contented, self-controlled, slow-witted, fortunate and of good character". Our example Ram has his Moon placed in Punarvasu as well and all of the above-mentioned attributes fit him perfectly.

* * *

8. Pushya   3°20' Cancer – 16°40' Cancer

8.

Pushya

(3º20' Cancer - 16º40' Cancer)

In the Sky :

Pushya comprises of three stars in the constellation of Cancer, known in modern astronomy as *Theta-Cancri, Gamma-Cancri* & *Eta-Cancri.* These are not very bright stars, as the brightest among them has a visual magnitude of 4.57. They, however, house the globular star cluster known as *M-44.* It is very clear that the ancient Vedic seers were privy to some knowledge about our neighbouring stars which we don't ascribe the same importance to. These stars are hardly visible to the naked eye. The ancient seers saw these three stars as resembling an 'udder of a cow'. The interesting thing to note is that they didn't choose the relatively bright stars normally associated with the sign of Cancer.

Name :

Pushya translates into the "Nourisher", the "Nurturer" or the "Yielding". This simple name carries within itself the essence of this nakshatra. Some scholars are of the opinion that Pushya also translates into "a flower". The flower conveys the same sense of gentleness and nourishment as the other translations.

Pushya's ancient name is "*Tishya*", which translates into auspicious. "*Sidhya*" meaning 'prosperous' is another name associated with this nakshatra. We can see that all these names are drawn from a common essence of benevolence.

Symbol :

Pushya's main symbol is the 'milk yielding udder of a cow'. We have already seen that the ancient seers saw its three stars as representing a cow's udder. Once we combine this symbol with its name, all the indications of this nakshatra are immediately clear i.e. its propensity and ability to nourish, nurture, care and give freely on all planes of existence.

Cows, as we know, provide their milk to others besides their own calf unselfishly. Cows are also a universal symbol of motherhood and were highly revered, especially in the ancient Vedic society. In India it is still considered the holiest amongst all animals. All the notions of fertility and productivity that are related to the earth on a material plane fall under the domain of this nakshatra. In many ancient legends, the earth is often equated with a cow.

Cows are intimately connected with the sign Taurus. This nakshatra is intimately connected with the sign Taurus and its qualities, even though it does not fall in that sign. As we shall find later, Moon in Taurus placement in a chart carries an energy similar to the energies of this nakshatra.

The practice of agriculture, the root of all civilization, can be equated with the domestication and milking of cows. From a universal perspective, it represents the power of the feminine goddess energy to provide for whatever is required. The milk which comes from the cow's udder represents all kinds of varied things like lifeforce, vitality and creativity. One can only give if one can produce and this nakshatra relates to all kinds of productive forces operating within our universe.

Its alternative symbol is a 'wheel'. The 'wheel' is an ancient symbol signifying movement in all its aspects, especially the movement of time. It can be seen as a motif for progress achieved in the course of time. The idea of progress or development always involves the passage of time. This nakshatra is very aware of the proper utilization of the time principle to achieve its productive, creative and nurturing objectives. From the modern day point of view, we can see that the use of automobiles have made people's lives much simpler than they used to be. This is just one of the numerous gifts from this liberal nakshatra.

Wheel is also an archetypal symbol for civilization, which once again emphasizes the prosperous, courteous and refined nature of this nakshatra. There's no place for brutality, savagery, vulgarity or animalistic behaviour in this nakshatra. Another obscure symbol of this nakshatra is a 'circle'. This generally reflects the circular essence of this asterism. This nakshatra is related to curves of all types. Breasts, the Moon, the Earth and a Cow's Udder are all circular and rounded. Natives with Pushya prominent in their charts usually show an obsessive streak for round things.

Some scholars ascribe a 'flower' to be one of Pushya's symbols. As we have already seen, flowering is one of the translations of Pushya. Pushya represents a flowering process of any type. For example, human beings are supposed to flower at the age of sixteen. The term "sweet sixteen" is usually used to describe this happy, cheerful, carefree period where the body, mind and emotions have matured or blossomed enough to make us step out of childhood. It is interesting to note that the sixteenth year is regarded as the maturation age of Jupiter, the planet most closely associated with this nakshatra.

Deity :

Brihaspati, the guru, priest and chief advisor of the gods, is the presiding deity of this nakshatra. Since he is the same as the planet Jupiter as understood in astrology, all the attributes and significations associated with Jupiter apply to him as well. It is not very hard to correlate Jupiter's basic nature with the kind and caring disposition of this nakshatra. All of Jupiter's benevolence such as generosity, compassion, joyfulness and optimism are manifested through this nakshatra. It is interesting to note that Jupiter relays all of its good qualities much more through this nakshatra in comparison to the nakshatras it is the planetary ruler of. This is very similar to the case of Moon reflecting most of its qualities through *Mrigasira* instead of the nakshatras it actually rules.

This point reveals the fact that the ruling deity is always more important than the planetary ruler when it comes to understanding the crux of any nakshatra.

Nature & Functioning :

Pushya is that place on our journey where we can rest safely and peacefully without anything to fear. It is the most nourishing of all nakshatras and brings us back to that state in our infancy where we are safely nestled in our mother's arms. That is why natives strongly ruled by Pushya are very maternal, kind, helpful, generous, protective and nourishing. They often end up in comfortable positions in life. Pushya relates to breasts and this conjures up the expression "Milk of human kindness". Kindness is what this nakshatra is all about. Pushya is a blissful and soothing nakshatra and the natives they produce are much sought after by others for their friendship and aid. Being ruled by Saturn, Pushya natives are very reliable, dependable stalwarts, who one can always turn to in times of need.

Pushya is simply the most loved and benign of all nakshatras. Like its neighbour Purnavasu, it loves life and expresses much contentment and sense of wellbeing, but it has the advantage of being able to manifest this fullness and expansiveness on the material plane, therefore giving rise to great material comfort and prosperity. This is due to the concrete nature of its ruler Saturn.

Pushya in its positive aspect is extremely nourishing and its energies, wherever they are directed, produce great expansion and growth. This is true for any area of life whether it be in the emotional realm, in one's creativity, spiritual development or on the material plane. As this nakshatra completely resides in Cancer, a sense of family, home and community are strong in Pushya natives.

On a less evolved level, these natives will be very generous and protective of kith and kin and ever ready to lend a helping hand to those in their immediate community, but may fail to see the bigger picture. On a higher level, evolved souls under its influence, will embrace the whole world as their family, nourishing the earth with their chosen talents and ceaseless gifts of caring. Pushya qualities of love, emotional wholeness, calmness, soothing, generosity and richness manifest through such souls with ease.

The negative side of this nakshatra makes one so comfortable in their own world, that they can become rigid, narrow-minded and orthodox in their attitudes towards anything or anyone outside of it, particularly in matters of religion, culture or other social conventions. Pushya has very few negative qualities attached to it, except the danger of it becoming overtly prejudiced, protective or bigoted. Suspicion and caution arises towards anything that does not fit its highly structured views or opinions.

Pushya expresses all the 'square-like' aspects of its ruler Saturn and the number "4" (relating to the fourth sign Cancer). Therefore it always tries to take a balanced and even approach to things. It has a sense of realism and sanity to it and will always react reasonably to most situations and problems, which is why it is the most helpful among the nakshatras. Helpfulness is its primary concern.

Natives here are highly productive and work patiently towards their goals. There is a sense of containment and safety inherent in this nakshatra, similar to the safety and containment inherent in the nakshatra *Shatabhishak*. The only difference is that Pushya's containment, shelter and safety arises from a very trusting situation, and Shatabhishak's arises out of a need for secrecy, and many a times, from a certain mistrust.

This number "4" influence is seen in Pushya's respect for its roots, foundations and traditions. It has more to do with respecting the conservative outer traditions of culture and religion, than the inner esoteric aspects of spirituality, which is more associated with the latter nakshatras. Jupiter is exalted in Pushya giving these natives a strong sense of ethics. They like to do the right thing and abide by accepted standards and laws. They are shining examples of hospitality, decency, courtesy, etiquette and are not likely to behave in any vulgar or extreme manner. However, in its negative aspect, Pushya can make one lethargic, needy, dependent and prone to addictions due to a lack of will power. If afflicted, Pushya natives tend to get victimized easily.

When this nakshatra influences the appearance of a native, it gives fleshy features, prominent chest/breasts, round faces and luminous lustre. Natives under its influence put on fat easily and are prone to bronchial disorders. They have a liking for good food, comfort and social enjoyment. They also like to surround themselves with material luxuries of all kinds. They are gentle, patient, docile creatures who are very attached to their family, especially the mother or mother figures.

In the universal scheme of things, *Pushya* relates to "*brahmavarchasa shakti*" - the power to harness the creative powers of *Brahma* (the universal creator). Its symbolism has sacrificial offerings above and the worshipper below. This re-emphasizes the priestly aspect of Pushya, where one does outer rituals like *homa* and *yagya* to get the favour of celestial entities and divine powers in general.

Mode of Functioning :

In keeping with its basic nature and disposition, ancient Vedic seers saw this as a Passive asterism. If we just picture the behaviour of a cow in our mind, we will come to understand the passive aspect of Pushya. Even though it is productive, it does not display the restlessness other light nakshatras like *Ashvini* and *Hasta* have. Pushya has a much more stable energy and tends to function without fuss. However, when occupied by afflicted planets, it can promote laziness, listlessness and paralyzing idealism.

Caste :

It belongs to the *Kshatriya* or warrior caste. It is perplexing why this seemingly *brahminical* (priestly) nakshatra should be classified in this category by the ancient seers. It is probably because of Pushya's intense involvement in politics and rulership, which is responsible for this classification. Politics and rulership is the *dharma* of the Kshatriya caste. Even Brihaspati, the ruling deity of Pushya, is supposed to have mastery over politics more than any other subject.

Gender :

It is a Male nakshatra. This is easily derivable from the fact that Brihaspati, a male deity, has the primary rulership of this nakshatra. Pushya, however, has a sensitive feminine side to it as exemplified by its strong relationship with cows. Cows are gentle, yielding and productive creatures. In countries like India, cows are treated with utmost reverence.

Bodyparts & Humor (Ayurvedic Constitution) :

The bodyparts it relates to the most are the Mouth and Face. Pushya is supposed to be intimately connected with facial expressions. Any affliction to Pushya therefore can limit our facial expressiveness or project the wrong image.

One may infer that because the Kshatriya class is predominantly effected by the "*Pitta*" (fiery) humor, the ancient seers ascribed the pitta humor to Pushya. They might, however, have had more direct cognition of Pushya's relationship with the digestive fires in the body and the fiery pranic airs.

Direction :

It is related to the directional arc that ranges from west to north.

Padas (Quarters) :

The first pada or quarter of this asterism 3° 20' - 6° 40' Cancer, falls in Leo Navamsa ruled by Sun. The first pada concerns itself with achievement, limelight, wealth and pride in one's family or ancestry. The luminaries, especially, give strong positive results in this pada. They make the native a father or mother figure or the native receives help from such figures.

The second pada or quarter of this asterism 6° 40' - 10° 00' Cancer, falls in Virgo Navamsa ruled by Mercury. The hardworking, service aspect of Pushya finds expression here. Since this is a Pushkara Navamsa pada, all planets barring Venus, give good results here, at least on the material plane. This pada can be called the Cook of the Zodiac.

The third pada or quarter of this asterism 10° 00' - 13° 20' Cancer, falls in Libra Navamsa ruled by Venus. The focus here is on home, comforts, luxury and sociability. Superficiality and conformity is the downside of this pada. Moon, Mercury, Venus and Saturn do well here.

The fourth pada or quarter of this asterism 13° 20' - 16° 40' Cancer, falls in Scorpio Navamsa ruled by Mars. This pada relates to the esoteric side of Pushya, which seeks connections with the celestial beings in the other world. It is the pada of mantras and rituals. In its negative aspect, most of Pushya's negative traits like dependence, victimization and bigotry find expression through this pada. Only unafflicted Jupiter and Venus do well in this pada.

Professions :

All those connected with the Dairy Industry; Food and Drink Merchants of all types; Politicians, Rulers & Aristocrats; Caterers and Hoteliers; All those in the Restaurant Business; Clergy, Nuns, Priests, Gurus, Spiritual Teachers; Psychologists, Counsellors and Psychotherapists; Managers; Those associated with Charitable Organizations; Professional Hosts & Hostesses; River and Lake related professions; Teachers and Education Experts; Child Care Professionals; Mothers; All Care Professions; Artisans; Those involved in all kinds of Business and Creative Activities requiring Finesse; Real Estate Agents; Farmers & Gardeners; Those making a living out of Orthodoxy, Traditionalism and Religious Bigotry.

Places :

Rivers, Docks, Wells, Reservoirs, Fountains, Pools, Canals; Boats and House Boats; Public Places; Nests; Homes; Breweries; Women's House Quarters, Hostels and Residences in general; Aquariums; Temples & Churches; Hotels & Restaurants; Foster Homes; Child Care Centres; Maternity Hospitals; Schools; Dairy Factories & Dairy Farms; Laundromats; Manors & Public, Government buildings like Parliament etc.; Charity Organizations; All places connected to the above professions.

Guna (Essence) and Tattwa (Element) :

It is supposed to be a *Tamasic* nakshatra. One can only say that the ancient seers were trying to highlight the inertia aspect of Pushya through this classification. It may relate to the involvement of

Saturn with this nakshatra. Pushya, just like the demi-gods *Indra* and his entourage, has an often overlooked indulgent, deceptive, cowardly, over idealistic, procrastinating and hyper aggressive side to it. A lot depends on the basic nature of the planet occupying Pushya.

For example, if Saturn (a natural malefic) having the rulership of the 6th house in a chart (a malefic house) is placed in Pushya, then Pushya's tamasic side will be in display. However if Moon (a natural benefic) having the rulership of good houses is placed in Pushya, the benevolent, compassionate and nurturing side of Pushya will be expressed.

It belongs to the Water element. The fact that Moon and Jupiter are primarily water planets makes Pushya a primarily watery nakshatra. Even Brihaspati, its ruling deity is often portrayed as a fat bellied watery type.

Gana (Type) :

It is considered a Divine nakshatra. It is appropriate that a nakshatra which is said to harbour all benevolent qualities should be seen as a representation of divinity.

Orientation & Disposition :

It is an Upward Looking nakshatra in keeping with its natural expansive nature. This is a nakshatra signifying increase and expansion. Planets placed in Pushya usually signify increase and expansion relating to the areas in the chart governed by that planet. It is said that any activity started when Moon is transiting this nakshatra will never fail.

It is a Light and Swift nakshatra. Just like Ashvini, Pushya is related to quick thinking and is supposed to be good for all activities requiring quickness of mind and body. This is probably one of the reasons why Pushya is regarded as one of the best nakshatras for all kinds of trade and business.

Lunar Month & Day :

It relates to the second half of the lunar month of *Pausha* which usually falls in January.

Pushya is also related to the *Dashami* (10th tithi or day) of the waxing and waning phases of the Moon's monthly cycle.

Auspicious Activities :

The best nakshatra for starting anything; Parties, Celebrations, Artistic & Creative activities especially Music and Dancing; Travelling; Dealing with Enemies (enemies are at their weakest in Pushya and cannot cause much harm); Seeking Legal Aid; Financial Planning & Transactions; Cooking & Food preparation; Gardening; Adoption & Purchasing Pets; All activities related to Children; All Healing, Soothing and Nourishing activities in general; Religious or Spiritual Endeavours like Initiations; Spending time with one's Mother; Good for worshipping Mother Goddess energies; Laying Foundation Stones and Starting Construction; Seeking help in general.

Inauspicious Activities :

Marriage is just about the only activity which is not seen favourable under this nakshatra; Generally unfavourable for harsh, cruel and negative activities.

Planetary Ruler :

The planetary influences affecting this nakshatra are Moon and Saturn. Saturn is its main planetary ruler. This comes more of a surprise in comparison to the planetary rulers of other nakshatras. The association of Saturn with Pushya reveals the hidden side of Saturn's functioning - its ability for grounded nurturing and painstaking care. Saturn nurtures through conservation, perseverance and limitations.

Moon represents emotions and Saturn represents stability and so the keyword here is "emotional stability". Moon is the mind and Saturn represents matter, which makes Pushya the asterism which connects mind with matter. This is the reason why it can give easy material expansion on the dictates of the mind.

It is important to consider Jupiter, the ruling deity of Pushya, in the equation here, because by itself the combining of energies of Moon and Saturn is likely to give melancholy and depression more than anything else. It is Jupiter's energies which make Pushya a very well balanced nakshatra. In its negative aspect however, the same Jupiterian energy manifests as dogmatism, shallowness and bigotry. On a higher level, Moon/Saturn/Jupiter influence together allow one to shape an idyllic world.

Saturn is a mass planner and so is Moon, a fact which makes Pushya the most mass-orientated of nakshatras. On a positive level, both Moon and Saturn promote the mindset and values which help foster an idealized civilized society. Moon and Saturn in their negative aspect make the masses tow the line, even in times when the ruling forces are dark and corrupt. Those with strong Moon-Saturn in their charts become mass leaders in today's times.

Moon/Saturn/Jupiter conjunction in a horoscope carry energies similar to Pushya. A well placed Moon, Jupiter, Sun, Venus and Saturn give excellent results when placed in Pushya. Mercury, Mars and the nodes do not give good results in this nakshatra.

Vowels and Alphabets

The first pada or quarter of this asterism 3° 20' - 6° 40' Cancer corresponds to "Hoo" as in Hoot.

The second pada or quarter of this asterism 6° 40' - 10° 00' Cancer corresponds to "He" as in Helen.

The third pada or quarter of this asterism 10° 00' - 13° 20' Cancer corresponds to "Ho" as in Hogan.

The fourth pada or quarter of this asterism 13° 20' - 16° 40' Cancer corresponds to "Dah" as in Darwin.

In the Sanskrit alphabet Pushya corresponds to "Ka", and consequently its mantra is "Om Kam".

Sexual Type and Compatibility :

Its sexual animal is a Goat. Despite the fact that its sexual animal is not seen as an emblem of sexuality, Pushya is supposed to be adept at all kinds of sensual and sexual activities. Its sexuality is more playful as opposed to intense.

For sexual & marital compatibility with other nakshatras, please refer to the tables on pages 468 & 469.

Esoteric :

Brihaspati, the priest of the gods, is the lord of *mantras* and all types of initiations like *yagyas* etc. He relates to the waters of inner life which nourish the soul. Pushya's spirituality relates to a high level of emotional maturity. Its emotional strength finds outward manifestation through powerful speech. Words generated from this nakshatra carry a certain spiritual energy, which tend to affect others on a deep level.

An ancient Vedic legend related to *Kamadhenu* (a wish fulfilling cow), reveals a lot about Pushya on all levels of its functioning:-

"A sage named *Vashishta* had a cow named Kamadhenu. A king along with his hundred brothers was hunting in the forest, when he came close to Vashishta's hermitage and happened to see this wonderful cow, which could produce anything you wished for. He immediately wanted to have the cow to himself, so he ordered his soldiers to get it for him.

The soldiers couldn't even budge the cow and came back empty handed. The king then decided to go with his whole army and all of his brothers to get the cow. Kamadhenu, in the meantime, had returned to her master, Vashishta, and had told him about the king's intentions. Seeing the approaching army coming, Vashishta ordered her to produce a whole army. Kamadhenu's army defeated the king's army in a very short spate of time and Vashishta personally killed the king's hundred brothers through the power of his staff.

The king was spared his life and he left the place bitter and revengeful. He was advised that the only way he can get stronger than Vashishta was through penance. He performed his penance and when he felt he had procured enough divine *astras* (celestial weapons) and yogic power, he went back to challenge Vashishta.

In the battle that ensued, all his weapons were effortlessly consumed by Vashishta's staff and he had to return disappointed and bereft of power. He vowed to himself that he would keep on doing his penance until he became equal to or better than Vashishta. In the course of his long arduous penance, he went through many adventures and most importantly, a change of heart, which earnt him the name *Vishwamitra* or "Friend of the World". By the time he had reached the same brahminical stature as Vashishta, he had already forgotten about his revenge and it was Vashishta himself, who conferred on him the title of *Brahmarishi,* (a Sage fit for *Brahmaloka*, the abode of the creator Brahma). "

This story reveals the fascinating dynamics between the Brahman (priestly) and Kshatriya (warrior class). Pushya, as we have seen, is a priestly nakshatra, which belongs to the Kshatriya class and is thus an ideal playing field for this dynamic. Kshatriyas are supposed to be subservient to the Brahman class, despite their martial prowess. Because of the power which the true sages and priests have, as a result of keeping in tune with the universal will, Pushya's strength, confidence and power arise from its willingness to function as per the dictates of the universal mind. No amount of penance, hardwork or suffering can make one rise above the smooth effortless power which arises out of the submission to the universal plan.

Gotra (Celestial Lineage) :

This nakshatra is related to the Sage *Marichi,* one of the seven celestial sages looking after the affairs of our galaxy. The name of this sage translates into "the light", which is in keeping with the light and swift aspect of this nakshatra and relates to the finesse part of this particular sage.

Remedial :

For those suffering from bad effects resulting from afflictions to this nakshatra, the best remedial measure is to pay reverence to cows, priests, gurus or brahmins. One can also worship a benign Mother goddess.

Repetition of the root mantra of this nakshatra - "Om Kam" 108 times when Moon transits this nakshatra and in the lunar month of Pausha, is sure to reduce suffering and bring enlightenment into a person's life.

Persons who are benefiting from the positive energy of this nakshatra can also increase the good effects through the above mentioned ways. It is helpful for them to wear colours like white, yellow, orange and golden shades. They should use its directions, lunar month and the days when Moon transits Pushya to undertake all important actions.

Example :

Pushya's sound and light can be experienced at -

http://osfa.org.uk/pushya.htm

Miscellaneous :

According to *Varahamihira*, those with Moon in Pushya are "lucky, learned, wealthy, ethical and of a peaceful nature."

* * *

Example

Harsha's sound and light can be experienced at

Miscellaneous

According to Varahamihira, those with Moon in Pushya are lucky, learned, wealthy, ethical and of a peaceful nature.

9. Ashlesha   16°40' Cancer ~ 30°00' Cancer

9.

Ashlesha

(16º40' Cancer - 30º00' Cancer)

In the Sky :

Ashlesha, the heralder of Mercurial energy, is represented in the night sky by a ring of stars in the constellation of *Hydra*, known in modern astronomy as *Epsilon-Hydrae, Delta-Hydrae, Mu-Hydrae, Rho-Hydrae, Sigma-Hydrae* & *Zeta-Hydrae*. These stars are easily visible in a dark sky from pollution free vantage points even though they are not bright stars, as the brightest among them, Zeta-Hydrae has a visual magnitude of 3.12. In essence the whole of the constellation Hydrae can be seen to be representative of this asterism.

Name :

Ashlesha is a term normally associated with serpent imagery and can be translated as "coiling", "clinging", "embracing" or "entwining". As we shall discover, all these terms directly define its nature and functioning. The name is probably derived from the serpent king/god "*Shesh*".

Symbol :

A 'coiled snake' (please refer to the image) is the main symbol of this asterism. Along with its name, this symbol makes it clear that the essence of Ashlesha lies in the serpent imagery, an imagery which can be found in every surviving ancient civilization.

Most cultures see snakes as secretive, creepy, wily, coldblooded, deceptive, insincere, hypnotic and poisonous creatures. All these qualities find their way into Ashlesha's functioning. On the positive side, serpents are seen as semi-divine creatures with access to other worlds. They are supposed to have great primordial powers of insight, intuition, perception, wisdom, cunning, concentration and sexuality.

Ashlesha, when functioning through its higher aspect, displays these qualities. In the present times when the worst side of everything is on display, one can usually expect only the forementioned, negative qualities to predominate.

Brain researchers have now been able to locate the most ancient part of the brain. It is known as the 'R' complex. 'R' here stands for 'reptilian'. All the above mentioned instinctual, negative qualities have been ascribed to this part of the brain. Thus a clear, tangible relation between reptiles, serpents and these types of human qualities is established.

It is interesting to note that DNA, the building block of our genetic code has a helical, coiled serpent shape. Thus Ashlesha has a lot to do with genetic heritage, the karma we have brought from previous lives and the scope of changes we are allowed to make in the present one.

Deity :

Ashlesha is supposed to be ruled by the celestial serpent kingdom as a whole. In Vedic mythology, *Nagas* (half serpent/half-human creatures) and other types of serpent beings abound throughout all the fourteen *lokas* (realms of existence). In some of the legends, these beings are supposed to reside on the earthly plane as well under lake, river or ocean beds. Mystery, being one of basic attributes of Ashlesha, it is no wonder then that all of these beings are shrouded in mystery. The legends however make it clear that the serpent beings or forces were necessary for the proper functioning of universal affairs. The readers can refer to the "Churning of the Ocean Legend" in the author's previous work "*The Rahu-Ketu Experience*" Sagar Publications, India or "*The Key Of Life*" Lotus Press, USA.

Even *Vishnu* always incarnates on earth with his serpent guard *Shesh*. When Vishnu incarnated as *Ram*, Shesh incarnated as *Lakshman*. It is interesting to note that Lakshman was born with Ashlesha rising on his Ascendant. His character reflects many of the qualities of Ashlesha (refer to the Vedic legend- "*The Ramayan*").

The negative type of serpents however need to be subdued and won over, just like the lower negative aspects of human nature are won over through knowledge, wisdom and understanding. *Krishn's* killing of the many headed snake called *Kaliya* (refer to the Vedic legend- "*The Mahabharat*") and in the Greek legend, *Hercules'* killing of the *Delphi* serpent illustrate this point.

The only other nakshatra directly associated with serpent energy is *Uttarabhadrapada*. Usually it is noticed that the higher, more refined aspects of serpent energy are displayed there, while Ashlesha epitomizes the more primordial and instinctual part of the serpent symbolism. Since *Patala Loka* (the realm ruled by serpent beings lying just below the earthly plane of existence), is supposed to be a seething pleasure ground (base and gross in comparison to the higher heavenly realm) meant for gratification and indulgence, Ashlesha often displays an unquenchable thirst for gratification on the earthly plane of existence as well.

Nature & Functioning :

The English words which use Ashlesha's alphabets ("Da", "Di", "Do") - "Demon", "Diabolical", "Darkness", "Debauchery", "Devouring", "Danger", "Deceit", "Deception", "Dastardly", "Dagger", "Decadence", "Degenerate", "Delinquent", "Destitute", "Defile", "Destruction", "Depression", "Damned", "Death", "Delusion", "Desperation", "Despotic", "Doom", "Devious", "Doctor" - sum up Ashlesha's nature and functioning. Much needn't be said after a thought is paid to each of these terms. Obviously this doesn't paint Ashlesha in a good light, but it is very hard for Ashlesha to function in a wholesome and healthy way when acting on a mundane level.

Ashlesha is perhaps the most difficult of all nakshatra energies to handle and channel correctly, especially in the present day and age. Even the ancient sages and scholars had very few kind words to say in relation to this nakshatra. It has its occult and esoteric significance, which the reader can look up in the Esoteric Section of this chapter.

Ashlesha rising gives a squarish face; parallel, straight, wide, thin lips; beady small eyes; a naturally suspicious look and a pale complexion. Despite lacking facial attractiveness, natives born under this nakshatra generally have sexually appealing bodies. Their movements are similar to that of snakes. They are very conscious of how they move and how their movement arouses sexual passion in others.

They are adept at putting up socially acceptable and amiable fronts. They use courtesy as a tool to flatter others. This good humour doesn't last for long, for once their objective is achieved, they are immediately cold and ruthless. They are always scheming and plotting when it comes to climbing the social ladder. Since they often work from very superficial levels, their chameleon like quality and deception is very evident to anyone having an above-average level of perceptiveness. The Ashlesha element in a personality can be easily spotted through the almost constant suspicion and mistrust prevalent in the background. Worry and caution follow them relentlessly.

On a positive level, their suspicious natures make them good observers. This power of observation is often combined with a natural intuition. However Ashlesha's intuitive and psychic capabilities tend to function best in situations where an element of danger is there. Natives can sense danger quickly and react quickly. On a negative level, their suspicion can turn into paranoia. In its extreme state, paranoia can become an illness. Paranoid schizophrenia is a disease whose roots lie in Ashlesha. Ashlesha natives can aid others in psychological exploration and understanding, but they also have a tendency to use their psychological perceptiveness to exploit others.

It is the predominance of Ashlesha energy which makes society a cradle of fear and suspicion. Ashlesha is about "lock your doors and mistrust your neighbour." It is due to this inherent mistrust that Ashlesha natives tend to remain hidden in regards to their true thoughts and feelings. They do not form intimate bonds with others and will mistrust their most closest confidantes and families. They are however highly protective towards their kith and kin and will ward off suspicious intruders in the most ruthless manner.

Ashlesha natives can be the most mean and stingy in regards to financial affairs. Their miserliness never pays in the end as they always end up having losses one way or the other. The presence of Ashlesha in a nativity works both ways; one deceives others and gets deceived by others. Many Ashlesha natives are victims, rather than the users, especially natives who have planets like Sun and Jupiter placed in Ashlesha.

Ashlesha is a glutton and shows great interest in food, especially when it is not Sattwic and prepared by others. Ashlesha natives find themselves at home in hotels, bars, restaurants and the like. They usually cannot bear any kind of hunger. They are the hoarders of the zodiac and dislike throwing anything away. They can go to real extremes in this regard and need to learn to put the material world into its proper perspective. They have a natural affinity for poisons. They do not mind drugs, pharmaceuticals, allopathy, doctors, antibiotics etc.

Ashlesha natives enjoy business activities which border on crookery. They never employ straight methods in business and want some type of cheating or deception to be involved. They find humour in tricking others. They like mental games and strategy. They delight in hoodwinking others.

If one thinks of the characteristics of cats and snakes it is not difficult to sum up an Ashlesha personality. Cunningness, calculativeness, caution, cold-bloodedness, wiliness, stealth are common traits amongst cats and snakes. The only way Ashlesha natives can use their singularly negative traits in a positive manner is by aligning themselves with universal will. The key for utilizing Ashlesha in a positive way is to overcome one's innate selfishness. Having done that, suspicion will turn into discretion and wiliness into wisdom. Ashlesha is the first step on the path of spiritual awakening.

The underbelly of nature is encountered here. One has to face all the dark demons of the inner psyche in order to come out shining and purified. Ashlesha's natural tendency to look under the surface has to be utilized for understanding the hidden elements of nature's functionings.

In the universal scheme of things, *Ashlesha* relates to "*visasleshana shakti*" - the power to inflict poison. Its symbolism has an approaching serpent above and trembling below. This relates Ashlesha with all kinds of sharp, venomous attacks made at one's enemy or prey. Once again the dangerous and naturally malefic potentiality of this nakshatra come to light.

Mode of Functioning :

Ashlesha is considered to be an Active nakshatra. Ashlesha on the surface often appears to be a passive nakshatra but that is only because all its activities are hidden. Even if an Ashlesha native seems to be physically passive, one will find that they are weaving many webs on the mental plane. Ashlesha's activities are subterranean in all senses of the world. In the present day and age where all the workings of the elite take place in secret away from the eyes of the public, one cannot help but see a dominant role of Ashlesha in the halls of power.

Caste :

It belongs to the lowest caste which is called *Mleccha* (outcaste). In its lower functionings Ashlesha is a sort of general menace to society in all the known forms like bandits, cheats, oppressors, exploiters etc. In its higher functioning it relates to the yogi who renounces the world in the search for enlightenment. In both ways Ashlesha doesn't seem to fit into the societal civilized structure.

Gender :

It is a Female nakshatra. Since the ancient Vedic seers have made this classification without enunciating a reason, we have to conclude that the intuitive, perceptive and deceptive qualities ascribed to Ashlesha relate more to the female of the species rather than the male. One can notice that even male natives under the prominent influence of Ashlesha have a feminine way about them.

Bodyparts & Humor (Ayurvedic Constitution) :

Bone Joints like Elbows, Knuckles, Knee Caps; the Nails and the Ears are the body parts related to this nakshatra.

It is a primarily "*Kapha*" (watery) nakshatra. This is due to its relationship with the sign Cancer. Most serpent deities are shown as having kapha characteristics like stagnation, laziness, indulgence etc.

Direction :

It is related to the directional range which covers the northwest to the north. Like all serpent energies it is strong in the Southwest as well.

Padas (Quarters) :

The first pada or quarter of this asterism 16° 40' - 20° 00' Cancer falls in Sagittarius Navamsa and is ruled by Jupiter. This pada has the ability to put in the most hard work. It has a lot to do with dealing with enmity, diseases and other 6th house affairs.

The second pada or quarter of this asterism 20° 00' - 23° 20' Cancer falls in Capricorn Navamsa ruled by Saturn. This pada is mostly involved in dealing with people. It is a highly ambitious pada which is usually liable to use all of Ashlesha's negative traits like trickery and deceit to get what it wants. An inability to let go of possessions is another unique aspect of this pada. Being a Ganda Mula pada, this pada is considered bad for finances.

The third pada or quarter of this asterism 23° 20' - 26° 40' Cancer falls in Aquarius Navamsa ruled by Saturn. Secrecy is the keyword to this pada. It however is most closely related to the occult side of Ashlesha, discussed in the Esoteric Section. This pada usually goes to unusual lengths and takes highly inventive approaches to scheming and plotting. Planets placed here adversely effects mother's wellbeing.

The fourth pada or quarter of this asterism 26° 40' - 30° 00' Cancer falls in Pisces Navamsa ruled by Jupiter. This is the pada relating to all kinds of illusions. The moral struggle is at its peak here. This is the place where the "serpent of Ashlesha" finally gets slain, and people under the strong influence of this pada, are more likely to get tricked by others, rather than deceive others. Such natives are always putting up fronts and hardly ever show their true nature. Planets placed here adversely effect the father's wellbeing.

Professions :

All professions dealing with Poisons; Petroleum Industry; Chemical Engineers; Cigarette Industry; Legal and Illegal Drug Dealers; Drug Pushers; All Self Serving professions like present day Politicians; Behind the Scenes Manipulators; Psychologists; Con Artists; Thieves; Swindlers; Pornography Industry; Prostitutes; Snake Charmers; Professions involving dealing with Reptiles; Allopathic Doctors & Surgeons; Pet Snake & Pet Cat Owners; Poachers; Secret Service Agents; Spies; Lawyers; Pawnbrokers; Physical Yog Teachers; Tantrics (usually beginner types); Hypnotists; Psychologists/Psychiatrists; Spirit Mediums; Charlatan Channelists/Psychics etc; False Gurus and Cult Leaders; Baseball Players.

Places :

All places where Snakes & Reptiles dwell; Secret service Institutions (CIA, FBI etc.); Hospitals; Law Firms; All Factories dealing with Poisonous Chemical Processes; Drug Stores; Pawn Shops; Sleazy Places where Illegal Prostitution & Drug Peddling thrive; False Cults & Religious Institutions like ISKON etc.; all places connected with the above professions.

Guna (Essence) and Tattwa (Element) :

It is supposed to be a *Sattwic* nakshatra. This classification might perplex the reader but the intention of the ancient seers can be understood thus - Ashlesha relates directly to the *kundalini shakti* (see the Esoteric section), which encodes all of our life, all of our previous lives' experiences. She (kundalini shakti) is our mother and our individual blueprint and so cannot be regarded as anything but purely sattvic.

It belongs to the Water element. There's not much to explain here as this classification is in keeping with its predominant kapha humor.

Gana (Type) :

It is considered a *Rakshas* or demonic nakshatra. This comes as no surprise as Hydra, Ashlesha's representative constellation in the sky, is said to be the abode of the most dangerous celestial demonic creatures. Ashlesha as we have seen already can be quite cruel and wicked and very rarely functions from an unselfish perspective.

Orientation and Disposition :

It is Downward nakshatra. It is common knowledge that snakes don't live above the ground. Ashlesha stands for and is interested in all things underground both literally and figuratively. Planets placed in Ashlesha often feel contained or constrained and often have to work in a behind-the-scenes fashion.

It is a Hard, Sharp and Dreadful nakshatra. This comes as no surprise considering the immensity of its negative potential. The reader can refer to the Nature Section of this nakshatra for the nitty gritty of it.

Lunar Month & Day :

It relates to the first half of the lunar month of *Magha*, a period which usually falls in the month of January in the solar (Gregorian) calendar.

Ashlesha is also related to *Navami* (9th tithi or day) of the waxing and waning phases of the Moon's monthly cycle.

Auspicious Activities :

All types of activities requiring harsh measures like Administering Poisons, Filing of Lawsuits etc; Good for Scheming & Plotting against One's Enemies; Good for Sexual Activity; Good for all Low Risk Short term activities; Good for Kundalini Yog .

Inauspicious Activities :

Generally unfavourable for all types of Beginnings & Auspicious Activities; This is a good time to lie low; Especially unfavourable for doing business; Bad for Borrowing or Lending money.

Planetary Ruler :

Moon and Mercury are the two planets connected with this nakshatra, Mercury being the main planetary ruler. Mostly the negative Mercurial traits like evasiveness, deception and deviousness get highlighted in this nakshatra. Ashlesha uses Mercury's alacrity, perceptiveness and calculating ability, more often than not, to further its own selfish ends. This is obviously the case in the present day and age, but the actual functioning of Mercury here is to control the mind (represented by the Moon).

Ashlesha is supposed to be the place where intellect develops itself to control and direct the vast subconscious and instinctual workings of the mind. In today's world, Mercury's ability to direct Moon is used for deceiving the masses (Moon) through the media (Mercury). This negative usage of Mercurial energy makes this one of the most dangerous nakshatras in *Kali-Yug* (present age/cycle of humanity). This is especially evident when seen in light of the fact that Mercury is representative of one of the preserving forces in nature. As a result, society/civilization and the natural world are thrown completely out of balance. Ashlesha is the battleground where the war between intellect and emotions, conscious and subconscious, reasonability and primevality takes place. Its turbulent energies make it very susceptible to decadence and taking the wrong path.

Moon/Mercury conjunction in a horoscope give similar results to Ashlesha. Ketu is supposed to give good results in Ashlesha when aspected by Jupiter. No other planet can be said to function well in this nakshatra. A well placed Mercury however, can make the native a shrewd and manipulative businessman.

Vowel s and Alphabets :

The first pada or quarter of this asterism 16° 40' -20° 00' Cancer corresponds to "Dee" as in Deena or Deer.

The second pada or quarter of this asterism 20° 00' - 23° 20' Cancer corresponds to "Doo" as in Doing .

The third pada or quarter of this asterism 23° 20' - 26° 40' Cancer corresponds to "Day" as in David.

The fourth pada or quarter of this asterism 26° 40' - 30° 00' Cancer corresponds to "Doh" as in Dorothy or Doctor.

In the Sanskrit alphabet Ashlesha corresponds to "Kha" and"Ga", consequently its mantras are "Om Kham" and "Om Gam".

Sexual Type and Compatibility :

Its sexual animal is a Cat. Cats are quite intensely sexual animals. One can easily see that even basic keywords for Ashlesha like entwining, clinging, embracing and coiling relate to sexual union. In the present day and age this nakshatra can be said to be responsible for most of the sexual exploitation.

Aside from its own nakshatra it is most sexually compatible with *Purnavasu*.

For sexual & marital compatibility with other nakshatras please refer to the tables on pages 468 & 469.

Esoteric :

We have already noticed the connection between Ashlesha and Hydra, the most feared serpent in the night sky. In Greek legends Hydra is supposed to be this many headed serpent which was finally subdued by Hercules. It is interesting to note that the royal nakshatra of Magha (see next chapter) lies right next to this serpent constellation. Ancient legends are trying to tell us that the crown and authority (represented by Magha) is only achieved after the dark serpent (vices and undesirable qualities) is subdued within each one of us. The lower nature has to be won over before we can tune into our higher nature. Ashlesha is therefore a crucial focal point for the battle between good and bad. It is the last among the first cycle of nakshatras (a new cycle begins in Magha).

Ashlesha relates directly to the kundalini. Kundalini is a serpent shaped, two and a half coils of astral /causal energy, which lies in the *Muladhara Chakra* (sacral root centre) at the base of our spines. It is the function of Ashlesha to arouse and activate this energy. Most of Ashlesha's field and scope of activity lies within the instinctual, primordial domain of the root centre.

The arousal of the kundalini is the first step on the way to enlightenment. This again re-emphasizes the point that Ashlesha is a point where a conscious choice is made. This choice of course relates to letting go of our baser, gross materialistic nature so that we can begin our journey on the path of wisdom and enlightenment. The journey of the kundalini, which begins in Ashlesha, culminates in *Uttarabhadrapada* (see Chapter 26.)

Gotra (Celestial Lineage) :

This nakshatra is related to the *Sage Vashishta*, one of the seven celestial sages looking after the affairs of our galaxy. The name of this sage translates into "possessor of wealth". According to Vedic texts most of serpent deities are said to guard treasure. According to ancient Vedic mythology most of the celestial serpent deities are shown as being enormously wealthy. Thus it is appropriate that the sage who has most to do with wealth presides over this nakshatra.

Remedial :

Paying reverence or obeisance to serpents or doing serpent rituals like *Sarpa Homa* is useful for gaining the favour of the energies of this nakshatra. In India, a special day known as *Narga Panchami* is reserved for feeding milk to snakes and worshipping serpent deities. Practicing kundalini yog (also known as *Raj yog*) is the best way of rising above the negative qualities of this nakshatra.

Repetition of the root mantras of this nakshatra - "Om Kham" and "Om Gam" 108 times when Moon transits this nakshatra and during the lunar month of this nakshatra is sure to reduce suffering and bring enlightenment into a person's life.

Persons who are benefiting from the positive energy of this nakshatra can also increase the good effects through the above mentioned ways. Ashlesha natives are usually attracted to dark shades of every colour. They are often seen wearing red and black. However they are advised to wear more sattvic shades even when they are using variegated colours. They should avoid gaudy shades.

Example :

Ashlesha's sound and light can be experienced at -

http://osfa.org.uk/ashlesha.htm

Miscellaneous :

According to *Varahamihira*, those born with Moon in Ashlesha are false, wicked, ungrateful, crafty and gluttonous, eating everything in sight.

Such things cannot be applied straight, everything depends on the soul evolution of the being in question.

* * *

10. Magha 0°0' - 13°20' Leo

10.

Magha

(0°00' Leo - 13°20' Leo)

In the Sky :

Magha, the brightest and largest amongst nakshatras, is represented in the night sky by a sickle-shaped group of stars in front of the royal constellation of Leo. The brightest among these is *Regulus* or *Alpha-Leonis*. With a visual magnitude of 1.41, it is one of the brightest stars in the night sky and is also known as the "Little King" or the "Little Sun". Its companions, which comprise the rest of the constellation, lie above it and are known in modern astronomy as *Eta-Leonis* (*Al Jabhah*), *Zeta-Leonis* (*Adhafera*), *Mu-Leonis* (*Rasalas*), *Epsilon-Leonis*, *Lambda-Leonis* (*Alterf*) & *Kappa-Leonis*. Ancient Vedic seers saw this constellation as a throne while other cultures saw it as a lion.

Name :

Magha translates into "mighty", "the beneficent", "the great", "the magnificent", "the most important" or "the bountiful". This translation immediately evokes a variety of meanings and feelings and as we shall see this nakshatra is true to its name

Symbol :

Magha's main symbol is a 'throne'. As a matter of detail one can say it is a 'royal chamber with a throne' (please refer to the image). This symbolism immediately conjures up a picture of royalty, power, status, honour and the like. We can see that all these interpretations live up to the meanings evoked by the name of this nakshatra. However the bottom line of this symbolism lies in one word - "achievement". After the struggles and tribulations of *Ashlesha* (previous nakshatra), it is now time for reaping rewards. In the material realm, Magha bestows this reward on natives under its influence through power, position, authority; and in the higher aspect, through self knowledge.

In a way the body is nothing but the throne of the soul. Most of us identify or attach our sense of self to our minds and bodies. Magha is the first nakshatra which relates to the individualization process. It represents all that we mean when we say "I". The soul uses the body and mind as its identity. The mind and intellect however are given the task to understand our true identities as eternal, everlasting souls. There's no greater accomplishment with the discovery of the "self". In its material aspect, Magha can bestow all kinds of worldly honours and prestige, usually through our ability to accomplish on the material plane.

In many cases Magha can bestow all of this as a result purely through hereditary means or some sort of succession. In ancient times it was implicit that the son of the king will be king and the son of a barber will be a barber. Even though things appear different today, they are still pretty much the same if one looks at the full picture.

Magha's throne denotes all that we have inherited, whether it be genes, roots, property, wealth, knowledge or status through our parents and ancestors. Magha is therefore the nakshatra which is most closely related to our sense of identity. It relates to who we are and where we are coming from.

Deity :

Pitris, or "the ancestors", are the main ruling deity of this asterism. It comes as no surprise that the world of the ancestors controls Magha. As we discussed earlier, we owe a lot to our ancestors in terms of our actual self identity and station in life, even without ever knowing or acknowledging it, as is the case in modern times. Ancestor worship was another one of the common strands which connected all ancient civilizations.

Our ancient ancestors obviously were not ungrateful fools like us and saw it as their duty and privilege to keep alive the knowledge of their roots, by honouring and in some cases bonding with their ancestors in the other realms. In the rural areas of countries like India, ancestor worship still remains a serious matter. In fact death rites usually involve rituals directly related to one's ancestry. Many families in India, especially *Brahmin* families, often trace their ancestries back to the original seven sages who were created by Brahma, at the very beginning of creation.

The modern science of genetics has made it clear that most of our abilities and capabilities are dependent upon our genetic code and that this genetic code is basically a sort of free gift from our ancestors. In the same way, Magha is known for bestowing liberal favours without any expectation of return. It is basically a nakshatra which deals with the past. We should however keep in mind that our ancestors are not frozen remains of the past, but are actually alive in one of the universal realms.

The *Puranic* texts tell us that there is a a heavenly realm called *Pitra Loka* or "world of the ancestors". This is the world where a lot among us go to after our physical deaths. It is sort of an intermediary station where souls meet their ancestors and rest for awhile, before returning to earth for another life or moving on to other lokas. This world of the ancestors finds vivid descriptions in all ancient cultures, especially among the present day native American Indian and aboriginal tribes. This world of the dead is supposed to overlook our affairs on the physical earthly realm and in some cases, some direct intervention and communication is experienced. Magha is a nakshatra relating both to our identity in the present life and our after death journey.

Nature & Functioning :

Common english words like "magnificent", "manor", "major", "mayor", "master", "magic" and "magnanimous" seem to have their root in the first two syllables of the word "Magha". The meanings of these words relate to Magha's functioning at some level or the other.

It is Magha's job to shape the present using the past. Wherever this nakshatra is placed in a chart one will experience the positive effects of one's past karmas. This may manifest as opportunities or favour from those in high positions. These favours are very sudden and based on impulse from those who bestow them.

Its fierceness corresponds to the fierce aspect of Ketu, which is akin to the fierce aspect of Sun. Ketu is the most fierce among planets. It can be as fierce as the mid-summer, mid-afternoon desert Sun. Fierceness as we know is also associated with authority at some level. Authority can either foster magnanimity or produce the merciless tyrants who are blinded by power and authority.

It is a human asterism which brings out the more worldly human side of esoterically oriented Ketu. This is very much a worldly nakshatra which is interested in human affairs. Ketu is known to us as a separative planet which disassociates one from worldly ties, but through this asterism it promotes involvement in mundane affairs for discharging one's worldly duties. It brings out the materially active side of Ketu which is very concerned about social status, prominence and discharging of one's worldly duties. This is why its pitfall lies in making one over ambitious in one's material pursuits. However when working through its higher principal, this asterism has a high degree of idealism even when surrounded by worldly attainments. Ketu is an idealistic planet when functioning in its solar aspect. Ketu is also a naturally rebellious planet and consequently this nakshatra is directly related to all types of revolts against authority.

This is an asterism connected to the sustenance and maintenance aspect of nature. Its primary impulse is to maintain established traditions, organizations and civilizations. This is usually the function of those in positions of authority whom this asterism represents.

Natives with Magha rising or strong Magha influence are easy to spot because of their big noses and regal demeanour. Magha people have middle stature and lion-like top heavy bodies. They have arrogant mannerisms which make them misunderstood in general. Their power lies in covering up weaknesses through reservedness. They usually align their selves with their ancestral lineage and derive pride through a sense of belonging. They are usually magnanimous to those below their station in life. Following a moral and ethical code is important for their inner peace of mind. Magha natives usually have a strong concern for the continuation of their family lineage through progeny. They have great expectations of their progeny and want them to bring pride and renown to the family.

In the universal scheme of things, Magha relates to "*tyaga shepani shakti*" - the power of the astral body to cut its ties with the physical body. Its symbolism has mourning above and the death process below. This relates Magha to all endings like physical death and new beginnings which arise as a result. Magha guides the souls to *Pitra Loka* (the realm of the ancestors) after one's death. Thus Magha is basically a facilitator in change of state.

Mode of Functioning :

Magha is considered to be an Active nakshatra. Magha's naturally fiery nature promotes activity and dynamism. It is Magha's striving for a sense of achievement and glory which makes it pursue an active way of life.

Caste :

Strangely enough, the ancient Vedic seers assigned the royal nakshatra of Magha the *Shudra* (servant) caste. Their line of thinking may be partially understood when one comes to the understanding that finally a king is nothing but a servant of his people. It is Magha's duty to be of service no matter what high throne it sits upon. This is best conveyed in the words of the contemporary songwriter *Bob Dylan*, "It may be the devil or it may be the lord, but you gotta serve somebody!"

Gender :

It is a Female nakshatra. It has been a tradition in the Vedic literature to view things like prosperity, fame and fortune as feminine. All these desired attainments in the material world are often depicted in the form of goddesses. It is interesting to note that even the word 'vanity' is seen as a predominantly feminine vice.

Bodyparts & Humor (Ayurvedic Constitution) :

Nose, Lips and Chin are the body parts related to this nakshatra. Readers thus can notice that people with prominent Magha influence in their charts usually have a big nose. It is not very difficult to see where the term "high nosed" came from!

It is a primarily "*Kapha*" (watery) nakshatra. It can be noticed that Magha has the ability to hide its ambitions, motives and fieriness under a calm exterior. A calm exterior as we know is often associated with water signs or the kapha element.

Direction :

It is related primarily to east, south, northwest and southwest.

Padas (Quarters) :

The first pada or quarter of this asterism 00° 00' - 3° 20' Leo, falls in Aries Navamsa and is ruled by Mars. This is the pada relating to the will power aspect of Magha. This is the pada where the throne is won after the killing of the many headed serpent of Ashlesha. Magha qualities like self assertion, leadership, courage and idealism are displayed here to their fullest.

The second pada or quarter of this asterism 3° 20' - 6° 40' Leo, falls in Taurus Navamsa ruled by Venus. After the throning, the king has to consolidate his position. This is a very ambitious pada, where the emphasis is on image, duty and materialistic organization. Planets placed here bring about favours from superiors.

The third pada or quarter of this asterism 6° 40' - 10° 00' Leo, falls in Gemini Navamsa ruled by Mercury. This pada relates to the often ignored intellectual side of Magha. After the throne is safe, the king indulges in more literary artistic pursuits and listens to discourses from learned men. The emphasis here is on mental activity and a quest for knowledge (knowledge of the ancients in the present times!). Planets placed here make one succeed through group activity, even though it is Magha's essential nature to go it alone.

The fourth pada or quarter of this asterism 10° 00' - 13° 20' Leo, falls in Cancer Navamsa ruled by Moon. This is the pada which brings out Magha's love of ritual, ceremonies, ancestor worship and family pride. The king here concentrates on the wellbeing of his subjects, his family life and looks for progeny to keep his lineage going. Planets placed in this pada make one derive pride from one's family, ancestors and one's charitability. Planets here are not very conducive to material prosperity and create upheavals through some form of self undoing.

Professions :

Administrators; Managers; Royalty and those in direct touch with Royalty; Those who bestow (or receive) honours like "knighthood" etc.; Those in high places in Government; People at the top of their chosen professions; Legends; Bureaucrats; Aristocrats; Officials; Chairmen (those in a position of authority); Lawyers; Advocates; Judges, Referees, Magistrates and like; Politicians; Historians; Librarians; Orators; Dramatists & Performers; Upholders of Traditions; Professions relating to Museums of all types; Occultists; Black Magicians; Exorcists; Astrologers; Dealers in Antiques of all types; Archaeologists; Genetic Engineering Experts; Professions related to using and researching Ancient Knowledge, Monuments etc; Those Researching & Documenting Lineages.

Places :

Deserts; Forests; Capital Cities; Libraries; Museums; Palaces; Ancient Monuments & Sites; Govt. Offices; Residences of Top Politicians; National Monuments; Stages & Performance Halls; Ceremonial Grounds & Buildings; Crematories; Places of Religious, Spiritual Significance.

Guna (Essence) and Tattwa (Element) :

It is supposed to be a *Tamasic* nakshatra. The primary reason why the ancient seers saw the active Magha as being predominated by tamasic energy is because of the fact that it relates more to the past. Many a times Magha can retard new growth as a result of being stuck in the past. Magha carries within itself all the inertia, temptations and trappings that the past more often than not manages to conjure.

It belongs to the Water element. It is a watery nakshatra in the sense that it is like an ocean and represents the expansive watery side of Ketu. Ocean is again symbolic of vastness and prominence inherent in this nakshatra. Water as we know is the secondary element of Ketu. It brings out the emotional side of Ketu, which manifests in qualities like compassion and benevolence. These are important qualities for those in authority positions.

Gana (Type) :

It is considered a *Rakshasa* (demonic) nakshatra. Through this classification the ancient seers are giving us a signal that the world of the ancestors is not all benign and godly. There are many *bhootas, pretas, pishachas* and other types of negative astral entities associated with this nakshatra. Most of the black magic practices involve the summoning and use of these negative entities. Most of these dark occult practices are often done in order to gain typical Magha goals - power, status, fame, fortune, prosperity etc. A statement of caution for the black magic practitioners - "every action has a reaction and everything has its price".

Orientation and Disposition :

It is a Downward Looking nakshatra. This basically relates to Magha's association with the past and in the same sense, all things down and under. As mentioned earlier, Magha can be quite a constrictive influence, a role which the bureaucracy and authority plays to the 'T' in the present times. It is interesting to note that a lot of research relating to the past involves digging underground, an activity normally associated with downward nakshatras.

It is an *Ugra* (fierce or aggressive) nakshatra. It is very clear that no throne is attained without overcoming numerous obstacles, enemies and the like. It is Magha's burning pride and ambition that makes it fierce and cruel. Magha sets itself no limits or boundaries when it comes to achieving its goals.

Lunar Month & Day :

It is related to the second half of the lunar month of *Magha*. This period usually falls in the month of February in the solar calendar. In India this part of the month of Magha is still used for ancestor worship.

Magha is also related to *Amavasya* (15th tithi or New Moon Day) of the waning phase of the Moon's monthly cycle.

Auspicious Activities :

Ceremonies of all kinds, especially those requiring pomp and grandeur; Marriage ceremonies; Stage & public performances whether it involves music, oratory or drama; Public displays; Coronations and other royal events; Parades; Award ceremonies; Researching one's lineage; Anything involving the past; Historical/classical studies & research; Taking on a new name; Upgrading to higher and better quality in possessions, jobs, etc.; Undertaking career strategies; Job promotions; Donating elaborate gifts; Studying ancient knowledge; Religious activities of all types especially those involving ancestor worship; Good for settling disputes or other warlike activities; A good time to seek favours from powerful persons, government and other authority figures.

Inauspicious Activities :

Not favourable for lending money; Not good for servile, mundane or common activities; Not good for futuristic planning and exploration; Not very conducive for dealing with new technologies.

Planetary Ruler :

Ketu is the main planetary ruler of Magha. One of Ketu's main symbols is a Flag, which directly relates to authority, eminence, fame etc. This favoured position in the present life is earnt due to meritorious past life deeds. Ketu as we know is the guardian of our past karmas and it releases the ones that are ripe enough to be experienced in the present life through this nakshatra.

The qualities and attributes of Ketu like deep perception, penetrating insight and independent spirit, which are similar to that of Sun, are exhibited by Magha. Sun as we know is the royal planet but mostly we don't see Ketu in that light. This asterism brings out the regal side of Ketu. This asterism can be seen as a combination of Sun's and Ketu's energies. Sun is related to Magha as a result of being the ruler of Leo, the sign Magha falls in.

Ketu as we have discussed earlier, is a genetic planet and represents the paternal grandfather and maternal grandmother in a chart. Our connection with our ancestors has a lot to do with our past lives which is again a Ketu domain. To sum it up, Magha has a lot to do with the genetic and past heritage aspect of Ketu. It also relates to the fact that Ketu is responsible for bringing the wisdom of the ancient ages and civilizations to the present.

Sun-Ketu conjunction in a nativity carries an energy similar to that of Magha. Fiery royal planets like Sun & Mars usually do well in Magha. Servant planets like Saturn however feel at sea in this nakshatra.

Vowel s and Alphabets :

The first pada or quarter of this asterism 00° 00' - 3° 20' Leo corresponds to "Ma" as in Magic or Marilyn.

The second pada or quarter of this asterism 3° 20' - 6° 40' Leo corresponds to "Mi" as in Mia.

The third pada or quarter of this asterism 6° 40' - 10° 00' Leo corresponds to "Mu" as in Mood.

The fourth pada or quarter of this asterism 10° 00' - 13° 20' Leo corresponds to "Me" as in Memory.

In the Sanskrit alphabet Magha corresponds to "Gha" and "Nga", consequently its mantras are "Om Gham" and "Om Ngam".

Sexual Type and Compatibility :

Its sexual animal is a Rat. It is interesting to note that the regal and pompous Magha becomes a rat in bed. Magha is always said to have a weakness for the opposite sex. Rats are highly sexually active animals known to produce scores of progeny. As we have discussed, Magha is very fixed on propagating its lineage and its rampant sexuality is both for procreation and recreation. It could be said that sexuality is just another show off medium for Magha, who in reality often doesn't match up to its partner's expectations in bed. It is mostly compatible with its fellow rat *Purva Phalguni.*

For sexual and marital compatibility with other nakshatras please refer to the tables on pages 468 & 469 .

Esoteric :

Magha is the 10th nakshatra and thus like the 10th house its spirituality lies in *Karma Yog*, which entails fulfilling one's duty in life. The star *Regulus*, the principle star of Magha, was revered in all the ancient cultures as the celestial seat of power. The constellation of Magha lay beside *Hydra*, the constellation relating to the demonic serpent forces and the previous nakshatra Ashlesha. This relates to the fact that the crown or throne of Magha is only achieved after overcoming the primordial negative part of our nature exemplified by Ashlesha.

In the Greek culture (an offshoot of the ancient Vedic culture), there are references to many celestial battles between the serpents and the Gods. The most famous of these battles relates to the killing of Hydra, the sea serpent with nine heads, by *Hercules*, the son of Jupiter. Hydra is the longest constellation in the sky and also covers the largest area. The astrological signs of Cancer, Leo, Virgo and Libra can be seen placed along its northern side. Hercules, the great warrior, is also a constellation in the sky placed close to the star *Vega*.

Krishn, an incarnation of *Vishnu*, kills a several-headed serpent called *Kaliya* in a story very reminiscent of the above-mentioned Greek legend. It was understood that subduing or winning over these forces was an important part of establishing oneself as being worthy of the throne, which allowed one to have influence over the masses. The whole point of Magha is to rise above the Cancerian pool of mass-mentality and discover one's own unique individuality.

The fact that our ancient ancestors who lived in the Golden, Silver & Bronze ages were supposed to be more highly evolved than us, makes the world of the ancestors a place where we could draw wisdom and knowledge from. Ancient native cultures like the Native American Indians and the Nordics have always known this fact. Any real change in the present day situation of hopelessness, confusion and misery will only come about after the knowledge of the ancients is properly understood.

Gotra (Celestial Lineage) :

This nakshatra is related to the *Sage Angiras*, one of the seven celestial sages looking after the affairs of our galaxy. The name of this sage translates into "the fiery one". Considering Magha's essential fiery nature, it is no wonder that it connects to this particular sage, who, as we recall, also presides over the fiery nakshatra of *Krittika*.

Remedial :

One straightforward way of getting Magha on your side is to be respectful and reverential towards elders and ancestors. Performance of a *Shradha* ceremony for one's ancestors in the prescribed tithi of the lunar month of Magha, is auspicious in the sense that one receives blessings from the world of the ancestors. Worship of *Kali* or *Shiv* is the best way of mastering the energy of this nakshatra.

Repetition of the root mantra of this nakshatra - "Om Gham" and "Om Ngam" 108 times when Moon transits this nakshatra and in the the lunar month of Magha is sure to reduce suffering and bring enlightenment into a person's life.

Persons who are benefiting from the positive energy of this nakshatra can also increase the good effects through the above mentioned ways. It is helpful for them to wear royal colours which includes dark and bright shades of gold, reds and yellows. They should use its directions, lunar month and the days when Moon transits Magha to undertake all important actions.

Example :

Magha's sound and light can be experienced at –

http://osfa.org.uk/magha.htm

Miscellaneous :

According to *Varahamihira*, those born with Moon in Magha have "lots of wealth, many servants, live a life of luxury and enjoyment, are persevering and devoted to gods and ancestors".

* * *

11. Purvaphalguni   13°20' – 26°40' Leo

11.

Purvaphalguni

(13º20' Leo - 26º40' Leo)

In the Sky :

Purvaphalguni is represented in the night sky by two bright stars in the back of the constellation of Leo. These stars can be seen forming a part of the lion shape usually associated with the constellation Leo. However ancient Vedic seers saw these two stars as representing the back legs of a cot (or the two poles of a swinging hammock). These stars are known in modern astronomy as *Delta-Leonis* (*Zosma*) & *Theta-Leonis* (*Chertan*). With a visual magnitude of 2.56, Zosma is the brighter one among them. It is very easy to locate these stars in the night sky as Leo is the brightest among the twelve zodiacal constellations. These stars are located to the left of the bright star *Regulus* where the hind legs of the lion figure of Leo are supposed to be. Zosma lies on top of Chertan.

Name :

Purvaphalguni translates into the "former reddish one", "the former" or "little fig tree". The colour red always evokes a wide variety of meanings and feelings and as we shall see, this nakshatra has a lot to do with the nature, qualities and temperament generally associated with the colour red. The "fig tree" translation is a more obscure one and relates to the procreative aspect of this asterism.

Symbol :

Its main symbol is the front legs of a couch or bed. The bed referred to here is not the bed we use for sleeping on during the night time, but a divan or bed/couch used for a daytime siesta or lounging around. Some astrologers also use a swinging hammock as one of Purvaphalguni's symbols. It is pretty clear from the above symbols that 'comfort' is the keyword for this nakshatra. In the cycle of the 27 nakshatras, the soul looks for comfort and enjoyment after attaining the 'throne' in the previous nakshatra.

Purvaphalguni relates to a time where we look for rest, relaxation and amusement after fulfilling our worldly duties and responsibilities (activities ruled by the previous nakshatra). The symbolism of the front legs of a bed/couch relates to the beginning part of this relaxation process. When we are very tired and hop onto a couch or a bed we usually go into a mode of complete relaxation in the beginning (the time period varies from individual to individual). Purvaphalguni relates to this beginning period where we feel like doing no activity and are completely intent upon renewing our energy. Purvaphalguni is thus strongly related with the forces of renewal, which ultimately link it to the process of creation itself.

It is difficult for some of us to understand how something can be creative without being active. All activity is dependent upon periods of non-activity. Nothing or no one can work all the time. It is the periods of rest which provide the impulse for the creative/active periods. A lot of scientists and researchers have found that the solution to a problem usually comes to them, not when they are actually working at the problem, but in the period when they have taken their mind off it and are in a state of complete relaxation. In the fast paced life of modern times, especially in cities, people have forgotten the importance of having adequate periods of rest between activities. This is probably the root cause for most of the physical and psychological traumas faced by the fast paced city dweller. However one must be careful not to amplify the Purvaphalguni energy, which usually results in excessive laziness and indulgence.

Deity :

Bhaga, one of the twelve *Adityas* (solar deities), is the main ruling deity of this nakshatra. He is often referred to as the "morning star", which might be a reference to the planet Venus. As we shall discover later, Venus is the planetary ruler of this nakshatra and was seen in ancient times as a planet representing the solar aspect of nature. Bhaga's name translates roughly into "delight". A similar sanskrit word called "*bhoga*" translates into "pleasure" or "indulgence". The term "Bhaga" finds use in "*bhagavan*" (full of delight), one of the sanskrit names often used for gods, incarnations and evolved souls. In keeping with his name, Bhaga is known for bestowing rest, relaxation, enjoyment, pleasure, affection, sexual passion and marital felicity. Thus Purvaphalguni is seen to promote all of the above indications.

Bhaga's strong relationship with enjoyment and merriment makes this one of the most carefree nakshatras. Purvaphalguni natives don't like to worry as long as they are comfortable, especially from a physical point of view. Bhaga's obsession with physicality often makes Purvaphalguni natives overtly concerned with their bodies. Bhaga's amorous nature gives Purvaphalguni natives a strong desire to appear beautiful and be appreciated. Bhaga stands for an easy life full of comfort and luxury and this is what all Purvaphalguni natives aspire for. Bhaga relates to that solar aspect of nature, which makes life worth living. If one removes the pleasure aspect from the universe, not many souls will be willing to take part in the game of life.

Bhaga is always usually invoked along with *Aryaman*, the ruling deity of *Uttaraphalguni*, the following nakshatra. As we shall discover later, these nakshatras form a pair in the same vein as *Mrigashira* and *Ardra*.

Purvaphalguni is directly connected to the *Shiv Lingam*, the most commonly worshipped form of *Shiv.* The fact that Shiv's penis is worshipped more than Shiv as a whole, relates to the penis being a regenerative symbol, representing creation and continuation of life; while Shiv as a whole is the god of destruction. Purvaphalguni thus relates to the creative and delightful aspect of Shiv, which can be easily understood through the stories and legends associated with him. It is interesting to note that the penis is the most delicate part of male anatomy. This fact brings out the essential tender quality of Purvaphalguni.

Nature & Functioning :

After the victory crown and throne achieved through intense battles in *Magha,* it is natural that rest, relaxation and enjoyment follow. This is what Purvaphalguni is all about. A period of rest follows every period of activity, just like a sunny calm follows a storm. Amongst all the nakshatras, Purvaphalguni is the most related to the recreational aspect of nature's functionings. It offers shelter from the vicissitudes of the drama of life.

The sense of self having been firmly established in Magha, self -absorption reaches a peak in this nakshatra. Just like a tired person looking for some place and time to rest, the concerns here are me, myself and I. The intensive absorption of this nakshatra makes it dramatic. The fact that it falls in the middle of the sign of dramatics, Leo, further encourages this tendency, making it the most theatrical amongst the nakshatras. Purvaphalguni natives have a strong desire to be noticed for what they are and what they do. This is the reason why a lot of Purvaphalguni natives fall prey to pretentious behaviour and attitudes. Learning anything, especially new things, becomes very hard for such natives as they don't want to look beyond their own little world, no matter how superficial it might be. If it wasn't for Purvaphalguni, terms like "vanity" and "pompousness" wouldn't exist.

Despite its self-indulgent eccentricity, Purvaphalguni is a social nakshatra. It likes to function within prevailing social standards. Despite its natural fixed character, it shows amazing flexibility when it comes to fitting the prevailing social norms. It likes the comfort and safety of blending in, rather than standing out. In its positive aspect, Purvaphalguni can be a warm, sustaining and nourishing influence on those around then. It is one of the cornerstone nakshatras which keep up the pillars of human society.

Having said this, it must be remembered that Purvaphalguni is a naturally cruel nakshatra and therefore natives under its strong influence can be expected to be capable of carrying out ruthless acts. Purvaphalguni's cruelty usually comes out when its rest, relaxation or amusement is disturbed by an outside agency. Natives under its influence get easily hurt and get extremely vindictive over small issues. This is especially the case if they don't get the requisite amount of attention from others which they think they deserve in their own minds.

Despite their limitations of pride, jealousy and vindictiveness, these natives are quite delightful creatures to be around when appreciating the finer enjoyments in life. They can be the most fun to hang around socially, as they radiate their Leonine warmth and beneficence from their position on the bed or couch. It is very easy to spot a Purvaphalguni native in a crowd as they will be the one in the most comfortable spot. They are usually in no hurry to begin the day's activities and like to lead lives of luxury, even if they can't afford to. They are not overachievers except in areas where little physical discomfort is demanded of them. They are happy idling about in the office, in the arts studio, making love or entertaining others with their personality. Most of their efforts go in trying to make themselves comfortable or exploring their own personal feelings, thoughts and emotions. They usually end up having a family but are often not very suited for the parental role. Their self-obsessive aspect usually makes them cruel or unnerving for their children.

In the universal scheme of things, Purvaphalguni relates to "*prajanana shakti*" - the power to procreate. Its symbolism has female above and male below. It is immediately apparent that Purvaphalguni is all about creation through union of the polar natural opposites. Its objective is creation of a family on the macrocosmic as well as microcosmic level.

Mode of Functioning :

Purvaphalguni is considered to be a Balanced nakshatra. Purvaphalguni balances creativity with relaxation, work with pleasure, aggression with gentleness. The aesthetically refined aspect of this nakshatra arises out of its ability to find a delicate balance with objects, colours and the like. As far as being active is concerned, it is a lazy nakshatra.

Caste :

It belongs to the *Brahmin* caste. Purvaphalguni relays the brahminical side of the brahmin planet Venus. *Shukracharya*, the presiding deity of Venus, is the preceptor of the demons and has the unique distinction of knowing *Sanjivinividya* (knowledge of bringing the dead back to life), which even *Brihaspati,* the preceptor of the gods, does not possess. A brahmin is someone who is supposed to understand the secret functionings of *Maya* and Venus's association with Purvaphalguni relates it to all kinds of occult knowledge.

Gender :

It is a Female nakshatra. Even though both of its ruling deities are male, the primary impulses of this nakshatra, like beauty, vanity, love of ease, comfort and luxury are all primarily feminine concerns. They come about due to this nakshatra's strong connection with Venus, which is seen in Jyotish as a feminine planet.

Bodyparts & Humor (Ayurvedic Constitution) :

The Sex Organs, the Lips and the Right Hand are the body parts related to this nakshatra.

It is a primarily "*Pitta*" (fiery) nakshatra. Its pitta quality arises out of its connection with Leo, a pitta sign and Sun, a pitta planet. Fire is the essence of desire.

Direction :

It is related primarily to the directional arc between south east and east.

Padas (Quarters) :

The first pada or quarter of this asterism 13° 20' - 16° 40' Leo falls in Leo Navamsa ruled by Sun. The emphasis here is on just I, I & more I. The evolved souls can use the warmth of their soul power to illuminate the minds of those around them, whereas for younger souls planets in this pada just heighten the ego. "Dignity" and "Regality" are the keywords here. Sun, Mars, Jupiter and Ketu can function strongly here and give some sort of executive ability.

The second pada or quarter of this asterism 16° 40' - 20° 00' Leo falls in Virgo Navamsa ruled by Mercury. This is the most sober and hardworking amongst all of these naturally pompous and lazy padas. The emphasis here is on trade and enterprise. A well placed Mercury here can give good common sense and heavy gains through trade.

The third pada or quarter of this asterism 20° 00' - 23° 20' Leo falls in Libra Navamsa ruled by Venus. This pada brings out the indulgent as well as creative Venusian aspect of Purvaphalguni. The emphasis here is on travel, harmony, relaxation, refinement, counselling, creation and appreciation of beauty. Since this is the Pushkara Navamsa pada most planets except Sun give good results here. Venus is especially strong in this pada.

The fourth pada or quarter of this asterism 23° 20' - 26° 40' Leo falls in Scorpio Navamsa ruled by Mars. The emphasis here is on intensified emotions, home and family life, self reflection and personal valour. Passions are very strong here and all things in life are approached with a martian spirit. Planets here usually give rise to a lot of unnecessary strife and complexity. Only a well placed Sun and Jupiter are capable of utilizing this pada's inner positive fashion.

Professions :

Animal trainers; Government Officials; Executives; Diplomats; Dealers in products related to women; Gemstone Industry; Entertainers; Beauticians; Make up Artists; Models; Photographers; Event Managers; Art Gallery Managers; Singers, mostly romantic types; Musicians (more into harmonies than other aspects of music); Creative Artists; Teaching profession in general; Dye makers; Physical Fitness Trainers; Interior Decorators and Designers; All professions connected with Marriages, Marriage Ceremonies & Childbirths; Nannies; Doctors (both Naturopaths and Allopaths); Sex-Therapists; Sleep Therapists; Masseurs; Those involved in Dating Agencies; Biologists; Leisure and Tourism Industry; People connected with Production & Distribution of Incenses, Toiletries and related Venusian Products; Goldsmiths & Jewellers; Wool, Cotton and Silk industry; Secretarial jobs.

Places :

Hot tropical landscapes; Flowery landscapes; Beaches; Entertainment halls; Exhibition places; Bedroom; Tourist resorts; Spas; Living rooms; Art galleries; Beauty parlours; Markets, especially the kind related to Venusian products; Pretty cottages, buildings and homes; All places connected with the above mentioned professions.

Guna (Essence) and Tattwa (Element) :

It is supposed to be a *Rajasic* nakshatra. Purvaphalguni is very engrossed on the material plane. Its planetary ruler Venus is supposed to be the most rajasic among planets. It represents the "desire" aspect of nature, which breeds life and makes the whole process of living exciting and delightful.

It belongs to the Water element. Purvaphalguni's connection with Venus, a watery planet, would account for this classification. Water breeds life (it is clear that all sentient life began in the oceans), and Purvaphalguni is representative of the creative potential in nature. Even sperm are carried by a watery fluid known as semen and the mating of sperm with the ova takes place in a watery medium.

Gana (Type) :

It is considered a *Manusha* or human nakshatra. Purvaphalguni's strong involvement with society, human relationships and procreation make it very concerned with what can be termed as human affairs. It is one of the nakshatras dedicated to sustaining the drama of life.

Orientation and Disposition :

It is an Upward nakshatra. Purvaphalguni fosters any kind of growth. The seed may lie beneath the ground, but the plant grows upwards. Purvaphalguni is intimately connected with the biological process of cell division, which is responsible for making a tree out of a seed, or a baby out of a sperm. Purvaphalguni natives always look upwards towards the sky, the gods and the creator for its inspiration and answers.

It is an *Ugra* or fierce nakshatra. It comes as a surprise that a soft, pleasure loving and comfort seeking nakshatra should have a fierce temperament. This relates to Purvaphalguni's tendency to get overtly disgusted when it does not get what it wants. As we have discussed earlier, Purvaphalguni natives are prepared to go to any lengths in order to secure the luxury and comfort which they think is their right. Disturbing Purvaphalguni's comfort zone is akin to disturbing a sleeping lion.

Lunar Month & Day :

It relates to the first half of the lunar month of *Phalguna*, which usually falls in late February in the solar calendar.

Purva Phalguni is also related to the *Trayodashi* (13th tithi or day) of the waxing and waning phases of the Moon's monthly cycle.

Auspicious Activities :

Marriage, sex, romance; Good for dealing with authorities and all kinds of persuasion; A good nakshatra for clearing out the air in relation to long standing disputes; Good for confronting enemies in a gentle appeasing way; Rest, relaxation and enjoyment; Artistic activities like painting, singing etc. ; Good for using charisma or personal power for gaining wanted ends; Good for buying property; Matters relating to property and construction in general.

Inauspicious Activities :

Unfavourable for all activities which require lessening down of ego; Not good for starting new things; Not good for intellectual activities; Not good for healing or curing diseases; Illnesses which start at this time are hard to overcome.

Planetary Ruler :

Sun and Venus are the two planets related to this nakshatra, Venus being its main planetary ruler. Venus's involvement with this nakshatra is obvious from the fact that the main functioning of Purvaphalguni is procreation. Venus relates to the force which produces attraction between the opposite sexes and the main focus of Purvaphalguni centres around this attraction. Sun, however, is connected with one's sense of self and is not very comfortable with the idea of losing one's self to another, something which Venus naturally stands for. Purvaphalguni is a battleground for the conflict between ego, love and harmony. It helps to know that the Venusian energy is stronger in comparision to Solar energy here (in *Krittika* it was the opposite way round).

The fact that Sun and Venus are natural enemies makes Purvaphalguni a volatile and turbulent nakshatra. The decision to be made here is how much of the self should be sacrificed in order for love and harmony to find their rightful place. Creativity is the only common meeting point between Sun and Venus. This is the reason why Purvaphalguni is able to be creative and constructive despite a plethora of inner rages and tumults.

Sun/Venus conjunction or exchange in a horoscope carries energies similar to Purvaphalguni. Sun, Mars and Venus usually give strong results here but as always a lot depends on the pada they occupy.

Vowels and Alphabets :

The first pada or quarter of this asterism 13° 20' -16° 40' Leo corresponds to "Mo" as in Mohicans.

The second pada or quarter of this asterism 16° 40' - 20° 00' Leo corresponds to "Ta" as in Taina.

The third pada or quarter of this asterism 20° 00' - 23° 20' Leo corresponds to "Tee" as in Tina.

The fourth pada or quarter of this asterism 23° 20' - 26° 40' Leo corresponds to "Too" as in Tooth.

In the Sanskrit alphabet Purvaphalguni corresponds to "Cha", consequently its mantra is "Om Cham".

Sexual Type and Compatibility :

Its sexual animal is a Rat, thus its sexual nature is similar to that of Magha, the previous nakshatra. As discussed earlier, rats are highly reproductive animals and produce scores of progeny. They are always busy scurrying around, which makes Purvaphalguni quite indefatigable when it comes to sexual or creative activity. Purvaphalguni is most compatible with the other rat nakshatra, *Magha*.

For sexual & marital compatibility with other nakshatras please refer to the tables on pages 468 & 469 .

Esoteric :

Purvaphalguni relates to the masculine creative spark which touches upon the passive feminine principle and puts it into creative motion. The feminine principle in nature is by itself passive (the quality which makes Purvaphalguni lazy), and needs an external force to set it alight. The Moon, which represents the feminine principle among planets, also needs a male source in form of the Sun in order to function.

All the *Puranic* stories relating to *Shiv's* phallus and the reasons why Shiv is worshipped in the phallic form relate to Purvaphalguni's functioning.

In a famous story, the seven sages living in a Himalayan pine forest in *Krita Yug* (the golden age) are tormented by Shiv who visits their hermitage in a wild, naked form and all the womenfolk get seduced by his erect hanging phallus. The sages in their puritanical narrowmindedness curse that Shiv's phallus should fall off. Shiv respects their wishes and lets his phallus get castrated. As soon as this happens the whole balance of the universe gets unsettled. Brahma intervenes and asks the sages to worship the *Lingam* (phallus) they had castrated in their moment of foolishness. Shiv pleased by their devotion and worship takes on his Lingam again and thus universal balance is restored.

Even in the present age, Shiv is still primarily worshipped in a Lingam form to make sure that puritanicalism never steps over the male primeval regenerative principle represented by the Lingam. Amongst the nakshatras, Purvaphalguni and *Uttaraphalguni* relate to this important aspect of universal functioning.

Purvaphalguni relates to the *Bhakti* path where the devotee likes to see the supreme governing entity as "the Beloved". The lives of bhakti saint figures like *Surdas* and *Meera,* who saw Krishn as a playmate and beloved respectively, illustrate Purvaphalguni's way of encountering the eternal divinity.

Gotra (Celestial Lineage) :

This nakshatra is related to the *Sage Atri*, one of the seven celestial sages looking after the affairs of our galaxy. The name of this sage translates into "one who consumes". As we have discussed in *Rohini*, the sage Àtri seems to have two opposing tendencies, creative and dissoluting. Along with *Rohini,* Purvaphalguni relates to the creative aspect of this sage.

Remedial :

Worship of *Laxmi* and other goddesses related to creativity and prosperity; worship of all fertility goddesses; worship of Shiv through his Shiv Lingam - are all good ways to harness the creative potential of this nakshatra.

Repetition of the root mantra of this nakshatra - "Om Cham" 108 times when Moon transits this nakshatra and in its corresponding lunar month is sure to reduce suffering and bring enlightenment into a person's life.

Persons who are benefiting from the positive energy of this nakshatra can also increase the good effects through the above mentioned ways. It is helpful for them to wear all light, variegated colours and pastel shades, especially yellows, pinks and whites. Predominantly feminine designs and accessories are good. They should use its directions, lunar month and the days when Moon transits Purvaphalguni to undertake all important actions.

Example :

Purvaphalguni's sound and light can be experienced at –

http://osfa.org.uk/purvaphalguni/htm

Miscellaneous :

According to *Varahamihira*, those with Moon in Purvaphalguni are "generous in bestowing liberal gifts, have sweet speech, pleasing manners, a habit of wandering and often serve the government in one way or the other".

* * *

12. Uttaraphalguni   26°40' Leo – 10°00' Virgo

12.

Uttaraphalguni

(26°40' Leo - 10°00' Virgo)

In the Sky :

Uttaraphalguni is the 12th asterism and consists of two very contrasting stars, known in modern astronomy as *Beta-Leonis* and *93-Leonis*. These two stars lie at the tail end of the constellation of Leo. *Denebola* (Beta-Leonis) is among the brightest stars in the night sky with a visual magnitude of 2.13. 93-Leonis on the other hand is a relatively faint star with a visual magnitude of 4.53.

Name :

Uttaraphalguni translates into "the latter reddish one" or "the latter fig tree". The month of *Phalguna* relates to the spring season. We can thus immediately associate Uttaraphalguni with all the feelings evoked by the spring season. Obviously Uttaraphalguni will relate more to the latter half of spring instead of the beginning, which would relate more to the previous nakshatra.

Symbol :

The main symbol of this nakshatra is the two back legs of a bed. Like *Purvaphalguni*, the bed referred to here is not the bed we use for sleeping on during the night time, but a divan or bed/couch used for a daytime siesta or lounging around. This nakshatra is similar to Purvaphalguni in many ways just as the symbolism suggests. In fact Purvaphalguni and Uttaraphalguni form a pair, the first in the sequence of nakshatras. They share similar names, symbolism, nature and quality although there a slight differences.

As we discussed in the previous nakshatra, the bed or hammock represents a place for rest, comfort and relaxation. The fact that Uttaraphalguni is related to the back legs and not the front legs of a bed, relates it to the second half of a siesta or lounging around. Usually this second half is much more active as one is mentally getting off the relaxation mode and preparing for work.

Uttaraphalguni is thus less comfort-oriented in comparison to its counterpart Purvaphalguni. It relates to someone lying on a couch talking, thinking, or contemplating or involved in some kind of activity like writing, reading, sexual etc.

The fully grown fig tree (refer to the image), represents the notion that Uttaraphalguni has the capacity to actually provide fruit, while Purvaphalguni, which is related to a growing fig tree, has the potential for bearing fruit, but is not actually ripe enough to do so. Uttaraphalguni can thus be seen as a productive rather than a purely recreational, enjoyment orientated and indulgent energy.

Deity :

Aryaman, one of the 12 *Adityas* (solar deities), is the main ruling deity of Uttaraphalguni. Aryaman is seen as a deity presiding over patronage, favours and kindness. Therefore the key motivation of this nakshatra is towards helping or receiving help from others. Aryaman is seen as the epitome of hospitality and congeniality, qualities which make Uttaraphalguni a very cultured, social and civilized nakshatra. Uttaraphalguni, like its presiding deity, is very concerned about etiquettes and social graces.

Aryaman is also seen as a deity who places strong emphasis on friendship. In Vedic rituals he is almost always invoked in a pair, either with *Bhaga* (the ruling deity of Purvaphalguni), or *Mitra* (the presiding deity of *Anuradha*). It is no wonder then that Uttaraphalguni along with Anuradha is known for its ability to promote and maintain friendships. Uttaraphalguni however relates more to a personal one-to-one bosom friendship, while Anuradha relates more to friendliness within a group.

Aryaman, being a solar deity, carries a lot of the natural significations attached to the Sun as an astrological entity. He acts like a patron but is bound to lose his temper and act harshly when firmly contradicted.

Nature & Functioning :

Most of the nature and functionings of Purvaphalguni apply to Uttaraphalguni as well. Other than that, the best way to understand Uttaraphalguni's nature and functioning is to understand the qualities normally associated with the king among the planets, Sun.

The names assigned to Sun in Vedic texts - the illuminator; the chief among the planets; the ever radiant; the shining one; the soul's significator; the cruel and sharp one; the intense one; bestower of prosperity, wealth and ultimate knowledge - give a clue to its basic energy and attributes. All these hold true for Uttaraphalguni as well.

Sun as we know is the light. It is a *sattwic* planet. *Sattwa* as we know is a quality of nature whose main objective is to further us along the evolutionary path, through balancing the other two qualities *Rajas* and *Tamas*. It is the mode of goodness which has the basic tendency to be helpful to everyone. Sun shines in the same way on the pauper or the king and is never shy of giving. In the same light Uttaraphalguni has a tendency to be free with its sharing, charity, benevolence and philanthropy.

Sun is the only graha which generates its own light. This makes it the most independent among the grahas, all of whom reflect the light generated by the Sun. This independence forms a part of its nature and can be witnessed in Uttaraphalguni. This independence relates to establishing one's own individuality rather than being part of the flock. A lot of us tend to imitate others instead of developing our own creativity, thoughts and opinions. The word 'self-reliant', which in today's world is only taken in its material aspect, actually refers to reliance on one's own soul for gaining knowledge and awareness. Uttaraphalguni natives are always seen trying to rise above the sea of mass consciousness. They are not the types to change their individuality just to stay in sync with whatever is happening.

Sun, as is common knowledge, is the father figure. This is clear from the fact that all life on earth is dependent upon the Sun. Like a typical father figure, Uttaraphalguni has a cruel and harsh side along with its benevolent life giving side. Uttaraphalguni is also a teacher and preacher at heart in much the same way as Sun and like Sun can be pompous and despotic in its negative functioning.

Most of the warlike qualities such as anger, valour, aggression, fearlessness, urge to conquer and competitive spirit are commonly shared by Sun and Uttaraphalguni. However Uttaraphalguni, unlike Sun's other nakshatra Krittika, has a more forgiving attitude and is always more interested in upholding harmony and honour rather than the final victory. The protective and nourishing aspect of the Sun manifests through Uttaraphalguni. It is gentle but firm.

Uttaraphalguni, having its main portion in the sign Virgo, is the meeting point of the energies of Sun and Mercury and thus allows for the expression of their blending. Mercury, the divine messenger, is the closest planet to the Sun. The prince (Mercury) is always the closest and dearest to the king (Sun). In fact Mercury is the only planet which is not afflicted by Sun's tremendous intensity, just like the prince is never awed by the presence of the king. Together they share the attributes of discrimination, intelligence, general awareness and the judgemental faculty. In a way both of them are intellectual planets, but Mercury carries a much more humorous and lighter energy as compared to the Sun. Intellect (Mercury) has the job of controlling the mind (Moon) but it takes its cue from the soul (Sun). Mercury can become a frivolous energy unless it establishes proper relations with the Sun. This situation is similar to a messenger without any message or source of news. Sun is the source from which Mercury has to derive its inspiration. Sun however lacks the communication ability of Mercury and cannot express itself properly without its help. This is the reason why the ancient seers extolled the Sun-Mercury combination. This blending of Sun-Mercury energies is very present in those natives born under Uttaraphalguni.

Uttaraphalguni, like Sun, is straightforward and unhesitating in its dealings. Like Sun, Uttaraphalguni is ready to serve but only from a position of superiority. There is a certain degree of ascetism inherent in Uttaraphalguni's nature. It is hard for many of us to imagine how a king can be an ascetic. An ancient Vedic story about a king called *Janaka,* in which he proved to a venerable sage that it is perfectly possible, is a case in point! :-

"He asked the sage to carry a burning lamp all around his palace in such a way that the fire is not extinguished. When the sage came back from his round the king asked him about the sights he had seen around his grand palace. The sage couldn't respond as all his concentration had been focused on the lamp. Janaka then told him that this is the way he rules his kingdom."

Krishn put forward the same doctrine of action without attachment in his discourse to *Arjun* in the legendary Vedic epic "*The Mahabharat*". Both Krishn and Arjun were kings in their own right and didn't exactly fit the role of an ascetic.

Uttaraphalguni, like Sun, assists in easy expression of the soul personality. This expression manifests in the outer world as self-confidence, self- assurance and creativity. In a negative sense it can manifest as selfishness, pride, self-aggrandizement or megalomania.

Nobility and dignity are also primarily solar traits which other planets cannot really imitate. There's no equal to Sun as far as sticking to one's word or pledge is concerned. Just like it rarely swerves from its celestial path, it always holds onto its word or promise. There are numerous stories of Sun personalities which illustrate this aspect of Sun's nature, which is also expressed through Uttaraphalguni. Another quality which sets it apart from others is its confidence and self-assuredness.

Sun also has a devious side to it, which most astrologers ignore. It is a master at fraud and lying. Uttaraphalguni has a lot to do with this part of Sun's nature because of its strong connection with the trickster Mercury. In the olden days the kings were supposed to master 64 arts; and lying, gambling and fraud were among these 64 arts. However it must be noted that Uttaraphalguni tries to use such tactics for a noble cause. Being the natural significator of the 9th and 10th houses, Sun is intimately connected with one's *dharma.* Uttaraphalguni is very concerned about fulfilling its duty and assigned goal. It is always very conscious of establishing its path and following it till the end.

In a nativity, Uttaraphalguni rising makes one generous and kind and a good friend towards others. It gives one a noble reputation and makes one skilful at their work. Popularity is due to the native's reliable and helpful nature. Their physical characteristics mirror that of the Sun, especially when the birth is in the Leo part of Uttaraphalguni. The Sun can be described as having honey coloured eye. It has a square body, sturdy bones and sparse curly hair. It has a majestic appearance and is not very tall. It has a courageous and steady look, its complexion is coppery reddish or golden. It has a proud demeanour.

The Virgo part of Uttaraphalguni adds mercurial traits like flexibility, humour, slenderness, agility and amiability to the Sun-like appearance of the native. The native appears more princely as opposed to kingly.

In the universal scheme of things, Uttaraphalguni relates to "*chayani shakti*" - the power of accumulation & prosperity. Its symbolism has wealth from one's own family below and wealth from one's spouse's family above. This relates Uttaraphalguni to all types of gains made through family, partnerships and unions. It is Uttaraphalguni's duty to utilize these resources properly, and be generous and fair in their distribution.

Mode of Functioning :

Uttaraphalguni is considered to be a Balanced nakshatra. Its balancing quality is pretty evident from the nature of its ruling deity Aryaman. One needs to have a balanced personality to have social graces, kindness, compassion and friendliness towards other living creatures. In a way Uttaraphalguni mirrors the sign Libra when it comes to all that is encompassed by the term "balance". The only difference is that Uttaraphalguni is more likely to hold onto its pivot or fixed centre, while the sign Libra is known to drown its essential nature in order to achieve balance and harmony.

Caste :

This nakshatra falls in the *Kshatriya* (ruling/warrior) class of nakshatras and makes one concerned about society and how to direct one's energy towards noble causes. It also suggests concern for some kind of accomplishment on the material plane so one can occupy a position of power or strength. Once again its Kshatriya qualities are derived from its association with the Kshatriya planet Sun.

Gender :

It is a Female nakshatra. This is a perplexing classification considering that both its ruling planet and ruling deity are male. When one considers that the bulk of this nakshatra falls in the feminine sign of Virgo, one can make some sense of the line of thinking behind this classification. Uttaraphalguni, as we have discussed earlier, is connected to predominantly feminine archetypes like grace, kindness, benevolence, consideration and receptivity.

Bodyparts & Humor (Ayurvedic Constitution) :

Lips, Sex Organs and the Left Hand are the body parts related to this nakshatra.

It is a primarily "*Vata*" (airy) nakshatra. The only reason, which seems to be behind this classification, is that the major part of this nakshatra lies in the predominantly vata sign of Virgo. Mercury, the ruler of Virgo, is also seen as a predominantly vata planet. We can however assume that the part of Uttaraphalguni lying within Leo would show *Pitta* rather than vata characteristics.

Direction :

The two directions it relates to most strongly are east and south.

Padas (Quarters) :

The first pada or quarter of this asterism 26° 40' - 30° 00' Leo, falls in Sagittarius Navamsa ruled by Jupiter. This pada relates to the Jupiterian side of the solar nature. It is like a Sun/Jupiter conjunction and gives a strongly ethical nature along with an advisory capacity. Planets placed here give fortunate, expansive results as long as they are in good *Shashtiamsha*.

The second pada or quarter of this asterism 00° 00' - 3° 20' Virgo, falls in Capricorn Navamsa ruled by Saturn. This pada is akin to a Sun/Mercury/Saturn conjunction and gives a tremendous organizational ability. Planets placed here usually give very good material results and a practical, hardworking nature.

The third pada or quarter of this asterism 3° 20'- 6° 40' Virgo, falls in Aquarius Navamsa ruled by Saturn. This pada relates to the philanthropic side of Uttaraphalguni. The keyword here is service. The intellectual abilities are sharp here and are usually used for the social good. Planets placed in this pada tend to work in a *Robin Hood* fashion.

The fourth pada or quarter of this asterism 6° 40' - 10° 00' Virgo, falls in Pisces Navamsa ruled by Jupiter. This pada is akin to a Sun/Mercury/Jupiter conjunction. Out here the intellectual abilities are always utilized for seeing the bigger picture and relating to others. A balance between the small and the big, matter and spirit, Virgo and Pisces is sought here. Since this is a *Pushkara* navamsa pada, planets placed here give strong, favourable results on a material as well as spiritual plane.

Professions :

Creative Artists, Musicians, Entertainers; Superstars & Male Sex Symbols; Managers; Leaders of all types & Public Figures like Sport Superstars; Those in high positions and held in esteem by others; Media & Entertainment industry; Priests; Heads of organizations; Mafia Dons; Teachers & Preachers; Philanthropists; Astrologers; Marriage Counsellors; Sex Therapists; Professions connected to United Nations; International Diplomats; Founding fathers and other Patriotic Figures; Bankers & Creditors; Social Workers; Professional Advisors in all fields.

Uttaraphalguni is highly flexible in regards to professions and can be seen in a variety of professions as long as it is in a commanding position.

Places :

Forests; Gardens; Estates; Public Buildings; Government Buildings; Stadiums; Entertainment Halls; Residences of Rich & Famous People; Palaces, Towers, Large Halls; Playgrounds; Cathedrals & other magnificent buildings; Public Assemblies; United Nation's Buildings; Libraries.

Guna (Essence) and Tattwa (Element) :

This nakshatra belongs to the *Rajasic* group of nakshatras. Not much needs to be said here, as Uttaraphalguni in its descriptions naturally comes out as an active, energetic nakshatra.

It belongs to the Fire element. This as we can see has a lot to do with its planetary ruler Sun and its solar deity Aryaman.

Gana (Type) :

It is considered a *Manushya* (human) nakshatra. Uttaraphalguni, as we have discussed earlier, is very involved in worldly affairs on the terrestrial plane. All human values like family, society, friendship etc. find expression through this nakshatra. Uttaraphalguni in a way is a harbinger of culture and civilization.

Orientation & Disposition :

It is a Downward nakshatra. Uttaraphalguni, because of its natural fixed character, is best for laying foundations. Its involvement with foundations and support of all types makes it a downward nakshatra. In a building, Uttaraphalguni will always relate more to the foundation stone or the foundation itself.

As mentioned previously, it is a *Dhruva* (fixed or permanent) nakshatra . Despite its receptivity, amicability and friendliness, Uttaraphalguni is quite fixed in its thinkings, opinions and functionings. This is probably the reason why it can always be relied upon. It tends not to sway away from vows and pleasures, especially those relating to friendship. This fixed quality obviously stems from its solar aspect.

Lunar Month & Day :

It relates to the second half of the lunar month of *Phalguna*, which usually corresponds to the month of March in the solar calendar.

Uttaraphalguni is also related to the *Dvadashi* (12th tithi or day) of the waxing and waning phases of the Moon's monthly cycle.

Auspicious Activities :

Favourable for sexual activity and marriage; Generally auspicious for beginning all things of a lasting nature like organizations, societies, etc.; Good for marriage and sexual activity; Good for dealing with higher authorities; Good for administrative actions of all types; Buying property or entering a new home for the first time; Openings/inauguration ceremonies & swearing-ins; Making promises; Performing sacred ceremonies & rituals; Wearing new clothes and jewellery; Acts of charity; Career related activities; Paternal activities; Good for activities requiring tact and diplomacy.

Inauspicious Activities :

Unfavourable for endings of all types; Not good for harsh activities like confrontation, retaliation or engaging with enemies; Not good for lending money if you are expecting it back.

Planetary Ruler :

Sun is the planetary ruler of this nakshatra. The solar aspect of nature comes into manifestation in the earlier nakshatra, Krittika. Uttaraphalguni relates to the process where the solar principle affects and organizes the material world, just like Sun's rays can cook food in a solar cooker. The primordial solar principle manifests as willpower in Krittika, but it takes the form of intelligence in Uttaraphalguni, with the aid of Mercury.

Mercury is associated with Uttaraphalguni, due to the fact that a major part of Uttaraphalguni lies in Virgo, a sign ruled by Mercury. Uttaraphalguni is all about the linking between soul and intellect. Under this nakshatra's influence, the solar energy is directed towards actual practical work in order to achieve certain goals which the soul has set for itself, and also help out others along the way as well. Just as all living life on our planet is dependent upon Sun's rays, all society and civilization is dependent upon the guidance of this nakshatra.

Sun/Mercury conjunction in a horoscope carries energies similar to Uttaraphalguni. Friends of Sun like Moon, Mercury, Mars & Jupiter do well here; while Venus, Saturn, Rahu and Ketu feel obstructed here, especially Venus, due to its in debilitation in the Virgo part of this nakshatra.

Vowels and Alphabets :

The first pada or quarter of this asterism 26° 40' - 30° 00' Leo corresponds to "Tay" as in Taylor.

The second pada or quarter of this asterism 00° 00' - 3° 20' Virgo corresponds to "To" as in Tohnamah or Toad.

The third pada or quarter of this asterism 3° 20'- 6° 40' Virgo corresponds to "Pa" as in Pascal.

The fourth pada or quarter of this asterism 6° 40' - 10° 00' Virgo corresponds to "Pee" as in Peter.

In the Sanskrit alphabet Uttaraphalguni corresponds to "Chha" and "Ja", consequently its mantras are "Om Chham " and "Om Jam (Jahm)".

Sexual Type and Compatibility :

The sexual animal associated with this nakshatra is a Cow, which suggests its nurturing and passive qualities. Although this nakshatra has noble qualities attached to it, it is said to give reputation or scandal through sexual adventures. This nakshatra has an adventurous element, which seems to express itself mostly in the sexual realm.

For sexual compatibility & marital compatibility with other nakshatras please refer to the tables on pages 468 & 469.

Esoteric :

The interesting thing about Uttaraphalguni is that it relates most closely to the visible physical Sun of our solar system, which we see rising every morning. The physical body of our Sun may have started forming around 5 billion years ago, but the actual causal solar entity we know as *Vivasvan,* might not have entered until a later time, just like the astral body only enters the physical body after the embryo has been developed up to a certain stage. This will also explain the fact that not every star in the sky has a solar system which breeds life! Only those stars which have an astral/causal entity housing them have the potential to breed life.

The names of the Sun's eleven brothers who are all born out of the union of sage *Kashyap* and his wife *Aditi* (translates into 'infinite space' and governs the nakshatra *Punarvasu*) are - *Aryaman, Dhatra, Tvastar, Pushan, Savitar, Mitra, Varun, Amasa, Bhasa, Vishnu* & *Shakra.* We can see that almost all of these solar deities are related with nakshatras - *Aryaman* with *Uttaraphalguni, Mitra* with *Anuradha* (the 17th asterism), *Pushan* with *Revati* (the 27th asterism), *Savitar* with Hasta (the 13th asterism), *Tvastar* with *Chitra* (the 14th asterism) and *Varun* with Shatabhisha (the 24th asterism).

The fact that this nakshatra has its first quarter in the sign Leo relates to the regal authoritarian side of this asterism. It is a doubling of solar energy. Since its last three quarters lie in the sign under Mercury, an intellectual bent is observed in the workings of this asterism. On a spiritual level, the main aim of this nakshatra is the harmonization of the intellect (Mercury) and soul (Sun), which aids evolutionary growth, along with bringing benefits on the material plane. This asterism relates to the culmination of the individualization process as it covers the final degrees of the sign Leo. After the individualization process is over the individual is expected to be of service to a greater whole. The service aspect of this asterism comes out through the sign normally associated with service, Virgo.

The characteristics usually associated with the number "12" in numerology are mostly borne out of the nature and functionings of this nakshatra. Uttaraphalguni forms the bridge between the numbers 5 & 6 and also between the numbers 11 & 12.

This asterism can be seen as the Egyptian *Sphinx*, which in a sense symbolizes harmonization of the energies of the signs Leo and Virgo. It relates to a period of time in history (around 10,500 B.C.), where the spring equinox was passing from the sign Virgo to the sign Leo. Many believe it to be a time of great upheaval and re-alignment, as the last great flood was supposed to have taken place around that time. This illustrates the importance of this nakshatra for human life on earth.

Gotra (Celestial Lineage) :

This nakshatra is related to the Sage *Pulasthya*, one of the seven celestial sages looking after the affairs of our galaxy. The name of this sage translates into "having smooth hair". The term 'smooth hair' may relate to the hair of the sophisticated, savvy nature of the Sage in question, which will then vibe well with the essential qualities of this nakshatra.

Remedial :

For those suffering from bad effects resulting from afflictions to this nakshatra, the best remedial measure is worship of the Sun. Recitation of the *Gayatri* mantra is very helpful for natives under strong Uttaraphalguni influence. People can refer to the author's previous work, "Sun - The Cosmic PowerHouse" (Sagar Publications, India) for remedial measures associated with the Sun. Worship of Durga and other warrior like feminine deities also suit this nakshatra.

Repetition of the root mantras of this nakshatra - "Om Chham" and "Om Jam" 108 times when Moon transits this nakshatra and in its corresponding lunar month, is sure to reduce suffering and bring enlightenment into a person's life.

Persons who are benefiting from the positive energy of this nakshatra can also increase the good effects through the above mentioned ways. It is helpful for them to wear all red, white, green and golden shades. The shade should be neither too bright, nor too dull, but fall somewhere in between. They should use its directions, lunar month and the days when Moon transits Uttaraphalguni to undertake all important actions.

Example :

George Washington, one of the founding fathers of America, was born with Uttaraphalguni rising on his ascendant. It is interesting to note that he fashioned the capital city of Washington (bearing his name) on the sign Virgo. We can assume that its foundation stone must have been laid with Uttaraphalguni rising for it to become the center of world power and have the permanence it has had.

Uttaraphalguni's sound and light can be experienced at -

http://osfa.org.uk/uttaraphalguni.htm

Miscellaneous :

According to *Varahamihira*, those with Moon in Uttaraphalguni "earn through their knowledge, are well liked and popular and live a life of comfort and luxury." The author of this book has His Moon placed in the fourth pada of Uttaraphalguni.

* * *

13. Hasta   10°00' Virgo - 23°20' Virgo

13.

Hasta

In the Sky :

Hasta consists of five prominent easily visible stars of the constellation known as *Corvi* (*the Crow*), which lies below the constellation of Virgo. These five stars, whose grouping was seen by the ancient Vedic seers as resembling the top of a hand (five fingertips), are known in modern astronomy as *Alpha-Corvi* (*Alchiba*), *Beta-Corvi*, *Delta-Corvi* (*Algorab*), *Gamma-Corvi* (*Gienah*) & *Epsilon-Corvi*. Beta-Corvi is the brightest among these stars with a visual magnitude of 2.66. The constellation representing this asterism Corvi can be located in the night sky below the constellation Virgo to the right hand side of the zodiacal belt. It lies very close to the right hand side of *Spica*, one of the brightest stars and can thus be easily spotted despite its relative faintness .

Name :

Hasta's main translation is "the hand". As we shall find in the course of this section, this seemingly general and inconsequential name conveys a major part of this asterism's nature, activities and approach.

Its alternative translation is "laughter". The root "*Has*" in Sanskrit means "to laugh". The ancient seers must have picked this name as a pun on a nakshatra most closely associated with pun. Its alternative names "*Bhanu*" and "*Ark*" translate into "Sun" and "Sun's Ray" respectively. The association of Hasta with Sun and the solar principle will become clear as we discuss its symbols and ruling deity.

Symbol :

Hasta has three main symbols. One symbol is "a hand with all five fingers spread-eagled". Through this symbol, the ancient seers are trying to emphasize Hasta's relation with fate. One can see all the lines in the palm when a hand is spread out. These lines in the palm as we know, relate to our destiny in the present life. Hasta is closely connected to the art of palmistry and by extrapolation, Astrology. The hand also simply relates to all activities done with the use of the hands. This will be expanded upon later. In ancient times the outstretched hand was a symbol of the Sun, with the fingers representing its rays. The relationship of this nakshatra with the Sun is established through its ruling deity .

The second symbol is "a clenched fist", which exemplifies secrecy and determination. Hasta, as we shall discover, is related to all kinds of activities like trickery, deceit and manipulation involving the use of the above two qualities. The clenched fist in its negative aspect represents greed, ambition and an inability to let go of things. In its positive aspect, it represents strength which is derived through unity and harmonious working of parts.

Hasta is the nakshatra most closely associated with cooperation in order to achieve the intended goal. This cooperation however has very little to do with friendship, as there is a distinct lack of trust in all Hasta bondings. It is no wonder that shaking hands is the most commonly used act for bonding in the modern times. This immediately reflects the modern world's obsession with cooperation without trust.

The third and more rarely used symbol of Hasta is "a potter's wheel". A potter's wheel has its obvious association with pottery making and all types of handicrafts in general. On an esoteric level the potter's wheel symbolizes the passage to time. Hasta is often very concerned about the proper utilization of time. It is very prone to go to extremes in relation to this issue and turn life into a clock. It is obsessed with time keeping, punctuality, repetition and other such robotic traits usually associated with the sign Virgo.

Deity :

Just like the previous two nakshatras, a solar deity presides over Hasta. This solar deity is named "*Savitar*". His name has two translations - "the impeller" and "the first rays of the rising Sun".

As an "impeller", Savitar is seen as a god who gives life. Hasta is therefore known as a nakshatra which aids childbirth. The "first rays of the rising Sun" represent the awakening potential of Hasta in all ancient cultures and civilizations. The first rays of sunrise were a signal for all people to begin their day's activities, its function being similar to an alarm clock today. We can thus infer that Hasta has all to do with the terms activity and alertness. Hasta is the proverbial 'wake up call', a term which should be read from both a material and spiritual perspective.

Savitar has a jovial, lighthearted type of persona. He is always portrayed with a laughing gesture. He is a playful deity into all kinds of tricks, amusements and games. This makes Hasta interested in all kinds of sports on all planes of existence. On the terrestrial earthly plane, Hasta relates to both mind games and physical sports.

Savitar is supposed to be extremely skilled with his hands. This makes Hasta directly associated with everything done with the hands. The reasoning behind the naming of Hasta should now be clear to us. Savitar is also considered to be a crafty trickster, taking pleasure in lying, gambling and fraud. These qualities don't seem like the kind which one would associate with a solar deity but the truth is that even the planet Sun has this cunning, crafty side to its nature, which is more often than not overlooked by astrologers. In the ancient times all kings (represented by Sun) were supposed to be well versed in the arts of lying, deceit, fraud, gambling and robbery. The readers can refer to the author's previous work (" *Sun-The Cosmic Powerhouse*" *Sagar* Publications, India) for more details on this aspect of the Sun's nature.

Savitar is almost mercurial in his approach, which does not come as a surprise since all of this nakshatra falls in Virgo, a sign ruled by Mercury. Savitar can be seen as a deity who fuses the energies of Sun and Mercury. His qualities are very similar to those ascribed to the *Budha-ditya Yog* (Sun/

Mercury conjunction in a sign or house). Again the reader can refer to "*Sun-The Cosmic Powerhouse*" for more information on this Yog.

In a way the nature and functioning of Savitar is akin to a bright sunny day where everyone is feeling good and are involved in creative activities of all kinds. This is what makes Hasta one of the most optimistic and creative nakshatras.

Nature & Functioning :

Common english words like "hand", "handy", "haste", "hassle", "haggle", "have", "hard", "harness", "hack", "harvest" - seem to have the same root as the word "Hasta". Their meanings relate to Hasta's functioning at some level or the other. The well known greeting "*Hasta Maniana*" sheds light on Hasta's jovial and easy going approach and its relationship with all kinds of endings.

Hasta follows Uttaraphalguni, the nakshatra in which a family is established. After the establishment of a family, issues like continuity and sustenance crop up. There are little and big things to be done on a regular basis to keep the household going. Hasta relates to all the little activities which make civilized living possible. It is no surprise that Hasta natives are the handymen of the zodiac. They also make excellent householders. Even though they take their work seriously, there is always some internal lightheartedness underneath. They are very good at carrying plain faces and stern exteriors. Even the comedians which use this nakshatra's energies, bring out humour through deadpan , straight, serious facial expressions.

When Hasta rises on the Ascendant it produces highly flexible and supple bodies capable of handling a variety of manual jobs. They often have some type of acrobatic skill. They have small eyes and roundish faces. They have mischievous smiles and like to squint a lot. They love to laugh and play the joker. They have quick, sharp minds which constantly process whatever they observe. They like to think along practical lines and have a tendency to look down upon romantically bohemian attitudes. Theirs is a world of classification, order and arrangement. Hasta natives have a tendency for overwork arising from an inability to sit still. They can get obsessive about keeping themselves busy, a trait which makes them invent unnecessary tasks or complicate relatively simple tasks. No other nakshatra comes close to Hasta when it comes to an eye for detail. They work at things painstakingly and expect others to do the same. They can be extremely critical when their high standards are not met. Hasta usually gives some sort of tension with progeny if related to the fifth house in any way.

In the universal scheme of things, Hasta relates to "*hasta sthapaniya agama shakti*" - the power to put one's object of desire in one's hands. Its symbolism has attainment of the object above and the process of attainment below. The symbolism makes it clear beyond words that Hasta promises immediate acquirement of one's object of desire through one's skill.

Mode of Functioning :

Hasta is a Passive nakshatra. This comes as a surprise but this can be understood in terms of its planetary ruler Moon. Moon has a strong, passive and receptive side to its nature, which is more on display in Hasta rather than Moon's other nakshatra, *Rohini.* Hasta's passivity can be seen through the following example character :-

"Hasta can be a timid, shy pottery maker who just spends all his time making pottery items without any desire for extraordinary gains. He gets paid much less than he deserves by cheating businessmen (another type of Hasta character). He never raises a voice against the injustice and accepts his fate of poverty and hard work lying down. "

Caste :

It belongs to the *Vaishya* (merchant/business) caste. This comes as no surprise because Hasta is predominantly associated with production, buying and selling of goods. It can be said that Hasta has the most businesslike approach to life in comparison with all other nakshatras. In the present day and age where business and commerce rules everything else, Hasta has a dominant role. However since corruption, deceit and greed form the back bone of most business in today's world, only the negative side of Hasta is on display. All of the big, multinational corporations and the ruling business elite are nothing but petty thieves and swindlers.

Gender :

It is a Male nakshatra. This classification is directly derived from its ruling deity. We have already seen that this is a predominantly solar nakshatra and thus has to have a male essence.

Bodyparts & Humor (Ayurvedic Constitution) :

Hands are the body parts related to this nakshatra.

It is a primarily "Vata" (airy) nakshatra. This is clear from the fact that all of this nakshatra lies in a predominantly vata sign, Virgo. One can also infer that Hasta derives its quick, light, agile and humorous disposition from its airy humor.

Direction :

It is related primarily to east, south, north and northwest.

Padas (Quarters) :

The first pada or quarter of this asterism 10° 00' - 13°20' Virgo falls in Aries Navamsa and is ruled by Mars. This pada gives abundant energy and makes one an expert at underhanded activities. Mathematical, Military and Surgical skills are enhanced here. A well placed Mars or Sun are strongest in this pada.

The second pada or quarter of this asterism 13° 20' - 16° 40' Virgo falls in Taurus Navamsa ruled by Venus. The emphasis here is on down to earth practicality. Planets here seek material arrangement and perfection as their dharma. Honesty and morality are more developed here in comparison to other padas. This pada supports artistic activities. A well placed Mercury, Venus and Saturn give good results here.

The third pada or quarter of this asterism 16° 40' - 20° 00' Virgo falls in Gemini Navamsa ruled by Mercury. This is the pada of the merchant, trader and business person. Emphasis here is on career. This is the most dexterous and clever amongst Hasta's padas. Well placed Mercury here gives extraordinary perception and intelligence.

The fourth pada or quarter of this asterism 20° 00' - 23° 20' Virgo falls in Cancer Navamsa ruled by Moon. The focus here is on family life and communal co-existence. This pada promises material security but at the same time promotes suspicion towards anything foreign. The best and worst of Hasta manifests through this pada. Only a well placed Jupiter gives strong results here especially in regards to having good progeny.

Professions :

Artisans; Manual Labourers; All professions requiring dexterity of hand; Mechanics; Jewellery makers; Origami Experts; Acrobats, Gymnasts and Circus performers; Fairy Tale Writers; Those involved in the invention and production of daily utility items; Inventors in general; Publishing & Printing Industry; Stage Magicians; Swindlers; Pickpockets; Stock Brokers; Packaging Industry; Paper Industry; Manicurists; All people working in share and stock markets; Casino dealers; Toy Makers; Carpenters; Professional Gamblers; Bookies; Small Shop Owners, Market Sellers, Small Scale Trade Persons, and Business men in all fields; Clerks; Bankers; Accountants; Typists; Cleaners; Housekeepers; Servants; Masseurs; Doctors; Physiotherapists; Chemical & Toiletry Industry; Textile industry; Tarot Card Readers; Palmists; Psychics; Astrologers; Auctioneers; Pottery & Ceramic industry; Interior decorators; Gardeners; Farmers & Agriculturalists; All professions connected with Food Production, Processing and Distribution Industry; Barbers, Hairdressers & Stylists; Sculptors; Masons; Those connected with Amusement Parks; Sales Persons in all fields; Professional Comedians; Satirical Novelists; Radio & Television Commentators; Speech Therapists; Newsreaders; Martial Artists; Forgers; Thieves; Robbers dealing with opening safes; All street smart professions in general.

Places :

Agricultural Fields; Grazing Pastures; Home Gardens; Art & Craft Studios; Marketplace; Stock Exchange (Wall Street etc.); Casinos; Betting Shops; Amusement parks; Fairgrounds; Factories; In general, places connected with the above professions.

Guna (Essence) and Tattwa (Element) :

It is supposed to be a *Rajasic* nakshatra. Hasta's immense immersion in worldly activities makes it a predominantly rajasic nakshatra. As we have mentioned repeatedly, it is a nakshatra very active on a material plane.

It belongs to the Fire element. This classification definitely relates to its association with Sun. Its fire energy manifests itself as innovation, quick thinking and an energetic approach to things.

Gana (Type) :

It is considered a *Deva* or godly nakshatra. Hasta's ruling deity Savitar is seen as a primarily benevolent deity. Hasta's divine quality can be judged from the fact that it never harbours any strong negative or cruel tendencies.

Orientation and Disposition :

It is a Level nakshatra. This has to do with the business aspect of Hasta. Most level nakshatras are supposed to be good for business of all kinds. They are also good for patching things up, an activity which Hasta greatly enjoys.

As mentioned previously, it is a Light and Swift nakshatra. This classification can be easily derived from its humorous, lighthearted nature. We have also seen that Hasta is associated with quickness in thought and action.

Lunar Month & Day :

It relates to the first 9 days of the lunar month of *Chaitra*, which usually falls in late March.

Hasta is also related to the *Dvadashi* (12th tithi or day) of the waxing and waning phases of the moon's monthly cycle.

Auspicious Activities :

Good for most activities done under the Sun; Arts & Crafts; Activities that stimulate laughter; All types of hobbies especially things like pottery and jewellery making; Planting seeds & Gardening in general; Domestic Work; Studying sciences & Astrology; Learning Languages; All activities requiring handskills and repetition; Magic Tricks; Playing games; All business activities requiring tact & shrewdness; Good for marriage; Buying & Selling, especially items like grains, textiles etc.; Good for getting a good bargain; Dealing with children; Thievery; Holistic treatments of diseases; Travel & Change of Residence.

Inauspicious Activities :

Planning longterm goals and objectives; Sexual Activity; Does not support Relaxation or Inactivity; Unfavourable for all activities requiring executive ability and maturity; Not good for most night-time activities.

Planetary Ruler :

The main planetary influences affecting this nakshatra are Moon and Mercury. Moon is the main ruling planet of Hasta. Moon imparts emotions, care and sensitivity to this nakshatra. It is this lunar influence which makes Hasta a doyen of home and family life. When working through its lower functioning, all the negative aspects of lunar energy like ultra conservatism, bigotry, fickleness, excessive attachment and inability to let go takes centre stage. However unlike Cancer, the lunar nature here is under supervision of Mercury, the planet of discrimination. Mercury's influence makes Hasta jovial and lighthearted thus saving it from the type of depression people with prominent Cancer placements go through. Hasta's discriminatory power also allows it to navigate its way through the waters of life more efficiently as compared to its nakshatra's counterpart in Cancer, *Ashlesha.*

Ashlesha and Hasta are the only two nakshatras where the energies of Moon and Mercury combine, the only difference being that Moon is the king in Ashlesha, while Mercury has the final say in Hasta. This means that intellect rules over the mind in Hasta, which is obviously the way universe prefers it. Moon can perceive but not derive conclusions, which is Mercury's doing. It is Mercury which guides the Moon while it is Moon which nurtures Mercury. Hasta is all about this interplay between Moon and Mercury.

Vowel s and Alphabets :

The first pada or quarter of this asterism 10° 00' -13° 20' Virgo corresponds to "Pu" as in Putin or Pure.

The second pada or quarter of this asterism 13° 20' - 16° 40' Virgo corresponds to "Sha" as in Shah or Sharon.

The third pada or quarter of this asterism 16° 40' - 20° 00' Virgo corresponds to "Nu" as in Nun.

The fourth pada or quarter of this asterism 20° 00' - 23° 20' Virgo corresponds to "Tu" as in Turtle.

In the Sanskrit alphabet Hasta corresponds to "Jha" and "Nya" consequently its mantras are "Om Jham" and "Om Nyam".

Sexual Type and Compatibility :

Its sexual animal is a Buffalo. Despite its dexterity and skill with hands and fingers, its sexual tendencies are usually not very refined. A lot of sexual exploitation takes place for making money under the energies of this nakshatra. It is however not prone to extreme sexual perversions like other cruel or fierce nakshatras. When it is working through its ascetic level, Hasta can be the most non-sexual amongst all nakshatras. Its sexual energies are most compatible with those of *Swati*.

For sexual and marital compatibility with other nakshatras please refer to the tables on pages 468 & 469 .

Esoteric :

Hasta is the handyman of the Universe and even esoteric things are nothing but exoteric when one truly understands the dictum - "As Above, So Below".

Hasta takes care of all the little things which keep the fourteen worlds running. "The divide between the devil and god is a matter of detail" sums up Hasta's approach on a macrocosmic level. Its painstaking efforts are however often overlooked on a personal as well as collective level, but such things don't bother it just like it doesn't bother Sun if its light is taken for granted.

Though this fact has not been brought up in any written text until now, Hasta has a connection with Rahu, the planet of *Maya*, magic and trickery. Hasta is partly the secret behind the deviously mischievous all-knowing smile on the face of *Vishnu*. Hasta is one of the few nakshatras which has the ability to see the whole of creation as a play and find enjoyment, merriment and laughter playing it the right way.

The legend of *Virgin Mary,* which obviously finds its parallels in all ancient cultures and civilizations, is all about the energies which come under Hasta's domain. Hasta is representative of the inner Sun which has the ability to hold, produce and foster the divine saviour (mainly incarnations of Vishnu). The term 'inner Sun' is used because Virgo is the sign of matter and the material world holds and hides the spiritual realm. Hasta therefore is the androgynous force which shapes the material world according to spiritual laws.

Being the 13th nakshatra, 13 is the number which Hasta relates to. It is common knowledge that 13 is a peculiar number associated with the occult, endings, death, regeneration etc. The concept of order and renewal inherent in Hasta can be understood best through its peculiar quality, which relates to the connections of events separated by time. For example, many things which happen to us in childhood are for a specific reason, which we only come to know about much later in life in our adulthood. For evolved souls, most events which happen in their childhood are silently building up a foundation and preparing for their purpose and destiny. It is usually very hard to understand the significance of these little, seemingly, meaningless, disconnected events until much later. It is within this phenomenon that the secret functioning of the number 13 and Hasta lies. The *Book of Solomon* states emphatically - "The one who understands the number 13, shall have power and dominion".

Gotra (Celestial Lineage) :

This nakshatra is related to the *Sage Pulahu*, one of the seven celestial sages looking after the affairs of our galaxy. The name of this sage translates into "connector of space". We can imagine that connecting space must be quite a detailed oriented job. It is also interesting to note that it is time which is the connector of space. Hasta as we have seen is directly connected with the passage of time, through its potter wheel symbolism.

Remedial :

One can strengthen this nakshatra's good qualities by worshipping the Sun as a creative force, at sunrise. All the remedial measures normally associated with the Sun can be applied to this nakshatra (See author's previous work - "*Sun, The Cosmic Powerhouse*", *Sagar* Publications, India).

Worship of *Vishnu* or any of Vishnu's incarnations is a way of getting in touch with the higher energies of this nakshatra. Repetition of the root mantras of this nakshatra - "Om Jham" and "Om Nyam" 108 times when Moon transits this nakshatra and in its corresponding lunar month is sure to reduce suffering and bring enlightenment into a person's life.

Persons who are benefiting from the positive energy of this nakshatra can also increase the good effects through the above mentioned ways. It is helpful for them to wear all lighter shades especially green. White is also good. Avoid bright shades. They should use its directions, lunar month and the days when Moon transits Hasta to undertake all important actions.

Example :

Hasta's sound and light can be experienced at –

http://osfa.org.uk/hasta.htm

Miscellaneous :

According to *Varahamihira*, "Moon in Hasta makes one energetic, daring, merciless, a drunkard and a thief".

* * *

14. Chitra   23°20' Virgo - 6°40' Libra

14.

Chitra

(23º20' Virgo - 6º40' Libra)

In the Sky :

Chitra is one of the few asterisms which are represented by a single star. Its star is commonly known as *Spica* (*Alpha-Virginis*), which lies in the lower back part of the constellation Virgo. It can be said to be placed around the region where the 'hips of the maiden' formed by the shape of the constellation Virgo would lie. It is one of the brightest stars in the night sky with a visual magnitude of 1.06 and can be spotted even in the polluted skies over big metropolitan cities. Ancient vedic seers saw this star as the residence of *Vishwakarma* (or *Tvashtar*), the divine architect.

Name :

Chitra conveys a wide variety of meanings in English ranging from "Glittering", "Brilliant", "Bright", "Art", "Artful", "Beautiful", "Many Coloured", "Variegated", "Illusory", "Visually Exciting" or "Magic". In a way this nakshatra conveys more of its inherent qualities through its name than any other asterism.

Symbol :

In keeping with its name, its main symbol is a 'big, bright, shining jewel'. Gemstones, as we know, are formed under conditions of intense heat and pressure acting over rocks and minerals for millions of years. On a material plane, the universe has to come a long way from the initial big bang to the stage where gems are produced on planets such as ours. A gem can thus be seen to be the apex of the universe's striving for beauty and perfection of form.

We have already seen that *Hasta*, the previous nakshatra, is related to artisans and those involved in light crafts like handicrafts. In Chitra, however, crafts are taken to another level and perfection of form is achieved. Chitra is therefore associated with the final appearance and form of everything in nature. Its ruling deity as we shall learn, was even responsible for giving our Sun its final present day form (refer to image). It is up to Chitra to finally oversee how a thing should look, whether it be a galaxy or a small leaf.

Its alternative symbol is a 'pearl'. Pearls, as we know, are formed in an oyster's moments of irritation, in much the same way art comes out of the artist's moments of irritation and depression. Chitra is thus related to the mysterious essence behind creativity, using its clear understanding of the laws of the universe. It has the ability to fashion new, wonderful and delightful things out of seemingly nothing at all. In its higher aspect, Chitra allows one to see beyond the illusion of form, thus giving access to the pearl of true knowledge.

Deity :

Tvastar, the celestial architect, is the main ruling deity of this asterism. He is usually referred to by the name Vishwakarma (creation worker) in most of the Vedic texts. He is said to be an adept in *Maya*, the illusory force which keeps alive the drama of life. Vishwakarma uses his knowledge of Maya to create, mutate and fashion new forms out of the pre-existing ones, an act which seems like magic to others. His workings are often done in secret and a shroud of mystery surrounds his character and persona. To understand his mysterious aspect better, we have to take our present day example; "most of the human population on our planet are completely unaware of how normal soil containing silicon is fashioned into a computer, a device which has the ability to do all these magic-like functions".

In the same way, most of the gods and other celestial beings do not have a clue as to how Vishwakarma creates magnificent structures using the most basic elements. Even on our planet we can see that the most important thing defining a civilization is its architecture. There's none better than Vishwakarma in material architecture and consequently none surpasses Chitra as far as arts, crafts, design, architecture, beauty and proportion are concerned. Chitra is the grand illusion maker creating delightful things, forms and objects, which make us want to live.

Vishwakarma, even though he is friendly to the gods, has no particular allegiance to anyone. He creates all *lokas* (planes of existence) for all races (human, godly, demonic, serpent etc.). It is Vishwakarma who fashions thunderbolts for *Indra*, the king of the heavenly hosts, but his twin brother *Trishiras* (three-headed) is a demon and an enemy of Indra. This duality finds expression through Chitra, a nakshatra which is very ambiguous and thus hard to classify in any fixed category of good, evil, crooked or saintly.

Like Vishwakarma, Chitra creates without a care for the far reaching implications of what it is creating. It was the palace, which Vishwakarma built for the *Pandavs* (refer to Vedic legend "The *Mahabharat*"), which in a way led to the final great war, commonly known as Mahabharat. Even in the present day and age, all kinds of new weapons of war are fashioned everyday by scientists, technicians and engineers. They however can't be held responsible for the way these weapons are used by politicians and the ruling elite.

Nature & Functioning :

"Balance" is a keyword in Chitra as this nakshatra falls in the middle of the nakshatras. It has 13 nakshatras on either side of it. The essence of Chitra can be summarized in the phrase "create, create and create". Chitra is a dynamic, energetic nakshatra which has very little ability to sit still. It likes to involve itself in one creative activity or another. When this creativity is in harmony with universal functionings all goes well for Chitra natives. However when this is not the case, Chitra natives can become unbalanced, selfish, indulgent creatures.

Chitra natives are obsessed with appearance, complexity, structure and form. Therefore this nakshatra has to do with *maya*, illusion and glamour. Chitra approaches things from an architectural, aesthetic point of view. There are different levels of maya. It can operate on the superficial external levels like a desire to project outer beauty, and in one's need to create harmony and balance in relationships with others. On both mundane or spiritual levels the point here is that Chitra natives can learn to play with universal energies and utilise its complex layers of perception and projection. It is due to this aspect that natives influenced by this nakshatra never reveal themselves in social situations. They are always projecting a front of some kind. Usually this is a dignified front with a hidden quality.

The Virgo part of Chitra has more core understanding of maya than the Libra part. The Libra part relates more to the form element, while the Virgo part is more concerned with the intricate detailed working of things. The Libra part of Chitra is more relationship oriented. Chitra loves admiration and is motivated by that in whatever it does, especially in the Libra part of this nakshatra. Chitra always has an element of doubt and uncertainty attached to it due to the Sun's weakness in the sign of Libra. Therefore its qualities and its needs to focus on structure and appreciation of form are motivated by this inherent doubt and uncertainty.

Chitra's love for understanding how things work and how all the parts fit together, generally place natives under its influence in scientific, technological and artistic fields. Japanese as a race are governed by this nakshatra, which can easily be seen in their technological obsession and their attention to detail. Chitra loves to create "magic". The Virgo part of Chitra will create the technological gadget and the Libra part will give it an outer form or garment to provide the aesthetic appeal. On a higher plane it is the Virgo part of Chitra which is more sincere in trying to understand the inner workings of the universe, whereas the Libra part can tend to keep one trapped in the maya aspect rather than going beyond it.

Natives with Chitra rising or having prominent Chitra influences usually have well-proportioned hairless bodies (if they have hair they are constantly pruning it), bright lustrous eyes, thin eyebrows and alluring mannerisms. They always have a glint in their eyes. They are born with a natural ability to dazzle. Chitra natives have a very strong ability to attract the opposite sex. They are usually passionate but also have the ability to fake passions when the situation demands it. They hold themselves with a certain degree of dignity which covers up their weaknesses. Chitra natives always make a special effort to come across as completely together type of individuals. Since all of them are not all together especially in the present Age of *Kali*, most of this effort is pretension.

Chitra can cause one a lot of frustration and angst whether it is functioning from a higher or lower level. Just like the oyster experiences irritation to produce a pearl, there is a certain amount of pain involved in stripping away the layers of illusion and going beyond maya. Again this pain only operates on the egoic plane, which itself is an expression of maya.

Mode of Functioning :

Chitra is considered to be an Active nakshatra. This does not come as a surprise, as Chitra's main motto is to simply "create, create and create". It is hyperactive and indefatigable. It constantly moves from one creative project to the next. In its positive aspect, this quality makes it hardworking and efficient, but in a negative aspect, it makes it obsessive and blind to the true meaning and function of life.

Caste :

It belongs to the Farmer caste. Even Vishwakarma, the divine architect, is in a way nothing but a "producer", in keeping with the wishes of the gods, or whosoever he is working for at any given point in time. The ancient seers obviously regarded creating and producing things, especially on a material plane, as a working class activity. In modern times, sculptures and architects are elevated to lofty positions in society, but in essence, they still remain puppets in the hands of the ruling elite who finance them.

Gender :

It is a Female nakshatra. Through this classification the ancient seers are hinting at Chitra's strong connection with maya, the feminine attribute of nature, which sustains the play of life. It can be seen that Chitra natives possess predominantly feminine graces.

Bodyparts & Humor (Ayurvedic Constitution) :

Forehead and Neck are the body parts related to this nakshatra.

It is a primarily "*Pitta*" (fiery) nakshatra. This is clear from its relationship with Mars, a primarily pitta planet. Chitra is a hot nakshatra and relates to all heat and energy producing processes in the body.

Direction :

It is related primarily to the range or arc that goes from south east ,

to south, to west.

Padas (Quarters) :

The first pada or quarter of this asterism 23° 20' - 26° 40' Virgo, falls in Leo Navamsa ruled by Sun. On a lower level, the emphasis here is on personal glamour, while on a higher level this pada strives for self perfection through self abnegation. This pada has a very strong ability to keep secrets, just like the *sphinx* (an ancient monument which is a combination of the signs Leo and Virgo) hides deep esoteric knowledge until humanity is ready for them. Planets here function in a very hidden non-apparent way. Sun, Mars, Mercury and Rahu are especially strong here.

The second pada or quarter of this asterism 26° 40' - 30° 00' Virgo falls in Virgo Navamsa ruled by Mercury. The emphasis here is on order, arrangement, maternity and duality. This is a very disciplined pada which likes to conclude whatever it begins. Saturn, Mercury and Rahu are strong here, although Saturn may make one excessively puritanical if working through its lower aspect.

The third pada or quarter of this asterism 00° 00' - 3° 20' Libra falls in Libra Navamsa ruled by Venus. On the material plane, the main focus of this pada is on relationships, self-absorption and equilibrium. This is a very self-centric and at the same time social pada, which likes to rise in life through manipulating its social circle. On a higher level it likes to promote love and harmony, especially in relationships. Planets here like to flaunt and dazzle. Mercury, Venus & Saturn are especially strong in this pada.

The fourth pada or quarter of this asterism 3° 20' - 6° 40' Libra falls in Scorpio Navamsa ruled by Mars. This pada relates to the magical and mysterious side of Chitra. More passion and secrecy is in display than what is usually associated with the sign Libra. Despite its non-acquisitive nature, planets here usually bring smooth sailing in regards to material affairs. Venus, Saturn, Rahu & Ketu give strong results here.

Professions :

All types of Craftsmen and Artisans; Sculptors; Architects; Designers; Fashion Designers; Models; Fashion Industry; Cosmetic Industry; Plastic surgeons; Surgeons in General; Photographers; Graphic Artists; Composers; Orators, Comperes and Broadcasters; All professions requiring special abilities and versality; Business Experts; Interior Designers; Jewellery makers; Vaastu/Fengshui Experts; All professions involving invention and production of all kinds of machinery; Builders of all kinds; Landscapers; Painters; Screenplay writers; Novelists; Production and Set designers; Art Directors; Those associated with Theatre or Theatre groups; Stage Managers; Performers of all kinds; Jazz Musicians; Musicians with an original and out of ordinary approach; Herbologists; Advertising Industry.

Places :

Capital Cities; Places of Architectural Importance like "Taj Mahal", "Eiffel Tower", "Empire State Building" etc.; Stages, Performance Halls and Theatres; Places frequented by artisans, merchants, consumers and women; Markets; Trade shows; Wardrobes, Closets; All places connected to the above professions.

Guna (Essence) and Tattwa (Element) :

It is supposed to be a *Tamasic* nakshatra. All illusions and delusions are classified under the Tamas aspect of nature. Thus the master of illusion itself would have to be seen in a tamasic light. From the perspective of the universal mind, creating just for the sake of creating does not reflect a very enlightened state of mind.

It belongs to the Fire element. This is directly derivable from its strong association with Mars. It is after all fire which creates a shining jewel out of plain rocks. The fire element directly relates to the creative principle in nature.

Gana (Type) :

It is considered a *rakshasa* or demonic nakshatra. In all the puranic mythologies, the demons are seen as superior to gods and humans when it comes to manipulation of maya, creating illusions or fashioning structures and weapons. The ancient seers are highlighting the indulgent aspect of Chitra through this classification.

Orientation & Disposition :

It is Level nakshatra. This relates to the balancing aspect of this asterism. Any perfection of beauty or form requires a sense of harmony, balance and proportion. Chitra is an absolute master in creating beauty through balance and harmony.

It is a Soft, Mild and Tender nakshatra. This comes as a surprise considering its martial element. In Chitra, the martian energy is used for constructive purposes rather than confrontation and destruction. We can see that half of Chitra lies in Libra, a mild, diplomatic sign. Its other half lies in Virgo, another non-violent sign.

Lunar Month & Day :

It relates to the middle 9 days of the lunar month of *Chaitra,* which usually falls in April.

Chitra is also related to the *Dvitiya* (2nd tithi or day) of the waxing and waning phases of the Moon's monthly cycle.

Auspicious Activities :

Health & body improvement measures; Buying new clothes and wearing them; Fixing up the home; Home designing; Any activity related to Arts & Crafts, Creative Activity in General; Any type of mechanical activities; Good for giving performances; Putting on gemstones and jewellery for the first time; Decorative Activities; Good for spiritual practices like visualizations; All issues relating to the opposite sex; Good for collecting herbs and preparing medicines; Good for all activities requiring charisma, elegance & personal charm.

Inauspicious Activities :

Unfavourable for direct confrontation; Marriage; Unfavourable for activities which require getting to the root of things; Bad for investigative activities as illusions are strong.

Planetary Ruler :

Mars is the main planetary ruler of this nakshatra. Mars is the energy required to fashion things the way we want them to. It would suffice to say that Mars is the powerhouse which runs Chitra's factory. The martian energy doesn't express itself in its natural confrontational way through Chitra as it is sublimated by Venus, the secondary ruler of this asterism. Venus is often regarded as the solar opposite of Mars. This view is only partially correct as Mars & Venus are complimentary to each other more than anything else. Together they are responsible for the reproductive process in nature. This gives us a clue as to where Chitra's creativity originates from. Venus refines the raw martian impulses. Chitra can thus be seen as the refinement-meter of the soul. Mars-Venus together promote sexuality, making Chitra one of the most sexually alluring and active amongst nakshatras.

Mercury comes into play in the first half of Chitra which falls in Virgo. The Mercury-Mars combo besides promoting technical skills, promotes skills relating to speech and words. Mercury uses Mars energy to go into the exacting details of nature's functionings. There is a Rahu element to this part of the zodiac which makes it more complicated than it looks on the surface. It is obvious that nature's secrets cannot be unravelled without Rahu's help. Mercury and Rahu always form a team when it comes to understanding maya (the universal play).

Mars/Venus, Mars/Mercury, Mars/Mercury/Venus and Mars/Mercury/Rahu conjunctions carry an energy similar to that of Chitra. Mars, Mercury, Saturn & Rahu are especially strong in the Virgo part of Chitra while Mercury, Venus, Saturn & Rahu are strong in the Libra section of Chitra.

Vowels and Alphabets :

The first pada or quarter of this asterism 23° 20' -26° 40' Virgo corresponds to "Pe" as in Page.

The second pada or quarter of this asterism 26° 40' - 30° 00' Virgo corresponds to "Po" as in Police.

The third pada or quarter of this asterism 00° 00' - 3° 20' Libra corresponds to "Ra" as in Ram.

The fourth pada or quarter of this asterism 3° 20' - 6° 40' Libra corresponds to "Re" as in Ray.

In the Sanskrit alphabet Chitra corresponds to "Ta" and "Tha" consequently its mantras are "Om Tam" and "Om Tham".

Sexual Type and Compatibility :

Its sexual animal is a Tiger. This points towards an aggressive and dominant attitude in sexual activities. Chitra however has a secrecy element attached to its sexual expression. It puts up a highly sexed or totally non-sexual image with equal ease, when the truth is always somewhere in between.

For sexual & marital compatibility with other nakshatras please refer to the tables on pages 468 & 469.

Esoteric :

Chitra represents the equilibrium point of everything. It represents the mid-point of our lives, the life of the universe and everything that exists. It is the midpoint between expansion and contraction. It is the point where the universe stops expanding and begins contracting. It lies directly opposite *Ashvini*, a nakshatra which can be seen as the big bang, which created the material universe.

Chitra is the architect of the Universe and thus relates closely to *Brahma*, the creator among the holy trinity. In fact Vishwakarma, the ruling deity of Chitra, is one of Brahma's direct mind-born sons. Chitra conceals within itself the laws and arrangement of the Universe on all planes of existence.

The fact that it connects the signs Virgo and Libra reveals that Chitra is the bridge between compassion and harmony. Even though compassion is one of the divine virtues, it is often forgotten that only a proper use of compassion brings about balance, understanding and harmony.

The number 14, which is the number of Chitra in the sequence of Nakshatras, has similar connotations in occult numerology. It is related to the "*Temperance*" card in Tarot imagery. The symbolism there depicts a winged angel mixing two heavenly fluids with one foot in water and one on dry land. Chitra has been assigned this delicate and precarious job of balancing seemingly opposing factions within the pool of universal constituents.

In the universal scheme of things, Chitra relates to "*punya chayani shakti*" - the power to accumulate merit. Its symbolism has truth below and law above. Chitra gains honour and merit through its hard work done in consonance with universal laws.

Gotra (Celestial Lineage) :

This nakshatra is related to the *Sage Kratu*, one of the seven celestial sages looking after the affairs of our galaxy. The name of this sage translates into "the inspirer". It is appropriate that a creative and inspiring sage should preside over the most creative among the asterisms.

Remedial :

Worship of feminine deities who ride a tiger like *Durga, Bhavani, Jagdamba* etc. is the best way of getting the best out of Chitra. On a higher level, worship of these deities helps us see through the illusions of maya, an important step on the road to enlightenment.

Repetition of the root mantras of this nakshatra - "Om Tam" and "Om Tham" 108 times when Moon transits this nakshatra and in the corresponding lunar month of Chaitra is sure to reduce suffering and bring enlightenment into a person's life.

Persons who are benefiting from the positive energy of this nakshatra can also increase the good effects through the above mentioned ways. It is helpful for them to wear all sparkly, bright, variegated and glittering colours. They should use its directions, lunar month and the days when Moon transits Chaitra to undertake all important actions.

Example :

Chitra's sound and light can be experienced at –

http://osfa.org.uk/chitra.htm

Miscellaneous :

According to *Varahamihira*, those with Moon in Chitra are found wearing bright clothes and garlands, with beautiful eyes and bodies.

* * *

15. Swati   6°40' Libra - 20°00' Libra

15.

Swati

(6º40' Libra - 20º00' Libra)

In the Sky :

Swati is once again among the few asterisms which are represented by a single star. Its representative is a yellowish star commonly known as *Arcturus* (*Alpha-Bootis*). It is the central star of the constellation of *Bootis* which can be said to lie on top of the gateway formed between Virgo and Libra. However, as we can see, this asterism occupies the heart of the sign Libra and has nothing to do with the sign Virgo. With a visual magnitude of 0.16, Arcturus is the third brightest among the stars in the night sky and can be spotted even in the polluted skies over big metropolitan cities. Ancient Vedic seers associated a lot of importance to this bright star and saw it as the abode of *Saraswati*, the goddess of learning.

Name :

'Swati ", like other sanskrit terms, evokes a wide variety of English meanings - "self-going", "good goer", "independent", "sword", "self -blowing", "delicate" and "tender". Each of these meanings relay a different side of this asterism's nature and functionings.

Symbol :

Its symbol is a 'young plant shoot blown by the wind'. The wind symbolism suggests the airy quality of this asterism which promotes restlessness, adaptability, dexterity and a roaming disposition. The young plant symbolism suggests delicacy. This is the reason why this asterism strives for strength and independence, just like a young plant shoot strives for maturity. Air is the balancing element among the five interacting elements in nature. This nakshatra is the balancing pivot of the zodiac in the sense that it is the middle most nakshatra, with thirteen nakshatras on either side. It represents the atmospheric aspect, where there's neither a lull nor a storm and a gentle breeze is blowing. Swati thus represents the period of our lives where smooth sailing takes place.

In ancient Vedic texts, wind also suggests an idea of force and ability to move things, like clouds. This implies that even though gentle, Swati is capable of applying force whenever required. The young delicate sapling is always growing to become a strong sturdy tree, which has very little to fear from nature's pressures like weather and animals.

A 'coral' is the alternative symbol of this nakshatra. The coral is a plant which makes its progeny out of its own body like bacterias and other micro-organisms. In the same way, Swati's creativity comes out of parting with a piece of itself. It is common knowledge that coral relates to the planet Mars. Swati has no direct correlation with the planet Mars, but through coral a connection is established. Just like wind gets the impetus to move through the imbalance between heat and cold, Swati gets its extraordinary mobility, energy and strength from the heating effect of the planet Mars.

Swati falls in the cardinal, achievement-oriented sign of Libra. This is why 'a sword' is also seen as a symbol of this nakshatra, to represent its cutting, fiery quality. In a way, it can be said, that in time this asterism transforms from the delicate young plant shoot into a hard and strong, razor sharp sword. Thus those with prominent Swati in their charts are late bloomers and have a stronger second half of life as compared to the first half.

Deity :

Its main presiding deity is *Vayu*, the god of wind. He is one of the five main gods residing in *Swarga* (heavenly astral plane), who are responsible for taking care of the five main elements of nature - earth, wind, fire, water & ether. All of Vayu's qualities, especially those relevant to the earthly plane, can be seen manifested through *Hanuman,* son of Vayu and one of the central characters in the Vedic epic, "*Ramayan".* Hanuman's qualities like extreme strength, morality, strong sense of ethics, moderation, fairness, resourcefulness, intelligence, wisdom, sense of propriety, loyalty and ability to serve without letting ego come in the way; apply to the highest aspect of Swati's functioning.

The "Ramayan" tells us that Hanuman was never consciously aware of his own prowess unless reminded of it by others. Swati, in the same way, is quite humble in its disposition and needs to be told about its potential for it to be able to express itself. This quality can be associated with its planetary ruler Rahu. Rahu as a planet represents the potential that is hidden from us, which we need to discover in the present life.

It is Hanuman's extreme loyalty and devotion to *Ram* (main character from the "Ramayan"), which still remains the strongest example of unconditional and unselfish service in the hearts and minds of people influenced by the Vedic way of thinking. It is no wonder then that the planet of service, Saturn, reaches maximum exaltation in Swati. *Bheem,* one of the central characters in the *Mahabharat* is also a son of *Vayu* (one must remember that in those days gods were still copulating with humans). He is a character similar to that of Hanuman, except that his qualities were not as sterling as that of Hanuman. This is however to be expected as the ages had changed from *Treta* (Silver) to *Dwapar* (Bronze).

Swati's relation to *Saraswati,* the goddess of music and learning, reveals the higher nature of this asterism, which is conducive for all sorts of learning - material, philosophical or spiritual. Just like its planetary ruler Rahu, when functioning through its higher aspect, this nakshatra is eager and open to learning - a rare quality.

Nature & Functioning :

Like *Chitra*, "Balance" is the keyword for natives born under the strong influence of this nakshatra. Balance is a double edged sword and many Swati types are seen to avoid taking any stance on any matter due to their extreme need to maintain harmony. Only very evolved Swati types are capable of decisive action. Extreme procrastination is one of the worst traits of this nakshatra. Inconclusive thinking is a feature which is apparent here more than any other nakshatra. Swati's openness to new thoughts and ideas make it ideal for all types of learning, but only a few acquire mastery over their chosen field.

In its lower aspect, Swati is the most airy fairy amongst the nakshatras. Swati natives always have to be conscious of growing towards a more stable centre and still this process usually takes a long time. Swati is usually in no hurry to achieve its objectives and this is the reason why Saturn finds maximum exaltation here. The emphasis here is on longterm planning. Most Swati natives are usually very good at sowing the seeds for the future, but only a few of them stick around to nurture the seed into a full grown tree.

Swati natives usually have slim and elegantly proportioned bodies. They can be easily spotted in group situations with a continuously fixed smile on their faces. Because of the emphasis of Venus and Rahu, Swati natives are born diplomats. They are the socialites of the zodiac. They usually go to any lengths to fit into prevalent social and cultural structures. They are strong advocates of social etiquettes, courtesies and civilized behaviour. They use their social charm to climb the ladder of success. Their catchphrase is "Who am I to blow against the wind?". It is this quality which makes them lose their inner centre and blindly follow mass trends. Often very intelligent Swati types behave in the same way, even after attaining a clear understanding of the worthlessness of trying to please everyone all the time.

'Swati' translates into 'independent' or 'self-going'. These meanings are self explanatory as this asterism promotes individuality. However this individuality is different from the individuality furthered by Sun's influence, as Sun has its maximum debilitation in this asterism. It is not a soul level individuality, but a more mental and material individuality based upon some skill or talent developed on these planes.

Many of the world's richest men are born with either Moon or other significant planets placed in this asterism. Working through its lower plane, this asterism can be overtly indulgent and function without any regard for morals. Law, sex and money - the three major Libran significations, form an integral part of the activities of this asterism.

Mode of Functioning :

It is supposed to be a Passive nakshatra. This obviously relates to its naturally shy and gentle quality. Swati is more of a "wait and watch" rather than a "run and get it" type of nakshatra. As we have already discussed, it is a patient energy, which is ready to wait for things to fall into place together, rather than aggressively put them in place itself.

Caste :

It belongs to the Butcher caste. It is hard to visualize what the ancient seers were trying to convey through this classification. In our opinion it must relate to the destructive and ruthless side of Swati. Even wind can be a highly destructive and unforgiving force when it takes the form of tempest, cyclones and tornadoes. Swati, as we have discussed earlier, is quite ruthless in its approach, especially when it gains strength and power over the passage of time.

Gender :

It is a Female nakshatra. Swati represents the female aspect of its planetary ruler, Rahu. It is directly associated with Saraswati, goddess of music and learning.

Bodyparts & Humor (Ayurvedic Constitution) :

The body part it relates to is the Chest, which emphasizes its connection with the air element and the process of breathing. On an astral level this is related to the flow of *prana* (life force) through the body.

Its constitutional type is "*Kapha*" (watery). This classification stems from the fact that all of this nakshatra lies in the predominantly kapha sign of Libra.

Direction :

It is connected with the west, southwest and the southeast.

Padas (Quarters) :

The first pada or quarter of this asterism 6° 40' - 10° 00' Libra falls in Sagittarius Navamsa and is ruled by Jupiter. This pada epitomises the restless and inquisitive aspect of Swati. It gives talent in writing, communications and promotes all kinds of travel. All planets give reasonably favourable results in this pada because of its eager and open-minded nature.

The second pada or quarter of this asterism 10° 00' - 13° 20' Libra falls in Capricorn Navamsa and is ruled by Saturn. This pada embodies the material aspect of Swati's functioning. It is the most rooted among the four padas and thus to an extent lacks Swati's inherent fragility. The concerns here are stability and material growth. It can be deemed as selfish when it comes to personal comforts and other forms of materiality. Planets here give a sound business sense.

The third pada or quarter of this asterism 13° 20' - 16° 40' Libra falls in Aquarius Navamsa ruled by Saturn. This is the most intellectual amongst the four padas of Swati. The emphasis here is on learning, creativity and cooperation. Planets here encourage any kind of group work in order to achieve one's chosen goals. Mercury, Venus and Saturn are especially strong in this pada.

The fourth pada or quarter of this asterism 16° 40' - 20° 00' Libra falls in Pisces Navamsa ruled by Jupiter. This is the most flexible and adaptable amongst Swati's padas. We have already seen that Swati's key to success lies in blowing with the wind and this pada is best suited for that. Being the Pushkara navamsa pada, it promises success through hardwork, ingenuity, flexibility and sociability. Planets here might seem flimsy in their approach but are service orientated and hardworking. All planets except Mercury give good results here.

Professions :

Businessmen and Trades people of all types; Wrestlers; All sports, especially those relying on breath control; Singers; Musicians playing Wind Instruments like Horns & Organ; Researchers; Inventors; Technology experts; Independent Enterprises; Government related Service Professions; Aeronautical Industry; Pilots; Professions connected with the Aviation industry; Transportation Industry; Socialites; Professions involving use of speech like Newsreaders etc. ; Computer & Software Industry; Professions requiring flexibility & quick ingenuity; Serving Professions like Housekeepers & Right-hand-man types; Kite Makers; Adventure Sports people like Skydivers, Balloonists etc.; Educators, Teachers; Lawyers; Judges; Politicians; Trade-Union & Working Class Leaders; Diplomats, Hosts, Hostesses.

Places :

High Cliffs; Places where winds blow strongly; Agricultural land; Coral reefs; Marketplaces; Business Centers; Banks; Financial Institutions; Sport Complexes; Airports (both civil & military); Educational institutions; Aeronautical facilities & testing grounds; Computer & Software related centres; Research facilities of all types; Diplomatic enclaves like Embassies, Consulates etc; Parliament Houses; Courthouses; Commuter places like Train Stations, Bus-Stations etc.

Guna (Essence) and Tattwa (Element) :

Rahu's Venusian side is usually quite materialistic which makes this asterism *Rajasic* (materially active). It is the best nakshatra for business and other financially profitable activities, as it always keeps its own interests above everything else.

It belongs to the Fire Element. The fact that it is fiery reveals a hitherto unknown aspect of Rahu, which is predominantly an airy and earthy planet. This fieriness relates to the inherent motivation of this asterism, which can range from learning, to acquiring financial gain, to getting worldly prominence.

Gana (Type) :

It is considered a *Deva* or godly nakshatra. Its godly nature stems from the fact that this asterism is very conducive to all types of learning. Rahu, its ruler, is the significator of knowledge and this aspect of its nature finds expression through this nakshatra.

Orientation & Disposition :

It is a Level nakshatra. Falling in the heart of Libra, it has a balancing quality. It thus relays the diplomatic, pleasing side of Rahu. It can always compromise to achieve its eventual ends. It can be seen as a combined Venus and Rahu energy and relays the Venusian side of Rahu's functioning. This makes it good in most Venusian related pursuits like music.

It is a Moveable nakshatra. Its moveable nature is borne out of its close association with the air element through planets Rahu and Saturn. As discussed earlier, its ruling deity Vayu corresponds to wind, which is one of the constantly moving elements in nature.

Lunar Month & Day :

It relates to the last 9 days of the lunar month of "*Chaitra*", which usually falls in late April, early May.

Swati is also related to the *Saptami* (7th tithi or day) of the waxing and waning phases of the Moon's monthly cycle.

Auspicious Activities :

Good for business & trade activities; Recommended for starting any educational venture; Good for learning in general; Social activities & events; Dealing with the public; Financial transactions; All activities which require a calm & flexible approach; The key here is to blow with the wind; Grooming and self adornment; Buying and Selling in general; Actions where diplomacy is required; Pursuing Arts & Sciences.

Inauspicious Activities :

Not good for travel; Fierce or warlike activities; Any type of aggressive behaviour is not likely to pay off in this nakshatra.

Planetary Ruler :

Rahu is the primary ruler of this asterism and its airy qualities are relayed through it. There is a strong urge for comfort and luxury when Rahu is manifesting its energies on an earthy plane. Earth is the secondary element of Rahu. Since Swati falls completely in the sign of Libra, Venus has a strong connection with this asterism. The Rahu-Venus influence together is a highly indulgent combination, which gives a strong urge for comfort and luxury. A love of show and pomp is seen when Rahu is functioning through its lower aspect. As discussed earlier, Swati natives often appreciate the finer things in life and uphold a certain degree of sophistication in their dress, mannerisms and tastes.

The primarily materialistic energy of Rahu and Venus combined gives Swati natives success in Venusian business pursuits. In its negative aspect, natives under the heavy influence of this nakshatra can become a slave to their desires and are guided by greed and deceit to gain their ends.

Rahu has a diplomatic nature, which is very similar to that of Venus. Rahu, like Venus, is by nature a social planet and enjoys company. Swati in this regard, can be the most pretentious among the nakshatras. Rahu is supposed to give an artistic temperament in much the same way as Venus, but as always with Rahu, there is a touch of unorthodoxy involved. Rahu's Venusian side is highlighted in any horoscope when it is either associated with Venus in a nativity, or is placed in the second/ seventh houses, or is posited in the signs Taurus/Libra.

In its higher aspect, Swati natives express higher Venusian qualities like diplomacy, compassion and a thirst for knowledge. Rahu is also very much capable of manifesting highest Venusian energies like universal love, compassion and harmony when working through its higher principle.

Rahu, Mercury, Venus and Saturn gives strong results in Swati. Sun and Mars are a little out of sorts here, while Ketu's energy is incompatible with the energies of this nakshatra. Jupiter and Moon are neutral and give results according to other factors in a nativity.

Vowels and Alphabets :

The first pada or quarter of this asterism 6° 40' -10° 00' Libra corresponds to "Ru" as in Ruth.

The second pada or quarter of this asterism 10° 00' - 13° 20' Libra corresponds to "Re" as in Rex.

The third pada or quarter of this asterism 13° 20' - 16° 40' Libra corresponds to "Ro" as in Robin.

The fourth pada or quarter of this asterism 16° 40' - 20° 00' Libra corresponds to "Ta" as in Tanya.

In the Sanskrit alphabet Swati corresponds to "Da" (pronounced as "The") and consequently its mantra is "Om Dam".

Sexual Type and Compatibility :

Its sexual animal is a Buffalo. This makes it fertile and it likes to play a dominant role in sexual activity. This nakshatra is often prone to exploit mild forms of sex and sexuality for business purposes. Swati can be said to be more of a tease rather than a whore.

For sexual & marital compatibility with other nakshatras please refer to the tables on pages 468 & 469.

Esoteric :

In our bodies, Swati relates to the five vital pranas or airs. These airs form an interface between the astral and the corporeal body. It is these airs which are normally referred to as the life force within us. The preliminary spiritual practices like *pranayama* are meant to create an equilibrium between these five vital airs, so that the mind can remain free from ripples when the real meditative process begins. Swati relates to the immense potential of these body airs, which when utilized properly, as done by sages in Ages gone by, allowed them to meditate unhindered for thousands of years and have lifespans which exceeded lifespans of the Ages.

In the universal scheme of things, *Swati* relates to "*Pradhvamsa shakti*" - the power to disperse like the wind. Its symbolism has roaming around above and change of form below. The relationship of Swati with the air element is stressed here. The *maya* element of Swati lies in its ability to adjust itself to any situation or circumstance without losing its own essence. Its free, detached, observant quality makes it easy for it to scatter away any negative buildup on any level of being. Swati can be seen as the universal vacuum cleaner.

Gotra (Celestial Lineage) :

This nakshatra is related to the *Sage Marichi*, one of the seven celestial sages looking after the affairs of our galaxy. The name of this sage translates into "Light". The "lightness" (as in swiftness) aspect of this Sage seems to connect well with Swati, considering that Air is a light element.

Remedial :

For those suffering from bad effects resulting from afflictions to this nakshatra, the best remedial measure is worship of Saraswati.

Repetition of the root mantras of this nakshatra - "Om Lam", "Om Ksham", "Om Am" and "Om Aam" 108 times when Moon transits this nakshatra and in its corresponding lunar month is sure to reduce suffering and bring enlightenment into a person's life.

Persons who are benefiting from the positive energy of this nakshatra can also increase the good effects through the above mentioned ways. It is helpful for them to wear all light, variegated colours and pastel shades. They should use its directions, lunar month and the days when Moon transits Swati to undertake all important actions.

Example :

Swati's sound and light can be experienced at --

http://osfa.org.uk/swati.htm

Miscellaneous :

According to *Varahamihira*, those born with Moon in Swati are "pleasant in speech, have a self-controlled nature and compassionate ways. The person is a merchant with principles".

* * *

16. Vishakha   20°00' Libra - 3°20' Scorpio

16.

Vishakha

(20º00' Libra - 3º20' Scorpio)

In the Sky :

Vishakha consists of four stars, which form the left half of the hanging scale shape formed by the constellation Libra. These stars are known in modern astronomy as *Alpha-Librae, Beta-Librae, Gamma-Librae* & *Iota-Librae.* Despite the fact that all of these stars are part of the constellation of Libra, a part of this asterism lies in the zodiacal sign of Scorpio. Among these, Alpha-Librae (*Zuben el Genubi* or the North Scale) and Beta-Librae (*Zuben el Hakhrabi* or the South scale) are the brightest, with visual magnitudes of 2.75 and 2.61 respectively. The easiest way to spot these stars is to locate them below the bright star *Spica*. Ancient Vedic Seers saw these stars as forming the shape of a forked branch and associated them with the abode of the gods under the rulership of *Indra*.

Name :

"Vishakha", like other Sanskrit terms, evokes a wide variety of English meanings - "forked", "two-branched", "poison vessel". Its alternative name is "*Radha*", which translates into "the delightful". Radha, as a name, has gained popularity by virtue of being the name of Krishn's beloved consort.

Symbol :

Its main symbol is a 'decorated arch' or 'gateway'. In depictions this gateway is usually decorated with leaves (refer to image). Such gateways are still a norm in marriage ceremonies in India. Consequently, one can infer that Vishakha has a lot to do with marriage. Most of Vishakha lies in the sign governing marriage, Libra. In the ancient times this gateway was symbolic of triumph. It symbolised the ending or attainment of a goal and the beginning of a new one. It was a reminder of the fact that challenges don't end once you pass through the gateway, after achieving your goal.

The challenges begin when one enters the gateway, just like the marriage ceremony is the precursor of the challenges to come in married life. The gateway also suggests that Vishakha always has its eyes fixed upon the final attainment of a goal. This goal can range from triumphing over one's external enemies to triumphing over one's inner demons. In the present day and age, where negative qualities of every nakshatra predominate, Vishakha usually functions as an obsessive, goal-oriented nakshatra with complete disregard for the nature of the means employed to achieve the desired end.

Despite its association with celebrations, Vishakha cannot be seen as a pleasant nakshatra. When striving towards a goal becomes the only objective in life, one is likely to have little peace of mind and will definitely miss the true essence of life.

Deity :

Vishakha, true to its forked quality, has two main ruling deities :- *Indra* and *Agni* (fire god).

In the puranic literature, Indra, the chief among the demi-gods, is often portrayed as a very goal oriented, fixated and offensive character, who would go to any lengths to achieve his desired ends. The funny thing is that many times his desired ends are completely ungodly and he is getting into all sorts of troubles as a result. This is a primary theme of Vishakha - pursuing unwholesome goals in questionable ways and creating bad karma as a result. Indra is also seen as a character who drowns himself in women, wine and other such pleasures. This indulgent side of Indra also finds expression through Vishakha.

Deceptiveness is also associated with Indra, in the sense that he doesn't shy away from putting his own near and dear ones in danger, in order to get what he wants. He is also often seen to act in a cowardly fashion at the first sign of real danger. It is helpful to remember that "Indra" is just a post which is occupied by different souls in different times in different universes. Vishakha people are always in search of a post which gives them dominion and pleasure and Indra is just a soul who makes it.

Agni, the fire god, basically represents energy in one of its many forms. It is because of Agni that Vishakha has the capacity to exert herculean efforts in order to attain its goal. Just like fire, when harnessed properly, can be used in a variety of constructive ways, Vishakha's strong energy can manifest as courage, determination and the capacity for hardwork directed towards wholesome pursuits. Fire in its negative aspect can run amok and burn indiscriminately. In the same way Vishakha can cause harm to others around it before finally getting consumed itself. Terms like " burning grief", "burning desire" and "burning passion" are all tailor-made Vishakha expressions.

Agni and Indra rule over heat and rain making Vishakha an agricultural nakshatra. It utilizes the forces of nature to produce crops and then goes on to derive intoxicants like wine and alcohol from these crops.

Nature & Functioning :

The nature of this Nakshatra can be summed in one word - "fixation". Even though its single-mindedness in pursuing its goals is unmatched, its achilles heel lies in "what goal it chooses to pursue". In the present day and age, the likelihood of forming unwholesome goals is intensively heightened, the presence of this nakshatra in a nativity becomes a cause for concern. Vishakha natives easily fall prey to excesses in regards to sex and alcohol. They are the ones who have an overwhelming need to flock to the local bar.

There is a certain jubilation aspect to Vishakha natives which shows itself in love of pomp and ceremony. Very often those among Vishakhas who choose the path of the senses end up becoming mad party types. Following *Swati*, the nakshatra where actual achievement takes place, Vishakha represents the exuberant victorious state after the achievement. It is common knowledge that a sense of emptiness follows any accomplishment. This sense of emptiness is a continuous feature throughout the lives of Vishakha natives. Fire is never satiated no matter how much or how long it consumes. They are always concerned about what they don't have, rather than making use of what they have. "The grass looks greener on the other side" mentality breeds a cogmire of unwholesome emotions. This emptiness and frustration drives some of the more evolved Vishakha natives away from blind worldliness in search of higher knowledge and truths.

Vishakha natives have a distinct fierce appearance with prominent slants and angles on the face even in case of the fairer sex. They usually have sharp eyes and features. Their external behaviour ranges from extremely courteous and jovial to completely nasty and obnoxious. Vishakha natives are very concerned about putting up fronts to gain their ends. This makes them hide their innate negative feelings towards others in their dealings with them. Most Vishakha natives easily fall prey to envy, jealousy, viciousness and can't help feeling useless in comparision to those around them. All these factors make Vishakha natives hard to get along with making them bereft of any real friends. These negative feelings arise from the same empty place which was mentioned above. The real problem lies in the fact that these natives become obsessive about these negative feelings and thoughts and can't let go of them. This is where the fire inside them starts burning their own selves instead of being put to any constructive use. Vishakha natives are pretty much defined by their obsessions, which can range from petty and soul-destroying to soul-nurturing and evolutionary.

The good thing about these natives is that once their mind is made up they are devoted to their cause and will go to any lengths to fulfill their objective. However it is noticed that life continuously presents them with two different paths, and they have to make a conscious choice to stay on the right one. Vishakha natives take life as a challenge of sorts. They usually make simple things complex and easy things difficult. The way they go about achieving their objectives does not follow the line of least resistance. They encounter lots of obstacles, which they are able to surmount by their one pointedness, but the process is not free from moans and complaints. The final paradox of this nakshatra lies at the point where after achieving what they set out to achieve, they are not sure if that's what they wanted to achieve.

Mode of Functioning :

Vishakha is considered to be an Active nakshatra. Pursuit of any goal requires constant activity. Vishakha is one of the most active nakshatras because of its obsessive approach to things. After attaining its desired goal, it sets itself another goal and so on and so on....its activity is ceaseless. This is probably the reason why a lot of Vishakha types cannot give a reason for some of the bad things they have done. It is as if some external force grips them and makes them act thoughtlessly without reflection. They are possessed individuals.

Caste :

It belongs to the *Mleccha* (outcaste) caste. It is clear from this classification that the ancient seers saw Vishakha as a natural trouble maker who could not function within society. It related either to bandits, revolutionaries or hermits retiring to the forest in order to perform *tapas* to obtain their wishes. None of these characters fit into the ideal society as envisioned by *Manu* (the grand overseer and law giver).

Gender :

It is a Female nakshatra. This classification seems to have its roots in its alternative name "*Radha*". Radha is the childhood consort of *Krishn* who spent the rest of her life pining for him. Vishakha carries within itself the primarily feminine attribute of "longing", "separation" and "catharsis". It is the longing for the unattainable, which characterises a Vishakha mindset. Its other qualities like possessiveness, jealousy and vindictiveness are also regarded as familiarly feminine qualities in Vedic texts.

Bodyparts & Humor (Ayurvedic Constitution) :

The Arms and the Breasts are the body parts related to this nakshatra.

It is a primarily "*Kapha*" (watery) nakshatra. This classification is borne out of the fact that Vishakha lies in two kapha signs, Libra and Scorpio. Vishakha, as we discussed earlier, is very good at hiding its fiery quality under a calm exterior. It is the kapha element which allows Vishakha to put up a diplomatic front even when a fiery storm is brewing inside.

Direction :

It is related primarily to west & north.

Padas (Quarters) :

The first pada or quarter of this asterism 20° 00' - 23° 20' Libra falls in Aries Navamsa and is ruled by Mars. This pada is all about energy, impulse, one pointedness and social ambitions. The focus here is on relationships, but passion and instinct are likely to dominate instead of commitment and depth. A well placed Mars or Venus are the most suitable planets for this pada.

The second pada or quarter of this asterism 23° 20' - 26° 40' Libra falls in Taurus Navamsa ruled by Venus. Endurance and durability are the hallmarks of this pada. Planets here tend to give success in Venusian pursuits. Material ambitions are strong here and since this is the Pushkara navamsa pada they are fulfilled to the degree allowed by the chart as a whole.

The third pada or quarter of this asterism 26° 40' - 30° 00' Libra falls in Gemini Navamsa ruled by Mercury. Vishakha's onepointedness channels itself through thoughts, communication, philosophical and religious attitudes. There's a definite conflict between two opposing forces here - one force demands the native to be lig thearted, open-minded and jovial, while the other promotes selfishness, deception and anxiety. Only well placed Mercury and Saturn can be counted on for giving good results in this pada.

The fourth pada or quarter of this asterism 00° 00' - 3° 20' Scorpio falls in Cancer Navamsa ruled by Moon. This is the most one pointed of all Vishakha's padas. The turmoil here takes place on the emotional plane, making this a highly volatile, transformative and dangerous part of the zodiac. In its lowest aspect, it is highly vindictive and revengeful and embodies most of the despicable human qualities. In its higher aspect, it can give penetrating insight, strong will power, executive ability and the conviction necessary to root out the dark forces. Only a well placed Jupiter can give the wisdom to navigate through the stormy waters of this pada.

Professions :

Bartenders; Alcohol & Liquor Industry; Manual Labourers; Fashion Models & Actresses; All professions involving use of speech like TV & Radio Broadcasters; Politicians; Marching Bands; Sports Persons especially sports requiring Herculean efforts; Cults & other types of Ideological Fanatics; Religious Fundamentalists; Professional Agitators; Soldiers; Dancers; Critics; Criminals & Mafia; Custom & Immigration Officials; Policing Jobs; Guards; Prostitution & Militant Revolutionaries.

Vishakha natives can be found in all types of professions but usually have a tendency to switch professions throughout their lives.

Places :

Rocky Rough Terrains; Mountains; Big Cities like New York; Breweries; Bars; Liquor Shops; Brothels; Theatres; Military Bases; Ceremonial Halls & Grounds; Interrogation Rooms; Warring Grounds; Danger Areas either in the City or designated by the Military; All places connected with the above professions.

Guna (Essence) and Tattwa (Element) :

It is supposed to be a *Sattwic* nakshatra. This relates to Vishakha's intense capacity for hardwork and penance. Vishakha is ready to sacrifice a lot for the attainment of its goals, a quality which is seen as sattwic from the universal point of view. Vishakha's sattwic quality is more liable to come out when planets like Sun, Moon and Jupiter occupy this nakshatra.

It belongs to the Fire element. Due to its close association with Agni (the deity presiding over the element fire), fire becomes the primary element of Vishakha.

Gana (Type) :

It is considered a *Rakshasa* or demonic nakshatra. Keeping in mind its basic nature and traits, it is not very hard to understand this classification. A complete disregard for others is considered a demonic quality and Vishakha is one of the nakshatras which displays it to the hilt. It is because of its selfish approach that it is classified as demonic even though both of its ruling deities are demi-gods.

Orientation & Disposition :

It is a Downward Looking nakshatra. Since downward nakshatras imply containment and contraction it is Vishakha's duty to contain its multifarious desires. Like all the nakshatras tenanting the signs Leo, Virgo and Libra, it is a very worldly nakshatra and thus has a lot of ambition in relation to its role in the world. Since it is a downward nakshatra, it goes about attaining these goals in a secretive and underhanded manner and most of its real intent and activities are concealed from others.

It is a Mixed (sharp and soft) nakshatra . This classification once again emphasizes the duality inherent in Vishakha as exemplified by meanings of its name. Its soft disposition relates to its pleasure seeking side while its sharpness relates to its fixidity of purpose. The softer side is often what stops Vishakha types from turning into complete psychopaths and at times it just acts as a disguise which lets them get away with their darker activities.

Lunar Month & Day :

It relates to the first half of the lunar month of *Vaishakha*, which usually falls in early May.

Vishakha is also related to the *Shashti & Saptami* (6th & 7th tithis or days) of the waxing and waning phases of the Moon's monthly cycle.

Auspicious Activities :

Aggressive or warlike activities; Any activity requiring executive ability; Getting things done which require an argumentative approach; Harsh activities in general; Any activity requiring strong mental focus; Working toward one's goals; All types of ceremonies, functions and parties; Awards or Decoration Ceremonies; Dressing up, Ornamentation, Decorating oneself; Romance & Sexual Activity; Performing penance; Making Resolutions.

Inauspicious Activities :

Not good for Travel; Marriage; Initiations of any kind; Activities requiring diplomacy or tact.

Planetary Ruler :

Venus, Mars, Pluto, Ketu and Jupiter are the three planetary influences connected to Vishakha. Jupiter is the main ruler of this asterism, while Venus, Mars, Pluto and Ketu rule the respective signs that Vishakha occupies.

Jupiter connects to this asterism through Indra, whose preceptor is *Brihaspati.* Jupiter supports most of Indra's objectives and ambitions, even the unwholesome ones, through this nakshatra. Its natural benevolence, grace and good fortune can be used for pompous extravagance under the influence of this nakshatra.

Venus, Jupiter's counterpart and adversary, is connected with the first three padas of Vishakha. It is the natural antagonism between the energies of these two planets which makes Vishakha a turbulent nakshatra. A lot of Indra's Venusian excesses as enumerated in numerous puranic legends are not sanctioned by Jupiter; and it goes without saying that Indra lands into some sort of trouble each time.

In the fourth pada, Mars co-rules along with Jupiter and thus the energy is more sorted out but has a militaristic tone to it. The Pluto/Ketu influence in the Scorpio part of Vishakha lends a great deal of impulsiveness, explosive drama and self destructiveness. Only when channelled into more occult areas can this energy act as a vehicle for transformation.

Venus-Jupiter, Venus-Mars, Venus-Mars-Ketu, Jupiter-Mars and Jupiter-Mars-Ketu-Venus conjunctions carry an energy similar to that of Vishakha. In the author's experience only Jupiter functions well in this nakshatra in the present day and age.

Vowels and Alphabets :

The first pada or quarter of this asterism 20° 00' -23° 20' Libra corresponds to "Ti" as in Tea.

The second pada or quarter of this asterism 23° 20' - 26° 40' Libra corresponds to "Tu" as in Tuesday.

The third pada or quarter of this asterism 26° 40' - 30° 00' Libra corresponds to "Te" as in Tailor.

The fourth pada or quarter of this asterism 00° 00' - 3° 20' Scorpio corresponds to "To" as in Tommy.

In the Sanskrit alphabet Vishakha corresponds to "Dha" and "Na" consequently its mantras are "Om Dham" and "Om Nam".

Sexual Type and Compatibility :

Its sexual animal is a Tiger. This points towards an aggressive and dominant attitude in sexual activities. It is mostly compatible with Chitra, the other tiger nakshatra.

For marital & sexual compatibility with other nakshatras please refer to the tables on pages 468 & 469 .

Esoteric :

The now globally famous *Radha-Krishn* love legend exemplifies Vishakha's inner core. This is the reason why Vishakha has "Radha" as one of its names. Radha was already married to someone when she fell in love with Krishn and romanced him in his childhood years. But since Krishn was Vishnu's incarnation this was no ordinary love. It epitomized a desire on Radha's part to merge with Universal energies, not as an inferior but as a lover. Vishakha's longing for perfection and enlightenment is always expressed in terms of love and relationships, which more often than not break societal conventions and moralistic taboos. Vishakha does not distinguish between fun, frolic and pain of such relationships and *tapasya,* the intense spiritual practice leading to knowledge and enlightenment. Above all else, its ultimate goal is experiencing the divine in and through relationship with the divine itself.

Being the 16th nakshatra in the nakshatra sequence, it relates to the number "16", a number which is seen as the number of tragedy, upheaval, ruin and turmoil. The destruction and ruin here is only of that which stands against the universal will. Nevertheless it becomes evident that Vishakha's path is not all romance and roses. This is clear from the fact that Radha spent a major part of her life pining for Krishn after he left for taking care of the purpose behind his incarnation. This intense longing and the pain of separation is Vishakha's tapasya and if it can keep the fire of love burning regardless of the outer circumstances, it achieves immortality like Radha did.

In the universal scheme of things, Vishakha relates to "*vyapana shakti*" - the power to make manifest and achieve various things. Its symbolism has harvest below and cultivation above. This makes it a fruitful nakshatra on the material plane, even though as we have just realized. its true spiritual path lies elsewhere. The material results here usually come with persistent and patient effort, just like the finest wine takes a long time to be ready for consumption after the grains have been put through the brewing process.

Gotra (Celestial Lineage) :

This nakshatra is related to the *Sage Vashishta*, one of the seven celestial sages looking after the affairs of our galaxy. The name of this sage translates into "possessor of wealth". We can imagine that Vishakha must relate to the sage's capacity for penance. As *Varahamihira* says, "Those with Moon in Vishakha are skilled at making money".

Remedial :

For those suffering from bad effects resulting from afflictions to this nakshatra, the best remedial measure is worship of the eight Vasus. Alternatively one can worship the half *Vishnu*, half *Shiv* form commonly known as *Hari Har*. The practice of *Raj Yog*, which involves the raising of the *kundalini* through the seven sacred centres, is one of the best ways to utilise this nakshatra's potential.

Repetition of the root mantra of this nakshatra - "Om Yam" and "Om Ram" 108 times when Moon transits this nakshatra and in its corresponding lunar month is sure to reduce suffering and bring enlightenment into a person's life.

Persons who are benefiting from the positive energy of this nakshatra can also increase the good effects through the above mentioned ways. It is helpful for them to wear colours like red, blue and gold. They should use its directions, lunar month and the days when Moon transits Vishakha to undertake all important actions.

Example :

Vishakha's sound and light can be experienced at -

http://osfa.org.uk/vishakha.htm

Miscellaneous :

According to *Varahamihira*, those with Moon in Vishakha are "jealous, greedy, clever with words, skilled at earning money, quarrelsome and incite quarrels among others".

* * *

17. Anuradha 3°20' Scorpio - 16°40' Scorpio

17.

Anuradha

(3°20' Scorpio - 16°40' Scorpio)

In the Sky :

Anuradha consists of three stars in a row, which were seen by the ancients as forming a shape similar to a staff. These three stars are known in modern astronomy as *Beta-Scorpionis* (*Acrab*), *Delta-Scorpionis* (*Isidis*) & *Pi-Scorpionis*. All of these stars lie in the beginning of the zodiacal constellation of Scorpio. Beta-scorpionis is the brightest among these stars with a visual magnitude of 2.62. All of these stars can be easily spotted in the dark night sky from the countryside, if one locates the bright star *Antares* in the constellation of Scorpio, close to the white stretch of the milkyway. These three stars lie directly above this bright star in a staff like formation (very close to a straight line).

Name :

"*Anuradha*" translates simply into "Another *Radha*" or "After Radha". Its alternative meaning is "Subsequent Success". This name, as we can see, has its root in the fact that it follows the asterism Radha (*Vishakha*). Even though it is not apparent straightaway, the often ignored fact is that these two asterisms (Vishakha & Anuradha) form a pair in the same way as *Purvaphalguni* and *Uttaraphalguni*.

Symbol :

A 'staff', the main symbol of this asterism, is directly derived from the shape ancient Vedic seers ascribed to its constituent stars. The staff has always been seen as a symbol of power and protection.

In the puranic lore most of the exalted sages carry a staff. It is in fact the only weapon that they carry, but it is usually more than enough as it carries within itself all the power of their penance.

The readers can refer to the puranic story of *Vishwamitra* challenging *Sage Vashishta*, where all of Vishwamitra's weapons including the *Brahmastra* (similar to a nuclear missile) were useless against Vashishta's staff. These sages never used a staff for offensive purposes. It is only used for self-defence. It typifies wisdom and learning and thus can only act in congruence with the Universal mind. This nakshatra relates to learning and the retention of learning. It also relates to one's relationship with the Universal force. The stronger the contact, the more powerful the effect of this nakshatra becomes.

A 'lotus' is another symbol ascribed by scholars and sages to this nakshatra. Since ancient times, the qualities of purity, auspiciousness, knowledge and enlightenment have been associated with the lotus. In fact *Saraswati*, the goddess of learning and *Laxmi*, the goddess of prosperity, are often depicted as sitting atop a lotus.

A lotus has the ability to grow in muddy waters. This represents the ability of this nakshatra to keep itself pure and *sattwic* in any surroundings. It also signifies the attainment of knowledge through the muddy puddles of mental, intellectual and emotional confusion.

A 'triumphant gateway adorned with leaves' is another alternative symbol of this nakshatra. The readers will remember that the preceding asterism, Vishakha, also has this as its main symbol. As we mentioned earlier, Vishakha is a sort of a ally or co-worker of Anuradha. Just like Vishakha, Anuradha also represents victory.

It is also a goal centred nakshatra in much the same way as its ally, but its goals are usually more in tune with universal plan. It also likes to attain its goals through group work rather than going it alone. This is probably the reason why Anuradha attains its goals more smoothly and effortlessly, in comparison to Vishakha. Vishakha is often reluctant to take help or cooperate with allies. In my experience, I have seen that Vishakha, more often than not, needs allies to attain its goals. In most cases this ally is Anuradha.

Deity :

Mitra, one of the twelve *Adityas* (solar deities) rules Anuradha. The name 'Mitra' translates into 'friend'. Thus it comes as no surprise that he is the solar deity related to friendships, good faith and cordiality. His qualities infuse this nakshatra with lightheartedness, warmth, leadership, friendliness, helpfulness and a generally optimistic view of life. Mitra's concern for friendship can be seen from the fact that he is never invoked alone. He is always invoked along with either *Varun* (the ruling deity of *Shatabishak*) or *Aryaman* (the ruling deity of *Uttaraphalguni*). One can easily deduce from the above that Anuradha is most friendly with these two nakshatras.

If it weren't for Mitra, the world would be a much more dangerous place to live in. All the natural qualities usually associated with the sign Aquarius correlate to Mitra as well as Anuradha. It is interesting to note that Anuradha lies in the 10th house for those born with Aquarius rising. Under the guidance of Mitra, sometimes even enemies can work together in order to achieve a goal. The readers can refer to the "Churning of the Ocean" story in the author's previous work "*The Rahu-Ketu Experience*", *Sagar* Publications, India or "*The Key Of Life*", *Lotus Press*, USA where bitter enemies, gods and demons agreed to work together for attaining certain ends.

Since Anuradha is so concerned with learning and accumulation of knowledge, *Saraswati,* the goddess of learning, can be said to be strongly connected to this nakshatra. This is the only way one can explain the musical prowess of this nakshatra. As we have seen earlier, Saraswati always sits on a lotus (a symbol of Anuradha) with a *Vina* (stringed instrument).

Nature & Functioning :

The keyword for Anuradha is 'exploration'. This exploration, however, is not a lonesome ordeal, but a joyous, communal combination of people and energies. Anuradha brings to life the hidden secrets of nature's functionings through establishing a bridge between naturally discordant energies.

Anuradha fosters communication between all the extremes - the young and the old; the mature and immature; the more evolved and the less evolved; the different races, castes etc. Anuradha can thus be seen as a universal solvent. Most of Anuradha's tendencies put it outside the orthodox , social gambit. This is the reason why it falls in the heart of Scorpio, a sign which questions and grows out of the social sensibilities represented by the sign Libra. In a way, Anuradha is the nakshatra of the revolutionaries, who rebel against outdated ways of thinking and being. In the present times, Anuradha is one of the nakshatras which has the ability to see through the reality behind all the fake media propaganda on social, economic and political levels.

The fact that Anuradha is open to all doesn't mean that it doesn't discriminate. Evolved Anuradha natives are in fact quite discriminative and cautious as to who they let into their inner circle. In the present day and age, where every nakshatra's energy has been utilized for negative ends, Anuradha falls prey to excessive openness and frivolous friendships.

The logic oriented approach of this nakshatra accounts for the fact that many Anuradha natives are attracted to material sciences like mathematics and physics. The ability of Anuradha to combine logic, intuition and freedom of thought produces deep thinkers in every field. Numbers are something which takes Anuradha's fancy like no other thing. A lot of Anuradha natives have a strong interest either in occult or mundane numerology or statistics. Anuradha always tries to broaden its horizons in relation to its area of interest. The more evolved the soul, the more all encompassing the vision.

Natives with strong influence of Anuradha on their ascendant are born with stout hairy bodies. They have prominent chest and thighs and have a tendency to develop a belly with age. Their face conveys a sense of friendliness and well-being. A slight hint of secrecy emanates from the eyes and the overall demeanour in general. Their social behaviour fluctuates between passivity and exuberance. Combining friendliness with aloofness is their special gift.

Anuradha natives are usually seen making special effort to put people at ease and love to act as a bridge between people, groups and organizations. They are very interested in anything to do with the occult and hidden issues in general. They are extremely sensitive on an emotional plane even though they like to put up a tough impenetrable exterior.

It is their ability to keep up solid exteriors which makes them good organizers. Anuradha natives are often seen to be the founders and leaders of organizations. They have original minds which are melting pots of myriad pieces of knowledge, understanding and experience.

Most Anuradha natives channel their emotional energy in the form of devotion to some higher deity, universal energy or cause. Anuradha natives are at their most versatile when they have to combine their talents with others. Despite their need for constant interaction, most Anuradha natives have to spend a lot of time alone at one time of their lives or the other.

Curiosity makes them travel a lot, especially to foreign lands. They have quite an easy time relating to and adjusting to foreign environments in comparision to other nakshatras. In fact, living in foreign lands is usually very satisfying and fruitful for them.

In the universal scheme of things, Anuradha relates to "*radhana shakti*" - the power of worship. Its symbolism has ascension above and descension below. This symbolism stresses upon Anuradha's ability to explore and understand both the lower and higher *lokas* through its devotion to universal energies.

Mode of Functioning :

Anuradha is considered to be a Passive nakshatra. By itself, Anuradha is a highly passive energy, just like a seesaw in its stationary balanced position. It usually requires an external agency in the form of co-workers/friends to put it into action. Its passive quality often results from Saturn overpowering Mars, while its activity results from the martian and saturnine energies being in equal balance.

Caste :

It belongs to the *Shudra* caste. This classification obviously relates to the fact that Saturn, the Shudra planet, is the planetary ruler of Anuradha. Anuradha is a service orientated nakshatra. Even a leader is nothing but servant to those he leads.

Gender :

It is a Male nakshatra. This classification relates to its male presiding deity and its association with the male planet Mars. Anuradha represents the masculine force, which tries to open up and look through the wheel of nature.

Bodyparts & Humor (Ayurvedic Constitution) :

Breasts, Stomach, Bowels and the Womb are the body parts related to this nakshatra.

It is a primarily "*Pitta*" (fiery) nakshatra. Anuradha relates to all the electrical and astral fires within our body. The astral fires are carried by the three channels *Ida*, *Pingala* and *Sushumna*.

Direction :

It is related primarily to north, south and west.

Padas (Quarters) :

The first pada or quarter of this asterism 3° 20' - 6° 40' Scorpio falls in Leo Navamsa ruled by Sun. The emphasis here is on understanding one's inner self and applying that understanding in the outer world through career etc. The tendency towards excessive pride or militancy has to be curbed here if one wants positive expression of the intense energy available here. Sun, Mars, Jupiter and Ketu are especially strong in this pada.

The second pada or quarter of this asterism 6° 40' - 10° 00' Scorpio falls in Virgo Navamsa ruled by Mercury. This pada is all about continuous learning, discipline, discrimination, group work and organization. This pada delves into the mysteries of the Universe and in doing so takes the mystery out of them. Numbers, calculation and classification are its domain. Being a Pushkara navamsa pada it promises fulfillment of objectives. Mercury & Rahu are especially strong here.

The third pada or quarter of this asterism 10° 00' - 13° 20' Scorpio falls in Libra Navamsa ruled by Venus. The concerns here can range from arts, music, bohemia to occult. There is always a certain degree of self-undoing and wastefulness associated with this pada. Planets here give a highly sociable nature. Venus and Saturn suit this pada's energies more than the other planets.

The fourth pada or quarter of this asterism 13° 20' - 16° 40' Scorpio falls in Scorpio Navamsa ruled by Mars. There is abundant energy available here to pursue all kinds of esoteric and exoteric goals. Only struggle here lies in channeling the energy constructively in tune with Universal functionings. Planets here function from a plane of excessive passion and emotion. They can give the ability to achieve much if the rest of the nativity supports it. Sun, Jupiter, and Ketu are better suited to handling the energy of this pada.

Professions :

Hypnotists & Psychic Mediums; Occultists; Institution & Organization Heads; Astrologers; Spies; All occupations involving Night Duty; Photographers; Cinema related professions in general; Musicians; Artists; Managers; Industrialists; Promoters; Counsellers; Psychologists; Scientists; Numerologists; Statisticians; Mathematicians; Explorers; Miners; Factory Workers; Diplomats; All professions connected with dealing with Foreign Countries, Travel and Foreigners; All professions requiring group activity.

Places :

Forests; Mountains; Caves & Caverns; Lakes; Isolated Landscapes; Old Ruins, Castles etc; Stadiums; Metropolis; Technological & Industrial areas; Study & Research Places; Temples & other places used for the Practice and Study of Religion and Occult/Spiritual Topics; Places of Occult Significance; Organization Headquarters; All places connected with the above mentioned professions.

Guna (Essence) and Tattwa (Element) :

It is supposed to be a *Tamasic* (inert) nakshatra. This classification comes about due to its relationship with Mars and Saturn, two inherently tamasic planets. It is Anuradha's job to create evolution through the balancing of two opposing tamasic tendencies. Evolution on all planes takes place by taking the middle path. Even though Anuradha is a tamasic nakshatra, it has the power to bring about spiritual flowering through inner gentleness and balancing of opposites.

It belongs to the Fire element. Its relationship with the fiery planet Mars is responsible for this classification. Anuradha's fire is more like fire over water, unlike the explosive petrol fire of Aries. Its fieriness is responsible for its warmth, friendship and associations.

Gana (Type) :

It is considered a *Deva* or godly nakshatra. This classification is clear from its soft, mild and tender mode of functioning. Anuradha is the nakshatra which strives to create harmony and understanding at all levels of existence. Besides making humans work with each other, it has the capacity to make the gods, demons, humans, serpents and sages all work together for a common cause.

Orientation & Disposition :

It is a Level nakshatra in keeping with its balanced nature. Since the main task of Anuradha is to balance out the energies of two contrary planets Mars and Saturn, it has to work in a level way.

It is a "*Mridu*" or soft, tender and mild nakshatra. The best way to understand this classification is to think about Anuradha's symbol, a lotus. A lotus is a soft and tender flower with a mild scent. This just goes to show that Anuradha's approach to uncovering the wheel of nature isn't that of a forceful warrior, but that of a gentle lover.

Lunar Month & Day :

It relates to the second half of the lunar month of *Vaishakha*. This month usually corresponds to middle or late May in the solar calendar.

Anuradha is also related to the *Dvadashi* (12th tithi or day) of the waxing and waning phases of the Moon's monthly cycle.

Auspicious Activities :

Group related activities; Research & Study in the sciences or occult subjects; Meditation; Exploring nature; Favourable for managerial activities requiring on the spot decision making; Good for travel; Immigration & dealing with all foreign affairs; Healing; Spending time with friends; Finances & Accounting; Quiet reflection; Secretive Activities.

Inauspicious Activities :

Marriage; Not good for activities requiring direct confrontation; Not good for inaugurations or beginnings; Unfavourable for routine, mundane activities.

Planetary Ruler :

Mars, Pluto, Saturn and Ketu are the planets connected to this nakshatra. Saturn is the main planetary ruler here and its strong influence is evident in the discipline inherent in Anuradha. Saturn makes Anuradha serious about life in general. It makes Anuradha natives go beyond superficial layers of regular social interactions and search for the answers to the mysteries of life. It gives them an ability to understand and then transcend the limitations of the material realm. A well-defined sense of purpose for one's existence is sought here through the influence of the two main karmic planets - Saturn and Ketu.

Ketu is responsible for this nakshatra's foray into occult and the unseen hidden realms of existence. Mars provides the initiative, impulse and energy necessary for any exploration. Pluto expands the conscious and sub-conscious boundaries allowing Anuradha to tap into collective rather than personal concerns.

Mars-Saturn conjunctions or mutual aspects, especially when they are placed in Saturnine signs or nakshatras, carry an energy similar to that of Anuradha. Saturn-Pluto, Ketu-Pluto, Saturn-Mars-Pluto conjunctions also partly carry energies similar to that of Anuradha.

All planets have an ability to function in a beneficial way in this Nakshatra. Like always, their level of beneficiality depends upon the overall tone of the nativity and the evolutionary status of the native.

Vowel s and Alphabets :

The first pada or quarter of this asterism 3° 20' -6° 40' Scorpio corresponds to "Na" as in Nassau.

The second pada or quarter of this asterism 6° 40' - 10° 00' Scorpio corresponds to "Ni" as in Nickel.

The third pada or quarter of this asterism 10° 00' -13° 20' Scorpio corresponds to "Nu" as in Nutan.

The fourth pada or quarter of this asterism 13° 20' - 16° 40' Scorpio corresponds to "Ne" as in Neha.

In the Sanskrit alphabet Anuradha corresponds to "Tam", "Tham" and "Dam" consequently its mantras are "Om Tam", "Om Tham" and "Om Dam".

Sexual Type and Compatibility :

Its sexual animal is a Deer. Deer qualities like shyness, gentleness, delicacy and fickleness are expressed in the sexual behaviour of those under the influence of this nakshatra. Anuradha is most compatible with the other deer nakshatra *Jyeshta*.

For marital & sexual compatibility with other nakshatras please refer to the tables on pages 468 & 469.

Esoteric :

Anuradha, being the seventeenth nakshatra, relates to the number '17'. This number is usually seen as a bringer of celestial waters down to the earth plane. It allows for a safe refuge from the vicissitudes of life. It must be mentioned here that Anuradha is the nakshatra presiding over the science of Numerology. The Universe, in a way, is a game of numbers and Numerology forms the backbone of all esoteric sciences like Astrology. Anuradha is a decoder of the secret functionings of the universe.

The real function of Anuradha, however, relates to the movement of *kundalini* (serpent energy) through the *chakras* (seven sacral centres). The awakening of the kundalini from its dormant state in the *Muladhara Chakra* happens under the energies of *Ashlesha*. After Ashlesha, Anuradha is the first nakshatra where a full scale exploration of all the chakras takes place. This exploration usually bears a lot of fruits within the same lifetime - one's old *karmas* get nullified and one gets access to universal functionings. The bodily nerves become capable of carrying direct, astral, causal impressions. In other words, one becomes friends with the universe.

Out of this friendship comes harmony and balance in one's thoughts and actions. If the full potential of Anuradha is utilized, there is no karma being birthed through actions and only a seeking for knowledge and enlightenment remains.

The story of how Anuradha becomes friends with the universe starts with its pair nakshatra *Radha* (*Vishakha*). Once one has utilized Vishakha's one pointed approach to dedicate oneself to one of the governing energies of the universe, it is but natural that a very friendly and intimate rapport will be established by the time Anuradha comes along.

More is expected out of Anuradha than just personal enlightenment. Anuradha is supposed to share its experiences and accumulated knowledge with its fellow beings (souls). This spreading of knowledge is meant to be in a coded form, so that it only reaches those who are ripe enough to receive it. The story of Sage *Vishwamitra* (the name translates into "friend of the whole world"), who went on to become a *Brahmarishi* (the highest post in the hierarchy of the sages) from an ordinary king, encompasses the various aspects of Anuradha's functionings from a universal standpoint.

Gotra (Celestial Lineage) :

This nakshatra is related to the Sage *Angiras*, one of the seven celestial sages looking after the affairs of our galaxy. The name of this sage translates into "the fiery one". The association of Anuradha with this particular rishi is not very apparent except for the fact that Anuradha falls in the sign Scorpio ruled by the fiery planets Mars, Ketu and Pluto.

Remedial :

For those suffering from bad effects resulting from afflictions to this nakshatra, the best remedial measure is worship of the eight *Vasus*. Alternatively one can worship the half *Vishnu*, half *Shiv* form commonly known as *Hari Har*. The practice of *Raj Yog*, which involves the raising of the kundalini through the seven sacred centres is one of the best ways to utilise this nakshatra's potential.

Repetition of the root mantra of this nakshatra - "Om Yam" and "Om Ram" 108 times when Moon transits this nakshatra and in its corresponding lunar month is sure to reduce suffering and bring enlightenment into a person's life.

Persons who are benefiting from the positive energy of this nakshatra can also increase the good effects through the above mentioned ways. It is helpful for them to wear colours like red, blue and gold. They should use its directions, lunar month and the days when Moon transits Anuradha to undertake all important actions.

Example :

Anuradha's sound and light can be experienced at -

http://osfa.org.uk/anuradha.htm

Miscellaneous :

According to *Varahamihira*, Moon in Anuradha makes one "wealthy, a traveller, living in foreign countries and one needs to satisfy their appetite immediately as they find it difficult to bear hunger".

* * *

18. Jyeshta   16°40' Scorpio - 30°00' Scorpio

18.

Jyeshta

(16°40' Scorpio - 30°00' Scorpio)

In the Sky :

Jyeshta, the senior most among the first eighteen asterisms, consists of 'three stars in a row', which were seen by the ancients as forming a shape similar to an ear-ring (or in some cases the top of an umbrella) . These three stars are known in modern astronomy as *Alpha-Scorpionis* (*Antares*), *Sigma-Scorpionis* and *Tau-Scorpionis*. All of these stars lie in the middle to end portion of the zodiacal constellation of Scorpio. Antares, the star with a reddish hue, is the brightest among these stars with a visual magnitude of 1.07 and was revered by all ancient cultures. It is in fact one of the brightest objects in the night sky, which makes it easy for one to spot this asterism in the night sky.

Name :

"*Jyeshta*" translates simply into the "Eldest" or "Seniormost". As is the case with some other asterisms, Jyeshta's name immediately reveals a lot about its nature and functioning. Jyeshta is considered the eldest among the first eighteen nakshatras. At some point of time in ancient history, only eighteen nakshatras were in use and Jyeshta was the final, the senior most or eldest nakshatra. Since then more nakshatras have been added, but the name has stayed.

Symbol :

Its main symbol is a 'round talisman'. In all the ancient civilizations and legends, one can see that a round talisman is seen as a symbol of divine protection. In many cases, one will find that it is also a symbol of an authoritarian position.

A circular earring is also a sort of round talisman and all the kings of the past were expected to wear big, round earrings. Thus an 'earring' can also be seen as a symbol of this nakshatra.

A round talisman, ring or earring are all considered to be related to the governing forces of the universe. As all wise men have known throughout the ages, everything in nature happens in circles. In ancient times, the king was supposed to be the person who is representative of the higher governing forces on earth. The fact that he used this circle symbolism showed that he was connected to these forces.

One can automatically infer that this nakshatra relates to all those in authority positions. This authority is usually conferred on one for their relative proximity to the governing universal forces. This may be the result of repeated past life efforts in the fields of karma, occult practices and penance.

The most important example of a circular occult symbol is the *Ouroboros*, a coiled snake swallowing its tail. The serpent symbolism relates to Rahu and Ketu and the *kundalini shakti*. The reader can refer to the author's *previous work "The Rahu-Ketu Experience"*, *Sagar Publications, India or "The Key of Life", Lotus Press*, USA.

An 'umbrella' is an alternative symbol of this nakshatra. The most basic function of an umbrella is to protect one from rain, sun or wind i.e. nature's forces. In the same way this nakshatra is supposed to provide protection against the universal forces. This is the reason why all kings and queens in olden days never went out without an umbrella on top of their head. It was the most visible royal insignia.

This protection usually comes about through a detailed understanding of the occult knowledge of Universal functions. In a way, the priestly class was the protective shield for a king. In today's day and age where most of the masses are totally ignorant of the occult and have little knowledge of Universal functionings, the truly protective aspect of this nakshatra is rarely seen. However the politicians and the ruling class of today do take the aid of occult practices in secret (away from public view), to protect their power and position.

Deity :

Indra, the scion of the Gods, is the main governing deity of this nakshatra. It is important to mention here that Indra is just a post, which different souls occupy at different times. A soul who has done enough penance is put on this post. In the same way Jyeshta has the capacity to bestow an authority position here on earth as a result of past life efforts.

The word "Indra" translates into "a celestial drop". This meaning can be looked at in different ways. Indra, even though he is a king of the gods, is a mere drop as far as the universe is concerned. On the other hand, we can see that this meaning relates well to the fact that Indra was regarded as the rain god in most of the ancient cultures.

Around five thousand years ago, Indra was the most worshipped among all the deities. The *Vedas,* especially the earlier ones, are full of remarks about his splendour and glory. His worship survived even up to a period around 500 B.C., as can be inferred from the fact that the Norse worshipped a thunder god known as "*Thor*". This thunder god was supposed to wield a thunder bolt in much the same way as Indra, who is always portrayed with a thunder bolt in his hand.

Rain was important to all civilizations because agriculture was directly equated with prosperity. It is no wonder then, that this nakshatra is related to prosperity on the material plane of existence. In a way this nakshatra also conveys a certain strong concern for prosperity, in much the same way as people in the olden days eagerly awaited the rains to fall. When the rainfall is irregular, it can destroy agriculture rather than support it. This brings out the fact that this nakshatra can, at many times, bring about depravity and hard times instead of prosperity. This can also be seen from the fact that when the rulers of a nation are corrupt and greedy, its subjects will encounter adversity.

With the invention of new technologies, the dependence of agriculture on rain diminished and so did the worship of Indra. *Krishn* can be said to be the first one who turned the common people away from the worship of Indra. He encouraged them to establish direct communication with the forces of nature instead. After all Indra's power only relies on his connection with these forces. Even today, the ruling elite go to great lengths to maintain this connection, while the common people toil away mindlessly.

Indra comes out as a robustious, proud, vain, tricky and unreliable character in most of the puranic stories. Most of the elements of his nature are conveyed through this nakshatra. In this way Jyeshta is very similar to *Vishakha*, the other nakshatra ruled by Indra. Jyeshta, however, is much more controlled, secretive and deliberating in comparison to Vishakha. One can say that Jyeshta functions in a positive or negative way depending on who the Indra is at any given point in time. In a birthchart however, an afflicted Jyeshta will tend to bring out the negative qualities like depravation, misuse of power and authority, unnecessary vanity etc.; while a well fortified Jyeshta will bring about prosperity, genuine concern and protectiveness towards others.

One peculiarity of Jyeshta is that it gives prosperity only through some occult, supernatural or extraordinary means. This arises from the fact that Indra always gets his position and power through penance and other occult activities. He even got his thunderbolt through the occult propitiation of a sage called *Dadhichi*. Interested readers can refer to "*Amar Chitra Katha*" comics for puranic stories related to Indra.

Nature & Functioning :

"A sense of arriving or becoming" characterizes Jyeshta. Jyeshta completes the second series of nine nakshatras beginning from *Magha*. This series is mostly to do with involvement in worldly activities on the earthly plane.

Jyestha is a nakshatra where keeping up an image is more important than anything else. Jyeshta natives usually do everything from a point of view which cares a great deal about how others are perceiving them. They want to gain respect in society and do whatever is necessary to adhere to the prevailing standards. In ancient times when real acts of charity, kindness and philanthropy were the stepping stones to a respectful position, Jyeshta functioned well. In the present day and age where excessive headless materialism is the standard, Jyeshta energy gets channelled in useless, self-destructive ways. The stereotypical mob leaders, corrupt and unwise politicians, beaurocrats and managers are all Jyeshta characters.

Natives with Jyeshta rising or having strong Jyeshta influence connected to the Ascendant, usually mature very quickly both physically and mentally. They have well proportioned bodies but are not able to hold onto their youth for long. Their upper body is usually stronger than their lower body. The easiest way to spot them is to pay attention to their penetrating and probing eyes.

Jyeshta natives are apt to magnify their troubles and woes. There is no beating Jyeshta when it comes to unnecessary, exaggerated moaning and groaning. The continent of Africa is under strong influence of Jyeshta energy. It is no wonder then that the "*Blues*" as a musical art form, came from this continent.

A revengeful and vindictive tendency is often noticed in Jyeshta natives. They also fall prey to jealousy very easily and are always on the lookout to put others down. A strong competitive spirit rather than an internal direction is what makes them manifest the full extent of their abilities.

The goodness of Jyeshta natives lies in their ability to be protective towards the weak, subordinate, helpless and underprivileged. They can purge themselves headlong into danger in order to protect others. Besides sticking to their word, they have a responsible attitude to the affairs that fall under their domain. However at times they can also carry their sense of responsibility and protectiveness to extremes. In today's day and age, most of Jyeshta's functioning is confined to the military, police and similar Martian pursuits. Since all these forces are guided and controlled by a dark elite there is no real sense in zealously identifying oneself with these branches.

Mode of Functioning :

Jyeshta is considered to be an Active nakshatra. Once again, we will take help from the policing profession to fathom Jyeshta's active nature. Being a policeman, one is expected to be ready and alert 24 hours a day as they can be called anytime for duty. It is a profession which involves constant vigil, activity and responsibility. It is noticed that Jyeshta types usually get depressed when their circumstances don't allow for constant activity of some kind.

Caste :

It belongs to the Servant caste. The servant caste was seen by the ancient seers as being involved in different forms of servitude. It is hard to understand why the supposed eldest among the first eighteen nakshatras should be relegated to servitude. The only reason we can think of is that Jyeshta is not skilled in any particular art, trade or profession. It is like Indra, whose activities can't be categorised under any of the four main castes *Brahmin*, *Kshatriya*, *Vaishya* and *Shudra*. Indra is neither a priest, nor a soldier, nor a businessman and he is no manual labourer either. We have already seen that Jyeshta types always end up in service professions like police officers, etc.

Gender :

It is a Female nakshatra. Jyeshta is often portrayed as the eldest and senior most queen. Even Indra as a character seems to have predominantly feminine attitudes and attributes. The old, seasoned, jealous, stern and lonely queen archetype fits Jyeshta like a glove.

Bodyparts & Humor (Ayurvedic Constitution):

The neck and right side of the torso are the body parts related to this nakshatra. In a lot of ancient cultures, the eldest queen was supposed to have the most elaborate neck ornamentation to signify her senior most status. Even today in some parts of Africa, huge necklings are used for signifying status. In some cases the necks are elongated by using larger and larger size necklings.

It is a primarily "*Vata*" (airy) nakshatra. This again must relate to its relationship with Mercury, a primarily vata planet. Jyeshta, as we have seen, belongs to the air element. Its classification under the Vata humor re-emphasizes its airy aspect.

Direction :

It is related primarily to north and south.

Padas (Quarters) :

The first pada or quarter of this asterism 16° 40' - 20° 00' Scorpio falls in Sagittarius Navamsa ruled by Jupiter. The emphasis here is on family concerns and interests. This pada is very concerned about financial affairs even though its prosperity in that area will swing from one extreme to the other. The lesson here is to take a more easy going attitude in regards to finances. A certain enthusiasm towards acquiring higher knowledge is noticeable here. The normally secretive Jyeshta tends to leak out secrets through Sagittarian carefreeness and frankness. The native is a risk taker. Generosity is more prominent in this pada in comparision to other Jyeshta padas. The native is chivalrous in terms of being protective towards kith and kin. Planets here have a sense of humour. Sun, Mars, Jupiter & Ketu are strong here and Jupiter tends to give the best results. Planets placed in this pada adversely affect the wellbeing of one's siblings.

The second pada or quarter of this asterism 20° 00' - 23° 20' Scorpio falls in Capricorn Navamsa ruled by Saturn. This pada is very rigid in regards to responsibility and doing the right thing. Natives here are fiercely protective and like to challenge others. This pada produces authority type figures. This pada can be selfish, stingy, materialistic and vengeful. The native is ruthless in regards to getting back at others. A strong sense of maturity is seen in the physical and mental make-up of the native from an early age. The native has an authoritative speaking voice. This pada is very serious and overbearing and will tend to take its time to achieve its goals. The native usually only achieves their goals late in life after much hardwork, perseverance and penance. Natives are cautious, slow and stern. They need to watch a tendency towards too much skepticism, melancholy and negative attitudes in general. Mars & Saturn are strong here in the sense that they give some sort of position of authority. Planets placed in this pada adversely affect the wellbeing of younger siblings.

The third pada or quarter of this asterism 23° 20' - 26° 40' Scorpio falls in Aquarius Navamsa ruled by Saturn. This pada gives a strong humanitarian instinct and allows the native to play roles which are beneficial or protective towards society. The native works best in professions which involve protecting the underdog or underprivileged. They like serving causes. The native can be very sacrificing when it comes to protecting others. This pada gives a love for researching science or mysticism. The native has their own peculiar brand of family values. The native enjoys espousing their personal philosophy to others. The native gets caught up in bizarre sexual encounters. Saturn, Mercury & Venus & Rahu are strong in this pada. Planets placed in this pada adversely affect the wellbeing of one's mother.

The fourth pada or quarter of this asterism 26° 40' - 30° 00' Scorpio falls in Pisces Navamsa ruled by Jupiter. This is a very emotional pada and the native is inclined to get carried away. The native can simply drown themselves. There is a danger of too much indulgence in fantasy, sexual intrigue and intoxication. The native may be able to channel their emotions into creative expression. The native carries their sense of responsibility and protectiveness to an extreme at times. In its lowest aspect, natives are apt to fantasize about their woes and troubles in life in an unhealthy way. In its highest aspect, this pada can give a strong sacrificing nature and a spiritual devotion to humanity. The native will be fond of children. The native will defend the rights of others and take an interest in occult exploration for liberation purposes. The only downfall is that the penance aspect which is so necessary for Jyeshta 's proper functioning is difficult to harness in this pada. However Jyeshta's capacity for material gain is stronger in this pada and its poverty aspect is decreased. This is true when strong benefics like Venus and Jupiter are placed here. Mars functions poorly in this pada, however Saturn, although giving material adversity, may be helpful in acquiring some sort of spiritual discipline. This pada tends to be the most self destructive, when working through its negative aspect.

Professions :

All Policing Professions; Government Officials; Administrative Posts of all types; Reporters; Radio & Television Commentators; Newsreaders; Talk Show Hosts; Actors; Orators; Firemen; Trade Unionists; Occultists (mainly Black Magicians); Detectives; Mafia; Politicians; Beaurocrats; Naval Professions; Forest Rangers; Military Professions in general; Salvation Army and other such 'Caring for the Aged' professions; Manual Labourers; Athletes, especially Sprinters; Telecommunication Industry related professions; Air Traffic Controllers and Radar Experts; Surgeons.

Places :

Hilly Inaccessible Terrain; Hot Tropical Jungles; Government Buildings; All places related to Telecommunications & Media in general; Airports; Hospitals; Military Bases; Capital Cities; Manors, Forts & Palaces; Old-Age Homes; All places connected with above-mentioned professions.

Guna (Essence) and Tattwa (Element) :

It is supposed to be a *Sattvic* nakshatra. This classification mainly relates to its elderly and protective aspect. As we have discussed earlier, Jyeshta is reverential towards its elders (or those more powerful than itself) and is protective towards its juniors or subordinates. Jyeshta is also sattwic in the sense that it is ready to sacrifice a lot of pleasures and enjoyments for the sake of its duties and commitments.

It belongs to the Air element. This relates to Mercury's strong association with Jyeshta. Behind its fixed and stern Mars exterior, Jyeshta is pretty light, floaty and airy in disposition. Jyeshta hankers for freedom and movement (which are natural qualities of the air element) but is usually constrained by its outer image, responsibilities or circumstances. For example, a police officer may like to join the crowd in a rock concert but he cannot do it because of his job and position.

Gana (Type) :

It is considered a *Rakshasa* or Demonic nakshatra. It is a surprise to find that the nakshatra whose ruling deity is king of the gods, is classified thus. A good look at stories and legends attached with Indra reveal that Indra at times surpasses the demons themselves, as far as demonic or unrighteous actions are concerned. Jyeshta's sense of right and wrong can get quite flawed because of its primarily selfish and self centred disposition.

Orientation & Disposition :

It is a Level nakshatra. Jyeshta's tendency to 'get even' is the first thing which comes up in regards to this classification. Jyeshta is always concerned with fair play, justice, balancing events and people. A policeman pursuing a murderer is in essence fuelled by Jyeshta's basic nature to get even. This 'getting even' tendency is found in gangster mentalities like the Mafia. The heads, dons or elders of Mafias are always playing the endless game of 'getting even' with each other.

It is a Hard, Sharp and Dreadful nakshatra. Just like the planet Mars, Jyeshta is not averse to activities requiring the above mentioned qualities. Jyeshta carries within itself most of the keywords associated with the sign Scorpio - hardness, coldness, focus, torture, punishment, attacking, arduousness and biting. Jyeshta represents the hard, stony and ferocious side of the sign Scorpio. Its brutality is well exemplified today by the police departments and the heads of organizations, corporations and institutions all around the world.

Lunar Month & Day :

It relates to the first half of the lunar month of *Jyaishtha.* This usually corresponds to late May/ early June in the solar calendar.

Jyeshta is also related to the *Saptami & Chaturdashi* (7th & 14th tithis or days) of the waxing and waning phases of the Moon's monthly cycle.

Auspicious Activities :

Harsh activities; Plotting; Spying; Scheming; Passing judgements; Getting even; Putting one's foot down over important issues; Taking control; Expressing one's authoritative nature out of a sense of caring; Administrative activities; Policing or monitoring situations; Occult activities; Acting responsibly; Acts of concern, care or protection; Associating with elders, especially giving assistance to the elderly; Taking care of family matters; Occult activities requiring a lot of penance; Holding discussions over serious issues; Grand planning; Acting restrained out of consideration for others; Setting disciplines for oneself.

Inauspicious Activities :

Wallowing in depression and resentment or having a hard done by attitude; Infidelity; Acts of selfishness or self-centricity; Taking advantage of others; Marriage; Healing; Too much rest or recreational activity; Any dealings which require a lot of tact, sensitivity and gentleness; Not good for travelling.

Planetary Ruler :

Mercury is the main planetary ruler of this nakshatra. Mercurial energy refines itself from its deceptive, cunning, childlike beginnings to a more serious energy, which tries to control the scattered functionings of the mind. Considering that Moon represents the mass mentality, Mercury's functioning here is directed to controlling that energy. It is no wonder then that Jyeshta natives feel like the police of the world.

Mars, the ruler of Scorpio, of course supports this policing mentality and provides the energy and initiative required for it. The Mercury-Mars combination can turn self-serving very quickly as the martian energy afflicts the perceptive and discriminative part of mercurial energy. Much of the deceit and misuse of power inherent in this nakshatra can be understood from the many tales about the unruly, boisterous behaviour of its ruling deity Indra, the scion of the demigods. Mercury makes Jyeshta a sort of a chameleon, whose values are not based upon any real understanding of things, but are dependent upon its surroundings.

Pluto and Ketu, being co-rulers of Scorpio along with Mars, also convey a part of Jyestha's energy in the form of self-destructive tendencies, outer and inner transformation, emotional upheaval and penance.

Mercury-Mars & Mercury-Mars-Ketu conjunctions in a chart, carry similar energies to Jyeshta. In the present day and age, most planets placed here need to be watched very carefully by the astrologer as they usually work against the native's peace of mind. Only a well placed Mercury can give good results here.

Vowel s and Alphabets :

The first pada or quarter of this asterism 16° 40' -20° 00' Scorpio corresponds to "No" as in Nora.

The second pada or quarter of this asterism 20° 00' - 23° 20' Scorpio corresponds to "Ya" as in Yagya.

The third pada or quarter of this asterism 23° 20' - 26° 40' Scorpio corresponds to "Yi" as in Year.

The fourth pada or quarter of this asterism 26° 40' - 30° 00' Scorpio corresponds to "Yu" as in Yule.

In the Sanskrit alphabet Jyeshta corresponds to "Dha" and consequently its mantra is "Om Dham".

Sexual Type :

Its sexual animal is a Stag. A stag is an aggressive sexual animal, as compared to a deer, which is the sexual animal for the previous nakshatra Anuradha. Jyeshta is supposed to have a cold, yet aggressively, passionate response towards lovemaking and likes to dominate the proceedings. It is not considered a very virile nakshatra even though it can get obsessive about sexuality.

For marital and sexual compatibility with other nakshatras please refer to the tables on pages 468 & 469.

Esoteric :

Being the 18th nakshatra, Jyeshta reflects the meaning associated with the number '18'. It is considered the culmination of Lunar energy. The tarot image associated with the 18th card, appropriately called "*The Moon*", depicts a night-time scene with two dogs howling at two towers, which form a gateway to a mysterious region beyond. A full moon hangs above on the horizon, while a crayfish is attempting to crawl out of a small pool in front. This predominantly dark imagery relates to a final confrontation with the hidden workings of the subconscious.

It is Jyeshta's task to constantly confront the mysteries, fears, illusions and pitfalls of the dark realms of the left hand side of nature. Jyeshta has to bring order into the scheme of things through the right use of the elemental forces. The catch here lies in knowing when to let nature take its course and when to interfere. Indra, along with the other elemental gods like *Agni* (fire deity) and *Varun* (water deity), is always trying to keep the balance in terrestrial affairs through confronting the dark demonic forces, who are repeatedly trying to disrupt nature's functionings. The danger here lies in folly, which arises out of an improper understanding of the Universal functionings. This is the point where the next nakshatra, *Mula*, takes over and tries to gain a root understanding of Universal functionings.

In the universal scheme of things, Jyeshta relates to " *arohana shakti*" - the power to rise above perils. Its symbolism has attack above and defence below. This imagery re-emphasizes the warrior aspect of Jyeshta. It is its task to conquer the demons of the subconscious and align the lower self in accordance with greater universal forces.

Gotra (Celestial Lineage) :

This nakshatra is related to the *Sage Atri*, one of the seven celestial sages looking after the affairs of our galaxy. The name of this sage translates into "one who devours". Going by the name, it seems that Atri has some sort of policing role in our galaxy and so it is appropriate that he presides over Jyeshta's energies.

Remedial :

For those suffering from bad effects resulting from afflictions to this nakshatra, the best remedial measure is the worship of *Vishnu* or fierce feminine deities like *Durga* and *Kali*.

Repetition of the root mantra of this nakshatra - "Om Dham" 108 times when Moon transits this nakshatra and during its corresponding lunar month, is sure to reduce suffering and bring enlightenment into a person's life.

Persons who are benefiting from the positive energy of this nakshatra can also increase the good effects through the above mentioned ways. It is helpful for them to wear colours like shades of blue, especially light blue, reds, black and dark green. They should use its directions, lunar month and the days when Moon transits Jyeshta to undertake all important actions.

Example :

Jyeshta's sound and light can be experienced at –

http://osfa.org.uk/jyeshta.htm

Miscellaneous :

According to *Varahamihira*, Moon in Jyeshta gives "an angry disposition, few friends, lustfulness, contentment and a sense of responsibility".

* * *

19. Mula 0°0' - 13°20' Sagittarius

19.

Mula

(00°00' Sagittarius - 13°20' Sagittarius)

In the Sky :

Mula, the first among the last nine asterisms, consists of a bunch of nine stars, which were seen by the ancients as forming a shape similar to a lion's tail. These nine stars are known in modern astronomy as *Lambda-Scorpionis (Shaula)*, *Epsilon-Scorpionis*, *Mu-1-Scorpionis*, *Iota-1-Scorpionis*, *Theta-Scorpionis*, *Eta-Scorpionis*, *Zeta-Scorpionis*, *Kappa-Scorpionis* & *Upsilon-Scorpionis* (*Lesath*). All of these stars lie in the end portion of the astronomical constellation of Scorpio, but astrologically they form the part of the sign Sagittarius. Their location corresponds to the center of the Milky Way which can be easily seen stretching across like a white river in the night sky. When we look at these stars in the night sky, we are basically looking towards the centre of our galaxy. Shaula and Lesath, having visual magnitudes of 1.63 & 2.68 respectively, are studded together and form the brightest part of this asterism.

Name :

"Mula" translates into "the Root", "the Center" or "the Innermost Core". In our view, nothing really needs to be said about this asterism's nature and functioning after its meaning is revealed. Mula is straight, direct and doesn't like to beat about the bush. However, we nevertheless have no option but to carry on with our dissection of its roots.

Symbol :

Its main symbol is a 'tied bunch of roots'. Both its name and symbol emphasize the word 'root' and this asterism literally relates to the 'root' of everything. The fact that the centre of our galaxy lies in it conveys the same idea. Just like its planetary ruler Ketu, this asterism deals with getting to the bottom/core of everything. In the trees and plants roots are usually hidden, which means that this nakshatra deals with all kinds of hidden things, realms, events, motives, propensities etc. The tied bunch of roots also symbolizes the restrictive aspect of this asterism.

The term 'root' has another meaning in the word 'rooted'. This nakshatra also relates to something properly rooted. This gives a strong foundation to the actions of this nakshatra. Its symbol also means collecting or tying up what belongs to one. Ketu, as we know, is the one who stores past karmas and releases the ones ripe enough to be experienced in the present life. It can help one collect the necessary tools from the past, which one requires in fulfilling one's goal in the present life. This is suggested by the symbolism of tied roots. Mula thus helps one put together in a meaningful way one's talents, which have developed in past lives.

Just as a tree's roots penetrate into the unseen realms beneath the earth's surface, Mula has a lot to do with investigation into things unseen or unknown. Along with its counterpart *Ardra,* (which lies directly opposite in the zodiac), Mula has the strongest and deepest sense of inquiry amongst all the nakshatras.

In ancient medicinal systems like *Ayurveda*, roots of various plants are used for medicinal purposes, thus Mula is directly associated with making medicines. In the same way, Mula also relates to the root of diseases, ie. microorganisms like virus, bacteria etc. Just like everything under Mula's jurisdiction, these microorganisms are invisible to the naked eye.

Finally, the fact that the roots are tied suggests an idea of constraint and limitation. As a result, Mula often does not allow too much freedom or scattering away of energies and makes one delve deeply within a limited sphere. In fact Mula is the most pinpointed in approach in comparison to the other nakshatras.

Deity :

Its presiding deity as per Vedic texts is the Goddess of dissolution and destruction known as *Nritti*, a name which translates into 'calamity'. She is supposed to be the daughter of *Adharma* (unrighteousness) and *Himsa* (violence) and the mother of *Mrityu* (death) and *Bhaya* (fear). Some texts also mention Nritti as a destructive demon, and some texts see her as *Alaxmi,* the opposite of *Laxmi* (goddess of wealth, abundance and prosperity).

In light of the above, it is not hard to see that this is not a very pleasant nakshatra. However, everything is not doom and gloom with this nakshatra. After all, it lies in the luckiest among the signs Sagittarius, which in turn is ruled by the greatest benefic Jupiter.

In the author's opinion, Mula is a very powerful nakshatra, even on the material plane. It can give worldly status, prosperity etc. The only thing is that it usually takes it all away from the native in question at some point. This, however, is not uncommon in the sense that death takes away all these things from everyone anyways.

Nritti shouldn't be seen as a goddess of poverty, misfortune and calamity. In fact, her nakshatra represents the peak of material achievement and the beginning of the spiritual impulse. Mula is the 19th nakshatra and '19' is a very lucky number for all types of material achievements.

Just like *Kali*, the fierce form of *Parvati*, her destructive aspect is always constructive in some sense. Her nakshatra promotes non-violence and all other such virtues after a proper understanding has been attained.

Nature & Functioning :

Mula's primary approach to life is to get to the root of things. It is a relentless nakshatra which will stop at nothing until it has exercised its will. Obviously not all natives under a strong influence of Mula are this extreme, but they do try to fully utilize whatever willpower is available at their command.

It is in Mula's nature to quickly cut out and destroy things that have lost their value. It is a very impulsive nakshatra. Much more often than not, it regrets its actions in hindsight. Only when its will is in tune with the Universal will, does Mula function in a wise Jupiterian way. The struggle between individuality and universality reaches its peak here, as individuality is at its peak expression.

The process of individualization begins in *Ashvini,* lionizes in *Magha* and culminates in Mula. The completed individual seeks experiences beyond the domain of ego and selfcentredness. Having said this, Mula is still quite a proud and haughty nakshatra. Mula natives, however, are unable to comprehend their own power and abilities. In some cases, this is a good thing, as their ability to inflict damage upon themselves and others is restricted by their ignorance.

Its dreadful and demoniac side comes from the negative functioning of Ketu in its lower aspects. It is a powerful asterism which can give dominion and lordship. This can sometimes breed ego, vanity and arrogance which can lead one to perform abominable and demoniac actions. *Ravan* and *Kamsa,* two main villainical characters in *Ramayan* and *Mahabharat* respectively, are associated with this asterism. They started harassing and killing without discrimination after gaining influence and power. This asterism can give power and influence, as it follows the nakshatra known as *Jyeshta* or the Eldest, which signifies the height of material accomplishment. This asterism relates to the state after one has successfully conquered the material realm.

Among the body parts, it relates to the feet, which emphasizes its capacity to take heavy responsibility, just as the feet take up the load of the body. As suggested by the symbolism of tied roots, it helps one put together in a meaningful way one's talents, which have developed in past lives. Although it may sound bizarre, it also promotes non-violence and protects the good. It is also a magical nakshatra, which either confers magical powers or helps those in need in sudden magical ways. This asterism gives both good or bad results in a blazing explosive way. It is usually triumphant in all sorts of warfare, but a downfall does take place at some point of time.

Natives with Mula relating to the ascendant have prominent noses, ears and thick lower lips. They can't be classified as attractive in the general sense of the word, even though they have a peculiar magnetism, especially in the case of highly evolved souls. It is usually quite easy to spot Mula types in a crowd. They usually display one form of arrogance or other in their dealings with others. Sarcasm, boldness and reservedness go hand in hand in Mula's behavioural patterns. There is a tendency to overtly dramatize or underplay situations. Mula natives have peculiar ways of looking at any given situation, which often puts them at odds with those around them. A degree of over-eagerness is seen when it comes to taking drastic actions or measures to resolve situations or problems. Their special talent lies in getting to the root of any matter at hand without any unnecessary beating about the bush. However, this straightforward, direct approach lands them in trouble when their judgement is skewed.

Mode of Functioning :

Mula is considered to be an Active nakshatra. Mula is essentially a seeker on all planes of existence. Just like the sign Sagittarius, it is very proactive in this seeking. It is its active nature which makes Mula more scary in comparison to the other demonic and *tamasic* nakshatras. As we have discussed earlier, Mula doesn't waste too much time in converting thoughts into actions. Since most of Mula's activities like death are feared, not many people are able to creatively harness its active energies.

Caste :

It belongs to the Butcher caste. This obviously is in reference to Mula's destructive quality. It is Mula's job to cut away anything which has outlived its usefulness. There are different types of butchery eg. a man cutting up animals in an abattoir, Kali cutting off demon's heads (refer to the image) or an ascetic cutting off his desires and attachments. Obviously we can see that there is a sense of right and wrong here and not all butcheries are bad. Death, which is essentially cutting the cord between the astral and physical body, is a kind of universal butchery, which in a way is a liberating and regenerative process.

Gender :

It is a Neutral nakshatra. As far as gender is concerned, Mula represents the neutral aspect of Ketu. This is why its presiding deity is sometimes seen as a goddess and sometimes as a male demon. After all, the centre of the galaxy and the root of all things cannot have a gender bias.

Bodyparts & Humor (Ayurvedic Constitution) :

Among the body parts it relates to the Feet, which emphasizes its capacity to take heavy responsibility, just as the feet take up the load of the whole body. It also relates to the left side of the torso.

It is a primarily "*Vata*" (airy) nakshatra. Trying to understand this classification is like trying to understand the nature of a black hole. One would expect Mula to be a primarily *Pitta* (fiery) nakshatra considering its connection with Ketu, Jupiter and Sagittarius. We will however try and give a small explanation here:

The Vata humor is directly connected to the *prana* (astral life force) in the body. The process of breathing is the essential dividing line between life and death. Since Mula relates to only the root processes, it has to relate to the Vata humor.

Direction :

It is related primarily to Southwest, Northwest, Northeast and East. However it is mainly connected with the "centre" or the "middle".

Padas (Quarters) :

The first pada or quarter of this asterism 00° 00' -3° 20' Sagittarius falls in Aries Navamsa ruled by Mars. This pada relates to all types of deep searches and probes. These can take place on material or spiritual planes depending upon the evolutionary status of the native in question. The outlook here is hopeful and optimistic if Ketu is well placed. A certain degree of erratic egotism and selfcentredness can be noticed when this pada is working through its lower aspect. Planets, especially Moon, when placed in this pada are supposed to be harmful for the wellbeing of the father. Sun, Jupiter, Mars and Ketu are strong here.

The second pada or quarter of this asterism 3° 20' - 6° 40' Sagittarius falls in Taurus Navamsa ruled by Venus. This pada has both occult and material implications. It can make one hardworking while pursuing material objectives. This same resoluteness and tenacity is seen when planets here concentrate on realms beyond material. A certain creative spark is seen when it comes to arts, music and other Venusian pursuits. Planets here usually cause some sort of strife and obstacles. They give bad results for the mother's well being. Jupiter, Mars, Moon and Venus do well here.

The third pada or quarter of this asterism 6° 40' - 10° 00' Sagittarius falls in Gemini Navamsa ruled by Mercury. This is the word play pada. In a way this is the most light amongst Mula's padas. The focus here is on communication, wordplay and relationships. Mula's need for dominion is transferred onto an intellectual plane. At their best, planets here can create a balance between material and spiritual values. This pada is generally against money and material acquisition of any sorts. Afflicted planets here can cause dire poverty. Jupiter, Mercury, Rahu and Ketu can give good results here.

The fourth pada or quarter of this asterism 10° 00' - 13° 20' Sagittarius falls in Cancer Navamsa ruled by Moon. This is the most tumultuous among Mula's padas. There's a constant struggle in trying to bridge the emotional realm with other planes. The emotional nature is too easily disturbed in this pada. The best option for the natives under the strong influence of this pada is to sacrifice their emotions for higher goals. According to ancient texts, this pada is harmful for the general wellbeing of a native and some propitiatory rites are required to harness its energy properly. Jupiter is the planet which is most conducive for channelling the energy of this pada.

Professions :

Shaman, Medicine men, Healers; Doctors and other such people who administer poisons, shots and vaccines; Dentists; Ministers, Preachers; Police Officers; Detectives and Investigators; Judges; Hitmen & Soldiers; Researchers, especially in the fields of Microbiology & Genetics; Astronomers; Morticians and those who perform Autopsies; Orators & Public Speakers; All professions involving oratorical ability like Mass Leaders, Rock Musicians etc.; Debaters & Contrarians; Those involved in Selling Herbs, Roots & Root vegetables like carrots, potatoes etc.; Bodyguards; Wrestlers; Homicide squads; Politicians; Those practising Tantra (especially *Aghoras*), Voodoo practitioners & Black Magicians; Nuclear Physicists; Mathematicians; Professional Agitators; Gold diggers & Treasure Hunters; Horse Trainers & all those involved in Equine Sports; Psychotherapists; Astrologers; Ascetics; Mining; Coal & Petroleum Industry; All professions involving investigation of any kind; Professions involving destructive activities.

Places :

Deserts; High Mountain regions where special herbs are found; Dense rainforests & other such inaccessible places; Frozen deserts like Antarctica; Bottom of oceans, lakes etc; Hidden subterranean caves; Earth's core & all layers beneath the Earth's surface; Small isolated islands & places; Big institution buildings; Supreme Courts & other courts of justice; Abattoirs; Cremation Grounds and Cemeteries; Places connected to Death & Death Rituals; Agricultural Wasteland; War grounds; Drought areas; Places where mass calamities have taken place; All places connected with the abovementioned professions.

Guna (Essence) and Tattwa (Element) :

It is a *Tamasic* asterism in the sense that it relates to the dark and passive aspect of nature. Thus it can cause all sorts of confusion, paranoia, fears etc., which fall in the domain of Ketu's significations. It also deals with all types of smoking and intoxication.

It belongs to the Air element. This is again a puzzling classification, as Mula is more strongly connected to fiery planets and signs. Since the air element is directly connected to the Vata humor, the readers can look up in the Body Parts & Humor section for an explanation.

Gana (Type) :

It is a *Rakshasa* or demonic nakshatra. It is a powerful asterism which can give dominion and lordship. This can sometimes breed ego, vanity and arrogance, which can lead one to do abominable and demoniac actions. The two Titan kings, who are the main characters in the two main Vedic historical texts, *Ravan* and *Kamsa*, are associated with this asterism. They started harassing and killing without discrimination, after gaining influence and power.

Orientation & Disposition :

It is a Downward nakshatra. Since roots grow down into the ground and not upwards, it makes sense that Mula is classified as a downward nakshatra. Mula, as we know, has energy which is always trying to move towards the centre or inner core. It involves digging, whether it be for earthly treasures like gold or petroleum, or more important things like enlightenment.

It is a Hard, Sharp and Dreadful nakshatra. Its sharpness relates to the sharp and often harsh way Ketu functions. This relates more to the destructive aspect of Ketu. Sometimes sharpness is necessary to initiate an important change and wake us up from our sleep. It is an intense nakshatra which initiates spiritual transformation. For understanding its hard and dreadful side, all one needs to do is look at its image.

Lunar Month & Day :

It relates to the second half of the lunar month of *Jyaistha*, which usually falls in June.

Mula is also related to the *Prathama* & *Chaturthi (1ˢᵗ* & 4ᵗʰ tithis or days) of the waxing and waning phases of the Moon's monthly cycle.

Auspicious Activities :

Any activity involving getting down to the root of a matter; Activities involving gathering together of knowledge, people etc; Singing, oratory and all activities requiring forcefulness and dynamism; Good for administering herbs & medicines; Suitable for planting, gardening and other agricultural activities; Suitable for laying foundations for houses, construction work, buying and selling homes; Good for expressing sexuality; Favourable for adventures; Good for getting even by cutting the chase; Favourable for contemplation, self-exploration & self-assertion; Favourable for meditation on death and fierce deities like *Kali* ; Good for initiation into occult realms & study of sciences like astrology.

Inauspicious Activities :

Does not favour any activity involving balance, tact, diplomacy; Not good for initiations or beginnings pertaining to materialistic matters; Unsuitable for marital ceremony; Especially unfavourable for borrowing or lending money and financial transactions in general.

Planetary Ruler :

Mula combines the energy of Jupiter and Ketu. Ketu is the main ruler of this nakshatra. Being a destructive asterism, Mula relates to the destructive potential of Ketu. Ketu's destructiveness is always benign in the sense that it either initiates a new beginning or a spiritual transformation. Ketu is the planet signifying the root underlying impulses of all thoughts and actions. It is also a planet which gives access and insight into the unseen realms as well as the invisible causes of visible things or events.

Jupiter's involvement with this nakshatra makes sure that transformations under Mula happen for the better. Although it may sound bizarre, Mula also promotes non-violence and protects the good.

It is a magical nakshatra, which either confers magical powers or helps those in need in sudden magical ways. Ketu loses much of its power to give bad results when associated with Jupiter in any way. In its negative aspect however, Jupiterian energy can foster and expand the wildly destructive and idiosyncratic tendencies of Ketu. Mula is a strong energy, which can either produce a benevolent sage or a demonic entity wanting to conquer everything.

Mula's fieriness relates to the fiery aspect of Ketu. Ketu, as we know, is a predominantly fiery planet. Through this asterism it gives both good or bad results in a blazing explosive way. Its fieriness makes it favourable for war and other similar activities. It is usually triumphant in all sorts of warfare but a downfall does take place at some point of time. Most prominent generals and military leaders have important planets placed in Mula.

Adolf Hitler's chart is a glaring example of the negative ramifications of the combined functioning of Jupiter and Ketu. He is one of the few people to have Jupiter-Ketu conjunction in Mula, which allows for a complete expression of the tremendous power inherent in this nakshatra. It is Jupiter's task to guide the Ketu energy in a wise and beneficial way. This is usually only achieved when the energies of Jupiter and Saturn are harmonized properly in a nativity (in Hitler's chart Saturn didn't aspect the Jupiter- Ketu conjunction, allowing for an uninhibited expression of the darker demonic energies of Mula).

Jupiter-Ketu conjunction carries Mula energy. A well placed Sun, Mars and Jupiter do well in Mula. Ketu almost always gives some extreme idiosyncratic tinge to the native, despite being very strong in its own nakshatra.

Vowel s and Alphabets :

The first pada or quarter of this asterism 00° 00' -3° 20' Sagittarius corresponds to "Ye" as in Yale.

The second pada or quarter of this asterism 3° 20' - 6° 40' Sagittarius corresponds to "Yo" as in Yog.

The third pada or quarter of this asterism 6° 40' - 10° 00' Sagittarius corresponds to "Bha" as in Bhang.

The fourth pada or quarter of this asterism 10° 00' - 13° 20' Sagittarius corresponds to "Bhe" as in Bhesh.

In the Sanskrit alphabet Mula corresponds to "Na", "Pa" and "Pha" consequently its mantras are "Om Nam", "Om Pam" and "Om Pham".

Sexual Type and Compatibility :

Its sexual animal is a Dog. It is more of a howling hound dog, rather than a Scottish terrier (please refer to the image). It is most compatible with *Ardra*, the other dog nakshatra.

For sexual & marital compatibility with other nakshatras please refer to the tables on pages 468 & 469.

Esoteric :

Mula is the first among the asterisms which symbolizes the spiritual journey of the soul. It follows *Jyeshta* (the 18th Nakshatra), which is the last among the second series of asterisms dealing with material involvement and accomplishments. Even the two Titan kings, *Ravan* and *Kamsa*, were finally initiated on a spiritual path after they were defeated in battle by the two incarnations of *Vishnu*, *Ram* and *Krishn* respectively.

The spirituality which Mula brings about is different from that of the previous nakshatras, in the sense that Mula goes for the 'root' of everything. In spiritual terms, this means that Mula settles for nothing less than the absolute merger with *Paramatman* (universal soul). Mula goes about this process through many extreme ways - sometimes it discards everything using the principle of *Neti Neti* (not this, not this). At other times, it goes for accumulating immense power in the three lokas (heaven, earth and the netherworld). It then misuses this power so that root deities like *Vishnu* have to personally intervene. In this intervention lies the key to its salvation.

The third way relates to the goddess *Kali.* On this path Mula goes after and destroys the demons and negativities within, without procrastination or mercy. Once this is done only *sattwa* remains and liberation is just a mere formality. Through this path Mula devotes itself to being a tool of the universal mind, rather than being a wayward rebel. The life story of *Anjaneya* (commonly known by his other name *Hanuman*), an incarnation of Shiv and a devotee of Ram (an incarnation of Vishnu), reveals the true spirituality of Mula.

Mula's association with the centre of the galaxy relates it to *Brahma,* the creator among the Trinity. Mula thus derives its power from this understanding of the original process of creation.

Being the 19th nakshatra, it relates to the number 19. '19' is seen as a solar number, which signifies both beginning and completion. '19' has the power to stand before the spiritual 'sun' because it has gone beyond the mundane lunar functionings, which reach their culmination in the number '18'. It is its association with the number 19 which gives Mula power and prosperity on a material plane, even though its presiding deity Nritti is supposed to be averse to material abundance and prosperity.

Gotra (Celestial Lineage) :

This nakshatra is related to the *Sage Pulasthya,* one of the seven celestial sages looking after the affairs of our galaxy. The name of this sage translates into "having smooth hair". Pulasthya appears to be a two sided sage. His lighter more benevolent side is expressed through his connection with *Mrigashira* and *Uttaraphalguni,* while his connection with *Mula* and *Purvabhadrapada* reveals a destructive aspect concealed underneath the benign posh exterior.

Remedial :

For those suffering from bad effects resulting from afflictions to this nakshatra, the best remedial measure is worship of fierce deities like *Kali* and *Rudra*. Contemplation and meditation on death in all its forms leads to constructive utilization of Mula energy.

Repetition of the root mantras of this nakshatra - "Om Nam", "Om Pam" and "Om Pham" 108 times when Moon transits this nakshatra and in its corresponding lunar month, is sure to reduce suffering and bring enlightenment into a person's life. "Om Eshte Nirate Bhagastam Jushsva" can be recited to cure the bad effects associated with Mula's first three padas.

Persons who are benefiting from the positive energy of this nakshatra can also increase the good effects through the above mentioned ways. It is helpful for them to wear a mixture of black, red golden colours or earth tones. They should use its directions, lunar month and the days when Moon transits Mula to undertake all important actions.

Example :

Ravan, the mightiest Titan king and sorcerer of *Treta Yug* (Silver Age) was born with his ascendant lord Sun placed in Mula. As narrated in the famous historical text, "*Ramayan*", he gained immense power and lordship over the three worlds through hard penances aimed at pleasing *Shiv*. This shows Mula's ability to gain power on a universal level through a close association with the root forces. He however fell prey to the haughty, bashful and unwise aspect of Mula energy and met his end as a villain in the hands of *Ram*, the 7th incarnation of *Vishnu*.

Hanuman or *Anjaneya*, the incarnation of the 11th *Rudra* (celestial deities presiding over universal affairs) in monkey form in the abovementioned *Treta Yug*, was born with Mula rising. His power surpassed even that of Ravan but he always selflessly offered it to righteousness, which in his time was represented by above mentioned *Ram*.

Both of these examples represent the different sides of Mula.

Mula's sound and light can be experienced at –

http://osfa.org.uk/mula/htm

Miscellaneous :

According to *Varahamihira*, Moon in Mula makes one "haughty, rich and happy besides giving a fixed, luxury loving and compassionate disposition ".

* * *

20. Purvashada 13°20' – 26°40' Sagittarius

20.

Purvashadha

(13º20' Sagittarius - 26º40' Sagittarius)

In the Sky :

Purvashadha, the pinnacle of Venusian energy, is represented in the celestial firmament by three bright stars, known in modern astronomy as *Epsilon-Sagittarii* (*Kaus Australis*), *Delta-Sagittarii* (*Kaus Media*) & *Epsilon-Sagittarii* (*Kaus Borealis*). All of these stars lie in a line (with a slight deviation) in the middle portion of the constellation Sagittarius. These stars can be spotted easily, as they are located close to the Milky Way as it stretches like a white celestial river across the night sky. Kaus Australis, having a visual magnitude of 1.81, is the brightest among these stars. Ancient Vedic seers saw these stars as forming the shape of a hand held fan.

Name :

'Purvashadha " translates into "the Former Invincible One" or the "Former Unconquered". Its name, like its successor, concentrates on the basic attribute of this asterism - invincibility.

The alternative name for Purvashadha is "*Aparajita*", which translates into "undefeated". We can see that this name goes along the same lines as the more commonly used name.

Symbol :

In congruence with the shape formed by its stars, a 'hand held fan' is the most famous symbol of this asterism. A fan can have four uses:-

1. As a decorative item popular in Japanese/Oriental cultures.

2. To cool oneself down in hot conditions.

3. To fan up a fire.

4. As a mask to hide oneself.

Its first use relates to the showy, glitzy and glamorous Venusian aspect of this nakshatra. In the ancient Orient, the type of fan one carried was directly related to social status. This conveys the superiority aspect of this nakshatra. It finds itself superior in comparison to all nakshatras before it, especially the earlier Venusian ones. The superiority of perfection achieved in the Venusian realm will however depend on the soul level of the native in question.

The second use corresponds to this nakshatra's ability to get through hard times. Fanning is essentially an act of aggression against heat. Thus this nakshatra is often associated with all kinds of aggressive activities. It is patient in adversity and aggressive whenever the opportunity arises.

The third use corresponds to this nakshatra's ability to keep a thing going. In its negative aspect this may manifest as exaggeration or over expansion. In its positive aspect it is an inspiring energy which knows how to keep the fire burning. As a result it is a very expressive and expansive nakshatra.

The fourth use relates to this nakshatra's ability to conceal facts, information, feelings, personality etc. It is in a way a shy and sensitive nakshatra, which likes to conceal its enthusiasm and bubbliness from the outside world as much as possible. Only after some initial reluctance and when it begins to gain confidence does it show its true colours.

A 'winnowing basket used for ridding grain of husks', is an alternative symbol, which more or less conveys the above mentioned meanings for a winnowing fan. This symbol brings out the aspect of this nakshatra related to uncovering hidden talents. This nakshatra is capable of shedding outer, unnecessary obstacles in order to bring out the useful part inside. This may relate to people, places or things.

Deity :

An obscure goddess by the name of *Apah* is the ruling deity of this nakshatra. "Apah" translates into "water". Very little is known about this goddess, as the surviving vedic texts don't mention her name much. However, her obscurity makes sense, when seen in the light of the fact that this nakshatra has a mysterious, hiding, secretive and shy quality about it.

Apah can be equated with the ocean goddesses of other cultures like *Aphrodite, Astartes* etc. It is interesting to note the "Aph" similarity in the names "Apah" & "Aphrodite". They seem to share the same roots as the name of the original celestial ocean "*Apas*". Even Purvashadha's alternative name "*Aparajita*" seems to have been derived from the same root. "Apa" is still the name for water in many languages around the world and many of the ancients saw water as the invincible element.

"Apah" and "Aphrodite" are both Venusian goddess figurines and can be seen as the female counterparts of the male ocean deity "*Varuna*". Both of them can be seen as part reflections of *Laxmi*, the universal goddess of prosperity. Laxmi is the spouse of *Vishnu*, the overseer of the celestial waters which sustain our universe. The image of Vishnu and Laxmi sitting on a snake bed on top of the ocean of celestial waters is an image which is directly related to this nakshatra.

The 'churning of the ocean legend' (refer to the author's previous work "*The Rahu-Ketu Experience*" *Sagar Publications/India, "The Key Of Life" Lotus Press/USA*) in which various treasures came out, signify the productive potential of Apah as a goddess. Her negative side is reflected by the deadly poison that came out as a result of the churning. Apah relates to the churning which goes on inside each one of us and the good and bad things which come out as a result.

Her flamboyant, enticing, invincible approach is reflected in the nature and functionings of Purvashadha. Like all primordial forces, Apah, though benevolent, is often cruel and harsh in her ways, which again can be seen to hold true for those having a prominent Purvashadha personality. Her grand, all-inclusive, all-embracing vision is where Venus derives its higher qualities like real love and compassion from. Purvashadha is the pinnacle of Venusian energy and thus the real aim of this nakshatra is to get to an all-encompassing level of awareness, at least from a Venusian point of view.

Apah is closely connected to the mythical sea creature now commonly known as mermaid. The qualities usually associated with mermaids like vain, alluring, sensitive, beautiful, mysterious, enticing, musical, freedom loving and adventurous can be applied to this nakshatra as well.

A Welsh folktale illustrates the same concern and reverence this nakshatra has for water. In that folk tale, "a mermaid who had spent three days with mortals on dry land, upon returning to her kith and kin, was asked what she had seen amongst those on land. She replied, "Nothing much, except that they are so ignorant as to throw away the very water they boil their eggs in."

Nature & Functioning :

The one characteristic which sets Purvashadha apart from all other nakshatras is its intense conviction that 'it can't lose'. Purvashadha feels that it has the ability to come out on top in wherever it directs its energies. As we have seen, there is a strong notion of invincibility attached with this nakshatra. This notion can however be misplaced at times like the famous character of *Don Quixote*.

Most of the qualities readily associated with the sign Sagittarius - leaps of faith, ambitiousness, adventurous spirit, wild exuberance, philosophical zeal, wanderlust - usually stem from the nature and functionings of this nakshatra. It is one of the most optimistic nakshatras, but its optimism does not have the tinge of impatience. It is always ready to bide its time until the wind blows in its favour. It is completely undaunted by setbacks and doesn't ponder on failure. At times this is a negative quality, in the sense that it hardly ever learns from its mistakes.

Many a times one finds that natives under the strong influence of Purvashadha have unrealistic hopes, ambitions and goals unless there are other balancing factors in the horoscope. For example, *Adolf Hitler*, who has Moon placed in Purvashadha, started a war with unrealistic aims way beyond the power of his army and resources. Purvashadha has a straight forward driving "just do it" type of energy, which doesn't always take everything into account, especially the feelings and concerns of those around them. This makes this nakshatra an insensitive one and even cruel in some situations. This is why this nakshatra is associated with declarations of war and other such actions which bring about destruction followed by sorrow and regret.

It has a cautious side to it in that it is slow to jump into new things and experiences, but once things are set in motion, it is the type which almost always ends up going overboard. At their best Purvashadha natives are an inspiration to those around them. In their presence one begins to realize that the universe is not such a bad place after all. Purvashadha natives usually have a fresh and unique approach to things, which has the power to instill life into the hearts and minds of those who are not as blessed. *Jyestha* is unhappy because it does not know the root of things. *Mula* makes one find the root and the centre, but it is only Purvashadha which holds the key to joy and happiness, after the centre has been found.

Purvashadha is the nakshatra which can be most associated with the joy of living. This doesn't mean that Purvashadha natives cling onto life like *Ashlesha* natives. It is just that they like to live each moment to its complete fullness without a care for the past or the future. They have a nonchalant attitude towards misery and thus are never phased by adverse circumstances. Obviously much depends on the overall tone of the chart as well, but the basic energy of Purvashadha is to shrug off adverse circumstances just like a fan shrugs off the misery caused by heat. As we can see, Purvashadha has a strong desire to live a good life and so the natives under its influence are always trying to improve their circumstances. It is usually seen that Purvashadha natives have little formal education and often have to rise from depravity or generally unpleasant circumstances in order to enjoy their "good life". Improvement of circumstances is the main concern for them.

They are the kinds who like to be exuberant once they have achieved their goals. At times this may seem like a show-off to other people, but in most cases the Purvashadha natives are only acting out their inner nature. They are born natural show-offs. Much depends on the refinement of Jupiter and Venus in the chart in terms of how their exuberance expresses itself.

In general, Purvashadha has a pleasant, artistic way of looking at things. They carry a certain proud and serious expression on their faces, but are ever ready to break into a smile or laughter. Their demeanour can change from jovial to serious in the twinkling of an eye. You can't always tell their inner thoughts from their outer expressions. They can be honest at times but they always like to keep a part of themselves secret, just as the ocean gods and goddesses like to have a mysterious touch about them. They have a flamboyant way about themselves which reflects through their dressing, communication and their work. One marked characteristic of Purvashadha is that they usually don't fare well at formal education and are often seen dropping out of schools and universities.

In the universal scheme of things, Purvashadha relates to "*varchograhan shakti*" - the power to bring about invigoration. Its symbolism has strength above and connection below. This imagery emphasizes the rejuvenation potential of the waters of life, which Purvashadha stands for. Just as the bathing process causes a renewal in our daily lives, the waters of cosmic consciousness bathe us internally so that most of our soul level hurts and confusions are washed away.

Mode of Functioning :

Purvashadha is considered to be a Balanced nakshatra. It is very unlikely for a Purvashadha native to overextend themselves, even in their *rajasic* pursuits. Jupiter and Venus, as planets, are not known to have an extreme attitude regarding activity in the same way that Sun or Mars does.

Caste :

It belongs to the *Brahmin* caste. This is one of the most evident classifications as Purvashadha is only related to the two brahmin planets, Venus and Jupiter. Purvashadha has a tendency to go for the most cushy positions or modes of existence available at any given time. In today's times, Purvashadha would rather take up the brahminical profession of being a rock star today! Purvashadha likes to maintain its position at the top of society and have a luxurious existence with the minimum of effort.

Gender :

It is a Female nakshatra. This obviously relates to its ruling deity, Apah, being feminine, and the fact that Venus is seen as a predominantly feminine planet.

Bodyparts & Humor (Ayurvedic Constitution) :

Thighs and Back (from neck to waist) are the body parts related to this nakshatra.

It is a primarily "*Pitta*" (fiery) nakshatra. This classification relates to Purvashadha's location within the predominantly pitta sign of Sagittarius. We have already talked about the fiery aspect of this asterism.

Direction :

It is related primarily to the directional arc ranging from northeast to southeast, via east.

Padas (Quarters) :

The first pada or quarter of this asterism 13° 20' - 16° 40' Sagittarius falls in Leo Navamsa and is ruled by Sun. This pada relates to the proud and confident side of Purvashadha. The spiritual urge is strong here and is accompanied by a strong sense of ethics. Planets placed here like to bring limelight in the issues related to them.

The second pada or quarter of this asterism 16° 40' - 20° 00' Sagittarius falls in Virgo Navamsa ruled by Mercury. This pada relates to the intellectual, alchemical aspect of this nakshatra. A lot of hard work is required here, but there is also the promise of great spiritual or material accomplishment. Barring Venus, planets placed here aid one's career in one way or the other.

The third pada or quarter of this asterism 20° 00' - 23° 20' Sagittarius falls in Libra Navamsa ruled by Venus. This pada relates to the easy going, luxury loving Venusian side of this nakshatra. The emphasis here is on reaping the fruits rather than working hard. This is a Pushkara Navamsa pada and barring Sun, planets posited here give good material results and promote all types of partnerships and group related activities.

The fourth pada or quarter of this asterism 23° 20' - 26° 40' Sagittarius falls in Scorpio Navamsa ruled by Mars. This pada relates to the haughty, secretive, hidden and mysterious aspect of this nakshatra. Herein lies the two extremes, great occult wisdom or material perversity. Planets posited here are good for occult attainments and foreign affairs.

Professions :

Hypnotists & Psychic Mediums; Sailors; Navy Personnel; Marine Life Experts; Shipping Industry; Fishing Professions; Professional Hosts & Hostesses; Entertainment Industry; Rock Stars; Professional Motivators and Inspirers; Teachers & Preachers of Motivational Philosophies; Managers of all types; Poets, Writers, Artists, Painters; All industries processing raw materials especially liquids; Refineries; War Strategists & Weapons Experts; Costume Designers; Fashion Experts; Hair Dressers; Para jumpers; Hot Air Balloonists; Flying profession especially in regards to civilian transport; Beauticians; Herbalists; Those working in Amusement parks; All professions associated with water and liquids in all its forms.

Places :

Oceans; Lakes; Aquarium Parks; Swimming Pools; Docks, Ports; Shipping Yards; Temples; Boats; High Class Estates; Air ports; Luxury Islands & Hotels; Beauty Salons; Amusement Parks; Art Galleries; Music Concert Halls; Places where pompous functions & high society gatherings are held.

Guna (Essence) and Tattwa (Element) :

It is supposed to be a *Rajasic* nakshatra. This fits well seeing its planetary ruler, Venus, is a primarily Rajasic planet. Purvashadha is a worldly energy in the sense that it can satisfy one's desires on a material plane through relentless activity. It is a sucker for the good things in life.

It belongs to the Air element. We have to go back to the fan imagery to understand this classification. In at least two of its functions, fan requires the involvement of air. Whether it is fanning the fire or alleviating oneself from the heat, the air element comes into play. After all it is air which keeps the fire burning and Purvashadha is a nakshatra which is most adept at keeping the fire burning.

Gana (Type) :

It is considered a *Manusha* or human nakshatra. Just like the human race, Purvashadha is a mixed up nakshatra displaying an extreme spectrum of good and bad qualities. Its human quality makes it very interested in terrestrial affairs. It is no wonder then, that 70% of our planet is made up of oceans and 70% of our bodies are made up of water.

Orientation & Disposition :

It is a Downward Looking nakshatra. Just like *Mula*, Purvashadha relates to all things which are hidden from view. When we look at our bodies, we can't really see the water in them, even though they are 70% water. Purvashadha's ruling deity Apah is supposed to reside under the surface of the ocean. It is Purvashadha's tendency to hide, which makes it a downward or under the surface nakshatra. One has to dive down to pick up the pearls of Purvashadha.

It is an *Ugra* (fierce and severe) nakshatra. As we have already seen, Purvashadha is associated with all types of aggressions like declarations of war. It is Purvashadha's naivete of acting without a care for consequences or repercussions, which makes it a dangerous nakshatra. It is quite a volatile nakshatra, which is very hard to control once it has caught fire. It presses on with its severe actions even after it has realized the futility of them.

Lunar Month & Day :

It relates to the first half of the lunar month of *Ashadha*. This month usually corresponds to late June in the solar calendar.

Purvashadha is also related to the *Trayodashi* (13th tithi or day) of the waxing and waning phases of the Moon's monthly cycle.

Auspicious Activities :

Facing issues which require courage; Taking a strong stance; Confronting enemies and opposition along with reconciliations and forgiveness; Settling debts; Going to war; Inspiring and inciting others into action; Renewal and revitalizing one's energies, goals and actions on the mental, spiritual, emotional or physical planes; Adventures including exploration into nature and sporting activities; Creative pioneering; Travelling over water, visiting water places and activities connected to water; Sailing and other water sports; Confidence boosting strategies; Worshipping female goddess energies; Showing off; Acts of bravery; Good for equine activities; Artistic performances; Decorating oneself or one's surroundings to spice it up; Visiting ancient sites; Spiritual & occult initiations/attainments; Favourable for agricultural activities; Good for marriage and invigorating sexual activity; All activities connected to its professions.

Inauspicious Activities :

Unfavourable for activities requiring tact and diplomacy; Not a time for calm reflection; Not good for endings unless the ending promises a brighter future or higher step up the ladder; Not especially good for land journeys.

Planetary Ruler :

Venus is the main planetary ruler of Purvashadha . Venus reaches its highest individual energy as a planet in this nakshatra (its peak expression however comes through Revati, where it reaches maximum exaltation).

Purvashadha is the power and purity of the childlike mind, which is represented by Jupiter in the form of faith and wonder. It is the child which stands before the universe. It is the power of renewed life that never grows old. That is why Mercury, the eternal youth, is intimately associated on the esoteric plane with this nakshatra. Wherever there is Venus to bring back life from the dead, there is Mercury behind it. The combination of Mercury/Venus and Jupiter is the Alchemist's secret. Alchemy first takes place in this nakshatra before reaching its completion in Revati (27th nakshatra). Purvashadha is the initiate of the occult mystery schools, Jupiter in this case being the student of Venus and Mercury. Everyone has to be blessed by Venus and Purvashadha to enter this school. Therefore Mercury has to function well with Venus in a horoscope for any type of real occult attainments.

In general astrological terms, Jupiter-Venus, Mercury-Venus, Jupiter-Mercury-Venus conjunctions carry an energy similar to that of Purvashadha. Mercury-Venus & Jupiter-Venus exchange also carries Purvashadha energy.

Besides Saturn, all planets usually do well in Purvashadha. Unless afflicted, even Saturn would do well in its 2nd and 3rd padas.

Vowels and Alphabets :

The first pada or quarter of this asterism 13° 20' -16° 40' Sagittarius corresponds to "Bu" as in Bootis.

The second pada or quarter of this asterism 16° 40' - 20° 00' Sagittarius corresponds to "Dah" as in Dahl.

The third pada or quarter of this asterism 20° 00' - 23° 20' Sagittarius corresponds to "Bha" as in Bhatt.

The fourth pada or quarter of this asterism 23° 20' - 26° 40' Sagittarius corresponds to "Dha" as in Dharma.

In the Sanskrit alphabet Purvashadha corresponds to "Ba" consequently its mantras are "Om Bam".

Sexual Type and Compatibility :

Its sexual animal is a Monkey. This makes it very playful in regards to sexual activities. It is most compatible with *Shravan*, the other monkey nakshatra.

For marital & sexual compatibility with other nakshatras please refer to the tables on pages 468 & 469.

Esoteric :

Purvashadha relates to surfing, whether its surfing the waves of time or waves of oceans that are different dimensions. Staying above these waves requires balance and discipline which can only arise out of humility to divine. There is a lot of surfing being tried out right now on the waves of the ocean called internet, but most are just sinking in it instead of reaching somewhere.

Purvashadha is the power and purity of the childlike mind, which is represented by Jupiter in the form of faith and wonder. It is the child which stands before the universe. It is the power of renewed life that never grows old. That is why Mercury, the eternal youth, is intimately associated on the esoteric plane with this nakshatra. Wherever there is Venus to bring back life from the dead, there is Mercury behind it. The combination of Mercury/Venus and Jupiter is the Alchemist's secret. Alchemy first takes place in this nakshatra before reaching its completion in Revati (27th nakshatra). Purvashadha is the initiate of the occult mystery schools, Jupiter in this case being the student of Venus and Mercury. Everyone has to be blessed by Venus and Purvashadha to enter this school. Therefore Mercury has to function well with Venus in a horoscope for any type of real occult attainments.

This is the 20th nakshatra. '2' represents Venus and the harmonising of two elements or two signs. '0' is the number of completion and infinity. Purvashadha is thus the infinity aspect of the Venusian energy. Purvashadha is the harmonising of Mercury/Venus and Taurus/Gemini, the two signs which form the gateway to the constellation of *Orion*. '2' relates to the 2nd sign of the zodiac Taurus and '3' represents Gemini, the third sign of the zodiac. This is why those who are born on the 23rd day of the month carry some of this Purvashadha energy. *Mrigashira*, the constellation which lies across the Taurus/Gemini axis also carries some of Purvashadha's energy. '2' is the feminine goddess energy, represented by the Moon. She is the "*Isis*" mystery, the *High Priestess* in the *Tarot* deck, the revealer of secrets and possessor of those secrets unrevealed. These secrets belong to the high initiates of the ancient mystery schools. This is why Mercury's role with Purvashadha is hidden from view. This hidden role is seen by the fact Gemini is placed opposite the sign of Sagittarius in the natural zodiac.

The seventeenth card of the Tarot deck known as "*The Star*", relates most closely to Purvashadha's energies. The female figure in the card expresses eternal youth and beauty and she pours the waters of life from heaven onto the earth. The motto of this card 'waters of life freely' speaks for itself in regards to its relation with Purvashadha."

Gotra (Celestial Lineage) :

This nakshatra is related to the *Sage Pulahu*, one of the seven celestial sages looking after the affairs of our galaxy. The name of this sage translates into "connector of space". Purvashadha's relationship with connectivity can be gleaned from the adhesive and connective role water plays in our bodies. Purvashadha relates to the same connecting force which holds space together in much the same way as it holds the water droplets together in the form of an ocean.

Remedial :

For those suffering from bad effects resulting from afflictions to this nakshatra, the best remedial measure is to worship Goddess *Laxmi*, and other Venusian deities like *Lalita* and *Tripurasundari*.

Repetition of the root mantra of this nakshatra - "Om Bam" 108 times when Moon transits this nakshatra and in its corresponding lunar month is sure to reduce suffering and bring enlightenment into a person's life.

Persons who are benefiting from the positive energy of this nakshatra can also increase the good effects through the above mentioned ways. It is helpful for them to wear ornate and decorative garments and jewellery, in variegated pastel colours. Mixtures of white, light pink and light blue are ideal. All psychedelic colours go well with the energy of Purvashadha. One should use its directions, lunar month and the days when Moon transits Purvashadha to undertake all important actions.

Example :

Purvashadha's sound and light can be experienced at -

http://osfa.org.uk/purvashadha.htm

Miscellaneous :

According to *Varahamihira*, Moon in Purvashadha "makes one have a loving and proud spouse while the native is of a proud disposition and steady in friendships".

* * *

21. Uttarashada 26°40' Sagittarius - 10°00' Capricorn

21.

Uttarashadha

(26°40' Sagittarius - 10°00' Capricorn)

In the Sky :

Uttarashadha, the pinnacle of solar energy, is represented in the celestial firmament by four bright stars, which the ancients saw as resembling an elephant's tusk. In modern astronomy they are known as *Sigma-Sagittarii* (*Ascella*), *Tau-Sagittarii, Phi-Sagittarii* & *Zeta-Sagittarii* (*Nunki*). These four stars lie in the end portion of the astronomical constellation of Sagittarius. However it must be noted that this asterism's influence extends into the first ten degrees of the zodiacal sign of Capricorn as well. Nunki, having a visual magnitude of 2.07, is the brightest among them. According to the legend, these stars correspond to the celestial area where the godly forces got their final victory over the demonic forces.

Name :

'Uttarashadha " translates into the "Latter Invincible One" or the "Latter Unconquered". This meaning reveals the crux of this asterism, which has more to do with the term "final victory" than any other asterism. It also reveals that it forms a pair with its predecessor *Purvashadha*, in the same way as *Purvaphalguni* and *Uttaraphalguni* form a pair.

Symbol :

Its primary symbol is an 'elephant's tusk'. The tusk is the most prized part of an elephant's anatomy. Elephants are usually very conscious of their tusks and zealously guard them. Researchers have found that the type, colour and size of the tusk has something to do with who becomes the leader of an elephant tribe. It follows that Uttarashadha has a lot to do with leadership issues.

Besides ornamentation, the tusk is useful to elephants for only one practical purpose - fighting. Just like its predecessor, Purvashadha, Uttarashadha has a lot to do with aggressive actions like declarations of war. As mentioned earlier, Purvashadha and Uttarashadha form a pair and some scholars regard the tusk of an elephant as a symbol for Purvashadha as well. They see the left tusk as belonging to Purvashadha and the right tusk to Uttarashadha.

In most ancient cultures where elephants were known, they were used as symbols of royal insignia. All kings, including *Indra*, the king of the gods, were supposed to ride on elephants during processions and sometimes even during warfare. Uttarashadha, therefore, has a direct relationship with kingship and all the responsibilities it entails. In a way, 'responsibility' is the most important keyword for this nakshatra.

For obvious reasons, an elephant's tusk is also regarded as a symbol of penetration. It signifies penetrating mental insight and the ability to enter new fields of endeavour. It also conveys a certain sense of fearlessness and a go ahead spirit.

Deity :

Uttarashadha has ten ruling deities known as the *Ten Vishvadevas*. Vishvadevas means Universal Gods. The names of these ten celestial beings translate into - "Goodness", "Truth", "Willpower", "Skill", "Time", "Desire", "Firmness", "Ancestors", "Brightness" and "Peak". It is clear that all these ten gods are extremely benevolent and are representative of the primary virtues of the original, divine, creative spark. They can be said to be the guardians of all that represents the word "good" in the universe. In the same way, Uttarashadha represents all that is good and benign on our planet.

All the qualities expressed through the names of the Vishvadevas find expression through Uttarashadha. This is what sets Uttarashadha apart from Purvashadha, even though most of Purvashadha's qualities and functionings apply to it as well. As a result of qualities like willpower and firmness, Uttarashadha has far greater permanence than its predecessor. It is easy to see that all these qualities are borne out of honest introspection, which makes Uttarashadha more introspective in comparison to the extroverted, flamboyant Purvashadha.

It is interesting to note that one of these gods is named "Ancestors". This must relate Uttarashadha to traditions as well as one's forefathers (see *Magha*). Uttarashadha is the first nakshatra which tries to encompass the qualities of all its predecessors (*Dhanishta* and *Revati* do the same). One can associate will power with *Ardra* and *Krittika*; skilfulness with *Hasta* and *Chitra*; time with *Bharani* and *Anuradha*; desire with *Bharani, Rohini, Mrigashira* and *Ashlesha*; goodness with *Ashvini, Purnavasu* and *Pushya*; Truth with *Uttaraphalguni*; Firmness with *Uttaraphalguni, Vishakha* and *Jyestha*; Ancestors to *Magha*; Brightness with *Rohini, Mrigashira, Purvaphalguni* and *Chitra*; and Peak with *Mula* and *Purvashadha*.

Ganesh, the elephant headed God, is the final presiding deity of this nakshatra. Ganesh is the only deity with an elephant's head. The story behind his getting an elephant's head reveals a lot relating to Uttarashadha's essence (refer to the Esoteric Section). Ganesh is always portrayed as having a full right tusk and a cut left tusk. This symbolises that Uttarashadha has a more complete and coherent energy in comparison to its mate Purvashadha. Ganesh can thus be seen as being strongly connected to both Ashadhas. Ganesh is seen as the "Lord of Beginnings" and "Remover of Obstacles" and his blessings are sought in all beginnings. Uttarashadha therefore relates to all kinds of beginnings. It is seen that activities started under the positive influence of this nakshatra are blessed with success and permanence.

Nature & Functioning :

Many of Magha's qualities like elegance, traditionalism, authority and respect for courtesies are similar to Uttarashadha. However, Uttarashadha has a more positive, introspective and enduring aspect. It shows a person of very good qualities who may be valued for their advice. It gives a talent for commencing new enterprises and seeing them through to completion. It is a very practical and pioneering type of energy as most of its quarters fall in the practical and achievement orientated sign of Capricorn. It is a nakshatra very concerned with structures, order and makes one adhere to activities and behaviour which are seen as respectable and sometimes conformist.

It's association with the ancestors shows a deep respect for traditional values and a desire to advocate these values in one's behaviour and life. However the Saturnine influence on this nakshatra can make a person rigid and harsh, just as the piercing symbol of the elephant's tusk suggests. It can show an intolerance for anything which does not follow normal respectable lines. Spiritual and philosophical motivations are directed towards finding practical solutions to life's problems

The sexual animal of this nakshatra, the mongoose, is one of the few animals which can defeat a snake. In a way, Uttarashadha can be seen as the very opposite of all that Ashlesha stands for. Since they are placed opposite each other (6th/7th/8th house relationship), there is open enmity and warfare between these two nakshatras. This nakshatra has little tolerance for underhanded or deceptive influences. However the mongoose is cunning in its own way and its symbol suggests that one is courageous and clever in finding ways to forge ahead in difficult, dangerous or complex situations. Natives under the strong influence of Uttarashadha tend to gravitate towards or attract situations in life which represent a lot of challenges. On a spiritual level it makes one very determined to pierce through the veil of illusion to uncover one's true soul nature.

In the universal scheme of things, *Uttarashadha* relates to "*apradhrishya shakti*" - the power to give permanent victory. Its symbolism has achievable goals above and the strength to achieve those goals below. This imagery is self-explanatory. The only thing worth mentioning is that this strength is not personal strength, but the collective strength which comes about due to an alliance with the higher forces of good, when one is wholeheartedly and unselfishly trying to establish righteousness over unrighteousness.

Mode of Functioning :

Uttarashadha is considered to be a Balanced nakshatra. This self evident classification does not require too much commentary. A centre is needed for any kind of balance and Uttarashadha, amongst all nakshatras, relates most closely to this centre, from both a universal and personal perspective. It is said that the "road to excess leads to the palace of wisdom", but one must remember that this palace of wisdom has balance as its foundation.

Caste :

It belongs to the *Kshatriya* (warrior) caste. This nakshatra is mostly concerned with attaining a place of position or strength in society. As we have already seen, it relates to leadership and the ruling class. According to *Manu* (the lawgiver for our planet), all kings and leaders came under the kshatriya caste. Uttarashadha has *brahminical* tendencies, but they often seem to manifest within a kshatriya framework. A good king is akin to a sage, but is still not a sage. In fact *Janak* is the only earthly king to have been awarded a brahminical title (refer to the Vedic legend "*The Ramayan*").

Gender :

It is a Female nakshatra. This classification defies all common sense as all of Uttarashadha's ruling deities and planetary rulers are male. The only way we can comprehend this is by considering the fact that all the ten good qualities are seen in a feminine light in Vedic texts. Vedic texts regard all qualities as being part of "nature", which in the end is considered to be the feminine principle of the absolute. Uttarashadha is a nakshatra which has more to do with the benign functionings of *Maya* rather than the male observer essence of the Absolute.

Bodyparts & Humor (Ayurvedic Constitution) :

Thighs and Waist are the body parts related to this nakshatra.

It is a primarily "*Kapha*" (watery) nakshatra. Elephants (closely associated with this nakshatra) are supposed to be the main representatives of the kapha humor. Kapha is a constitution, which is derived from the combination of earth and a little bit of the water element. The earth element is provided by the sign Capricorn (which most of Uttarashadha lies in) and the little bit of water element is provided by Jupiter (part of Uttarashadha falls in Sagittarius, Jupiter's sign).

Direction :

It is related primarily to south, west, north-east and east.

Padas (Quarters) :

The first pada or quarter of this asterism 26° 40' - 30° 00' Sagittarius falls in Sagittarius Navamsa and is ruled by Jupiter. Righteousness, confidence and expansiveness are the hallmarks of this pada. Nothing seems impossible when one is working through the energies of this pada. It has supreme faith in its ability, knowledge and understanding. Being both a pushkara navamsa pada and a vargottama pada, planets placed here give strong material/spiritual results. Sun, Jupiter, Mars and Ketu are especially potent here. Jupiter gives the best results.

The second pada or quarter of this asterism 00° 00' - 3° 20' Capricorn falls in Capricorn Navamsa ruled by Saturn. The emphasis here is on concretization and material expression of one's thoughts, plans and desires. Planets placed here give nerves of steel. Most of the issues of this pada circle around one's own self and personality and how it is expressed in the outer world. It is the goal rather than the means which becomes important here. An exaggerated attention or attachment to worldliness and power structures can be noticed. Mars and Saturn have the ability to best utilize the energies of this pada.

The third pada or quarter of this asterism 3° 20' - 6° 40' Capricorn falls in Aquarius Navamsa ruled by Saturn. The emphasis here is on accumulation, whether it be knowledge or material possessions.

A strong attachment to the concept of family can be noticed in this pada. Planets here give good results if one works towards one's goals through involving other people. Group and team work are essential for the proper functioning of this pada. Rahu, Mercury and Saturn feel comfortable in this pada. Saturn gives the strongest results.

The fourth pada or quarter of this asterism 6° 40' - 10° 00' Capricorn falls in Pisces Navamsa ruled by Jupiter. This pada promotes physical prowess, short travels, courage and philanthropy. There's a constant conflict between material and spiritual values as the native strives to achieve a balance. In the present times, more often than not, materiality prevails. Planets placed here give abundant energy for pursuing one's goals. Moon , Mars and Saturn seem best equipped to handle the energies of this pada.

Professions :

Preachers, Priests; Counsellors; Astrologers; Lawyers (of an ethical nature); Judges; Government officials; Psychologists; Military Professions; Equine professions; Pioneers; Explorers; Wrestlers, Sword fighters and other combat sports; Athletes; Elephant trainers; Business Executives; Organizers; Defence Industry; Authority figures of all types; Teachers; Guards, High class Servants; Bird watchers & enthusiasts; Body Guards, Security Personnel; Rangers; Hunters; Construction Industry; Cricketers; Holistic Physicians; Politicians (as good as they get in the present day and age); All professions requiring a sense of responsibility and ethics.

Places :

Prairies; Flat Savannahs; Mountainous Forests; National Parks; Wildlife Sanctuaries; Bird Sanctuaries; Reservations; Government Buildings & Grounds; Courts; Temples, Churches and other religious buildings; Universities; College Campuses; Military Bases; Traditionalistic Towns & Cities; Elite Gentlemen Clubs & Societies; Sports Stadiums; Cricket Grounds; All professions connected with the above places.

Guna (Essence) and Tattwa (Element) :

It is supposed to be a *Sattwic* nakshatra. The sattwic and benevolent nature of this nakshatra can be seen clearly through its ruling deity, the Ten Vishvadevas.

It belongs to the Air element. This definitely must relate to its connection with the airy planet Saturn. Besides ether, air is the most all encompassing element. Uttarashadha, which has more to do with responsibility, equality and justice, has to have an all encompassing framework to manifest its ten golden qualities.

Gana (Type) :

It is considered a *Manusha* or human nakshatra. The fact that its ruling deities are known as Vishvadevas, coupled with the fact that *Vishva* is one of the common terms used for terrestrial affairs on our planet; reveals the intensive involvement of this nakshatra with human affairs on the earthly realm. It is said that one can only truly understand and develop the ten qualities associated with Uttarashadha in a human birth. It is for this reason that a lot of astral beings like demi-gods are vying for earthly incarnations under suitable conditions.

Orientation & Disposition :

It is Upward nakshatra. All upward nakshatras are considered good for things which grow or progress over time. We have already mentioned that all activities commenced under the positive influence of Uttarashadha grow in leaps and bounds and achieve permanence. Another way of looking at it is that Uttarashadha takes its cue from up above.

It is a *Dhruva* (fixed or permanent) nakshatra. If there is any nakshatra which can be considered as the 'doyen of permanence', it is Uttarashadha. In fact all the qualities associated with the character Dhruva (son of a demon king who was an ardent worshipper of *Vishnu*), are the same as those belonging to Uttarashadha. In honour of this character, the pole star was known as *Dhruvatara* in

Vedic texts. In the same vein, one can understand that Uttarashadha is the pivot of good qualities around which the game of life revolves.

Lunar Month & Day :

It relates to the second half of the lunar month of *Ashadha*, a period which usually falls in late July in the solar calendar.

Uttarashadha is also related to *Purnima* (15th tithi or Full Moon day) of the waxing phase of the Moon's monthly cycle.

Auspicious Activities :

Planning new beginnings; Laying out plans for anything; Initial plans for any activity; Beginning things anew; Laying foundations; All spiritual/religious activities & rituals; Putting one's affairs in order; Activities requiring great discernment and correct judgement; All types of Business affairs; Signing Contracts; Promotions; Acting authoritatively; Artistic Ventures; Marriage; Sexual Activity; Entering a new residence; dealing with authority; Public, Political or Legal matters; One of the best nakshatras for initiating any kind of activity.

Inauspicious Activities :

Unfavourable for travel; Not good for concluding matters/endings. Uttarashadha is generally good for everything except committing unlawful activities. Unethical, rude, impetuous and primitive behaviour is not allowed here.

Planetary Ruler :

Sun is the main planetary ruler of this nakshatra. The solar principle, which was born in Krittika, reaches its zenith in this nakshatra. Theoretically it is suffice to say that the Sun does not exist after this nakshatra. It means that the soul's ability to effect its surroundings reaches a peak in this nakshatra. In its highest aspect, the individual will is completely tuned with the universal will and thus all the actions on a worldly plane are taken without the involvement of ego and selfishness. The sense of right and wrong which is required here is not related to personal human laws but to the divine laws of the universal mind. This is the nakshatra where the ego and individuality is sacrificed for the sake of the greater good.

Since this nakshatra lies in the signs Sagittarius and Capricorn, Jupiter and Saturn have a strong relationship with it. We can note that Jupiter and Saturn also rule the four padas of this nakshatra. The combination of expansive Jupiter and contractive Saturn signifies moderation and practicality. Since Jupiter reaches maximum debilitation in the Capricorn part of this nakshatra, it is implied that this part of the nakshatra is not suited for too much hope, idealism, expansiveness or outer religious displays and rituals. In simple language, this is the place for action, not words. The concrete practical action, which takes place here, shapes the material world according to universal laws.

Jupiter/Saturn, Sun/Jupiter, Sun/Saturn & Sun/Jupiter/Saturn conjunctions carry energies similar to Uttarashadha. Planets Mercury, Venus and Jupiter, unless operating from their higher aspect, can make one too materialistic if placed in the Capricorn part of this nakshatra. All planets when placed in this nakshatra, are prone to excessive and misplaced idealism, unless the individual will is working in harmony with the universal will. Every error one makes under the influence of this nakshatra is magnified, due to the enormous capacity of this nakshatra to influence the material world.

Vowels and Alphabets :

The first pada or quarter of this asterism 26° 40' -30° 00' Sagittarius corresponds to "Be" as in Beth.

The second pada or quarter of this asterism 00° 00' - 3° 20' Capricorn corresponds to "Bo" as in Bohemian.

The third pada or quarter of this asterism 3° 20' - 6° 40' Capricorn corresponds to "Ja" as in Jar.

The fourth pada or quarter of this asterism 26° 40' - 10° 00' Capricorn corresponds to "Ji" as in Jingle.

In the Sanskrit alphabet Uttarashadha corresponds to "Bha", consequently its mantra is "Om Bham".

Sexual Type and Compatibility :

The sexual animal related to this nakshatra is the Mongoose. Uttarashadha is not very sexual in the first place, which is clear from the fact that the mongoose has no compatible sexual animal amongst the other nakshatras. To put it simply, sexuality is not Uttarashadha's domain.

For sexual & marital compatibility with other nakshatras please refer to the table on pages 468 & 469.

Esoteric :

The legend of the birth of *Ganesh* carries within itself all the tragedy, valour, divinity, esotericism, enforced sacrifice, renewal and regeneration inherent in Uttarashadha. In short the story goes like this:-

"*Parvati* created a mind borne son and instructed him to stand as a guard and not to let anyone in while she was bathing. Her husband *Shiv*, returning home, was barred entry by Parvati's son. Shiv had not seen this boy before and did not know who he was, and the boy in turn did not recognize Shiv. Harsh words were exchanged and a battle erupted. Shiv could not defeat this boy and had to retreat. He felt humiliated after being defeated by a mere child and sought the help of *Vishnu* and other Gods to defeat the child.

In the battle that ensued, all of the Gods together were unable to defeat him. Vishnu finally came up with a plan that someone should fight with the boy from the front, while he flew from behind to stealthily take the mace out of the boy's hand. Vishnu's theory was that the boy couldn't be defeated until the mace was taken out of his hand. The plan worked, as Shiv was able to cut the boy's head with his trident as soon as Vishnu's vehicle *Garud* (celestial eagle) snatched the mace.

Since he was Parvati's mind borne son she immediately came to know of his death and the whole story flashed before her mind's eye. She became enraged and summoned all the *Shaktis* (feminine forces) of the universe to create havoc on Vishnu, Shiv and the rest of the Gods. The whole creation went completely haywire and all the Gods were scared out of their wits. Vishnu realized that the whole universe would collapse if Parvati was not appeased quickly. This could only be done if the boy was brought back to life.

Vishnu instructed the Gods to descend on earth and bring back the head of the first thing they saw. They saw an elephant and swiftly returned with its head. Vishnu and Shiv attached the elephant's head to the trunk of the boy's body, which resurrected him. Finally Parvati's anger subsided and order was restored in the universe. The boy was named 'Ganesh', which translates into 'the leader of all tribes', and was given the boon to be worshipped first before any other Gods."

As the 21st asterism, Uttarashadha relates to the number 21. According to the ancients the number 21 is called 'The Crown of the *Magi*. The 'Crown' here obviously refers to the seventh sacral centre, *Sahastrar,* which is the final resting place of the *kundalini.* The Pythagoreans see it as a special number because it is a multiple of the two sacred numbers 3 and 7. We know that there are three channels *Ida*, *Pingala* and *Sushumna,* which carry the lifeforce within our astral bodies through the seven sacral centres. 21 can be seen as a summation of the passage of these three channels through the seven sacral centres. Uttarashadha therefore relates to perfection on all levels, physical, mental and spiritual.

In the *Tarot* Deck, the 21st card is "*The World*", which is seen to represent the whole earthly plane of existence with all its complexities and diversities. It also represents perfection and finality from a universal perspective. We can easily relate this symbolism with Uttarashadha's ruling deities, "The Ten Lords or Overseers of the World".

Gotra (Celestial Lineage) :

This nakshatra is related to the *Sage Kratu*, one of the seven celestial sages looking after the affairs of our galaxy. The name of this sage translates into "the inspirer". In a way, inspiring others is one of the main functions of Uttarashadha, as its own goodness sets examples for others to follow. Since the Sage Kratu is associated only with benign nakshatras, we can infer that he has a similar role in celestial circles.

Remedial :

For those suffering from bad effects resulting from afflictions to this nakshatra, the best remedial measure is worship of Ganesh, the remover of obstacles and bestower of wisdom.

Repetition of the root mantras of this nakshatra - "Om Bha" & "Om Bham" - 108 times when Moon transits this nakshatra and in its corresponding lunar month is sure to reduce suffering and bring enlightenment into a person's life.

Persons who are benefiting from the positive energy of this nakshatra can also increase the good effects through the above mentioned ways. It is helpful for them to wear all orange, yellow and light blue colours and whites. They should use its directions, lunar month and the days when Moon transits Uttarashadha to undertake all important actions.

Example :

Uttarashadha's sound and light can be experienced at -

http://osfa.org.uk/uttarashadha.htm

Miscellaneous :

According to *Varahamihira*, those born with Moon in this nakshatra are "modest, graceful, grateful, fortunate, abide by dharma and have many friends".

* * *

22. Shravana   10°00' Capricorn – 23°20' Capricorn

22.

Shravan

(10°00' Capricorn - 23°20' Capricorn)

In the Sky :

Shravan, the apex of lunar energy, is represented in the celestial firmament by three bright stars in the constellation known as *Aquila*

(the Eagle). In modern astronomy these stars are known as *Alpha-Aquilae* (*Altair*), *Beta-Aquilae* (*Alshain*) & *Gamma-Aquilae* (*Tarazed*). These three stars can be seen huddled together on top of the constellation of Capricorn. Altair, having a visual magnitude of 0.93, is one of the brightest objects in the night sky making Shravan a very easily visible asterism. According to the puranic legends, these stars correspond to the three steps taken by *Vishnu* in his *Vaman-avatar.*

Name :

'Shravan" translates into two very unrelated terms - "hearing" and "the one who limps". The limping meaning is in obvious reference to Vishnu's three steps (please refer to the story below in the Esoteric Section); while "hearing" as we shall discover, forms the crux of what this asterism is all about.

Its alternative name is "*Ashvattha*", a term used for the sacred *Pipal* tree (*Ficus Religiosa*). In Vedic texts, this tree is always given extraordinary significance. It is worthwhile to mention that *Buddha* received enlightenment meditating under this tree.

Symbol :

There are three main symbols for this nakshatra. One is a 'row of three uneven footsteps', which as we can see from the nakshatra's image, are represented by its constituent stars. These three steps were supposed to be taken by Vishnu in one of his incarnations, the purpose of which was to establish order in the universe through the restoration of the heaven to the gods and earth to the human beings. We will discuss this story in more detail when we discuss the esoteric aspect of this asterism. These three steps can be seen as the threefold law through which the cosmic intelligence maintains order in the universe. Nature, as we know, operates in three modes and this threefold law relates to the three interactions between these modes.

A 'trident' is the alternative symbol of this asterism, which once again reiterates this asterism's connection to the number '3'. Most numerologists know that '3' is the number of communication and is the energy responsible for establishing order in the universe. This is why all ancient cultures had three main deities responsible for overlooking universal affairs.

An 'ear' is a commonly used symbol for this asterism, which we can see is derived directly from its name. The communication aspect of this asterism is therefore more focused on listening than speaking. Listening is the one and only way one can learn anything. To emphasize this aspect, some wise men assigned three ears as its symbol. The reader can see that in the nakshatra's image the tree is 'full of ears'. In the ancient Indian Vedic tradition, knowledge was orally transmitted and so (*shruti*), the power of listening, automatically became the most important quality an individual could possess. It is because of these oral transmissions that Vedic knowledge is available today in its pristine state. From this we can conjure that this asterism has a lot to do with preservation, in keeping with the nature of the sign it falls in. When a native has a strong Shravan influence in their horoscope, the astrologer can safely advise that person to learn to listen more to others, or pay attention to one's inner voice in order to grow or progress in life.

Deity :

Vishnu, the preserver among the Trinity, is the main presiding deity of this asterism. His relationship with this nakshatra is already established from the symbolism and mythology associated with this nakshatra. It is because of this strong relationship with Vishnu that this nakshatra gets its strong organizational ability, which is normally associated with the sign Capricorn. In keeping with Vishnu's nature, this nakshatra likes to bring order through tact and cleverness and in many a case, through any which way possible. It allows one to be able to listen, assimilate and contemplate on a problem to arrive at the solution. Like Vishnu, this asterism does not believe in hurrying with things and is ready to sit and wait until the time is ripe.

Saraswati, the goddess of learning, is also strongly associated with this nakshatra, even though very few scholars acknowledge this fact. This nakshatra is not all about listening. It is also related to speech and the ability to put learning into words. Someone has to speak for someone to listen! This relationship with Saraswati connects this nakshatra to the use and study of languages, music and a fascination for all media connected with education.

Nature & Functioning :

On a positive level Shravan is an amicable nakshatra, which tries to be reasonable and keep its peace with its surroundings. It is calculative, but in its higher expression this calculativeness does not have selfish motivations. Even its stubborn, unyielding nature is directed towards a higher cause in its positive aspect. It is a persevering nakshatra which doesn't like to leave things in the middle or undone. This is probably the reason why it is said that any activity started in this nakshatra always reach its completion.

In its negative aspect, all its qualities like perseverance, shrewdness and knowledge are used for purely selfish means. Its power to listen, learn and teach meaningful things is usually lost in gossip, backbiting and manipulation. Since it is a very goal oriented nakshatra, it becomes dangerous when its goals are unwholesome and unethical. Narrow-mindedness is one of the strong traits to emerge out of the negative functionings of this nakshatra. This nakshatra requires toning down of the ego, as listening without preconceptions is the only way to learn. There is always a danger with this nakshatra that a person under its influence may not always learn the right things. A person born under a strong influence of this asterism should always be very careful of the company they keep. There is always some foolhardiness attached with Shravan. The native can easily fall prey to deception and bad advice.

In its highest level of functioning, this asterism relates to acquiring universal knowledge and applying it to bring about order in the material world. It usually bestows very strong powers of erudition and sagacity. Oratory and other forms of lecturing come naturally and effortlessly to such natives. In the present times, much of the organizational ability of this nakshatra has been used for destructive and degenerative ends. This asterism is connected to all forms of media and in today's world most of the media is used for propagating falsehood, lies and devoluting influences.

Shravan is a socially active nakshatra which revels in public dealings. It has a very business like approach to things, even though maintaining cordiality is its primary objective. If this nakshatra is rising on the Ascendant, the person is likely to be mature in their approach, cunning, well mannered and receptive with an alert look. The appearance is a mix of Moony softness and Saturnine rigidity. Such people are usually clever in conversation and are skilled at putting others at ease quickly. In the present day and age, most of them can be seen spending a whole lot of time on the telephone! Whether a native under the influence of this nakshatra will listen more or speak more, depends upon the planet posited in this asterism. For example, if Saturn is posited in this nakshatra, one will tend to listen more and may find speaking difficult, while a person who has Mars placed in this nakshatra can be quite a chatterbox, but may not be well-versed in the art of listening .

Philosophical and religious attitudes which rely heavily upon phrases like "Word is God ..." and "In the beginning, there was the word, from which arose everything else ...", corresponds to this nakshatra's line of thinking. It is true that "*Om*" (or *Aum*) was the first sound at the beginning of creation, but it is important to remember that the seed of the universe lay in a silent state before that. The "word" is not "god", but just one of the many expressions of the ultimate causative principle, commonly known as "god".

The downfall of this nakshatra usually lies in excessive generosity which leads to debts and poverty. It can also make enemies through bigotry, narrow-mindedness or extreme ethical stances. This nakshatra is not favourable for having and raising children. This seems to hold true in charts where this asterism falls in the fifth house. When Ascendant or Moon is placed in this asterism, or it is placed in the fifth house, or the fifth lord is placed in this asterism, it usually denotes few children and the native derives little happiness from them. On the contrary, they are always a source of anxiety for them.

In the universal scheme of things, Shravan relates to "*apradhrishya shakti*" - the power to give permanent victory. Its symbolism has achievable goals above, and the strength to achieve those goals below. This imagery is self explanatory. The only thing worth mentioning is that this strength is not personal strength, but the collective strength, which comes about due to an alliance with the higher forces of good, when one is wholeheartedly and unselfishly trying to establish righteousness over unrighteousness.

Mode of Functioning :

It is supposed to be a Passive nakshatra. Its passivity relates to the fact that it is receptive and takes time to listen to others. In fact, much of its organizational skill comes from a passive approach to things. It tends to let things organize themselves rather than poke its head into the process too much.

Caste :

Its caste is *Mleccha* (outcaste). It might surprise some that this amicable and worldly nakshatra should be regarded as an outcaste. The thing to note here is that this nakshatra was in some way connected with the lower Capricornian type working class in ancient times. It was related to people who had to basically listen to orders and carry them out. On the higher levels this nakshatra relates to individuals who listen to and follow the inner voice without caring much for the social order of their times, which again puts them in an outcaste category !

Gender :

It is a Male nakshatra. This can easily be seen from the fact that its primary ruling deity is Vishnu, one of the three bearers of the masculine principle. It carries a sense of objectivity, a very masculine quality. It does have a soft, feminine side to it since Saraswati, one of the three main feminine archetypes, is also connected with it. Saraswati's feminine principle again relates to logic, reason and learning, but her influence imparts some sensitivity.

Bodyparts & Humor (Ayurvedic Constitution) :

The primary body parts it relates to are the Ears and Sex Organs. In our view, it can be seen as the primary indicator of ear and secondary indicator of sex organs. Considering its symbol and imagery, its relationship with the ears comes as no surprise. Besides being the organs of listening, ears are the balancing organs for the body. This again highlights the balanced nature of this asterism. Its relationship with the sexual organs is mainly connected to its connection with procreation as a means of preservation.

Shravan is also related to one's gait. Capricorn, as we know, is the sign related to gait, but it is only the Shravan part of it which relates to gait. Any affliction to this nakshatra can result in limping or lameness, especially if the lords of the 9th, 10th, 11th or 12th houses are involved.

It is a primarily "Kapha" (watery) nakshatra due to its strong relationship with the Moon.

Direction :

Its primary directions are south and northwest.

Padas (Quarters) :

The first pada or quarter of this asterism 10° 00' - 13° 20' Capricorn falls in Aries Navamsa and is therefore ruled by Mars. Someone born under this pada expresses an underlying Martian quality in relation to the nakshatra, which is expressed as logic, initiative and a career conscious or ambitious approach.

The second pada or quarter of this asterism 13° 20' - 16° 40' Capricorn falls in Taurus Navamsa, ruled by Venus. Therefore the Venusian qualities such as diplomacy, tact and courtesy are dominant influences in the way this nakshatra expresses itself. This pada corresponds to Pushkara Navamsa and any planet posited in this pada will give the best results as far as this asterism is concerned. This pada relates to those involved in organizational aspects of the entertainment industry, especially the music business.

The third pada or quarter of this asterism 16° 40' - 20° 00' Capricorn falls in Gemini Navamsa, ruled by Mercury. This pada brings out the part of Shravan which is flexible, cunning, versed in speech and conversation and eager to learn. This pada relates to those working in the mass-media and other communication oriented occupations.

The fourth pada or quarter of this asterism 20° 00' - 23° 20' Capricorn falls in Cancer Navamsa, ruled by Moon. This pada brings out the part of Shravan which is receptive, sympathetic and understanding. It is the most mass-oriented pada of this asterism and thus relates the most to those holding important public offices or those in lunar-occupations like hoteliers etc.

Professions :

Teachers, Preachers and Educators in all fields; Scholars, Students and all those associated with universities; Linguists, Language Translators and Interpreters; Story Tellers and Narrators; Comedians; Those involved in the Music Business and Recording Industry (mainly Producers and Sound technicians); Telephone Operators and all those earning their livelihood by some kind of phone job; Those involved in the preservation of ancient traditions and those pursuing classical studies; Those involved in organizational capacities in big and small corporations; Gossip Columnists, News Broadcasters, Talk Show Hosts and others involved in the radio/television business; Modern day Counsellors, Psychiatrists, Psychoanalysts and Psychologists; Radio Operators in different fields (even those who are involved in catching signals from other civilizations in the galaxy!); Travel Agents and all those involved in the Transportation and Tourism industry; Those working in the Hotel/Restaurant business; On a higher level Healers and Practitioners of holistic medicine and on a lower level those involved with allopathy, hospitals and the medical profession in general; Those connected with Charitable organizations, clubs and societies.

Places :

Universities; Libraries; Schools; Colleges; Public Auditoriums and other places of public gatherings; Recording Studios; Hospitals; Telephone Companies; Basically all the places connected to the above mentioned professions.

Guna (Essence) and Tattwa (Element) :

It is a primarily *Rajasic* nakshatra. This means that it is active on the worldly plane. This activity can be motivated either by universal interests or purely selfish interests, depending upon the evolutionary level of the soul in question. This is a good nakshatra for attaining wealth and worldly accomplishments in general. If a person under a strong influence of this asterism is poor, one can infer that this poverty is self inflicted, rather than being fated.

Its element is Air, which again emphasizes the communication aspect of this nakshatra. It usually relates well to the fire nakshatras like *Uttaraphalguni* etc.

Gana (Type) :

It is a Godly nakshatra. This is evident since Vishnu, the harbinger of all godly qualities, presides over this asterism. This relates to its gentle, kind, amicable, liberal minded, prosperous, reasonable and sociable nature. Shravan natives always think twice about doing harm to others and are not prone to take the lead in any sort of cruelty.

Orientation & Disposition :

It is an Upward Looking nakshatra. This relates to its expansive attitude in relation to life in general. After all, Vishnu took three very expansive steps (refer to the story in the Esoteric Section) to take away the control of all the three worlds from *Bali* (the demon king). This expansiveness in today's world tends to boil down to ambition.

This is a Moveable nakshatra. This is thus a nakshatra which promotes travel, mostly in relation to the career. A lot of natives under its strong influence go touring as part of their job, which may involve lecturing and teaching. Natives may enjoy the hotel/tourism side of travelling with this nakshatra placement.

Lunar Month & Day :

Its energies correspond to the first 9 days of the lunar month of *Shravan*. This period usually corresponds to the month of August in the solar calendar.

Shravan is also related to the *Trittiya* (3rd tithi or day) of the waxing and waning phases of the Moon's monthly cycle.

Auspicious Activities :

Religious rituals and performances; Beginning new ventures; Entering a new house or buying property; Medical actions and remedial measures; Taking preventive measures of all kinds; Listening to advice (listening in general); Social interactions and public involvement; Learning, study of languages and classical traditions; Reading and writing; Music, philosophy & meditation; Good for sexual activity; Making peace; Organizing in general; Making and taking herbs and medicines; Politics; Purchasing new clothes, items and equipment for home or business; Initiations in spiritual learning; Giving and receiving counselling; Important phone calls; Favourable for travel, especially towards its ruling directions; Taking a new name; Humanitarian actions in general; Worship of Vishnu or Saraswati.

Inauspicious Activities :

Unfavourable for aggressive, uncertain or risky activities such as lawsuits, wars etc.; Not good for creative activities involving manual work; Not good for lending, making promises, oaths etc.; Not good for putting an end to things like demolishing old structures; Not good for worshipping fierce deities like *Rudra*; It is not considered favourable for marriage ceremonies or adopting children.

Planetary Ruler :

Moon and Saturn are the two planets governing this nakshatra. Moon is the nakshatra's main planetary ruler and Saturn rules Capricorn, the sign that it falls in. Moon relates to the receptive and gentle part of Shravan, while Saturn relates to its persevering and organizational aspect.

Both Moon and Saturn are intimately connected with the masses and mass mentality. This is where this nakshatra gets its ability to influence mass opinions. This is probably the reason why a lot of politicians are under a strong influence of this nakshatra. The 10th house, which has a similar energy to Shravan, bestows position and influence so that one may educate the masses in universal values and truths. In today's world however, where the majority among the masses are ignorant and the leaders dumb and selfish, only the negative aspects of this nakshatra come to life. In its higher aspect, it relates to dissemination of universal truths and knowledge through entertaining and easy to understand Vedic epics like the *Mahabharat* and *Ramayan*.

The lunar energy attains completion in Shravan. In numerology, '2' is considered to be the Moon's number. Shravan is the 22nd asterism and the double '2's' signify the summation of the lunar energy. This means that all the best and worst of the lunar qualities are expressed through this nakshatra. Due to its extreme receptivity, error in judgement is very likely with this nakshatra. Other negative lunar traits like changeability, vacillation, imaginary fears and phobias are also seen in their extreme expression here. Only in evolved souls do the positive lunar qualities of universal compassion, motherly nurturing and complete receptivity to the universal mind are witnessed.

Moon in Capricorn, Saturn in Cancer or Moon/Saturn together in any sign or house, are the placements and combinations which carry an energy similar to that of Shravan.

Moon, Saturn, Mars, Mercury and Venus do well in Shravan. Venus however can make one too materialistic unless there are other elevating factors.

Vowels and Alphabets :

The first pada or quarter of this asterism 10° 00' - 13° 20' Capricorn, corresponds to "Ju" as in Jupiter or Justin.

The second pada or quarter of this asterism 13° 20' - 16° 40' Capricorn, corresponds to "Je" as in Jennifer or Jet.

The third pada or quarter of this asterism 16° 40' - 20° 00' Capricorn, corresponds to "Jo" as in Joe.

The fourth pada or quarter of this asterism 20° 00' - 23° 20' Capricorn, corresponds to "Gha" as in Ghana or Ghastly.

In the Sanskrit alphabet Shravan corresponds to "Mam", and so its mantra would be "Om Mam".

Sexual Type and Compatibility :

Its sexual animal is a Monkey, which indicates more affinity towards affection and playfulness than the actual sexual act. Those under the influence of this nakshatra can be exhibitionist in regards to sexual activities. They are prone to talk more about it rather than actually indulge in it.

For sexual & marital compatibility with other nakshatras please refer to the table on pages 468 & 469.

Esoteric :

The main puranic story connected with this asterism is as follows:-

"A demon king called Bali had taken over all the three worlds (earth, heaven and the netherworld) through his might and prowess. The beaten *devas* (demi gods) appealed to Vishnu for help. Vishnu assured them that he would restore their heavenly abode to them and rid the universe of the rule of the demons. He waited until Bali was performing a big *Yagya* (elaborate religious ceremony). One of the rules of this Yagya was that Bali could not refuse the demand of any *brahmin*. Keeping this in mind, Vishnu went to this Yagya in the form of a young brahmin boy. Like all the other brahmins present there, he was honourably received by Bali and asked what he could do for him. Vishnu in his *Vaman* form (young Brahmin boy form) asked Bali for land which he could cover within his three strides. This demand amused Bali as he thought, "Why would this little Brahmin boy want something as little as three foot strides of land, when he could ask me for millions of other things?"

Bali's preceptor, *Shukracharya*, could see through Vishnu's act and warned Bali not to give into the innocent looking brahmin boy's request. Bali was a man of his word and told his preceptor that even though he honoured and respected him, he couldn't go against his vow, and had no option but to fulfil the brahmin boy's wish. Shukracharya became furious with Bali for not paying heed to his advice and left the assembly. When Bali was pouring the sacred water from his pot as a ritual marking for granting the boy's wish, Shukracharya assumed a tiny form and stuck himself in the pot's spout so that no water could come out of it. Vishnu obviously knew what was going on and so he took a sharp blade of grass to clear the obstruction. It is said that this blade of grass destroyed one of Shukracharya's eyes, and this is the reason why he is always portrayed as having one eye ever since.

With the obstacle removed and the ritual over, it was time for the brahmin boy to take his three strides worth of land. Suddenly the boy's size started increasing until it got so big that no one could see his head anymore. In one stride he took both the netherworld and the earth, and in the second stride he took heaven. Then Vishnu turned around to Bali and said, "Now where do I put my third foot?" Bali knowing that he had no other place to give, offered his own head for him to put his third stride. Vishnu smiled and put his foot on Bali's head.

Bali was immediately transported into the lowest among the fourteen *lokas*. Vishnu had now restored the earth to humans and the heavens to the gods. He was however very pleased with Bali's magnanimity and devotion to universal laws. He conferred on him the status as the doorkeeper of the 'outer most universal sheath'. He also promised to help him out whenever he was in need. At a later point in time, Vishnu actually took the job of a doorkeeper in Bali's palace at his behest ! "

If one just contemplates on this story, it reveals everything about the nature, functioning and quality of Shravan. Vishnu taking the form of an innocent brahmin boy relates to the amiable, innocent front projected by this nakshatra. This nakshatra is clever in achieving its goals in much the same way as Vishnu was about achieving his. This nakshatra keeps to its word the same way Bali kept his word.

One interesting thing which comes out of this story is that Venus doesn't like to be placed in this asterism, seeing how this incident was detrimental to Shukracharya, who is intimately connected with the planet Shukra (Venus). This might seem odd as Capricorn is a friendly sign to Venus. In our view Venus does better in other parts of Capricorn in comparison with the Shravan part.

This story also brings out the highest expression of this nakshatra, which is upholding the universal law at all costs. Since '21' is seen as the number of perfection, the number '22' is regarded as '0' or a new beginning by ancient mystery schools. Even in the Tarot deck, the 22nd card does not exist. Instead there is a '0' card known as "*The Fool*". "The Fool" is a character, who is ready to jump into any unknown or foreign situation without any concern for the past, future or its consequences. If this character is receiving its impulses from the universal mind, then all the actions undertaken are fruitful and necessary. On the other hand, if this character is guided by the ego or other false external influences, the outcome is disaster. This character is what Shravan is all about.

Gotra (Celestial Lineage) :

This nakshatra is related to the *Sage Vashishta*, one of the seven celestial sages looking after the affairs of our galaxy. The name of this sage translates into "possessor of wealth", so the prosperity aspect of this nakshatra is reinforced from this angle as well.

Remedial :

For those suffering from bad effects resulting from afflictions to this nakshatra, the best remedial measure is worship of Vishnu, the preserver and maintainer of all creation. This worship can be done through use of mantra and meditation on any or all of Vishnu's incarnations and aspects.

Repetition of the root mantra of this nakshatra - "Om Mam" 108 times when Moon transits this nakshatra and in its corresponding lunar month, is sure to reduce suffering and bring enlightenment into a person's life.

Persons who are benefiting from the positive energy of this nakshatra can also increase its good effects through the above mentioned ways. It is helpful for them to wear colours like white and light blue. They should use its directions, lunar month and the days when Moon transits Shravan to take all important actions.

Example :

Shravan's sound and light can be experienced at -

http://osfa.org.uk/shravan.htm

Miscellaneous :

According to *Varahamihira*, Moon in Shravan makes a person "learned, rich, famous and prosperous; and gives the native a liberal minded spouse".

* * *

23. Dhanishta   23°20' Capricorn ~ 6°40' Aquarius

23.

Dhanishta

(23º20' Capricorn - 6º40' Aquarius)

In the Sky :

Dhanishta, the zenith of martian energy, is represented in the celestial firmament by four stars in the constellation known as *Delphini* (the Dolphin). These four stars are arranged in a *rhombus* shape, which the ancients saw as signifying a drum. In modern astronomy these stars are known as *Alpha-Delphini, Beta-Delphini, Delta-Delphini* & *Gamma-Delphini*. This asterism can be seen lying in the dark empty space above the constellations of Capricorn and Aquarius. Beta Delphini, having a visual magnitude of only 3.63, is the brightest among these stars, making Dhanishta less bright in comparision to other asterisms. However it can be easily spotted as there are no bright constellations in its vicinity.

Name :

'Dhanishta "translates into - "the wealthiest" or "the most beneficient". The reader can already understand the basic energy of this asterism through this simple meaning. Its alternative name is "*Shravishta*", a sanskrit term, which translates into "the most heard of" or "the most famous". This again is a self-explanatory meaning, which directly hints at the extremely lucky quality of this asterism. The name Shravishta implies that Dhanishta forms a pair with the previous nakshatra *Shravan*.

Symbol :

All scholars agree on the fact that a musical drum is the main symbol of this nakshatra. However there is a difference of opinion in regards to the type of musical drum. Some equate the drum with a *tabor*, some with a *tabla*, some with a *mridanga*, but in our view the drum is actually a *damaru*. Damaru is Shiv's favourite drum.

The drum (damaru) conveys two main attributes - music and hollowness. Hollowness here relates to receptivity to outer influences. In its highest expression this receptivity allows one to be an instrument of the universal mind without letting the ego interfere with the process. Since this nakshatra follows Shravan, it relates to the process where what we have listened to is synthesized. This gives this nakshatra the ability to actually accomplish things like playing music etc. In its lowest expression, this nakshatra is susceptible to receiving lower level influences, and thus its outer works are not as elevating as they are in its highest expression. A drum as we know is a rhythmical instrument, which can be associated with time, and time is the rhythm of the universe. This is why this nakshatra is said to have immaculate timing.

Its alternative symbol is a flute, which again emphasizes the fact that music is produced through hollowness, in much the same way as celestial music is created through the hollowness of universal space.

Deity :

Dhanishta is presided over by a group of eight gods called the *Vasus*. "Vasu" translates into "superb", "excellent or "wealthy". Their names are:-

Apa, which translates into 'water'. He is a male deity usually related to *Apah*, the water goddess of *Purvashadha*.

Dhruv, which translates into 'the fixed', and is related to the pole star at any given point in time.

Dhar, which translates into 'a bearer' or 'a stream of water'. This deity is akin to 'the man pouring water from a pot' - the symbol of Aquarius.

Anil, which translates into 'wind'. This deity is the same as *Vayu,* the wind god who is the ruler of *Swati.*

Som, which translates into 'the Moon'. He is the same as the Moon deity associated with *Mrigashira.*

Anal, which translates into 'fire'. This deity is another manifestation of *Agni,* the fire god who rules *Krittika.*

Pratyush, which translates into 'dawn'. He is the male counterpart of *Usha,* the solar goddess who rides in front of the Sun.

Prabhas, which translates into 'light'. This is another solar deity related to the morning time.

As we can see, all these eight deities carry within them the energies of different nakshatras. This makes Dhanishta a sort of compendium of the energies of earlier nakshatras i.e. specifically *Ashvini,* Krittika, Mrigashira, Swati and Purvashadha. These eight Vasus are supposed to be wealthy and skilled at music. This conveys this nakshatra's mastery over the material plane and relates it with the rhythmical, musical functionings of the universal mind. This is probably the reason why a lot of scholars associated the signs of astrology with this asterism, which in a way is understanding the rhythm of the universe.

Shiv is the ultimate presiding deity of this asterism. This can be easily understood from the fact that part of this asterism lies in Aquarius, a sign completely under the influence of Shiv. Ancient puranic scriptures are full of stories of Shiv's immense musical ability. Shiv, even while wreaking havoc and destruction, does so in a graceful and rhythmical dance form known as *tandav,* exemplified by his famous *nataraj* posture. In fact, two of the main Indian classical dance systems directly originate from Shiv.

In a way, this nakshatra can be seen as a bridge between *Vishnu's* and Shiv's energy. It can thus be related to the half -Vishnu, half- Shiv form which can still be found in some temples in India. Vishnu relates to its mastery of the material world, while Shiv relates to its musical and bohemian aspect.

Nature & Functioning :

Much of the nature of this nakshatra can be derived from the nature and qualities of the eight gods presiding over it.

From Apa, it derives its musical ability, confidence, invincibility and a warrior-like disposition, which in its negative aspect can manifest as vanity and obstinacy. This can sometimes lead this nakshatra to 'beat its own drum'.

From Druv, it derives the fixed part of its nature, which relates to its reliability, perseverance and good organizational ability. In a negative aspect it manifests as stubbornness. Dhanishta natives do not like to be told what to do !

From Dhar, it derives its wisdom, charitable nature and conversational ability. In its negative aspect it makes one a chatterbox, or having a tendency to disperse their energies in unconstructive, unwholesome ways.

From Anil, this nakshatra derives its business acumen, resourcefulness and motivation to accomplish things. In its negative aspect this can make one self seeking or generally worried about their prospects.

From Anal, it derives its energy, mental acumen and discrimination. In its negative aspect it can make this nakshatra bad tempered and consequently capable of hurting others.

From Pratyush, it derives its radiance, happiness, joy and hopefulness. Nature expresses unbounded joyfulness through sunrise, which this nakshatra usually tries to accomplish through music and dancing.

From Prabhas, it derives its lightheartedness, purity, good nature and wholesome aspirations.

From Som, it derives its gentleness and sensitivity, which sometimes can manifest as fickleness, deceptiveness or extreme indulgence.

The reader can easily infer from the above that Dhanishta is all about living a good life. The reader can also infer how it is not easy to put the Dhanishta personality in a box. It has many diverse aspects to its nature, making it one of the most expressive among the nakshatras. It has an ability to adapt itself to any situation in which it finds itself.

Those born with Dhanishta rising on the Ascendant usually carry a rich, liberal, radiant expression on their faces. They exude confidence and nobility. They have a peculiarly captivating smile, which conveys a feeling of deep satisfaction at some inner level. In some cases they can have roving eyes.

Being good conversationalists, Dhanishta natives can always put the other person at ease very quickly. This will hold more true of those natives who are born under the Aquarius part of this nakshatra. The Capricorn part has a more worldly orientation and thus lacks in the more refined, divine aspects.

All those who have Dhanishta happening in their chart, one way or the other, have a good sense of rhythm and enjoy music and dance. It is very easy for them to excel in these fields if they work at it. Dhanishta natives tend to be good at sports because rhythm and timing are the key to almost all sports. This holds especially true for track and field athletics, ball games and gymnastics. Natives are especially good at sports like gymnastics, where grace is a prerequisite.

This is a social nakshatra, which likes to be part of groups. It is not a loner and likes to mingle with people. Since it is naturally ambitious and is always conscious of its 'dharma', it very rarely shows escapist tendencies. It would rather confront things, which can make it appear argumentative at times.

When Moon occupies this asterism, the person concerned often goes for mates or partners who are very different in personality and outlook to them. This obviously leads to a lot of conflict in these issues. This can be seen to be most true when Moon occupies the Capricorn part of this asterism. A lot of scholars are unanimous regarding the peculiar property of this asterism in promoting marital discord.

Since this asterism carries so many good qualities, such a thing does not make sense straight away. In our view the martian aspect of this asterism is responsible for this problem.

Mars is regarded as the most unfavourable planet for marital harmony. Once again the Capricorn part of this asterism has more problems in this regard as compared to the Aquarius part. This is simply because Aquarius has a more accommodating nature as compared to Capricorn. These marital difficulties are usually enhanced when either Mars, Saturn, Rahu or Ketu are placed in this nakshatra, especially the Capricorn part. If this placement has some connection with the seventh house, it might be impossible for such a person to have a smooth married life. In our experience, most Cancer Ascendants, whose Ascendant falls within 16° 40' - 30° 00', have difficulty in married life or sometimes don't marry at all. This is because Dhanishta falls on the seventh house cusp. Those under the strong negative influence of the Capricorn part of Dhanishta often end up hating the opposite sex.

Ram, one of Vishnu's avatars, who is regarded as the epitome of good conduct and righteousness, faced numerous problems in his married life. In his chart, Mars is placed in the Capricorn part of Dhanishta in the seventh house. He had to fight a big war to rescue his kidnapped wife *Sita,* and even after things returned to normal, he had to abandon her on some very flimsy ground. The readers can refer to the ancient Vedic epic of "*Ramayan*" for the whole story.

Dhanishta always has the ability to tune into some source. The most important aspect of this is the source it tunes itself into. In the present day world where media acts as the primary influence for the masses, and provides them with ever declining and degenerating standards of culture, music, dance, fine arts etc., most Dhanishta kinds find themselves tuning into these unwholesome influences. This is the reason why the higher expressions of this nakshatra, which come about by direct tuning in with the universal mind, are a rarity nowadays.

In the universal scheme of things, Dhanishta relates to " *khyapayitri shakti*" - the power to give fame and abundance. Its symbolism has birth above and prosperity below. This symbolism and imagery re-emphasizes the beneficial and positive aspect of this nakshatra. Dhanishta can be seen as the zenith of worldly achievements, a characteristic often attached with the sign Capricorn. It goes without saying that only when these worldly achievements are in tune with universal requirements do they have any lasting meaning.

Mode of Functioning :

In keeping with its basic nature and disposition, ancient Vedic seers saw this as an active asterism. Even infants born under a strong influence of this nakshatra are more active than other infants. They start to respond to music from a much earlier age than others. This is a nakshatra meant for getting out in the world and doing things.

Caste :

It belongs to the Farmer caste. It is puzzling for everyone to understand why such a wealthy and well endowed asterism should be assigned to the working caste. This relates to the fact that this nakshatra falls in Saturn's sign, a planet which was seen as belonging to the working class. Dhanishta is involved in all farmer like, creative activities, which deal with actual production of goods etc.

Gender :

It is a Female nakshatra. This is odd considering the fact that all its presiding deities are male. This is because this nakshatra relates more to the energies of its deities, rather than the actual deities themselves. These energies are their '*shaktis*' and are always feminine. It is a feminine force which presides over all creative arts like music and dancing. It is no wonder then, that all male dancers of the classical forms are quite feminine in their appearance and disposition !

Bodyparts & Humor (Ayurvedic Constitution) :

The bodyparts it relates to the most are the back and the anus. The spinal cord as we know is directly related to the planet Saturn and the sign Capricorn. The *kundalini* energy rises from the area around the anus and travels upwards through the back to the top *chakra* on the head. This is the only way for human beings to tune into the universal mind. As discussed earlier, this nakshatra requires one to do that in order to express its qualities.

It is a primarily "*pitta*" (fiery) nakshatra due to its strong relation with Mars.

Direction :

It is related to east, south east, south, west and southwest.

Padas (Quarters) :

The first pada or quarter of this asterism 23° 20' - 26° 40' Capricorn, falls in Leo Navamsa and is ruled by Sun. This portion relates to the ambitious part of this asterism. It combines the energies of Sun, Mars and Saturn and directs one towards worldly accomplishments. Since Sun as we know is not a favourable planet for marriage, this pada is not good for marital harmony. It can also be too aggressive. This pada assures easy success in one's undertakings, and often brings the native under its influence into some kind of limelight.

The second pada or quarter of this asterism 26° 40' - 30° 00' Capricorn, falls in Virgo Navamsa ruled by Mercury. It relates to the skilful and communicative part of this nakshatra. This is a highly adaptable pada which often gives a lot of success in one's chosen pursuits, however once again Mercury's mutability is not good for marital harmony. The rulership of Mercury gives this pada good mind-hand coordination, which promotes musical and athletic skill.

The third pada or quarter of this asterism 0° 00' - 3° 20' Aquarius, falls in Libra Navamsa ruled by Venus. This relates to the amicable, optimistic, happy, social, musical, group orientated and wealthy aspect of Dhanishta. Since Venus is the natural significator of harmony, this pada promotes marital harmony. This is the pada which carries the most refined and subtle attributes of this nakshatra. It relates to those involved in music, fine arts, divination and astrology.

The fourth pada or quarter of this asterism 3° 20' - 6° 40' Aquarius, falls in Scorpio Navamsa ruled by Mars. This pada has excessive martian energy and relates to the rhythmical aspect of this asterism. It is helpful in creative arts requiring a lot of energy like drumming etc. This pada is sympathetic to the underdog, however this pada is not good for marital harmony due to its excessive aggressiveness. This pada has a warrior's attitude and gives sporting prowess and athletic ability.

Professions :

Musicians, Dancers and Performers; All those involved in the Management side of the entertainment industry; Drummers and those involved in the rhythm sections of bands and orchestras; Creative Artists of all types; Those involved in military bands and other types of marching bands; Gemstones and Precious Metal Dealers; Athletes and other Sports Persons; Group Coordinators in all fields; Those in the Real Estate Business; Landscape Artists; Those who deal in Financial Transactions; Scientists and Physicists; Computer Professions; Warriors and Military people; Poets, Songwriters and Reciters of rhythmical incantations; Makers of musical instruments; Vocalists with more emphasis on delivery the melody; Astrologers and Divinators; Psychic Channellers & Mediums; On a higher level those involved in Holistic Healing through Kundalini Yog; On a lower level Surgeons and Medical Practitioners; Professions involving high tech devices and electronic equipment; Professions requiring versatility and multiple task ability; Managers in general. The immense versatility of this nakshatra allows it to be involved in all types of professions, especially those involving large monies.

Places :

All places related to music and other creative arts ranging from Schools to Studios to Dance Halls etc; Meditation Rooms; Managerial Offices; Real Estate Agencies; Gardens; Science Labs; Factories with high tech equipment or producing high tech equipment; Amusement Centres and Sports Stadiums; All places related to sports; Financial centres and institutions like Banks etc.; Safes where wealth and valuables are stored.

Guna (Essence) and Tattwa (Element) :

It is supposed to be a *Tamasic* nakshatra. This is clear from the fact that two inherently tamasic planets, Mars and Saturn, govern this nakshatra. This however does not mean that this nakshatra is averse to activity. It just means that this nakshatra is more geared towards dissolution, than creation or maintenance.

It belongs to the Ether element. The ether element can mingle and cooperate with all the elements. This is what gives this nakshatra its all encompassing quality, just as space and ether pervade everything. This nakshatra likes to keep its horizons as wide as possible.

Gana (Type) :

It is considered a Demonic nakshatra. Once again, this can be attributed to its close relationship to the two natural malefics, Mars and Saturn. It carries an energy which always tries to bring about change in the present. Most godly nakshatras are related to maintaining the status quo, so in the present times however, this seemingly negative quality of this asterism is definitely positive from a universal point of view !

Orientation & Disposition :

It is an Upward Looking nakshatra in keeping with its natural expansive nature. This is a nakshatra signifying increase and expansion.

It is a Moveable or Ephemeral nakshatra. This means that it relates to travelling and change in all its forms. This is probably the reason why some scholars say that this nakshatra does well in foreign countries. A person with a strong influence of this nakshatra is likely to travel a lot and attain success in a foreign land.

Lunar Month & Day :

It relates to the middle portion (the middle 9 days) of the lunar month of Shravan. This period usually corresponds to the month of August in the solar calendar.

Dhanishta is also related to the *Ashtami* (8th tithi or day) of the waxing and waning phases of the Moon's monthly cycle.

Auspicious Activities :

Religious rituals and performances; Creative activities in general, especially musical and dancing; Group activities of all kinds; Mega celebratory events involving huge crowds like concerts, opening ceremonies etc.; All activities involving pomp and splendour; Purchasing moveable and immoveable property; Travelling - good for both short trips and long journeys; All activities requiring aggression and a pro-active attitude; Lending money and all kinds of financial transactions; Meditation and Yog; Gardening; Buying new clothes, gemstones, jewellery etc.; Favourable for treating diseases and commencing educational ventures; Career activities involving fame and recognition; Learning how to use high tech equipment and weapons.

Inauspicious Activities :

Unfavourable for sexual activity or marriage; Activities of a fixed or restrictive character like giving up old habits etc; Not a good time to form new partnerships; Homely activities like cleaning etc; Dealings with people requiring tact, cleverness and gentleness.

Planetary Ruler :

The main planetary influences affecting this nakshatra are Mars, Saturn, Rahu and Uranus, Mars being its primary ruler. It represents the pinnacle of Martian energy. Consequently bravery is a quality strongly associated with this nakshatra. This is the reason why it connects with warriors, weapons and military personnel. Courage is a prerequisite for a lot of sports as well such as adventure sports or mountain climbing, and so this nakshatra finds its expression through people involved in such activities.

Saturn's rulership relates to the persevering nature and organizational ability of this nakshatra. It usually sets itself longterm goals, which it likes to fulfil at any cost. Discipline, as we know, is a key to excelling in any of the creative arts as well.

Dhanishta is the nakshatra which finally accomplishes the difficult task of harmonizing the divergent energies of Mars and Saturn. The martian energy is at its absolute refinement here and this is why Dhanishta is the pinnacle of Martian energy. It has the wisdom to use energy (Mars) constructively over time (Saturn), a quality which brings about all its other good qualities and its ability to gain wealth. We can see how keeping rhythm while playing drums is a very similar activity. Dhanishta understands the rhythm of life, and its capacity to stick to the rhythm/tune makes it reap all the best the universe has to offer.

Its relationship with Rahu and Uranus connects it with the mass media, and this is the reason why a lot of top people in the entertainment industry have a strong Dhanishta influence in their chart. It likes to make people wealthy and respected in their chosen fields, and in the present day and age Rahu and Uranus are keys to astounding success in any field.

In general astrological terms, Mars in Capricorn, Mars in Aquarius, Rahu-Mars conjunction and Mars-Saturn conjunction in nakshatras like Rohini, Mrigashira, Purnavasu, Pushya, Chitra, Anuradha or Uttarabhadrapada carry an energy similar to that of Dhanishta. Rahu-Mars-Saturn conjunction completely carries the energy of this nakshatra.

Moon, Mars, Saturn, Mercury, Venus and Rahu usually do well in Dhanishta. Moon and Mars do better in the Capricorn part while Mercury, Venus and Rahu fare better in the Aquarius part. Saturn's positioning in this nakshatra will make success slow to come and may totally deny marital pleasures.

Vowel s and Alphabets :

The first pada or quarter of this asterism 23° 20' -26° 40' Capricorn, corresponds to "Ga" as in Galileo.

The second pada or quarter of this asterism 26° 40' - 30° 00' Capricorn, corresponds to "Gi" as in Guitar.

The third pada or quarter of this asterism 0° 00' - 3° 20' Aquarius, corresponds to "Gu" as in Google.

The fourth pada or quarter of this asterism 3° 20' - 6° 40' Aquarius, corresponds to "Ge" as in Gate.

In the Sanskrit alphabet Dhanishta corresponds to "Yam" and "Ram", consequently its mantras are "Om Yam" and "Om Ram".

Sexual Type and Compatibility :

Its sexual animal is a Lion. As we will discover later in the Esoteric Section, this nakshatra has a strong connection with the lion, which goes far beyond its sexual preferences. On a sexual plane this type does not relate well with other nakshatras, except the lion/tiger nakshatras - Dhanishta, Chitra, Vishakha and Purvabhadrapada. In keeping with its animal, it is not very enthusiastic about sexual activity even though it might have multiple partners.

For sexual & marital compatibility with other nakshatras please refer to the tables on page .

Esoteric :

The stars of this nakshatra lie very close to the constellation of *Andromeda,* where a lot of godly and *asuric* (demonic) forces are said to reside. However the eight Vasus, which preside over the stars of the constellation of Delphinus, are all godly in nature. Delphinus is associated with Dolphins, the most intelligent and benevolent among all the sea creatures. This nakshatra shares a lot of its traits with dolphins. Even dolphins are known for their permanent mysterious smile!

This constellation sort of lies on the borderline between Shiv's and Vishnu's territory. From an astrological point of view, it connects the signs of Capricorn and Aquarius. Capricorn or the 10th house as we know relates to karma, while Aquarius or the 11th house corresponds to the fruits of karma. This nakshatra thus relates to the fulfilment of one's goals, desires and ambitions as a result of good karma from previous births. It is the balancing point between the forces of maintenance and destruction.

This is the 23rd nakshatra and '23' is a number associated in numerology with the phrase, "the royal star of the lion". This obviously alludes to the star *Regulus*, which forms the core of the nakshatra "*Magha*". In the zodiacal belt, "Magha" lies directly opposite the Aquarius part of this nakshatra. Thus these two nakshatras can be seen as partners. Magha, as we know, is the nakshatra related to royal honours and exalted status. Dhanishta, especially its latter half, also carries within itself these qualities. One can see that the lion is an animal strongly associated with both of these nakshatras. '23' is regarded in numerology as a very fortunate number signifying completion. Both these nakshatras carry the completion aspect of this number, which makes them become the best in their chosen fields, due to repeated past life efforts or having more *paramatmamsha* (the part belonging to the eternal absolute one).

Gotra (Celestial Lineage) :

This nakshatra is related to the *Sage Angiras*, one of the seven celestial sages looking after the affairs of our galaxy. The name of this sage translates into "the fiery one", which is in keeping with the martian aspect of this asterism.

Remedial :

For those suffering from bad effects resulting from afflictions to this nakshatra, the best remedial measure is worship of the lion-riding Goddess *Durga*, or *Hari-Har*, a deity with a half-Vishnu, half-Shiv form. Alternatively one can worship the eight Vasus. The practice of *Raj-yog,* which involves the raising of the *kundalini* through the seven sacred centres, is one of the best ways to utilise this nakshatra's potential.

Repetition of the root mantras of this nakshatra - "Om Yam" and "Om Ram" 108 times when Moon transits this nakshatra and its corresponding lunar month, is sure to reduce suffering and bring enlightenment into a person's life.

Persons who are benefiting from the positive energy of this nakshatra can also increase the good effects through the above mentioned ways. It is helpful for them to wear colours like red, blue and gold. They should use its directions, lunar month and the days when Moon transits Dhanishta to undertake all important actions.

Example :

The Life of *Bheeshm,* one of the major characters in the Vedic epic, *"Mahabharat",* exemplifies the functionings of Dhanishta. He took and observed the vow of lifelong celibacy and was unconquerable in battle; was generous even to his competitors and showed immaculate courage till his dying breath.

Dhanishta's sound and light can be experienced at –

http://osfa.org.uk/dhanishta.htm

Miscellaneous :

According to *Varahamihira,* Moon in Dhanishta makes a person "liberal, brave, rich and adept at music and other fine arts".

* * *

24. Shatabhisha   6°40' Aquarius - 20°00' Aquarius

24.

Shatabhisha

(6°40' Aquarius - 20°00' Aquarius)

In the Sky :

Shatabhisha, the apex of Rahu's functioning, is represented in the celestial firmament by a faint group of stars in the heart of the constellation of Aquarius. The ancients designated a hundred among these faint group of stars as belonging to this asterism. The brightest among this group with a visual magnitude of only 3.85, is a star known in modern astronomy as *Gamma-Aquarii* (*Sadachbia*). Despite its faintness, the general location of this asterism can be gauged by its neighbouring bright star, *Alpha-Aquarii* (*Sadalmelik*). Sadachbia lies slightly above on the left hand side of this bright star.

Name :

'Shatabhisha" (also spelt as "*Shatabhishak*") translates simply into - "the hundred physicians", "the hundred medicines", or "possessing a hundred healers". Though this bizarre name conveys a part of this asterism's functioning, it doesn't completely convey its vast connotations. Its alternative name is "*Shatataraka*" which translates into "possessing a hundred stars". This is in obvious reference to the fact that the vedic seers saw this asterism as a collection of a hundred stars, with each one of the stars representing one physician/medicine.

Symbol :

Its main symbol is an 'empty circle'. This circle can be seen either as a round magical charm or as a representation of the infinite void of creation. A circle can represent many things - the circle of life; the circle of the zodiac; the circle of creation, maintenance and dissolution.

The importance of the circle can be seen from the following words spoken by *Black Elk*, an *Oglala Sioux* holy man - "You have noticed that everything an Indian (native American indian) does is in a circle, and that is because the power of the world always works in circles, and everything tries to be round ... the sky is round, and I've heard that earth is round like a ball, and so are all the stars. The wind, in its greatest power whorls. Birds make their nest in circles, for theirs is the same religion as ours ... even the seasons form a great circle in their changing, and always come back again to where they were. The life of a man is a circle from childhood to childhood, and so it is in everything where power moves."

Besides these universal ideas, the circle also suggests an idea of containment or circulation. There is an idea of protection and hiding related to this asterism. The circle can act as a boundary and protect one from the dangers outside its circumference. A circle can conceal and hide things just like an opaque jar hides the liquid inside. This nakshatra is thus related with secrets and the ability to conceal secrets.

A circle also carries the idea of identity through segregation. A shoreline separates the ocean from land and thus allows for its identity. This asterism thus relates to all enclosed water bodies like lakes and oceans. It however does not represent rivers, as rivers are not enclosed on all sides. In the same way the idea of containment can be seen in our own beings, as the physical body houses and offers protection to the soul or astral body.

This asterism has a lot to do with the idea of protection, which can operate on many levels of existence. The part in the Vedic epic, the *Ramayan,* where *Lakshman* drew a line around the hut for *Sita's* safety and asked Sita not to cross it, is a wonderful example of the magical containment and protection connotation of this asterism.

Deity :

Even though this nakshatra is related to a hundred physicians through its name, its main deity is *Varun,* the lord of the oceans. In essence, Varun can be seen as the representative deity of the water element in nature. This fact automatically relates this nakshatra with all kinds of liquids in the physical as well as astral realm. Varun can be equated with the planet Neptune, as it is seen in modern astrology. Varun like Neptune is the lord of the cosmic and terrestrial waters.

In this nakshatra's image, Varun can be seen holding a pot. This pot contains *Som* - the preferred drink of the gods. This drink is the heavenly ambrosia, which suggests the idea of rejuvenation and intoxication. We can easily see that the liquids we consume in our day to day life produce the same two effects. In the other hand Varun is seen holding some medicinal herbs. This is where the hundred physicians come into the picture. This asterism has a lot to do with healing on all levels of existence, whereas the herbs only signify healing on a physical level.

The idea of magical cures through divine waters is common to all cultures. Our everyday glass of water is a vital rejuvenator in the sense that it keeps us alive. Oceans have always been seen in the Vedic texts as a repositor of herbs which can cure every possible disease. Some of these herbs came out during the churning of the ocean undertaken by the gods and demons collectively (Please refer to the author's previous work "*The Rahu-Ketu Experience*" *Sagar Publications*/India; "*The Key of Life*" *Lotus Press*/USA). Even *Amrit,* the elixir of eternal life, came out of the ocean during this churning.

On the highest level, this asterism falls under the jurisdiction of *Shiv,* the lord of the ascetics. Shiv, as we know, presides over the sign Aquarius, and since this asterism falls in the heart of the sign Aquarius, it automatically falls under Shiv's domain. Consequently it carries within itself Shiv's mystical, contemplative, ascetic and dissoluting nature.

Nature & Functioning :

Secrecy is the one quality which immediately separates Shatabhishak from other nakshatras, even though a lot of other nakshatras like *Anuradha*, *Jyestha* and *Purvashadha* can be secretive. Shatabhishak, however, is in a league of its own when it comes to hiding thoughts, motives, self or anything else. In fact, Shatabhishak derives almost all of its power from what is hidden. Whether it be the herbs in the ocean or secret formulaes of nature's functionings, Shatabhishak always tries to gain access to whatever is hidden and in doing so attains its power. Shatabhishak is not always very ready to share the hidden secrets it has discovered and tries to hide them just like the ocean covers up many a treasure.

As we shall discover, Shatabhishak is one of the main nakshatras presiding over media in all its forms, especially electronic media. In today's world, media as we know, functions on the twin principles of secrecy and deception. The people "running the show" obviously know about the truth regarding the actual seat of power, whilst all that the masses get is a smokescreen. Shatabhishak is the ultimate con artist.

Shatabhishak's essential nature is to view everything with suspicion. Natives under the influence of its energy usually take their time to get accustomed to new things, thoughts, places and people. Their suspicious nature often makes them be on guard, thus making them capable of shielding themselves from harm. Once again, the circle symbolism comes into play. Shatabhishak natives usually draw a hard to penetrate boundary around themselves which makes it difficult for others to approach them. The reclusive aspect of Shatabhishak arises directly from its inclination to create these walls and boundaries.

Natives are generally solitary, eccentric, reclusive, and introverted. The plus side to this aspect is that its reclusivity gives it the capacity to be alone. Being alone gives rise to contemplation, which in turn produces wisdom and enlightenment. In negative cases, this seclusion can only translate into pessimism and self pity. Shatabhishak is as keen on unravelling secrets as it is on keeping secrets. This is why most Shatabhishak natives enjoy activities like solving puzzles or those which involve the pursuit of something hidden.

Shatabhishak loves to get to the truth of anything in much the same way as *Mula* loves to get to the root of everything. Even though Shatabhishak natives are usually quiet and undemonstrative, (which one should expect them to be since they are supposed to be the masters of secrecy); they often blurt out harsh truths at the most inopportune moments. This is in fact one of the major problems Shatabhishak natives face in climbing the ladder of success, especially material success. Refinement and sensitivity is not their forte.

It is noticed that most natives under the strong influence of Shatabhishak lack proper grooming and education in their formative years. They often have to make their own rules for dealing with today's rough world, which adds to their innate roughness. They have extremely cold, calculating heads and there is a marked tendency to completely suppress the emotional nature.

Shatabhishak in a way represents the culmination of the air element. It is thus the master of the mental, analytical and logical. In its higher mode, Shatabhishak can be all pervasive, just like the air. This ability to relate to everyone without preconceptions, judgements and prejudice is what makes a philosopher out of Shatabhishak. Their philosophy is usually heavy on intellectualism, but the evolved souls understand that emotional and mental bodies need to be integrated in order for any true understanding to occur.

Those with Shatabhishak rising have their own particular brand of magnetism, even though they lack conventional charm and beauty. They are often unkempt in relation to their appearance and clothing. Their countenance is usually calm, quiet, shy and reserved but they however have a tendency to explode every now and then. Absentmindedness is one of their marked features. They usually convey a sense of aloofness even if they are genuinely attentive from the inside. Their negative traits include laziness, addictions, perversions and vulnerability to all types of mental/emotional/psychological disorders. Their positive qualities include enterprise, moderation, discrimination, philosophical attitude, truth seeking and unbounded vision.

On a material plane, Shatabhisha has a tendency to make a "zero" out of the things it affects in a nativity. For example if someone has their second lord placed in Shatabhisha they might experience a pauper state or a complete loss of family at some stage of their lives.

In the universal scheme of things, Shatabhisha relates to "*bheshaja shakti*" - the power of healing. Its symbolism has pervasiveness above and support below. This obviously relates to the three worlds - heaven, earth and the nether world. This symbolism shows that Shatabhisha is even more pervasive than *Purvashadha*, a power which it uses to heal the three worlds. The healing process here is different from *Ashvini*, in the sense that it happens through genuine repentance, and sustained effort is required over comparatively longer periods of time. The all-pervasive power that media has in today's world is basically Shatabhisha's power and since this power is in the wrong hands, it is not being used to heal or teach but to fool, chain, dumb down and devolute.

Mode of Functioning :

This is an Active nakshatra. Its active disposition springs directly from its moveable nature. Aquarius as we know is an electric sign. This nakshatra embodies electricity in all its different forms. In the present day and age where most of the communication is electronic, this asterism assumes tremendous importance. This nakshatra is active and fast in much the same way as the fast moving world of electricity.

Caste :

It belongs to the Butcher class and is thus involved in all butcher like or harsh activities, ranging from advanced medical treatment of complicated diseases to just plain killing and hunting. The natives highly influenced by this nakshatra can also be butcher like in their own self mortification or have some twisted tendencies in regards to people and things. Since this nakshatra is not cruel or fierce it is comparatively benevolent despite belonging to the butcher class.

Gender :

It is a Neutral or Eunuch nakshatra, which means that it has a balance of masculine and feminine attributes. Of course one would expect zero or nothingness to be genderless. Since it is a neutral nakshatra it doesn't promote childbirth if it is connected with the 5th house or Jupiter in a nativity. This neutral quality also makes it very dextrous in regards to its dealings with people, which is ideal for media related activities.

Bodyparts & Humor (Ayurvedic Constitution) :

The body part it relates to the most is the Jaw, which emphasizes its relation to the acts of eating, drinking and speaking. It is also related to the Right Thigh.

It belongs to the *Vata* (airy) humor. This classification is clear from Shatabhisha's strong association with primarily vata planets Saturn and Rahu.

Direction :

Its direction is from southwest to southeast.

Padas :

The first pada or quarter of this asterism 6° 40' - 10° 00' Aquarius, falls in Sagittarius Navamsa and is ruled by Jupiter. This relates to the happy go lucky, optimistic and philanthropic side of this nakshatra. This pada has a tendency to get carried away and so it is important for those under the influence of this pada to choose the right thing to get carried away with. They are the kind who will go about fanatically espousing their cause or belief.

The second pada or quarter of this asterism 10° 00' - 13° 20' Aquarius, falls in Capricorn Navamsa ruled by Saturn. This conveys the more practical and organizational aspect of this asterism. This is the pada which relates to all material activities under the domain of Shatabhisha. One has to watch out for excessive ambition in relation to the planets posited in this pada.

The third pada or quarter of this asterism 13° 20' - 16° 40' Aquarius, falls in Aquarius Navamsa ruled by Saturn. This pada relates to the visionary, futuristic and philosophical side of this nakshatra.

In its negative aspect it can be too eccentric and rebellious. Planets placed in this pada often do well on the material plane as this is a vargottama position.

The fourth pada or quarter of this asterism 16° 40' - 20° 00' Aquarius, falls in Pisces Navamsa ruled by Jupiter. This pada relates to the expansive, hallucinatory and illusory side of this nakshatra. When favourable it can give great powers of healing and compassion. When afflicted it can make one too ambiguous. Planets placed in this pada can often make the native lose themselves in one form of intoxication or other. It is however good for activities relying on imagination like filmmaking etc.

Professions :

Electricians and all those who work with electricity; Technology Experts; Radar & X-ray Experts; Chemotherapists; Astronauts; Astronomers & Astrologers; Space Research; Pilots; Radio Operators; Martial Art Instructors & Martial Artists; Aeronautical, Rocket or Space Engineers; Aeronautical Industry; Those who work in the Film and Television Industry; Movie Stars; Trend Setters; Photographers; Science Fiction Writers & Enthusiasts; Nuclear Physicists and Physicists in general; Those working in the Drug & Pharmaceutical Industry; Physicians & Surgeons; Herbologists; Professions connected with the Production & Distribution of Alcohol; Drug Dealers, Pushers; Waste Disposal & Recycling Industry; Pimps & Prostitutes; Those who work in the Production of Plastics; Petroleum & associated Industries; Bikers & Motor Sports; Automobile Industry; Sea Faring Professions; Detectives, Puzzle Experts; Explorers, Hunters & Inventors; Yog & Meditation gurus; Zen Experts.

Places :

High-tech Studios & Environments; Off Shore Drilling Stations; Space Stations; Airports; Observatories & Planetariums; Physics & Chemistry Labs; Bars & Nightclubs especially Techno Clubs; Factories; Hospitals; Nuclear Waste Dumps and Waste Dumps in general; Recycling Stations; Herbal Centers; Water Treatment Plants & Reservoirs; Oceans; Sea-Side; Temples, Meditation, Yog & Zen

Centres; Outer Space; Film & Television Studios; Processing Labs; Hunting Grounds; All places connected to the abovementioned professions.

Guna (Essence) and Tattwa (Element) :

Its basic essence is *Tamas,* which relates to inertia on all levels of existence. The quality of inertia in this nakshatra relates to its capacity for meditation and zen practices. It also relates to its introverted and reclusive nature and on the negative side, a tendency towards intoxication with drugs, alcohol, sex etc.

Its element is Ether. Ether is the element in nature which can mingle with every other element. This associates this nakshatra with broad vision and wide open space. It relates to its meditative capacity and the ability to attune oneself to the omnipresent emptiness.

Gana (Type) :

It is a *Rakshasa* (demonic) nakshatra. This means that this nakshatra primarily seeks independence and can be eccentric or overtly negative in its outlook. It should not however be seen as an overtly evil asterism since it is mild by nature. Its demonic side is usually used for breaking through attachments and conventions.

Orientation & Disposition :

It is an Upward nakshatra. This means that it is an expansive nakshatra and most of its activities happen above the ground. Since this asterism rules all telecommunications in general, one can see how this fits in. One just has to look at the professions connected with this asterism to understand its upward and expansive outlook.

Lunar Month & Day :

It can be seen as the co-ruler of the month *Shravan*, which is generally said to be ruled by Shravan. One can expect the energies of this asterism to be stronger during the last 9 days of the lunar month of *Shravan,* a period which corresponds to the month of August in the solar calendar.

Shatabhisha is also related to the *Chaturdashi* (14th tithi or day) of the waxing and waning phases of the Moon's monthly cycle.

Auspicious Activities :

Good for signing business deals & contracts, land & housing deals; Education or learning activities; Travel (especially over water); Bike riding; Acquiring new vehicles; Recreational ventures; Meditation & Yog; Sexual activity; Studying astronomy & astrology; Medicine, therapies, rejuvenation & life enhancing activities; Media events; Technological activities; Visiting the sea-side.

Inauspicious Activities :

Not good for beginnings in general; Marriage; Childbirth; Fertility treatments; Law suits, arguments; Negative or wrathful action; Not beneficial for too much socializing unless it is work related; Not good for financial matters; Not good for buying new clothes or jewellery; Not good for domestic activities.

Planetary Ruler :

Shatabhisha is ruled by the planets - Saturn, Rahu and Uranus. Rahu is the main ruler of this asterism. Shatabhisha is the pinnacle of Rahu's energy.

In its highest aspect this nakshatra relays the most knowledgeable and philosophical side of Rahu. Rahu, being a child of *maya*, carries within itself the complete knowledge of nature's hidden and complex functionings. The humanitarian, all inclusive, philosophical disposition of this asterism, when it is functioning through its higher aspect, is very in tune with Rahu's disposition in its higher aspect. Rahu is that force that attempts to break down all boundaries of race, age, status, nationality and religion to usher in a feeling of oneness of humanity, which in a sense embodies the spirit of Aquarius. Functioning through its lower aspect, it relays the aspect of Rahu, which is responsible for consumption and manufacturing of all types of alcohol, intoxicants and drugs. All the significations of Rahu dealing with poisonous chemicals and substances also fall under the domain of this asterism. How planets posited in Shatabhisha will function in a nativity depends on Rahu's functionings and intentions.

Saturn is associated with this nakshatra being the ruler of Aquarius. Saturn, as we know, is a planet associated with coldness, slowness, practicality, organization, melancholy, stillness, discipline, introversion, perseverance and detachment. All these qualities find expression through this nakshatra. However the emphasis here is on stillness, introversion, contemplation, seclusion and philanthropy instead of the Capricorn-Saturn traits like materiality and organizational capacity.

Uranus is the co-ruler of Aquarius and is a planet which relates to sudden events, eccentricity, electricity, science and high technology. Shatabhisha, as we have seen, rules most of the electronic media in today's world. Since most of the electronic media is dependent upon advancements in technology, the relationship between Uranus and Shatabhisha is immediately clear.

It is interesting to note that Vedic Astrologers have chosen the name Varun for Uranus. Varun as we have seen earlier is the ruling deity of this nakshatra. Another interesting aspect to this correlation is that the name "Uranus" is derived from the Greek root "*Ouaronus*". Just like Varun, Ouaronus was the God of the sky, seas and oceans. Linguistically, it is pretty evident that the sanskrit term 'Varun' metamorphosized into Ouaronus during the transference of Vedic knowledge through ages and civilizations.

Rahu-Saturn, Rahu-Uranus and Saturn-Uranus conjunctions in a chart convey similar energies to Shatabhisha.

Mercury, Venus and Rahu do best in this nakshatra. Saturn also does well here but it can make one too melancholic.

Vowels and Alphabets :

The first pada or quarter of this asterism 6° 40' - 10° 00' Aquarius corresponds to "Go" as in Going.

The second pada or quarter of this asterism 10° 00' - 13° 20' Aquarius corresponds to "Sa" as in Sanskrit.

The third pada or quarter of this asterism 13° 20' - 16° 40' Aquarius corresponds to "Si" as in Sea.

The fourth pada or quarter of this asterism 16° 40' - 20° 00' Aquarius corresponds to "Su" as in Sue.

In the Sanskrit alphabet Shatabhishak corresponds to "Lam" and consequently its mantra is "Om Lam".

Sexual type & Compatibility :

Its sexual animal is a Mare. This makes it most compatible with *Ashvini*, whose sexual animal is represented by a horse. Ashvini and Shatabhisha share a deep relationship on many levels. For example, they are the two nakshatras which deal with healing and rejuvenation. It is the view of the ancient seers that diseases which begin in Shatabhisha can only be cured in Ashvini.

For sexual & marital compatibility with other nakshatras please refer to the tables on pages 468 & 469.

Esoteric :

The etheric aspect of this asterism relates to the subtle electric forces of the etheric or heavenly realm. It is a deeply mystical asterism which can open one's consciousness to the highest realms. Its empty circle symbolism highlights the truth that all creation arises from nothingness and dissolves into nothingness.

The present day phenomenon of "crop circles", is, in the author's view, directly connected with this nakshatra. These crop circles remain a big mystery to all those who don't want to accept any reality other than material. 90% of them are formed in the wheat fields of a small agricultural area in England, known as the *Wiltshire Plains*. The interesting thing is that many ancient sites like *Stonehenge* and *Silbury Hill* lie within this small area.

Many of these crop circles are complicated geometrical patterns based on universal mathematical principles like the golden ratio 1.618, aka. the 'golden mean'. Some of them are very similar to the ancient mandalas and the petalled sacred *chakras* which lie within our astral bodies. They are called crop circles just because of the extensive use of circle in their complicated patterns. The important thing about them is that they are all made with unerring finesse and not a single wheat plant is damaged or out of place in the finished patterns.

The crop circles, some of them spreading over 1000 ft, are formed within seconds and only one has ever been filmed forming. Many people who think they are hoaxes have failed to make even a simple accurate circle in the fields in one whole night. The film clearly showed four roundish white lights (earth spirits) making a circle within 2-3 seconds. The film's validity is confirmed by the fact that the newly formed crop circle was open for public viewing on the same day.

Shatabhisha, as we know, likes to baffle through mysteries and puzzles, and in that way leads people into discovering the real truths of the universe. Despite all the hopelessness in our times, there seems to be hope for the future, considering that the other side is still communicating with us even if in a secretive playful way. The messages of these crop circles are very clear to those who have real knowledge and the moment a certain number of people reach that understanding, we would all be living in a different world.

Gotra (Celestial Lineage) :

This nakshatra is related to the *Sage Atri*, one of the seven celestial sages looking after the affairs of our galaxy. The name of this sage translates into "one who devours", which is in keeping with the essential demoniacal nature of this nakshatra. Shatabhisha has a dissoluting nature and is very much in keeping with the job assigned to this particular sage.

Remedial :

Healing measures can be used for those suffering from the bad effects of this nakshatra, which may manifest as health problems related to the body parts it rules, or problems with drug and alcohol addiction etc. One can also strengthen this nakshatra's energy to increase one's chances for fame in the media or progress in meditation.

The best way is to recite its root mantra "Om Lam" 108 times on Saturday and during its lunar month. While doing this, one should sit facing south west or south east. The other more potent way is worship of *Lord Shiv* in any form one is attracted to.

One can wear all shades of blues and neon electric colours when undertaking activities related to this asterism.

Example :

Shatabhisha's sound and light can be experienced at -

http://osfa.org.uk/shatabhisha.htm

Miscellaneous :

According to *Varahamihira*, "those with Moon in Shatabhisha are truthful but harsh and cruel in their speech. They are always eager to conquer their enemies and suffer much grief in isolation. They have independence of thought and action but are often seen acting without thought."

* * *

25. Purvabhadrapada   20°00' Aquarius ~ 3°20' Pisces

25.

Purvabhadrapada

(20°00' Aquarius - 3°20' Pisces)

In the Sky :

Purvabhadrapada, the culmination of Jupiterian energy, is represented in the celestial firmament by two bright stars in the constellation of *Pegasus,* which the ancient vedic seers saw as being representative of the front legs of a funeral cot (or sleeping bed). Pegasus itself was seen as a full funeral cot (or sleeping bed). These two stars are known in modern astronomy as *Alpha-Pegasi* (*Markab*) and *Beta-Pegasi* (*Scheat*). The bright constellation of Pegasus lies directly on top of the astronomical constellations of Aquarius and Pisces.

The two stars of this asterism make a straight line (almost perpendicular to the ecliptic belt) at the juncture of the constellations Aquarius and Pisces. This is in harmony with the fact that this asterism connects the signs Aquarius and Pisces. Alpha-Pegasi, which can be said to represent the part in Aquarius, lies closer to the zodiacal ecliptic and has a visual magnitude of 2.49, while Beta-Pegasi, which can be said to represent the part in Pisces, lies further away and is slightly brighter with a visual magnitude of 2.47. Both of them can be easily located in the night sky.

Name :

'Purvabhadrapada "translates into - "the former (one who possesses) lucky feet". Its alternative name is "*Purvaproshthapada*", which translates into "the former (one who possesses) the feet of a stool".

These translations clearly highlight the problems one encounters when translating Sanskrit terms into English. The above translations seem odd and confusing and don't seem to convey much regarding the nature or functioning of this asterism. As we shall find out later they just relate to its ruling deity.

Symbol :

Its main symbol is the 'front part of a funeral cot'. A funeral cot denotes our exit from the world. In astrology, the sign Pisces, or the 12th house in the chart signifies this exit. Since this asterism begins the sign of Pisces, it is appropriate that it is ascribed the front legs of the funeral cot. The front part of a normal sleeping bed can also be seen as the symbol of this asterism. Since the 12th house relates to sleep, which can be seen as a temporary form of death, a sleeping bed would also relate to this asterism. It signifies the moment in time when after doing our worldly duties and mingling with friends (Aquarian or 11th house activities), we prepare for retiring to bed in the night.

Its alternative symbol is 'a man with two faces'. As you can see in the image for this nakshatra, one face wears a benign look while the other one appears mad, violent and destructive. This relates to the *Jekyll* and *Hyde* character of this asterism. It can always put up a normal, socially acceptable and cheerful front on the outside while holding its darker side inside at all times.

A 'sword' is also used as its symbol by many scholars. The sword obviously relates to the process of "cutting off". The cutting off process relates to the destructive, dissoluting side of nature and associates this nakshatra with all kinds of pains, injuries, accidents, deaths and endings.

Another alternative symbol for this asterism is 'a single ray of Sun'. This relates to the gloomy, desolate aspect of this nakshatra where all hope is at the minimum and the light at the end of the tunnel is very faint. Those readers who are conversant with the novel "*Count of Monte Christo*" by *Alexander Dumas*, can easily see how this applies to the experience of the lead character *Edmund Dantes*, while he was imprisoned on the remote island of *Elba*.

Deity :

It has an obscure ruling deity with the name of *Aja-Ekapada*, which translates into "the one footed goat". Its alternative meaning, which carries a cosmic pun, is "the one footed unborn one." This mysterious creature is a goat headed monster with one leg, who forms part of the entourage of *Rudra* (the fierce form of *Shiv*).

Surprisingly, Aja-Ekapada, a Vedic character, can be easily found on the card *no. 15* in the Western *Tarot* pack. This card is called "*The Devil*" and is supposed to signify the evil and dark side of life in general. This goat headed creature carries much of the same meanings from the Vedic point of view, except the fact that the destruction and ruin it brings is supposed to be divinely ordained. We can see that the name of this asterism also relates directly to this one footed deity.

The sign Pisces is seen to symbolise feet and since this asterism has only one part in Pisces, it can be said to have only one foot. It is interesting to note that this one footed dark deity has gained enormous prominence in the present world age of *Kali-Yug*. It can be seen in all major important centres of the Western civilization. All the secret societies and brotherhoods like the *Freemasons*, *Club of Rome* and the *Illuminati* consider this goat god as their main deity. In these circles he is known as *Baphomet*.

Since our present day world is run by a secret elite group, which has strong connections with the above mentioned secret societies, it is not hard to understand why there is so much unnecessary violence and bloodshed being perpetuated on our planet. Aja-Ekapada can be seen as the ruling deity of all types of black magic and that is why individuals deeply influenced by this asterism are attracted to or practise black magic.

In the image representing this nakshatra, the reader can see skulls and bones lying all around, which form a secondary symbol for this asterism. One can see that the skull and bones symbol has always been associated with danger as it is displayed in dangerous places like high voltage areas etc. In this light it is interesting to note that there's a secret order in the United States known as the "*Skulls & Bones Society*", of which prominent American presidents have been members!

Finally, the supreme ruling deity of this asterism is Rudra, the fierce form of Shiv. This asterism carries the destructive aspect of Shiv in much the same way as *Ardra*. The difference is that here Rudra represents the final dissolution on all planes, while in Ardra the chaotic destructive energy only operates on the mental, emotional planes. As a result, this asterism can be much more cruel and merciless in comparison to Ardra. This can be said to be the place where the Universe loses its mind!

This is basically a purificatory energy. When the old has fallen into decay it has to be destroyed for the new to take birth. The destructive fires of Rudra aim to achieve exactly that. On a more personal level, souls pay for their past life bad karmas through penance and retribution under the burning fires of this nakshatra.

Nature & Functioning :

If there is one word which could sum up this nakshatra it would be 'diabolical'. A lot of the so called negative human traits like paranoia, pessimism, debauchery, violence, hedonism, thirst for the macabre, lying, deceit, cruelty and morbidity can be ascribed to this nakshatra. This nakshatra is mainly concerned with transformation. Those under the strong influence of this asterism have the huge task of witnessing and understanding the lower dark side of life without getting their hands dirty.

Although most scholars don't recognise this fact, this is the most intense amongst all the nakshatras. Since all its negative aspects can only in essence be manifested through the ego, humility becomes the most important thing for Purvabhadrapada natives. One of the few good qualities of this nakshatra is that it is devoted to those it respects. This again however is a double edged sword, since many a times its object of veneration is not very wholesome.

Ramakrishn Paramahansa (the famous 19th century saint), who has his Moon in Purvabhadrapada, was devoted to *Kali*, the fierce goddess. The dark deity Kali, despite being fierce, is ultimately benevolent. This devotion helped him rise above all the negative Purvabhadrapada characteristics, but many under this nakshatra's influence take to worshipping demonic and devilish deities and spoil their karma for many lives. Thus we can see that it is very important for the natives under this nakshatra to find the right thing to get devoted to from the very beginning.

Another good quality of this nakshatra is that it is very sincere and hardworking, even if its goals are not so wholesome. It has tremendous perseverance and will go to any lengths to achieve its objective. In fact a lot of Purva Bhadrapada natives end up engaging in bad karma because they are ready to do 'just about anything' to obtain their objectives.

If a case study of mass murderers, homicides and genocides was carried out, it would be found that most of the people involved would have some strong connection with Purvabhadrapada. This nakshatra relates both to the persecuted and the persecutor.

More evolved souls usually use this nakshatra's energy to mortify themselves instead of others. All the sages like *Vishwamitra,* who underwent extreme penance, are basically utilising this nakshatra's energy. Even today in India, one can see a lot of *sadhus* involved in intense practices involving self torture and self mortification. A Purvabhadrapada native is ready to stand on one foot for ten years or even more, if they are convinced that it is going to bring them their desired result.

After reading the above description, the reader may be surprised to know that a lot of times Purvabhadrapada natives cannot be distinguished from the rest, just because they have a very strong capacity to fit in with the contemporary societal structure. They are normal people with nine to five office jobs, who speak, eat and dress like everyone else, and no one can suspect the kind of things they are up to in their private lives. They usually keep their idiosyncrasies and nefarious activities secret.

The only way of spotting a Purvabhadrapada person is their highly strung, nervous demeanour along with an overtly serious look. They are the ones who are likely to snap first in any confrontational situation. They however try to carry a happy look and act amicably in social gatherings.

They are basically two faced people, the kind who work on normal day jobs, and in the nights they can be found in fetish clubs, banging heads at hard core heavy metal concerts, entertaining macabre fantasies, practising dark tantric rituals or plotting and carrying out violent or criminal activities

... Purvabhadrapada natives are very susceptible to extreme views and often end up being part of extreme fundamentalist groups.

Not every Purvabhadrapada person gives physical expression to their negative energies. The more evolved souls learn to fight the battle between light and dark within their own minds and hearts. A lot of common everyday Purvabhadrapada pada people, instead of being the perpetrators, end up being the victims. Creative artists who have this nakshatra strongly placed in their charts, can often be seen channeling its energy, by implementing all the dark side of life in their art, whether it be writing, music or drama.

Purvabhadrapada natives, like everything else, tend to oscillate between extremes in the sexual sphere. All kinds of sexual perversions and phobias are seen to originate in this nakshatra.

Regretfulness is another of the prominent qualities of this nakshatra. Being contemplative at some inner level, its natives are often seen brooding over the past, tormenting themselves for all the wrongs they have done.

On a material plane such natives are stingy in regards to money. However their one peculiarity is that they are always ready to place all of their wealth at the disposal of their spouse, partner, teacher or cause. Their capacity for revenge holds no equal among nakshatras. Once again Alexander Dumas's novel, "Count of Monte Christo", reveals how this emotion can be taken to the extreme.

In the universal scheme of things, Purvabhadrapada relates to "*yajamana udyamana shakti*" - the power to raise the evolutionary level. Its symbolism has humanity above, and the astral regions below. This imagery suggests that Purvabhadrapada acts as a bridge between the consciousness on the material and non-material planes. It is this bridge which is blocked in majority of the humanity in the present times. Purvabhadrapada has the power to raise one's evolutionary level through internal purification brought about by the raging celestial fires of penance.

Mode of Functioning :

It is supposed to be a Passive nakshatra, but this does not mean that it does not or cannot act when required. Its passivity relates to the fact that it takes its time in forming and visualizing its goals and does not act in haste. It is usually in no hurry to achieve its ends.

Caste :

Surprisingly, this asterism is given the *Brahmin* caste by ancient Vedic seers. It is however easy to understand the why of it with a closer look. It is ruled by Jupiter, the most brahminical among planets. It is related to the universal law, that power and knowledge can be achieved through penance, and this asterism is very capable of achieving both. What it finally does with that power and knowledge is another matter.

Gender :

It is a male nakshatra in keeping with its male deities. Even Jupiter, one of its planetary rulers, is a male planet.

Bodyparts & Humor (Ayurvedic Constitution) :

It mainly relates to the Sides of the Body. This includes the Ribs, Abdomen and the Sides of the Legs. It is also an indicator of the Left Thigh and Soles of the Feet. It is interesting to note that patting the left thigh was considered an invitation for war or an aggressive act meant to cajole or humiliate others. In the Vedic epic *Mahabharat*, *Duryodhan* did a similar gesture when he asked *Draupadi* to come and sit on his thigh, and *Bheem* took a vow to break off his thigh in battle and drink the blood from it (a very Purvabhadrapada act!)

It is a predominantly *Vata* (Air) nakshatra in keeping with its expansive nature.

Direction :

Its directions are west and southeast, leaning a little closer towards east as compared to south.

Padas (Quarters) :

The first pada or quarter of this asterism 20° 00' - 23° 20' Aquarius, falls in Aries Navamsa and is ruled by Mars. This pada brings out the most aggressive side of this nakshatra. The energy here is more mental. Such natives will do well to control their temper, aggression and violence. It gives tremendous determination to achieve one's objective.

The second pada or quarter of this asterism 23° 20' - 26° 40' Aquarius, falls in Taurus Navamsa ruled by Venus. This pada relates to the more indulgent side of this nakshatra. The energy here is more earthy and the natives are likely to give some physical expression to the aforementioned dark sides of this nakshatra.

The third pada or quarter of this asterism 26° 40' - 30° 00' Aquarius, falls in Gemini Navamsa ruled by Mercury. This pada expresses this nakshatra's energy through more communicative means and makes the native curious. This is the lightest pada of this intense nakshatra.

The fourth pada or quarter of this asterism 0° 00' - 3° 20' Pisces, falls in Cancer Navamsa ruled by Moon. This pada has an extremely diabolical quality, in the sense that it can be extremely benign or extremely dangerous. It relates both to the persecuted and the persecutor. Such natives can be found in all walks of life and are most socially adept in comparison with the other three padas.

Professions :

Morticians and all professions relating to death or the death process like Coffin Makers, Cemetery Keepers etc.; Surgeons and contemporary Medical Practitioners (basically those who administer poisons as remedies); Fundamentalists, Radicals, Fanatics, Terrorists etc; Horror, Mystery and Sci-Fi Writers;

Present day Psychiatrists (who often end up making things worse); The dark side of the entertainment industry; The dark side of the ruling elite; Pornographic Industry; Weapon Makers and Users; Occultists dealing with the dark side, Black Magicians; Perpetuators of dark technologies; Leather Industry; Extreme Ascetics involved in self mortification (like the famous Aghoras); Police Departments particularly Homicide Squads; Soldiers; Metal Industry; All professions involving the use of fire and high temperatures; Those who deal with toxic substances and highly polluting waste products; Enemies of the environment like Lumber Jacks; Environmental Activists; Pharmaceutical Industry.

Places :

Cemeteries, Morgues, Cremation Grounds; Factories; Heavy industries of all types; Land Fills; Dark Alley Ways; Centres for Occult Studies and practices of a dark nature; Operation Theatres and Terminal Illness Wards; Asylums and Penitentiaries; Churches; Top Secret Military Research Bases; Atomic Power Plants; Places where high technology equipment is kept; Night Clubs and all other places associated with dark entertainment; The places related to the above mentioned professions in general.

Guna (Essence) and Tattwa (Element) :

The ancient Vedic seers saw it as a *Sattwic* nakshatra. Once again, this classification relates mainly to its capacity for penance, detachment and generosity. It must be kept in mind that its generosity only extends to those close to it by family or association.

It belongs to the Ether element. This is primarily to do with its planetary ruler Jupiter, who also has a primarily etheric constitution. This element relates to the dissolution aspect of this asterism. In a way even murdering a person is nothing but an act of separating their etheric, subtle body from their physical body.

Gana (Type) :

It is a *Manusha* (human) nakshatra. Going by its qualities one would expect it to be a demonic nakshatra, but it is important to remember an old dictum from Vedic wisdom here - "Humans are capable of more demonic acts than the demons and more godly acts than the gods."

Orientation & Disposition :

It is a Downward nakshatra. This means that it is concerned with what is below the surface of things. It also suggests a person whose glance is downwards instead of upwards. It also relates to its capacity for deep research of all kinds. Natives predominantly influenced by Purvabhadrapada are very good at keeping secrets and can't be taken on their face value.

Vedic seers regarded it as an *Ugra* (cruel & fierce) nakshatra. This doesn't come as much of a surprise after understanding its essential nature.

Lunar Month and Day :

It can be seen as the ruler of the waning part (first nine days) of the month known as *Bhadrapada*. This period usually corresponds to the month of September in the Solar calendar.

Purvabhadrapada is also related to *Chaturdashi* (14th tithi or day) of the waxing and waning phases of the Moon's monthly cycle.

Auspicious Activities :

All dangerous, uncertain and risky activities; All activities of a mechanical or technological nature; Holding funeral services; Putting an end to things; Exploring Death Issues; Agricultural activities; All activities connected with water like sailing etc.

Inauspicious :

Generally unfavourable for most activities except those mentioned above; Especially unfavourable for beginning new things or initiations of all kinds; Not good for travelling, sex, marriage and dealing with the government or higher authorities. Most of the actions carried out under its influence often end up causing pain, anxiety, regret, sorrow or extreme difficulty.

Planetary Ruler :

The planets associated with this nakshatra are Saturn, Jupiter, Uranus, Neptune and Ketu. Jupiter is its main planetary ruler. Saturn and Uranus are connected to this asterism because of their corulership of Aquarius, while Neptune and Ketu connect to the portion of this asterism which falls in Pisces.

It is important to note that even though Rahu is a co-ruler of Aquarius, Rahu does not relate to the part of Aquarius where this asterism lies (20° to 30°). Rahu's energy culminates in the previous asterism Shatabishak (6° 42' to 20° Aquarius).

Saturn primarily relates to the grief causing and disciplined aspect of this asterism. It also points to the fact that this asterism always tends to physically carry out its dark functionings. Saturn also provides the detachment aspect, which can be best seen through the self-tormenting ascetic standing on one foot (see the nakshatra's image).

Uranus relates to the futuristic and technological aspect of this asterism. The most famous among the modern science fictions, "*Star Wars*", displays the Uranian aspect of this nakshatra. It can be seen that this nakshatra has a tendency to go overboard with technology, and in its hands technology always ends up being used for destructive purposes. This is the asterism which furthers anti-nature and dehumanizing technologies like microchipping, androids and mindless genetic manipulation.

It is hard for some people to understand how a benefic planet like Jupiter can rule such a malefic asterism. In order to explain this mystery, we would like to once again bring into the picture the two faced nature of this asterism. This nakshatra is very capable of putting up a Jupiterian, socially acceptable, well mannered and conservative front. It is also skilled at earning money and Jupiter as we know is the natural significator of wealth. However its means of earning money are always questionable. It is an expansive asterism in keeping with Jupiter's natural tendency. It however uses its expansiveness for furthering darker/destructive causes. Its Jupiterian side also comes out when it is ready to place all of its belongings and resources at the disposal of its partners or those whom it admires and respects.

Jupiter's energy culminates in this nakshatra. This means that at some stage, Purvabhadrapada goes beyond the Jupiterian values which uphold society. Once the moralistic and preservative influence of Jupiter is finished, the stage is set for destruction and dissolution. This process can be seen as *Vishnu* stopping his preservation activities, which sustain the drama of life, so that Shiv's destructive energies are let loose without restraint.

Neptune relates to the fantasy aspect of this nakshatra. All its Uranian futuristic visions like "Star Wars" have been made into hugely successful movies. Neptune, as we know, rules the cinematic realm and this asterism has a strong hold over the modern day showbiz capital, *Hollywood*. One can plainly see the energy of this asterism being relayed through 90% of the movies being churned out by Hollywood, especially in the last 20 years or so. Its fantasy aspect goes into other areas as well, which we have already mentioned in its nature and disposition.

Ketu comes in touch with this nakshatra through the "little foot" it has in the sign Pisces. Ketu, as we know, is the most destructive and detached among all the planets, and this asterism requires that energy to be able to inflict torture upon itself or others. When it is working on an internal, benefic level, the attachments are destroyed without any self mortification. When it is working on an individualized but external, benefic level, this nakshatra tries to control and sublimate inner desires through external means like tormenting the body through extreme penance. When working in a malefic, externalized way, it wreaks havoc on its surroundings, and this is where we get the cold blooded murderer, serial killer, the war general or behind-the-scenes manipulator.

In general astrological terms, the conjunctions of Mars/Saturn/ Rahu/ Ketu/Uranus or Neptune in cruel and harsh nakshatras have an energy similar to Purvabhadrapada.

Not many planets fare well in Purvabhadrapada. Only a well aspected, well fortified Jupiter is good here. Saturn can also give okay results in Purvabhadrapada, if Jupiter is well placed in the chart. A well placed Ketu, especially in the Pisces part, can generate detachment in a positive way.

Vowels and Alphabets :

The first pada (20° to 23° 20' Aquarius) relates to "Se" as in the name "Seth".

The second pada (23° 20' to 26° 40' Aquarius) relates to "So" as in the name "Somalia".

The third pada (26° 40' to 30°00' Aquarius) relates to "The" as in "Then".

The fourth pada (0° to 3° 20' Pisces) relates to "Di" as in the name "Diwali".

In the Sanskrit alphabet Purvabhadrapada corresponds to the letters "Vam" and "Sham", and consequently its mantras are "Om Vam" and "Om Sham".

Sexual type & Compatibility :

Its sexual animal is a Lion, which points towards an aggressive sexual nature and attitude. It likes to be the dominant partner in sexual union and in many cases does not have a healthy respect for its partner. One can notice in the image of this nakshatra, the lion is a roaring lion and not a tame, gentle one as is the case with *Dhanishta*.

For sexual & marital compatibility with other nakshatras please refer to the tables on pages 468 & 469.

Esoteric :

Its ruling deity, as we have seen earlier, is a mysterious figure and finds little mention in the Vedic texts. Surprisingly, it is a much revered deity in the present time and human sacrifices are carried out under its name by today's ruling elite. This may come as a shock to many of the readers, but as the saying goes, "Fact is always stranger than fiction!"

This asterism relates to all the dark deities of all ancient cultures, who were supposed to require sacrifice of some live thing, in the form of an animal or human being. The blood sacrifices of the *Mayan* civilization are notoriously famous.

This nakshatra is the consummation point of Jupiter's energy, which in effect means that Jupiter's benefic nature cannot intervene in the destructive acts of this asterism. The universal function of maintenance, so dear to Jupiter, holds little meaning for the destructive, dissoluting energies of this nakshatra. Since this nakshatra relates to the extremely destructive types among Shiv's entourage, it deals specifically with the unrestrained aspect of Shiv.

The imagery of the 'two-faced man' (refer to the image), on an esoteric level, refers to the dying process. Each of us when we die get to face all our actions in the earthly realm, and at the same time we get to peer into the astral plane, commonly referred to as "the world of the dead."

Gotra (Celestial Lineage) :

This nakshatra is related to the *Sage Vashishta*, one of the seven celestial sages looking after the affairs of our galaxy. The name of this sage translates into "the possessor of wealth". This seems to be apt considering the fact that this nakshatra seems to be good at acquiring wealth; especially in today's world, as Purvabhadrapada seems to have taken complete control of all the resources of our planet. On the other hand, Vashishta is renowned for his extreme penances in keeping with Purvabhadrapada's essential inclinations.

Remedial :

For those suffering from bad effects resulting from afflictions to this nakshatra, the best remedial measure is worship of Shiv. The practice of *Karma Yog*, which involves carrying out one's divinely ordained path in life, is the best way to neutralize the bad effects of this nakshatra.

Repetition of the root mantra of this nakshatra - "Om Vam" and "Om Sham" 108 times when Moon transits this nakshatra and in the waning half of the lunar month of Bhadrapada is sure to reduce suffering and bring enlightenment into a person's life.

Persons who are benefiting from the positive energy of this nakshatra can also increase the good effects through the above mentioned ways. It is helpful for them to wear light colours like light blue. Leather apparels and black colours should be avoided as much as possible.

Example :

Death & thrash metal bands represent the energy of this nakshatra.

Purvabhadrapada's higher aspect sound and light can be experienced at -

http://osfa.org.uk/purvabhadrapada.htm

Miscellaneous :

Varahamihira states that "those who have Moon in Purvabhadrapada are good at earning money, are stingy and are liable to place their wealth at the disposal of their partners. They speak distinctly but tend to suffer from grief." All these characteristics would easily fit in with 90% of the present day ruling elite !

* * *

26. Uttarabhadrapada   3°20' Pisces - 16°40' Pisces

26.

Uttarabhadrapada

(3°20' Pisces - 16°40' Pisces)

In the Sky :

Uttarabhadrapada, the apex of Saturnine energy, is represented in the celestial firmament by two bright stars, one of which lies in the constellation of *Pegasus*, while the other is seen as being part of the constellation *Andromeda*. The ancient vedic seers saw these stars as being representative of the back legs of a funeral cot (or sleeping bed). Also the ancients saw these two stars forming a rectangular bed (which is now known as the "*Square of Pegasus*"), along with the two stars of *Purvabhadrapada*.

These two stars, which lie in Pegasus and Andromeda respectively, are known in modern astronomy as *Gamma-Pegasi* (*Algenib*) and *Alpha-Andromedae* (*Alpheratz*). They can be seen lying directly above the constellation of Pisces. Gamma-Pegasi has a visual magnitude of 2.84, and lies closer to the zodiacal ecliptic. Alpha-Andromedae is the brighter of the two with a visual magnitude of 2.06 and lies farther away from the zodiacal ecliptic. Both of them can be easily located in the night sky through spotting Andromeda, one of the brightest constellations in the night sky.

Name :

'Uttarabhadrapada "translates into - "the latter (one who possesses) lucky feet". Its alternative name is "*Uttaraproshthapada*", which translates into "the latter (one who possesses) the feet of a stool". These names and meanings are a direct result of this asterism forming a pair with the the previous asterism *Purvabhadrapada* and don't convey much regarding the nature or functioning of this asterism.

Symbol :

Its main symbol is the 'back part of a funeral cot'. A funeral cot denotes our exit from the world, and the sign Pisces, or the 12th house in the chart, signifies this exit. Since this asterism forms the heart of the sign of Pisces, it is appropriate that it is ascribed the back legs of the funeral cot, while its counterpart, Purvabhadrapada, is ascribed the front legs. In a way it represents our initial state after death, while Purvabhadrapada can be seen as relating to the actual process of dying. The back part of a normal sleeping bed can also be seen as the symbol of this asterism. Since the 12th house relates to sleep, which can be seen as a temporary form of death, a sleeping bed would also relate to this asterism. Uttarabhadrapada signifies the deep sleep state, in which the dream activity is at the minimum, and we go to the depths of our unconscious. It can however be also representative of all dreams and dreamlike states.

In our view, its alternative symbol is a serpent with two and a half coils (see the image), symbolizing the *kundalini*, the primeval life force lying at the base of the spine in humans. This asterism symbolizes enlightenment through the awakening of all the seven vital centres through the movement of the kundalini. This process of kundalini awakening is actually started in *Anuradha*, which can be seen as an associate asterism, in the sense that Saturn rules both of these asterisms. As we discussed in the section dealing with Anuradha, Anuradha is the initiator of this process, while Uttarabhadrapada is the culmination point of this process.

Deity :

Its deity is known by the name *Ahir Bhudhanya* and in keeping with the basic energy of this asterism, is a figure shrouded in mystery. His peculiar name roughly translates into "Serpent of the

Depths" or "Serpent that lies beneath the surface of the earth". Most of the Vedic texts don't say much about him, except the mention of him being a serpent god dwelling in the primeval depths. Even the west has its own share of imagined or otherwise mysterious underwater serpent creatures like Scotland's *Lochness Monster*. Vedic mythology, however, is replete with stories of serpent beings which reside at the bottom of bodies of water like lakes, rivers and oceans. These beings also reside in all the nether worlds. Ahir Bhudhanya can be seen as a collective composite of all these serpent beings.

There is an obvious connection of the serpent forces, revered by all ancient cultures, with this asterism. The reader can refer to the author's previous work, "*The Rahu-Ketu Experience*" *Sagar Publications*, India/ "*The Key Of Life*" *Lotus Press*, USA) for gaining a more detailed understanding of how these forces are central to the universal plan. Ahir Bhudhanya was seen as the deity responsible for maintaining the fertility of the earth. The symbolism of a serpent lying at the core of the earth, who maintains earth's structure and fertility, can be found in all ancient cultures. In the west, Pluto, the planet seen as the lord of the underworld, was given a similar portfolio.

Ahir Bhudhanya is a more wise and compassionate deity in comparison with *Aja-Ekapada* (please refer to the section on Purvabhadrapada). Its essential nature is akin to the western Neptunian god-figure, which is not very interested in revealing itself. Like Neptune, it presides over the celestial ocean. Even *Vishnu*, the preserver among the Trinity, has a similar symbolism as can be seen from his lying on a serpent bed on top of the celestial ocean image.

Finally *Shiv*, the destroyer among the cosmic Trinity, can be seen as the main presiding deity of this asterism, even though its symbolism relates to Vishnu. This asterism has a dissolution aspect to it in the guises of death, transformation and enlightenment through destruction of forms - Shiv's domain. Shiv also carries a serpent around his neck !

Nature & Disposition :

The first thing which must be said here, is that it is very hard to pin down the exact nature of this nakshatra. It can function in a variety of ways and fashion itself according to its needs and surroundings.

Since wisdom is the key word for this nakshatra, the native strongly under its influence acts according to the needs of the moment rather than from any instinctual archetype.

The real motives of this nakshatra are always very hard to know. Natives under its strong influence are as elusive as the serpent of the deep sea. Just like the ocean carries a whole different variety of plants and creatures, this nakshatra has room for many different qualities, natures and expressions.

Despite its apparent flexibility, it is quite a fixed nakshatra, which is usually very determined to achieve its set goals. Flexibility here is just a means to an end. This is the wise old man amongst the nakshatras. It never acts hastily. In fact many a times it can postpone actions too long for its own good. In a lot of cases it can just be plain lazy, in both physical and mental matters.

A lot can be understood about this nakshatra by understanding the nature and role of the old wise chief archetype of indigenous native tribes. Its wisdom has been gained from experience. It is calculative when it comes to achieving its ends. These natives always try to keep the big picture in mind while making plans, decisions and the like. Uttarabhadrapada likes to do everything in a controlled fashion with care and restraint. Its intentions are usually benevolent. Its ambitions are not self serving and it is full of qualities like empathy, understanding and sympathy.

Uttarabhadrapada natives usually make very good counsellors. Water as we know has the ability to extinguish any fire. In the same way the cooling waters of this nakshatra can ease and cool out all fiery emotions like anger, revenge, jealousy etc. Even in all the native tribes of the past, everyone used to turn to the elder or wise man of the tribe to find solace and direction in their troubled times. The level of compassion this nakshatra can show will obviously depend upon the evolutionary status of the soul in question.

The calculative aspect of this nakshatra connects it to all the sciences concerned with understanding the functionings of the universal mind, like Astrology, Numerology, Yog, Meditation, Divination etc.

Natives with Uttarabhadrapada rising on the Ascendant usually have a serene and calm countenance. They try their best to remain happy even in difficult, disturbing and unfavourable circumstances. Uttarabhadrapada has a tendency to give one a large body with broad shoulders. This can be gauged from the fact that oceans are quite expansive. Such natives are usually short in height, with a tendency towards weight gain, especially with age. Uttarabhadrapada usually produces shy, reluctant and passive personalities. Such natives are usually in no hurry, a tendency which in its lowest aspect can make them lazy and prone to inaction in times where action is indispensable.

Much depends on the placement of Saturn in ascertaining how this nakshatra will function in a particular nativity. The serpent of the depths is quite an immobile and inert creature, and it requires some external agency or force to arouse it. This is why the presence of fiery optimistic planets like Mars, Sun and Jupiter in this nakshatra help it overcome its latent inertia. In fact, the placement of any planet in this nakshatra makes it dynamic.

Uttarabhadrapada can initiate destructive or seemingly evil actions, but unlike its predecessor, Purvabhadrapada, it usually does so for some wholesome reason. Uttarabhadrapada, even when causing destruction, puts less emphasis on cruelty and depravity as compared to its predecessor. Uttarabhadrapada's anger is more sublimated and thus its actions are not mindless.

Reasonability is another key to this nakshatra. It likes to come out with the best possible solutions, which are fair to all parties. The interesting thing to note about this nakshatra is that it usually has an eye for the needs of others, but almost always ends up benefitting from others. Natives born under its strong influence usually benefit from gifts, donations and inheritance etc. One interesting thing to note about this nakshatra is that it is usually fortunate with making and handling money.

This nakshatra relates to the *Vana Prastha*, the third stage of life according to the ancient Vedic texts, in which the native is supposed to cut off their worldly chords and retire to the forest in order to seek enlightenment. It has secretive, reclusive tendencies, which may sometimes make the native under the strong influence of this nakshatra prematurely retire from their worldly duties. No matter what the evolutionary status an Uttarabhadrapada native has, there is always some seeking towards some higher awareness.

In the universal scheme of things, *Uttarabhadrapada* relates to "*varshodyamana shakti*" - the power to bring about rain. Its symbolism has raining clouds above, and growing plants below. This imagery obviously has more to it than just being a common fertility reference. The rain here connects with the soothing universal vibrations which can flow through our astral and causal bodies if we open ourselves to them. This spiritual rain comes about from the celestial ocean of consciousness when the hot Sun (representing our *Atman*) touches upon it. The reader can refer to the image of Uttarabhadrapada to understand the whole process better.

Mode of Functioning :

It is supposed to be a Balanced nakshatra. We have already seen that this nakshatra takes its time before acting. When well disposed, it can give one the wisdom to put things in their proper perspective. When afflicted, it can make one too conservative and too afraid to confront reality or face transformation.

Caste :

This nakshatra belongs to the *Kshatriya* or warrior caste. It is strange that a prudent nakshatra like this should be assigned this caste. This comes about because of its association with the energies of Pluto and Shiv. Uttarabhadrapada is always a warrior, but not in any aggressive, cruel sense like its predecessor Purvabhadrapada. It works in the typical Kshatriya fashion of setting goals and attaining them.

Gender :

It is a male nakshatra. The rulership of Jupiter gives this nakshatra its male quality. Also its presiding deities are both male.

Bodyparts & Humor (Ayurvedic Constitution) :

It mainly relates to the Sides of the Body, including the Sides of the Legs, the Shins and the Soles of the Feet.

It is a primarily "*Pitta*" (fiery) nakshatra. This association comes from its symbol of a funeral cot. As we discussed earlier, it is related to the earth's core, which as we know is the hottest part of our planet.

Direction :

It covers the range from west to north.

Padas (Quarters) :

The first pada or quarter of this asterism 3° 20' - 6° 40' Pisces, falls in Leo Navamsa and is ruled by Sun. It represents the active, illuminating, proud and achievement oriented side of this nakshatra. Just like the rising or setting sun on the oceanic horizon (refer to the image), the function of this pada is to spread around the light of its experience.

The second pada or quarter of this asterism 6° 40' - 10° 00' Pisces, falls in Virgo Navamsa ruled by Mercury. This relates to the analytical, calculative and planning side of this nakshatra. It tends to find wisdom in small things, and planets here are more likely to stay in the background then reveal themselves.

The third pada or quarter of this asterism 10° 00' - 13° 20' Pisces, falls in Libra Navamsa ruled by Venus. This relates to the passive, balance seeking and equilibrium-oriented side of this nakshatra. Planets placed here seek wisdom through balance and objectivity. They might however become too passive and may lack the energy to let their findings be known.

The fourth pada or quarter of this asterism 13° 20' - 16° 40' Pisces, falls in Scorpio Navamsa ruled by Mars. This relates to the occult, mysterious and hidden aspect of this nakshatra. This pada can go to extremes -depths of confusion or depths of wisdom. Whichever way it operates, it always has the ability to aggressively externalise its energy. Everything is intense here and things are usually likely to get to fever pitch in relation to whatever area this pada is influencing (planet or house).

Professions :

Yog and Meditation Experts; Counsellors & Therapists of all types; Shamans; Healers; Practitioners of Tantra and other Occult Sciences; Divinators; Renunciates; Monks, Hermits; Those working in Charity Organizations; Researchers; Philosophers; Poets, Writers, Musicians and Artists; Those working in professions requiring extraordinary abilities, whether it be patience, insight, erudition or awareness; Professions involving little movement like Shop Clerks, Night Watchmen, Doormen; Historians; Librarians; Those who are unemployed and relying on inheritance, legacies or charity.

Places :

Libraries, Temples & Museums; Occult Book Stores; Ancient ruins; Historical Places; Cremation Grounds; Holy Sites and Pilgrimage Places; Caves; Mountainous Caverns; Meditation Centres; All places suitable for meditation and quiet activities; Charity Organization Compounds; Forests, High Mountain Ranges and other uninhabited solitary places; Bottoms of Lakes, Deep Seas & Oceans; Social Welfare Centres; Centres for Psychic and Spiritual Research.

Guna (Essence) and Tattwa (Element) :

It is supposed to be a *Tamasic* nakshatra. Its basic inert quality and the fact that it deals with dissolution on all levels of existence, made the ancient Vedic seers ascribe this guna to it. We have seen earlier that Shiv, the overlord of *Tamo Guna*, is the main presiding deity of this nakshatra.

The Ether element predominates for Uttarabhadrapada, as is the case with the last group of nakshatras starting from *Dhanishta.* Its relation to Ether is clear from its wisdom and all encompassingness.

Gana (Type) :

It is a *Manusha* (human) nakshatra. This goes to show that Uttarabhadrapada has a strong involvement in human affairs, even though it relates to other finer realms of existence. It is one of the nakshatras which form a bridge between the *astral, causal* and physical realms, bringing in higher, universal truths into the material human frame of existence.

Orientation & Disposition :

It is an Upward Looking nakshatra. This mainly relates to the expansive nature of this asterism. Activities begun under the influence of this nakshatra are more likely to grow and expand with time.

It is a Fixed nakshatra in keeping with the nature of its ruling deity Ahir Bhudanya. As mentioned earlier, he is a very fixed sort of character, who literally and figuratively budges only when absolutely necessary.

Lunar Month and Day :

It can be seen as the ruler of the middle 9 days of the month known as *Bhadrapada*. This usually falls in the solar calendar month of September.

Uttarabhadrapada is also related to *Navami* (9th tithi or day) of the waxing and waning phases of the Moon's monthly cycle.

Auspicious Activities :

Quiet peaceful activities; Research, Meditation, Psychic Development & Astral Exploration; Good for making promises, pledges and commitments including Marriage; Beginning construction activities - homes, offices etc; Financial dealings; Beginning activities requiring support from others; Artistic ventures; Treatment of diseases; Sexual activity; Entering a new home; Naming children, organizations etc; Planting & gardening.

Inauspicious Activities :

Unfavourable for travelling; Litigation; Dealing with enemies; Activities which require quick, swift action in general; Speculation & gambling; Bad for lending money; Too much physical movement or exertion.

Planetary Ruler :

The planets associated with this nakshatra are Saturn, Jupiter, Neptune and Ketu. Saturn is the main ruler of this asterism. In fact this nakshatra represents the culmination of Saturnine energy. This is the place where Saturnine lessons learnt under the signs Capricorn and Aquarius, are synthesized and transformed into true wisdom and enlightenment. Saturn's role here is not that of a hard task master, but that of a wise, old teacher who teaches through patience, perseverance and example. The most refined aspects of Saturn's functionings are expressed through this nakshatra. At times this nakshatra can give abundant material prosperity, as one reaps the fruits of hard work done in previous lives. In more evolved souls however, this prosperity is bestowed as a result of functioning in tune with the universal will. This is the nakshatra where Saturn becomes Shiv and can no more be seen as an outcaste, slow, troublesome, painful deity of sorrow.

Jupiter lends an expansive quality to this nakshatra. Uttarabhadrapada does not believe in boundaries, and carries within itself all higher Jupiterian virtues like compassion, caring, sensitivity and acceptance of the divine will. This nakshatra has a lot to do with the final balancing of the energies of Jupiter and Saturn, the two planets regarded by some astrologers as being the most important.

Neptune as we know is directly related to the celestial ocean, which houses the manifest universe. Uttarabhadrapada as we have seen earlier, is directly related to this ocean through its presiding deity Ahir bhudanya. Uttarabhadrapada is one of the few nakshatras which sets the stage for the drama of life. In a way it can be seen as a director of the movie called life. This is the reason why natives under the strong influence of this nakshatra often take up filmmaking in today's media heavy society.

Ketu relates to the spiritual/detachment/enlightenment aspect of this asterism. On closer inspection, one finds that Ketu has a strong connection to the way this nakshatra goes about achieving its spiritual goals. Uttarabhadrapada relates to *Raja Yog*, which involves harnessing of the *kundalini shakti* and opening of the seven *sacral* centres. Ketu is the planet which relates directly to kundalini shakti, and the seventh and final centre known as *Sahastrar* (please refer to the author's previous work "*The Rahu-Ketu experience*" *Sagar* Publications, India or "*The Key Of Life*" *Lotus Press*, USA for more insight on Ketu's role in this regard).

Active dynamic planets like Sun, Mars and Rahu do best in Uttarabhadrapada. Saturn also does well here if it is aspected by active planets like Mars and Jupiter. Jupiter, Mercury and Venus can also do well in this nakshatra when associated with active planets.

Jupiter-Saturn conjunction and conjunctions of Ketu and Neptune with Jupiter and Saturn carry an energy similar to this nakshatra. Saturn-Ketu conjunction however would relate more to Purvabhadrapada.

Vowels and Alphabets :

The first pada (3° 20' - 6° 40' Pisces) relates to "Du" as in the name "Durga".

The second pada (6° 40' to 10° 00' Pisces) relates to "Tha" as in the name "Thatcher".

The third pada (10° 00' to 13°20' Pisces) relates to "Jha" as in the name "Jhanci".

The fourth pada (13°20' to 16° 40' Pisces) relates to "Na" as in the name "Natasha".

In the Sanskrit alphabet Uttarabhadrapada corresponds to the letters "Sha", "Sa" and "Ha", and consequently its mantras are "Om Sham", "Om Sam" and "Om Ham".

Sexual type and Compatibility :

Its sexual animal is a Cow, which indicates a docile and passive sexual nature. It is not a very sexually active nakshatra. It however can be quite interested in sex from a *tantra* point of view.

For sexual & marital compatibility with other nakshatras please refer to the table on pages 468 & 469.

Esoteric :

As a meeting point of the energies of *Vishnu*, the preserver; and *Shiv*, the destroyer; this nakshatra carries a very special influence. It relates to the harmonizing aspect of the universal mind, which often times uses destruction as a means of preservation. Even *Krishn*, Vishnu's incarnation, used destruction (Shiv's means) to set things right.

This nakshatra relates to the *sahastrar* or crown centre, the topmost amongst the seven chakras. It is the final destination of the kundalini, the serpent force residing at the base of the spine. Thus the whole symbolism of this nakshatra relates to the journey of the kundalini from the base of the spine (which can be equated with the bottom of the sea), to the crown chakra (which can be equated with the surface of the celestial ocean).

The left (*Ida*), right (*Pingla*) and middle (*Sushumna*) channels converge and become one at the third eye centre. These three channels can be equated with the trinity of Shiv, *Brahma* and Vishnu respectively. Thus this nakshatra has a special affinity with the third eye chakra (*Agneya*). It is at the third eye centre where perfect equilibrium is established between nature's three *gunas*. This allows one to directly comprehend the functionings of the universal mind. This is the nakshatra where wisdom is gained, and as a result all the mental, intellectual and emotional thirsts are quenched. After the third eye chakra, there is only one channel, the centre one, leading up to the crown chakra, which means that this nakshatra readies an individual for supreme enlightenment, putting them on a singular path.

The 'serpent of the depths' is often equated with 'a stream in the *Milky Way*'. This, besides suggesting a path which leads us through the darkness of space, hints at the fact that the serpent imagery is present on all levels of existence - it is the kundalini within our bodies, the stream in the Milky Way within our galaxy, and Ahir Budhanya in the celestial ocean.

Uttarabhadrapada is the unfathomable darkness of space in which the material universe dwells. It is the nothingness from which everything is born. It is where the answer to the most basic questions eventually encountered by all thinkers, scientists, spiritualists and philosophers alike i.e. "how did creation come out of nothingness and what existed when nothing existed", lies.

Gotra (Celestial Lineage) :

This nakshatra is related to the *Sage Pulahu*, one of the seven celestial sages looking after the affairs of our galaxy. The name of this sage translates into "the connector of space". This makes sense when we recall that Uttarabhadrapada presides over all the dark space which harbours creation.

Remedial :

For those suffering from bad effects resulting from afflictions to this nakshatra, the best remedial measure is worship of Shiv, *Durga* or Vishnu. The practice of *Raja Yog*, which involves the raising of the kundalini through the seven sacred centres is one of the best ways to utilise this nakshatra's potential.

Repetition of the root mantras of this nakshatra - "Om Sham", "Om Sam" and "Om Ham", 108 times when Moon transits this nakshatra and in its corresponding lunar month, is sure to reduce suffering and bring enlightenment into a person's life.

Persons who are benefiting from the positive energy of this nakshatra can also increase the good effects through the above mentioned ways. It is helpful for them to wear shades of blue and yellow. It is the nakshatra which encompasses everything classified under the term "psychedelic", so imagery, patterns and colours associated with "psychedelia" are good for conveying this nakshatra's energy. One should use its directions, lunar month and the days when Moon transits Uttarabhadrapada to undertake all important actions.

Example :

Uttarabhadrapada's sound and light can be experienced at -

http://osfa.org.uk/uttarabhadrapada.htm

Miscellaneous :

According to *Varahamihira*, Moon placed in Uttarabhadrapada denotes "a happy disposition. Such natives usually end up having lots of children and grandchildren. They are virtuous and make convincing speakers. They are supposed to prevail over their enemies".

* * *

27. Revati 16°40' Pisces ~ 30°00' Pisces

27.

Revati

(16°40' Pisces - 30°00' Pisces)

In the Sky :

Revati, the culmination of Mercurial energy, in fact all zodiacal energies, is represented in the celestial firmament by a group of very faint stars in the constellation of Pisces. The exact number of these stars is not specified in the ancient texts, although 27 seems like an automatic choice! The ancient vedic seers saw that these stars made a shape similar to a *dhol* (drum strung across the neck with a strap and played with both hands, used for carrying in processions).

The brightest among these faint stars is known in modern astronomy as *Zeta-Piscium*, which has a visual magnitude of only 5.20. It is located close to a comparatively brighter star, *Mu-Piscium*, around the fag end of the tail of the fish formed by the constellation Pisces. This asterism is not easy to locate in the night sky, but one can always utilize the fact that Zeta-Piscium lies almost exactly on the planetary ecliptic (the path of the planets around the zodiac); in order to locate it in a very clear new moon night sky.

Name :

'Revati "has a simple translation - "wealthy". As we shall discover later, this name conveys a lot about this asterism on all levels, even though it is not apparent straightaway why the final asterism representing complete dissolution be related to something as transitory as wealth. Its alternative translation is "to transcend", which is more in keeping with this being the final nakshatra.

Symbol :

Since this asterism has a lot to do with duality, it has two and not one main symbol - a " fish swimming in the sea" and a "drum".

A fish swimming in the water is an obvious choice as a symbol for this nakshatra, as it falls completely in the sign of Pisces, which as we know is represented by two fishes swimming in opposite directions. The symbolism of a fish swimming in the sea has been used from time immemorial to show the soul's journey in the waters of the universe. *Vishnu*, the preserver among the Trinity, is often shown sitting atop the sea of consciousness.

The fish swimming in the sea also suggests a path. This nakshatra has a lot to do with paths of all kinds, whether it is just a path to one's house or the whole life-path itself. As declared by all wise men and incarnations, knowing and following one's path in life is the biggest penance of all. In a way it is the one and only path to liberation.

This nakshatra, as we know, is the last among nakshatras and thus has a lot to do with moksha and final enlightenment. It should be noted here that moksha doesn't actually mean liberation from cycles of births and deaths, as is enunciated by many schools of thought. Even after final enlightenment, one might have to take birth in some cycle of some universe. To find one's true path in life, one has to learn to see the bigger picture. This happens through connecting oneself with the universal mind, which in turn is tuned to the collective consciousness. This nakshatra represents collective consciousness. This however is a little different from the mass consciousness represented by the sign Cancer.

A drum as we recall is the symbol for *Dhanishta* as well. There's a lot of similarity between Revati and Dhanishta. One similarity which stands out immediately is that they are both regarded as wealthy. Please refer to the symbol section in Dhanishta for understanding the signification of a drum as a symbol. Revati's drum is similar to a *Naggada* (a type of Indian drum played with two sticks), and other types of modern drums used by marching bands (refer to the image).

It can be seen that Revati's drums are always played by sticks of some kind instead of by hand. They also have a connotation of bringing news, which the Dhanishta drum doesn't have. In all the ancient cultures, any news of importance to the community was always announced accompanied by the sound of drums. In some cultures, drum beats were even used as a way of sending signals in much the same way as morse code. We can thus infer that 'communication' is one of the key aspects of this nakshatra.

Deity :

Pushan, a solar deity, similar to the Sun god, is considered the main presiding deity of this asterism. He is supposed to light up all paths. This gives him rulership over as diverse a thing as streetlights, which light up the road; a lighthouse, which keeps the ship from getting lost; to the rulership of the inner light of the soul, which lights up one's life-path. He is always portrayed as standing at the beginning of all paths and beginnings (refer to the image). This is the reason why he became popular as the deity connected with safe travel. Consequently this nakshatra relates to all kinds of travelling - physical, mental, emotional, astral or causal.

Pushan is supposed to be a more nourishing, softer deity than our Sun god and is said to give wealth, prosperity and completion. It is not hard to see see how fruitful journeys or fruitful life-paths will bring these to us automatically.

Finally *Vishnu*, the preserver among the Trinity, is the overseer of this nakshatra. At the time of the final dissolution, it is Vishnu's job to gather together all of the universal life force and consciousness. It is the gathering quality of this nakshatra which makes it wealthy, whether it be in terms of material wealth, knowledge or experience. Vishnu as we know is the husband of *Laxmi*, the goddess of wealth and prosperity, which again brings this nakshatra in touch with the principle of abundance. Mercury, the planetary ruler of this nakshatra is supposed to be directly connected with Vishnu. Communication is a forte of Mercury and Vishnu and as we have seen earlier, of this nakshatra as well. The image of Vishnu and Laxmi sitting on a snake bed on top of the ocean of celestial waters is an image which can very much sum up this nakshatra.

Nature & Functioning :

Common English words like "reverie", "reverent", "revolving", "reverend", "revelry", "represent", "resolution" - seem to have the same root as the word "Revati". We can easily see that their meanings relate to Revati's functioning at some level or other.

Revati is one of the most pleasing and benevolent of nakshatras. It is an extremely fortunate nakshatra and this helps it see life in a positive light. It is the eternal optimist and remains completely unflustered even in the face of big setbacks. It has an innate trust in divine providence. It knows how to keep the faith but in some cases it has a tendency to not do anything else except having faith. In such cases this usually positive quality turns out to its detriment.

A lot of the natives born under this nakshatra tend to rely too much on belief and their beliefs are not always real. It is seen that some Saturn influence is required to give a realistic groundedness to this nakshatra. Let us take two cases. In one nativity, Jupiter is placed in this nakshatra aspected by Saturn and in the other, Jupiter is placed in this nakshatra without having an aspect of Saturn. The former is more likely to reap all the expansive benefits of this nakshatra, while the latter will be more prone to idle fantasies.

This is the nakshatra of the dreamer. It can create whole worlds around itself. This is because of its strong association with *Maya*, the illusory quality related with Vishnu, which sustains the drama of life. A lot of natives with prominent Revati tend to live in universes of their own creation. It is a case of Maya within Maya, which is not very conducive for enlightenment. The best thing Revati natives can do is to see things as they are.

Revati people are always supportive of others and since one reaps what one sows they often get supported as well. The peculiar thing about Revati natives is that they always get support when they need it most.

Revati can be seen as the apex of civilization. Its natives place special emphasis on refinement, sophistication, grooming and civilized behaviour. They like all the things which constitute civilization, and abhor primitive behaviour. A lot of Revati natives are born into rich, aristocratic or refined families. Unless there are other conflicting factors in the chart, Revati promotes good childhood, upbringing, early education and physical felicity.

Revati natives seem to have pleasing social personalities and are usually well liked within their social sphere. This is to be expected from someone who has had a good upbringing. No other nakshatra comes close to Revati as far as being a socialite is concerned. They are very good hosts and their friendships last long because of their responsible nature. They are very understanding of other's problems and like to be as helpful to as many people as they can. However, sometimes they take too many people's problems on their shoulders, and can exhaust themselves mentally, emotionally or physically as a result.

They are always soft and polite in conversation and only spiteful if hurt or jealous. Revati is one of the most tender nakshatras and so has a tendency to get hurt very easily. Despite this they are often good counsellors and have a knack for solving people's problems or showing them their right path.

Revati natives usually have a lustrous and luscious body and a smiley, lighthearted demeanour. One can refer to the picture of Pushan in the nakshatra image, or look up an image of Vishnu, for getting a general idea of the appearance of Revati natives. Revati is a soft but indulgent asterism. It is the nakshatra which derives the most fun and joy out of the drama of life. It must be said that while more evolved souls learn to keep themselves on an observer status, the younger, less evolved souls tend to immerse themselves completely in the maya of life.

This nakshatra doesn't actually have a sense of limits and so it is very easy for it to do too much of anything. This nakshatra likes to exude power through its speech and other forms of communication. It is the most charming and enchanting amongst all the nakshatras and its charm lies in completely engaging another person's attention. This engagement can at times be so extreme that the other person may feel that nothing but the two of them exists. It is also a master at appearing intensely engaged in things, even though its attention might be scattered in a million directions. Among the nakshatras, Revati has the strongest ability to cast illusions, while at the same time in its lower aspect it can just as easily get caught up in illusions itself.

Revati is the most tricky and clever amongst the nakshatras. It is a chameleon which can put on any act at any given point in time. The more evolved souls use this ability for serving universal causes, while the less evolved souls end up using it for selfish motives.

Revati natives are proverbial "*Richie Rich*" characters. People often take them to be very financially well off even when they are penniless.

To sum it up, Revati can be seen as the height of civilization with all its upsides and downsides.

If there is one asterism which can see the bigger picture, then this is it. Since it is the last nakshatra, it has the ability to understand and even mimic the energies of every other nakshatra. Revati is a complete display of all possibilities of existence. It is the only complete nakshatra in the sense that it contains all the wisdom and knowledge there is. There's nothing which is beyond the scope of Revati's domain and thus it is very difficult to label it, stereotype it, or put its nature and activities in a box. It always surprises others by turning into something completely different just as it is being put into a category.

It is a nakshatra dealing with infinity of time, space and everything else. This is the reason why it is hard to pin this nakshatra down, as some new light is always shining on the horizon.

The most significant thing about Revati is that it has the ability to see and understand every other nakshatra. Its most important keyword is "summation". It is the *sigma* and the *omega*. Other nakshatras can only fathom where they are at, but Revati can fathom where everyone is at. Obviously this all seeing capacity is restricted by the evolutionary state of the soul in question. The more evolved the soul, the more all encompassing the vision.

In the universal scheme of things, Revati relates to "*kshiradyapani shakti*" - the power to nourish through milk. Its symbolism has cows above, and calves below. This imagery emphasises the nourishing and sustaining aspect of Revati. However, if one pays attention to the fact that Vishnu, the sustainer amongst the holy trinity, sits atop the celestial ocean known as *kshirasagar,* a whole new interpretation opens up. Revati then relates to the *shakti* which sustains the celestial ocean in which all the fourteen *lokas* play the game of life.

Mode of Functioning :

Revati is considered to be a Balanced nakshatra. This relates to its love of society and its conservative and balanced approach to fostering civilization. It also relates to its wisdom aspect, which after seeing all sides of a situation, takes the middle path. Finally all philosophical and religious schools of thought consider the middle way to be the best way. It is this nakshatra's task to accommodate and resolve the duality inherent in existence.

Caste :

It belongs to the *Shudra* caste. This is the case because ancient seers saw it as a service orientated nakshatra. As mentioned earlier, Revati natives are always willing to give assistance to others. In fact this is one of the few nakshatras which doesn't mind helping out even their enemy. In a way, Vishnu is also doing service to the universe by maintaining harmony and keeping the game of life alive.

Gender :

It is a Female nakshatra. It represents the sum total of all the feminine force which sustains the universe.

Bodyparts & Humor (Ayurvedic Constitution) :

Feet, Ankles, Abdomen and Groin are the body parts related to this nakshatra. Its association with the feet and ankles is clear from its relationship with Pisces. In our view it must relate to the abdomen because of the positioning of the *manipur* (navel) chakra. Vishnu is the presiding deity of this chakra. We are not very clear about the reason why some scholars associate groins with this nakshatra.

It is a primarily "*Kapha*" (watery) nakshatra. This is clear from the fact that it falls completely in a water sign and is associated with watery planets like Jupiter and Neptune.

Direction :

It is related primarily to north and north-east.

Padas (Quarters) :

The first pada or quarter of this asterism 16° 40' - 20° 00' Pisces, falls in Sagittarius Navamsa and is ruled by Jupiter. This relates to the happy go lucky, optimistic and philanthropic side of this nakshatra. This pada has a tendency to get carried away and so it is important for these natives to choose the right thing to get carried away with. They are the kind who will go about fanatically espousing their cause or belief.

The second pada or quarter of this asterism 20° 00' - 23° 20' Pisces, falls in Capricorn Navamsa ruled by Saturn. This conveys the more practical and organizational aspect of Revati. This is the pada which relates to all time-related sciences like Astrology etc. Natural benefics maintain a sense of balance here, while natural malefics can give too much ambition. This is the most realistic pada within this nakshatra and has a tendency to not be swayed by blind belief.

The third pada or quarter of this asterism 23° 20' - 26° 40' Pisces, falls in Aquarius Navamsa ruled by Saturn. This relates to the bohemian and humanitarian aspect of Revati. This pada finds it difficult to express its workings on a material plane.

The fourth pada or quarter of this asterism 26° 40' - 30° 00' Pisces, falls in Pisces Navamsa ruled by Jupiter. This is the eternal dreamer. It can only give good material results if natural malefics like Mars and Saturn occupy it. Like the first pada, this pada has a tendency to get swayed easily.

Professions :

Hypnotists & Psychic Mediums; Creative Artists of all kinds including Painters, Musicians etc.; Actors, Entertainers & Comedians; Linguists; Conjurors, Illusionists, Magicians; Watchmakers; Road Planners and those working in Rail & Road Construction Business; Time Keepers; Calendar/Ephemeris Makers; Astrologers; Divinators; Managers; Professional Hosts & Hostesses (especially air hostesses, ship stewards etc.); Gemstone Dealers; Those involved in the Pearl Industry; All kinds of Shipping and Marine Industry; Those involved with Foster Homes & Orphanages; Driving or Transport Professions; Those involved with Religious Institutions; Air Traffic Controllers, Traffic Cops; Light House Workers; Those involved with Road Safety; Driving Instructors.

Places :

Roads, Railroad Tracks, Airports; Oceans, Seas, Beaches; Shipping Yards; Stage; Cinema; Orphanages; Monasteries; Ships, Aeroplanes, Trains, Cars etc; Bus Stations, Transport Industry; Public Auditoriums; Clock Towers/Watch Towers; Light Houses; Driving Instruction Schools; All places connected with the above mentioned professions.

Guna (Essence) and Tattwa (Element) :

It is supposed to be a *Sattwic* nakshatra. This comes as no surprise as this nakshatra has primarily sattwic ruling deities and is associated with benefic sattwic planets like Jupiter, Mercury and Neptune.

It belongs to the Ether element. This again comes as no surprise as the Ether element has an all encompassing quality, and can mingle and cooperate with all the other elements, which is what the essence of Revati's functioning is.

Gana (Type) :

It is considered a *Deva* or godly nakshatra. This fact is quite apparent from its general benefic nature and the benefic quality of its ruling planets and deities.

Outlook and Disposition :

It is a Level nakshatra. This relates to the balanced nature of this asterism. We have already discussed how it is a soft nakshatra, which automatically means that it doesn't go to extremes. The Level aspect also relates to its innate capacity to maintain a regular equilibrilized flow of life force on all planes of existence.

As mentioned previously it is a Soft nakshatra. This basically relates to its mild, tender, easy going and pleasure loving nature.

Lunar Month & Day :

It relates to the last 9 days of the lunar month of *Bhadra Pada*, which usually falls in September.

Revati is also related to *Purnima* (15th tithi or day) of the waxing phase of the Moon's monthly cycle.

Auspicious Activities :

Initiating all activities of a positive nature; Business activities and financial dealings; Anything involving exchange of goods; Good for marriage & sexual activity; Religious rituals; All kinds of travelling; Good for dealing with gemstones (putting them on for the first time etc.); Buying cars, homes and other valuable goods; Creative activities like music, drama etc.; Good for kind, charitable and soft activities; Learning, especially spiritual or occult; Healing and treatment of diseases; Rest and relaxation; Good for leisure activities like gardening; Good for completion of all types (putting the final touches on things).

Inauspicious Activities :

*The last two quarters of this nakshatra should be avoided for beginnings of all kinds.

All activities requiring harshness and boldness should be avoided. Not good for overcoming difficulties, obstructions, enmity or calamities; Not good for negative, sharp actions like surgery; Not good for strenuous activities of any kind like mountain climbing.

Planetary Ruler :

Mercury is the primary ruler of this nakshatra along with its sign rulers Jupiter, Neptune and Ketu. As mentioned earlier, Revati represents the culmination point of Mercurial energy. Since it is the last amongst the nakshatras, it can be seen as the culmination point of all zodiacal energies. Mercury's function here is not so much analytical as it is discriminatory. Mercury's function here is to categorize/classify and give everything its own unique place in the scheme of creation. Mercury doesn't lose its sense of humour here despite the fact that its task here is enormous. Mercury has to evolve and become a Buddha (enlightened one) here. It is interesting to note that Buddha is the sanskrit name originally assigned to Mercury by the ancient Vedic seers. They had set and encoded its goal in its name itself! Mercury has to become Vishnu, the maintainer of universal affairs, who, while being in the game is still out of the game.

Mercury however cannot achieve this feat without the help of Jupiter, the harbinger of wisdom and compassion. It is Jupiter which gives an understanding of the basic laws of nature, as Mercury gives no cognizance to rules - universal or otherwise. The blending together of the energies of Jupiter and Mercury creates the Neptunian field. One ancient school of astrological thought says that the three outer planets act as secondary Suns and in turn control two of the inner planets. According to this school of thought, Neptune presides over the functioning of Jupiter and Mercury. One can easily see that this line of thought is validated through Vedic Mythology and Astrology. Vishnu is in essence a Neptunian deity and most of the schools of *Jyotish* relate the planets Jupiter and Mercury with Vishnu.

Together Neptune, Jupiter and Mercury rule over the intellectual realm and share the responsibility of connecting our individual consciousness with the collective universal consciousness.

Ketu is the planet of the beginning and the end. Since Revati represents the end, Ketu's relationship with this nakshatra is not very hard to establish. Ketu is the planet most intimately connected with dissolution of our past *karmas* and it achieves that using the energy of Revati.

Jupiter, Mercury, Venus and Moon usually do well in Revati. Ketu's placement here is good for spiritual pursuits. Conjunctions like Jupiter/Mercury; Jupiter/Mercury/Ketu; Jupiter/Neptune; Jupiter/ Ketu; Mercury/Ketu; Mercury/Neptune; Ketu/Neptune; mirror this asterism's energy.

Vowels and Alphabets :

The first pada or quarter of this asterism 16° 40' -20° 00' Pisces corresponds to "The" as in The.

The second pada or quarter of this asterism 20° 00' - 23° 20' Pisces corresponds to "Tho" as in Though.

The third pada or quarter of this asterism 23° 20' - 26° 40' Pisces corresponds to "Cha" as in Charlie.

The fourth pada or quarter of this asterism 26° 40' - 30° 00' Pisces corresponds to "Chi" as in Chile.

In the Sanskrit alphabet Revati corresponds to "La", "Ksha", "A" and "Aa", consequently its mantras are "Om Lam", "Om Ksham", "Om Am" and "Om Aam".

Sexual Type and Compatibility :

Its sexual animal is an Elephant. In fact many of these nakshatras' qualities can be gauged from the essential nature and behaviour of elephants. The fact that elephants prefer level grounds rather than uneven terrain, once again reiterates the level aspect of this nakshatra. Elephants are the largest among all land animals. In the oceans their counterparts, the blue whales, will also fall under the auspices of Revati. One can do a study of the sexual nature of these creatures to understand the sexual nature of this nakshatra.

For sexual & marital compatibility with other nakshatras please refer to the tables on pages 468 & 469.

Esoteric :

Revati corresponds to the universal point in time where the material as well as astral are drawn into the causal realm and after the process is completed, the causal is drawn into the supreme eternal void. On a more personal level, Revati relates to the assimilation of life experiences from many previous lives, so that a synthesis can take place and a state of completeness achieved.

Revati can thus be associated with the seventh sacral centre known as *Sahastrar*. A state of complete awareness is achieved after the kundalini opens every petal of this thousand petalled lotus centre. After achieving this, the kundalini breaks through the top part of the head known as *Brahma Randha*. At this point the will of the soul achieves complete harmony with the universal will, and the personal consciousness is submerged into the collective universal consciousness. In other words, the drop joins with the ocean and can no longer be traced as an individual drop. In its highest aspect, Revati relates to this state and process.

In a relatively lower aspect, Revati relates to the 'ocean of illusion' associated with the third sacral centre often known as *Manipur Chakra* (or the navel centre). This is the place where the *chi* (life force) is supposed to reside as per Zen principles. This centre is representative of all the activities on a worldly/material plane. Only after the mastery of this oceanic field does a soul gain true knowledge about the higher planes of existence. Once again the image of Vishnu sitting atop the ocean of illusion best characterizes this aspect of Revati.

Revati represents the celestial ocean in which the creative force rests, after *Mahapralaya* (universal dissolution). On a smaller scale, cycles of destruction and dissolution take place on our planet as well. In each such *Pralaya*, where the oceans are engulfing all the land, Vishnu is supposed to incarnate as a fish and save seven sages and all the plants and animals required for the recontinuation of life. This can be said to be a very Revati operation. In fact the process of earthly death also requires Revati's services, as all the actions of this life and all the vital pranas (life forces) are accumulated within the astral/causal center before the chord between the material body and the astral body is cut.

Finally, Revati conceals the answer to the ultimate question - "Why all of this creation, for what purpose, and for whom ?"

Gotra (Celestial Lineage) :

This nakshatra is related to the *Sage Kratu*, one of the seven celestial sages looking after the affairs of our galaxy. The name of this sage translates into "the inspirer", which is in harmony with the fact that Revati is one of the most optimistic and inspirational nakshatras.

Remedial :

For those suffering from bad effects resulting from afflictions to this nakshatra, the best remedial measure is worship of Vishnu.

Repetition of the root mantras of this nakshatra - "Om Lam", "Om Ksham", "Om Am" and "Om Aam" 108 times when Moon transits this nakshatra and in its corresponding lunar month is sure to reduce suffering and bring enlightenment into a person's life.

Persons who are benefiting from the positive energy of this nakshatra can also increase the good effects through the above mentioned ways. It is helpful for them to wear all oceanic, light, variegated colours and pastel shades. They should use its directions, lunar month and the days when Moon transits Revati to undertake all important actions.

Example :

Revati's sound and light can be experienced at -

http://osfa.org.uk/revati.htm

Miscellaneous :

According to *Varahamihira*, Moon in Revati "gives one perfect body and physical felicity. The native is supposed to be blessed with purity, luck, wealth and a heroic disposition." One will generally find that those having Moon or Ascendant in Revati are usually gentle, kind and pious unless there are other overwhelming factors to the contrary in the chart.

* * *

Abhijit

Abhijit is a nakshatra which comes into picture when a 28 Nakshatra system is used. This system was discarded by the Vedic seers for a variety of reasons. Firstly, the division of 360 degree zodiacal arc by 28 gives an incomplete fraction. This makes it impossible to specify the exact degreecal range of each nakshatra, which makes an unequal size system the only possibility. Even if one unwantingly accepts that each nakshatra would have a different size, one is faced with the strange task of dividing 28 Nakshatras among 9 planets. Even if one manages to get over this obstacle by assigning 4 nakshatras to one planet and 3 to the rest, one finds that the exceedingly accurate *Dasha* system falls to pieces. In other words, it makes perfect sense to use a 27 nakshatra system. All this has a lot to do with the fact that 27 is a more perfect number than 28, but a discussion on that is beyond the scope of this work. The average time it takes Moon to complete one revolution through the zodiac is 27.3217 days, a figure which is closer to 27 than it is to 28. Thus a 27 nakshatra system also fits in with the Lunar calendar much better than a 28 nakshatra system. It is interesting to note that the Chinese and Arabic astrologers are still using this borrowed 28 lunar mansion system, which has no sense besides the fact that it fits in with the seven day-four week solar calendar (7 x 4 = 28).

Abhijit can be seen as an attempt to highlight the speciality of a certain portion of the zodiac. This certain portion lies between 0 and 12 degrees of the sign Capricorn, which would place Abhijit between Uttarashadha & Shravan. The English translations of the term "Abhijit" can range from "the undefeatable", "ever-conquering", "complete victory" & "final victory", but they all point towards the same general area of triumph and achievement. No wonder then that Krishn says in Bhagavad-Gita, "Amongst the nakshatras I am Abhijit". It is in this part of the celestial firmament that Indra and the Gods achieved a final & lasting victory over the Demons.

One finds that the triumphant aspect of Abhijit is very similar to that of Uttarashadha. Also Abhijit more or less lies within the last 10 degrees of Uttarashadha. Uttarashadha is the nakshatra where a conclusive triumph of good over evil takes place. Abhijit then can just be seen as a specific part in Uttarashadha where there is absolute domination of all that is good from the universal perspective.

* * *

Afterword

It has been my endeavor to write the majority of this book in harmony with nature's everchanging & time-bound functionings. Each nakshatra was dealt with only when Moon was passing through that particular nakshatra. The same is the case with the visualization and drawing of the nakshatra images.

Best to state again that each nakshatra works on 2 levels - Divine (higher aspect) & Evil (lower aspect). Ashlesha can be used as a kundalini raising tool or for unnecessary stalking. Purvabhadrapad can be used for discipline in divine path or just hellish tortures on the road of evil. Same applies for all of them.

The study of nakshataras has a vast scope beyond natal astrology. The esoteric sections in this work are nothing more than mere signboards pointing towards the hitherto unknown galactic level functionings which nakshatras encode and the ancient sages were privy to.

* * *

Bibliography

Sage Parashara, Brihat Parashara Hora Sastra: Volume I. Translation by G. C. Sharma, Sagar Publications, New Delhi, India.

Sage Parashara, Brihat Parashara Hora Sastra: Volume II. Translation by G. C. Sharma, Sagar Publications, New Delhi, India.

Sage Jaimini, Jaimini Sutram, Translation by P. S. Shastri.

Varahamihira, Brihat Jataka, Translation by Usha-Shashi, Sagar Publications, New Delhi, India.

Mantreswara, Phaladeepika, Translation by S. S. Sareen, Sagar Publications, 1992, New Delhi, India.

Rama Daivagya, Muhurta Chintamani, Translation by Girish Chand Sharma, Sagar Publications, New Delhi, India.

Pt. Dhundhiraj, Jataka Bharnam, Translation by Girish Chand Sharma, Sagar Publications 1998, New Delhi, India.

Taittriya Samhita, Translation & Commentary by Bhattabhaskara Mishra.

Prashna Marga, Vol. I & II, Translated by B. V. Raman, Motilal Banarsidass Publishers, Delhi, 1985.

* * *

Sexual Compatibility Table

YONI/SEXUAL ANIMAL	Horse	Elephant	Sheep	Serpent	Dog	Cat	Rat	Cow	Buffalo	Tiger	Hare	Monkey	Mongoose	Lion
Horse	4	2	2	3	2	2	2	1	0	1	3	3	2	1
Elephant	2	4	3	3	2	2	2	2	3	1	2	3	2	0
Sheep	2	3	4	2	1	2	1	3	3	1	2	0	3	1
Serpent	3	3	2	4	2	1	1	1	1	2	2	2	0	2
Dog	2	2	1	2	4	2	1	2	2	1	0	2	1	1
Cat	2	2	2	1	2	4	0	2	2	1	3	3	2	1
Rat	2	2	1	1	1	0	4	2	2	2	2	2	1	2
Cow	1	2	3	1	2	2	2	4	3	0	3	2	2	1
Buffalo	0	3	3	1	2	2	2	3	4	1	2	2	2	1
Tiger	1	1	1	2	1	1	2	0	1	4	1	1	2	1
Hare	1	2	2	2	0	3	2	3	2	1	4	2	2	1
Monkey	3	3	0	2	2	3	2	2	2	1	2	4	3	2
Mongoose	2	2	3	3	1	2	1	2	2	2	2	3	4	2
Lion	1	0	1	2	1	1	2	1	2	1	1	2	2	4

One can see from this table that nakshatras sharing the same sexual animal are the most compatible. Apart from comparing the Moons of each partner for sexual compatibility, one can also compare the planets relating to lovemaking/sex in the horoscopes such as 12th lord, 5th lord, Venus etc.

Marriage Compatibility Table

Bridegroom's Star → / Bride's Star ↓	ARIES Aswini / Bharani / Kriittika	TAUR Krittika / Rohini / Mrigashira	GEMIN Mrigashira / Ardra / Punarvasu	CANC Punarvasu / Pushya / Ashlesha	LEO Magha / Purvaphal / Uttaraphal	VIRG Uttaraphal / Hasta / Chitra	LIBRA Chitra / Swati / Vishakha	SCOR Vishakha / Anuradha / Jyestha	SAGI Mula / Purvaash / Uttarashad	CAPR Uttarashad / Sravana / Dhanish	AQUA Dhanish / Shatabish / Purvabhad	PISCES Purvabhad / Uttarabhad / Revati
Aswini	28 33 27	17 23 22	25 16 17	22 30 27	20 24 14	9 10 12	22 28 22	18 24 13	12 24 23	25 26 20	19 14 15	14 23 26
Bharani	33 28 23	18 26 14	17 25 25	30 22 24	19 17 24	19 18 3	13 28 21	18 17 19	19 17 25	27 28 10	9 19 23	22 4 25
Krittika	26 28 28	18 10 16	19 19 19	24 26 22	15 10 20	15 14 14	27 14 19	16 19 25	25 19 11	13 13 25	24 25 18	17 14 10
Krittika	19 19 19	28 18 26	17 17 17	21 23 19	19 21 22	20 18 23	22 9 14	21 24 30	22 15 7	12 10 24	29 30 23	20 22 13
RohinI	23 23 11	20 28 30	26 23 22	26 27 12	10 24 27	25 25 18	17 15 8	14 29 23	13 19 11	16 18 19	24 24 29	26 27 19
Mrigashira	23 14 18	27 35 28	18 23 22	26 19 21	19 15 24	23 25 11	10 9 17	23 21 24	14 10 16	21 26 12	17 26 28	25 18 27
Mrigash	28 17 21	19 26 19	28 33 31	18 11 13	22 18 27	31 34 20	13 27 19	13 13 14	23 19 23	19 24 10	12 21 22	24 17 26
Ardra	18 26 21	19 24 25	34 28 25	12 20 12	21 27 20	24 24 27	20 27 20	13 19 5	15 28 27	21 22 17	19 12 17	18 26 26
Punarvasu	18 25 21	19 22 23	31 24 28	14 21 15	21 25 19	23 24 26	19 27 21	14 20 6	14 27 27	21 22 16	18 13 16	17 26 26
Punarvas	21 28 24	21 24 25	17 10 13	28 34 28	16 20 14	16 17 19	19 26 20	19 25 10	7 20 20	16 27 21	12 5 9	18 25 24
Pushya	29 20 26	23 25 18	10 18 24	34 28 29	18 14 23	15 25 11	11 25 20	19 17 20	17 12 20	26 27 13	4 13 17	26 18 26
Aslesha	25 23 21	18 11 19	11 11 13	27 28 28	15 15 17	19 19 24	24 11 16	14 19 25	22 15 7	13 13 26	18 18 11	17 20 12
Magha	19 19 15	16 9 17	20 20 19	16 18 16	28 30 26	14 14 19	23 10 15	24 24 32	24 19 8	3 4 17	23 24 17	17 18 12
Purvaphal	25 17 19	20 23 15	18 26 25	22 16 10	30 28 34	24 20 5	23 22 24	22 22 24	20 17 24	19 18 5	9 18 23	23 16 24
Uttaraphal	15 25 20	21 26 24	27 19 17	14 23 18	26 34 28	16 15 12	16 25 16	22 30 16	9 25 25	20 20 11	17 10 15	15 26 24
Uttaraphal	11 21 16	20 25 24	31 21 23	17 20 20	15 23 17	28 27 24	16 25 16	18 28 12	14 29 29	24 24 15	16 9 14	17 28 26
Hasta	11 18 16	20 23 21	32 18 23	18 26 21	16 20 15	26 28 28	29 26 18	20 26 13	15 27 23	23 24 18	19 10 13	15 26 24
Chitra	12 4 18	23 18 10	18 22 24	21 11 25	20 6 13	24 27 28	19 19 25	27 11 25	27 13 21	15 17 15	16 24 16	19 10 19
Chitra	22 14 28	23 18 10	12 20 18	19 11 25	24 10 17	27 20 20	29 27 33	22 6 20	27 13 21	23 25 23	18 26 18	12 3 12
Swati	20 28 16	11 14 24	26 26 27	27 20 13	12 24 25	25 27 21	28 28 20	9 21 15	23 27 19	21 22 26	21 22 25	18 19 11
Vishakha	21 22 20	15 9 17	18 20 20	20 20 17	16 18 17	17 18 26	33 19 28	16 16 21	27 21 13	15 15 29	24 26 20	13 12 4
Vishakha	16 16 14	19 13 21	11 12 12	18 18 14	24 22 21	17 18 26	21 7 15	28 27 31	21 15 7	11 11 25	24 25 19	19 18 9
Anuradha	23 14 18	23 27 20	10 15 19	25 17 20	24 20 28	24 25 11	6 20 16	28 28 31	15 13 21	25 26 12	11 20 24	24 17 26
Jyestha	10 17 23	28 22 29	12 2 4	9 19 25	31 23 15	11 11 24	19 14 10	31 30 28	14 16 16	20 20 25	24 17 10	9 20 20
Mula	11 19 25	19 12 12	21 14 12	7 17 23	24 18 9	13 13 26	26 21 26	22 16 16	28 28 13	13 14 19	28 21 14	16 24 26
Purvashad	25 17 19	14 18 10	19 26 27	22 14 16	19 17 25	28 27 12	12 27 20	16 15 17	27 28 34	22 22 5	14 23 28	20 22 30
Uttarashad	24 25 11	6 10 16	25 26 27	22 22 8	8 24 25	28 28 20	20 19 12	18 23 17	25 35 28	16 15 13	22 23 28	20 30 22
Uttarashad	27 28 14	12 16 22	19 24 21	28 28 14	4 20 21	24 24 15	22 31 14	12 27 21	14 24 17	28 27 25	15 16 21	29 30 22
Shravana	28 27 14	12 17 26	23 19 21	28 28 14	5 18 20	23 24 17	24 21 14	12 27 21	14 22 15	26 28 27	17 17 20	28 29 23
Dhanishta	20 11 26	23 19 11	18 16 14	21 13 27	18 4 10	15 17 15	29 24 28	26 12 26	20 6 14	25 27 28	17 23 17	24 15 22
Dhanishta	19 10 25	30 25 17	11 18 17	12 4 18	24 10 18	17 19 17	18 20 24	25 11 25	20 15 23	16 18 18	28 33 27	16 6 13
Satabhisha	14 20 26	31 25 26	20 12 12	6 13 19	25 19 11	10 10 25	20 21 26	26 20 18	22 24 24	17 17 24	33 28 29	8 24 15
Purvabhad	17 24 19	24 30 30	23 17 17	11 19 12	18 26 16	15 15 17	18 26 20	20 26 11	15 29 29	22 22 27	16 27 29	16 22 19
Purvabhad	11 21 16	19 25 25	24 17 17	17 25 17	16 22 14	16 16 18	11 18 12	19 25 9	14 28 28	28 28 24	15 7 15	28 33 30
Uttarabhad	23 25 18	21 26 18	17 25 26	26 19 20	17 25 25	27 26 9	2 19 11	18 18 23	23 21 29	29 29 14	5 24 21	33 28 33
Revati	25 23 10	13 17 26	25 24 25	24 26 13	12 22 22	24 25 19	12 10 4	10 20 21	26 28 20	23 21 22	13 15 17	29 33 28

Look down the first column to find the Moon nakshatra of the bride. From here travel across the page horizontally until the Moon nakshatra of the bridegroom is reached. The number that intersects at that place is the number of compatibility units.

High compatibility = 25 +   Good compatibility = 20+   Average compatibility = 15 - 20

Low compatibility = 10 - 15   Very Poor compatibility = below 10

OSFA

Orion School & Foundation for Astrology

OSFA is dedicated to enhancing public awareness about *Jyotish* (aka. Vedic Astrology & Indian Astrology) and its related fields through research, writings, media and courses.

OSFA accepts donations. Those wanting to help or contribute can write directly to us at astrology@karmablueprint.com

OSFA is open to all who would like to further the cause of Astrology. OSFA is an open forum for all those who want to share their thoughts on Astrology and other Esoteric subjects. You can send us your Piece or Article via Email

For more information about OSFA please visit -

Website Homepage : www.osfa.org.uk

Online Course: www.osfa.org.uk/onlinecourse.htm

Publications: www.osfa.org.uk/book-19.htm